Thomas W. Kniesche (Ed.)
Contemporary German Crime Fiction

Companions to Contemporary German Culture

Edited by
Michael Eskin · Karen Leeder · Christopher Young

Volume 7

Contemporary German Crime Fiction

A Companion

Edited by
Thomas W. Kniesche

DE GRUYTER

ISBN 978-3-11-042655-7
e-ISBN (PDF) 978-3-11-042660-1
e-ISBN (EPUB) 978-3-11-042225-2
ISSN 2193-9659

Library of Congress Control Number: 2019944705

Bibliographic information published by the Deutsche Nationalbibliothek
The Deutsche Nationalbibliothek lists this publication in the Deutsche Nationalbibliografie;
detailed bibliographic data are available on the Internet at http://dnb.dnb.de

© 2019 Walter de Gruyter GmbH, Berlin/Boston
Cover image: Götz George as Schimanski. Image: WDR/Michael Böhme. WDR Fernsehen
SCHIMANSKI – "Blutsbrüder", directed by Hajo Gries (30.12.02).
Typesetting: Integra Software Services Pvt. Ltd.
Printing and binding: CPI books GmbH, Leck

www.degruyter.com

MIX
Papier aus verantwor-
tungsvollen Quellen
FSC
www.fsc.org   FSC® C083411

Preface

At a meeting of the German Studies Association some years ago, Jochen Vogt asked me whether I would be interested in editing a volume on contemporary German crime fiction. He thought it would be a great way to draw the attention of English-speaking audiences to a realm of writing that had seen tremendous momentum since the 1980s, in terms of not only its quantity but also its quality. I was working on another book on the topic at the time and readily and enthusiastically agreed. This is how this book was conceived.

The volume is divided into eleven longer chapters and fourteen short author portraits. While the longer chapters are primarily concerned with broader developments within the genre and with providing overviews of certain trends in German crime fiction (such as the *Soziokrimi*, the *Regionalkrimi*, the *Frauenkrimi*, etc.), the short chapters in the last section will familiarize readers with some of the most interesting German-speaking crime novelists writing today.

Whenever the titles of books written in German are mentioned, an English translation is provided in brackets. If the translated title is followed by an asterisk (*), the book has *not* been translated into English; otherwise an English translation of the book is available.

The bibliography contains the titles of the primary and secondary sources referred to in the book and invites readers to expand their knowledge of crime fiction from German-speaking countries. The index will allow readers to navigate the pages of this volume easily and to look up the names of authors and concepts of special interest.

I would like to extend my heartfelt thanks to the friends and colleagues who contributed the chapters that comprise this *Companion to Contemporary German Crime Fiction*. I would also like to thank Dr Manuela Gerlof at De Gruyter and the editors of *Companions to Contemporary German Culture* for including this book in the series. Special thanks go to Lydia J. White for her help in copyediting the typoscript for this book.

The publication of this volume was made possible by generous grants from the Humanities Research Fund at Brown University.

https://doi.org/10.1515/9783110426601-201

Contents

Thomas W. Kniesche

1 Introduction: German and International Crime Fiction

International crime fiction vs. crime writing in Germany

Crime fiction has long been considered a literary genre dominated by the Anglo-American writing tradition. This tradition started with Edgar Allan Poe's stories featuring C. Auguste Dupin, followed by the singular phenomenon of the best-known fictional detective of all times, Arthur Conan Doyle's Sherlock Holmes. It continued with the authors of the 'golden age' of crime fiction (Agatha Christie, Dorothy Sayers, Philo Vance), the American hard-boiled school of the 1920s and 1930s (Dashiel Hammett, Raymond Chandler), the police procedural (Ed McBain, P.D. James), the spy thriller (Ian Fleming, John le Carré), the forensic thriller (Patricia Cornwell, Kathy Reichs) and the serial-killer thriller (Thomas Harris, James Patterson). The importance of other distinct national traditions of crime fiction, such as the French, Scandinavian, and Italian traditions, has now also been recognized, and writers from Spanish-speaking countries have had considerable success with English-speaking audiences. On the other hand, many still view crime fiction written in German as a case of a 'missing literary tradition'.[1] A chapter on 'Crime Writing in Other Languages' in an otherwise comprehensive recent companion to crime fiction briefly mentions the Swiss author Friedrich Dürrenmatt but makes no reference to any other German-speaking writers.[2] The widespread understanding, however, that there is no tradition of crime fiction in Germany is a misconception. It is time for a more differentiated narrative to replace the myth of the missing tradition of German crime fiction.

---

1 Cf. Julia Karolle-Berg, 'The Case of the Missing Literary Tradition. Reassessing Four Assumptions of Crime and Detective Novels in the German-Speaking World (1900–1933)', *Monatshefte* 107.3 (2015), pp. 431–454.
2 Cf. Sue Neale, 'Crime Writing in Other Languages', in *A Companion to Crime Fiction*, ed. by Charles J. Rzepka and Lee Horsley (Chichester: Wiley-Blackwell, 2010), pp. 296–302 (pp. 298–299). Elsewhere in this volume, Erich Kästner's *Emil und die Detektive* [1929, *Emile and the Detectives*] is discussed as an important contribution to 'crime and detective writing for children'. Cf. Christopher Rutledge, 'Crime and Detective Literature for Young Readers', pp. 321–331 (p. 328).

https://doi.org/10.1515/9783110426601-001

Due to the immense popularity of detective fiction modelled on the stories and novels of Edgar Allan Poe, Émile Gaboriau and Arthur Conan Doyle, and the dominant role played by the Anglo-American authors of the 'golden age', until the 1950s, crime fiction was largely seen as an extension of the concept of the 'whodunit'.[3] Crime fiction that employed the formulas and conventions of the 'whodunit' also gained a large following in German-speaking countries in the nineteenth century, but this was a time when other forms of crime writing also developed, competing with detective fiction. During the eighteenth and nineteenth centuries, documentary literary styles depicted crime as realistically as possible, illuminating both the social and psychological backgrounds to criminality and the way the penal system functioned. This was largely a didactic literature that was interested in contributing to ongoing discussions of judicial, sociological and psychological concerns. These texts clearly distinguished themselves from detective fiction in other European countries and in the US, which was written and read as a literary game, where the reader would compete with the detective to solve the mystery.

The strong separation in German cultural history between 'serious', 'high' literature and 'mere' entertainment or genre literature is another reason why the notion that crime fiction has no tradition in German-speaking countries gained so much traction. Novellas and novels such as Friedrich Schiller's *Der Verbrecher aus verlorener Ehre* [1792, *The Criminal of Lost Honour*], E.T.A. Hoffmann's '*Das Fräulein von Scudery*' [1819, 'Mademoiselle de Scudery'], Annette von Droste-Hülshoff's *Die Judenbuche* [1842, *The Jews' Beech Tree*], Theodor Fontane's *Unterm Birnbaum* [1885, *Under the Pear Tree*] and Jakob Wassermann's *Der Fall Mauritius* [1928, *The Mauritius Case*] all tell tales of crime, criminals and detection. However, these texts have never been considered candidates for possible inclusion in the tradition of crime fiction and are instead allocated to the canon of 'high' or 'true' literature.

A third explanation for why crime fiction is missing from the German literary tradition is that, after the downfall of the Nazi regime in 1945, translations of Anglo-American writers dominated the crime fiction market. Authors writing in German had a hard time gaining recognition and it was only in the mid- to late 1960s that readers in Germany would take notice of home-grown crime fiction.

---

3 Martin Priestman defines the 'whodunnit' as 'primarily concerned with unravelling past events which either involve a crime or seem to do so. The present action is largely static, and major attention is given to the detecting activity itself, which may be performed by virtually anyone – police of amateur – who enjoys the final approval of the law'. (*Crime Fiction from Poe to the Present* [Plymouth: Northcote House, 1998], p. 1). Other terms used for these kinds of texts include 'tales of ratiocination' (Poe) or 'clue puzzles'.

A very short history of crime writing in Germany and elsewhere

In order to elucidate and illustrate these issues we have to look back at how crime writing in German has developed and compare it with other national traditions. Just as in other European countries, in German-speaking countries, writing and publishing about crime for a wide audience goes back to the early days of printing. As sensational stories about murder and mayhem were becoming popular material for pamphlets and broadsheets in England in the sixteenth and seventeenth centuries,[4] they were also quickly gaining a captive audience in German readers. These broadsheets often featured illustrations made from woodcuts in order to include the many illiterates among the population in their audience.[5] However, the stories told in this format were not what we would consider crime fiction. They focussed on the criminal act itself, its brutality and the sordid motivations behind it. No process of detection took place; instead, it was usually an act of divine revelation that connected the criminal to the crime, for example, the corpse of the murder victim would start bleeding as the culprit approached. Broadsheets described the punishment in revolting detail in order to deter the audience from contemplating criminal acts themselves.

This situation changed in the seventeenth century, as legal scholars began employing a new narrative form, the case history, to explore crime in a fresh light. In 1649, the legal expert and poet Georg Philipp Harsdörffer published a compilation of novellas,[6] in which sinful behaviour resulting in crime was invariably met with draconian punishments. Most of the stories in Harsdörffer's collection were translations and adaptations of anthologies of novellas that the French bishop Jean Pierre Camus had been publishing since 1630. The case history combined what we now refer to as 'true crime' with elements from a variety of discourses (legal history, forensics, psychology, philosophy, etc.) to create a narrative form that would be of interest both to legal scholars and a wider audience of middle-class readers. The latter wanted to be entertained while also being informed about the origins of crime, criminal acts themselves and how the legal system would deal with them. The widespread interest in case histories

---

4 Cf. Stephen Knight, *Crime Fiction 1800–2000. Detection, Death, Diversity* (Houndmills, New York: Palgrave Macmillan, 2004), pp. 3–5.

5 Cf. Waltraud Woeller and Bruce Cassiday, *The Literature of Crime and Detection. An Illustrated History from Antiquity to the Present* (New York: Ungar, 1988), pp. 13–20.

6 Georg Philipp Harsdörffer, *Der Grosse SchauPlatz Jämerlicher Mordgeschichte. Mit vielen merkwürdigen Erzehlungen/ neu üblichen Gedichten/ Lehrreichen Sprüchen/ scharffsinnigen Hoffreden/ artigen Schertzfragen und Antworten etc.* (Hamburg: Nauman, 1649).

and their printed anthologies was a truly transnational phenomenon that has survived in other forms to the present day.[7] Other early examples of these fictionalized forms of true crime were the stories that would later be collected in the *Newgate Calendars*[8] (starting in 1728) and in the twenty-volume *Causes célèbres et intéressantes* [*Famous and Interesting Cases*], compiled by the French lawyer and writer François Gayot de Pitaval (1673–1743) and appearing between 1734 and 1743. Pitaval went to the archives and searched for cases that had already caused a stir in their own time. He dug out the legal documents pertaining to the cases and combined them with excerpts from the judicial literature and vivid descriptions of the culprits, the crimes and their punishments. Pitaval was the first to augment the bare facts of famous historical cases with fictionalized accounts of their psychological underpinnings, the perpetrators' sociological backgrounds and the public's response to the crimes. The formula Pitaval found would prove enormously successful and influential. The first German translation had already appeared by 1747, and in 1792, one of the iconic writers later associated with German literary classicism, Friedrich Schiller, published a four-volume selection with a preface. Schiller praised the fictionalized case history's potential for exploring the deepest recesses of the human mind and for gaining insights into anthropology, psychology, pedagogics and the medical sciences. In Germany, the Pitaval tradition continued well into the nineteenth century with the publication of the *Neuer Pitaval* [*New Pitaval*] by the novelist and lawyer Wilhelm Häring (aka Willibald Alexis, 1798–1871) and the legal expert Julius Eduard Hitzig (1780–1849). These stories first appeared in 1842 and became so popular that sixty volumes had been published by 1890.

In the nineteenth century, crime writing underwent a process of differentiation that generated a number of distinct narrative forms. In countries like Great Britain, France and Germany, these new crime stories met with varying levels of popular success, creating the impression that there was a preponderance of separate national traditions of crime fiction. The Anglo-American tradition of modern crime fiction is said to have its origins in Edgar Allan Poe's (1809–1849) stories, which feature the brilliant, eccentric amateur detective C. Auguste Dupin. Poe's 'tales of ratiocination' ushered in a new literary form, the detective story, and created a school of writing that found its adherents in novelists and writers such as Charles Dickens, Wilkie Collins, Gilbert Keith Chesterton and Arthur Conan Doyle. Together, the detective story and the novel, the latter usually

---

7 Cf. *Kriminalfallgeschichten*, ed. by Alexander Košenina, *Text + Kritik* Sonderband (Munich: edition text + kritik, 2014), pp. 5–6.
8 Cf. Knight, *Crime Fiction 1800–2000*, pp. 5–9.

featuring a charismatic amateur detective, constituted the dominant narrative form in crime fiction until the end of the 'golden age' of the 1950s. This period gave rise to enormously popular writers such as Agatha Christie, Dorothy Sayers, Margery Allingham, John Dickson Carr, Ngaio Marsh, S. S. Van Dine and Ellery Queen.

This tradition also heavily influenced German crime fiction, and the works of these writers appeared in translation and became just as successful as in their home countries. Crime fiction that originated in German-speaking countries, however, followed a different trajectory. The case histories of the Pitaval tradition had attempted to introduce legal thinking and an understanding of legal procedures into mainstream middle-class discourse. They had set out to engage an audience of non-experts in the exploration of legal issues and thus tried to mediate between the arcane discourse of legal scholarship and the harsh reality of crime in modernizing societies. Case histories relied mostly on authentic legal cases, which authors then supplemented with fictional material to provide a wider audience with a more interesting reading experience. However, the more fictional material the compilers and writers of case histories included in their stories, the more they were criticized for stooping to the base instincts of a mass-audience that was only interested in cheap thrills. Clearly, in a developing literary market, case histories would not be able to satisfy everybody's tastes. There was room for other forms of crime writing.

Since the 1820s, and therefore almost a generation before Poe, the crime novella (*Kriminalnovelle*) had been gaining a strong foothold in German literature. The German crime novellas of the nineteenth century highlighted the moral, psychological and social causes of crime. They used fictionalized accounts of crime to explore the moral and psychological dimensions of criminal behaviour. The most important example of the early crime novella in German is E.T.A. Hoffmann's *Das Fräulein von Scuderi* [1819, *Mademoiselle de Scudéry*]. Based on an authentic seventeenth-century string of poisonings in pre-revolutionary France, Hoffmann makes use of the historic setting and protagonists, up to and including the French king, but centres his story not on the poisonings themselves, but on a number of fictional murders, for which the widespread hysteria caused by the poisonings merely provide the background. The eponymous Mademoiselle de Scudéry takes it upon herself to investigate the baffling murders and, by using a combination of psychological insight and common sense, she ultimately manages to expose the killer. According to some literary scholars, 'Mademoiselle de Scudéry' was the first detective story, appearing more than twenty years before Poe's tales of ratiocination were published, but Stephen Knight has rightly pointed out that in Hoffmann's novella 'there is no real detection' and that the elderly heroine merely 'supervises the unraveling of the mystery by the plot itself'.[9] More important than establishing who wrote the first detective story, however, is that Hoffmann was primarily interested in exploring the societal ramifications of crime in a given historical setting and, even more so, in fathoming the depths of unconscious desire that drives the murderer in his novella. Hoffmann's tale is not one of detection or the amazing feats of a brilliant and daring detective, but of what drives a killer to commit his crimes. 'Mademoiselle de Scudéry' is among the first in a long list of works of crime 'literature' in German, which includes Annette von Droste-Hülshoff's 'Die Judenbuche' [1842, 'The Jew's Beech Tree'], Theodor Fontane's *Unterm Birnbaum* [1885, *Under the Pear Tree*], Ricarda Huch's *Der Fall Deruga* [1917, *The Deruga Case*], Jakob Wassermann's *Der Fall Maurizius* [1928, *The Maurizius Case*], Heimito von Doderer's *Ein Mord den jeder begeht* [1938, *Every Man a Murderer*] and Patrick Süskind's *Das Parfum* [1985, *Perfume*]. However, due to an ingrained practice of distinguishing between high-brow or 'true' literature and 'trivial' literature or mass-produced 'trash' written merely for entertainment purposes – a practice that has formed an integral part of German cultural history – none of these works are considered 'crime fiction' in Germany.[10]

Starting in the late eighteenth century, another type of crime writing became popular in German-speaking countries. The *Kriminalerzählung* or *Kriminalgeschichte* (both translate as 'crime story') were 'accounts of authentic cases according to what is stated in the files' ('"aktenmäßiger Behandlung" authentischer Fälle').[11] One of the first writers of crime stories in this vein was the legal scholar and professor of aesthetics August Gottlob Meißner (1753–1807). Between 1778 and 1796, he published fourteen volumes of *Skizzen* [*Sketches*], in which he explored the societal background behind criminal acts. Although based on authentic cases, Meißner used his literary skills to probe the motivations of the perpetrators and to question the cruel methods of investigation and punishment. As an adherent of the Enlightenment, he promoted rational thought in dealing with crime and condemned the use of torture to extract (often false) confessions.

---

9 Knight, *Crime Fiction 1800–2000*, p. 19.
10 For a discussion of twentieth-century German novels that feature crime see *Experimente mit dem Kriminalroman. Ein Erzählmodell in der deutschsprachigen Literatur des 20. Jahrhunderts* ed. by Wolfgang Düsing (Frankfurt am Main, et.al.: Peter Lang, 1993).
11 Cf. Jörg Schönert, 'Kriminalgeschichten in der deutschen Literatur zwischen 1770 und 1890. Zur Entwicklung des Genres in sozialgeschichtlicher Perspektive', in *Der Kriminalroman. Poetik, Theorie, Geschichte*, ed. by Jochen Vogt (Munich: Wilhelm Fink, 1998), pp. 322–339, (p. 327).

Meißner had many followers in his attempt to make a literary contribution to a legal discourse that was feeling the effects of the philosophical, technological and societal changes brought about by modernization. His brand of 'Justizkritik' (criticism of the legal system) served as the inspiration for two types of fictionalized crime writing that emerged in the nineteenth century in German-speaking countries.[12] Stories of detection and the hunt for the criminal focused less on the perpetrator's psychological background or questions of morality in connection with the criminal act and more on the figure of the professional investigator. Two of the most important writers of this school were the lawyer, journalist and dramatist Adolph Müllner (1774–1829) and the Prussian judge and law professor J.D.H. Temme (1798–1881). Müllner's *Der Kaliber* [1828, *The Caliber*] has been called 'the first genuine detective story in the German language'.[13] Temme was forced into exile in Zurich after the failed revolution of 1848 and published thirty-four crime stories between 1855 and 1868, reaching a widespread audience. In these stories, he applied his robust knowledge of legal procedures while advocating for a practice of fair trials and the importance of civil rights.[14]

The other type of crime story that developed during the nineteenth century in German-speaking countries was that of the criminal career. Writers such as Ernst Dronke (1822–1891) and Hermann Kurz (1813–1873) embodied this type of crime writing. After obtaining his law degree, Ernst Dronke went to Berlin and launched his career as a writer. He, too, was forced into exile and finally settled in Liverpool. His literary work was heavily influenced by his socialist convictions. In this respect, and similar to Eugène Sue's *Les Mystères de Paris* [1842–1843, *The Mysteries of Paris*], Dronke's *Polizeigeschichten* [1846, *Police Stories**] are a collection of novellas that show human beings as products of their social environment. Often, crime is the result of bureaucratic overreach or the actions of corrupt police officers.

What these nineteenth-century crime narratives from German-speaking countries have in common and what separates them from the Anglo-American and French traditions of crime writing is a desire to educate the public about

---

12 For the following, cf. Schönert, 'Kriminalgeschichten', p. 328.
13 Cf. the note by the editors in: *Early German and Austrian Detective Fiction. An Anthology*, ed. by Mary W. Tannert and Henry Kratz (Jefferson/NC and London: McFarland, 1999), p. 9. An abridged translation of *Der Kaliber* is available in this volume (pp. 9–53).
14 Cf. Volker Neuhaus, 'Die Schwierigkeiten der Deutschen mit dem Kriminalroman', in *Mord als kreativer Prozeß. Zum Kriminalroman der Gegenwart in Deutschland, Österreich und der Schweiz*, ed. by Sandro M. Moraldo (Heidelberg: Universitätsverlag Winter, 2005), pp. 9–19 (p. 11).

the intricacies of the legal system, its procedures and strengths, its challenges and shortcomings, but also to awaken readers' interest in crime's psychological and social background. They also strive to entertain, but this appears to be almost an afterthought. A completely different strand of crime fiction, 'the dime novel', emerged during the second half of the nineteenth century in the US. Printed on cheap paper (like its successor, the pulp magazine), it featured all kinds of adventurous and sensationalist stories, beginning with Westerns, horror stories and fantastic tales. During the 1880s, detective stories and mystery stories became the dominant types of dime novel, featuring private detectives like Nick Carter (in German translation since 1905) and Sexton Blake (in the United Kingdom since 1893). Influenced by Poe's tales of ratiocination and by Émile Gaboriau's (1832–1873) model of the French *roman policier*, dime novels soon acquired a mass following in Germany. Seen as cheap 'trash' that presented a threat to the intellectual and cultural well-being of the people (*Volk*), detective stories became the object of systematic vilification carried out by pedagogues and self-appointed guardians of good taste.[15] In spite of these efforts, translations of detective fiction written by British, American and other international authors still had a strong following in Germany at the beginning of the twentieth century. In the 1920s and 1930s, writers such as Arthur Conan Doyle, Agatha Christie, G.K. Chesterton, Edgar Wallace (1875–1932), Ellery Queen, and Sweden's Sven Elvestad (1884–1934) were household names in Germany.

What is not well known, however, is the fact that detective fiction written by German-speaking authors also had a large following from the nineteenth century to the beginning of the Nazi-period.[16] The names of German authors of crime fiction who were quite successful during the interwar period, such as Ernst Reicher, Alfred Schirokauer and Paul Rosenhayn, have now been forgotten.[17] During the interwar years, another development changed the landscape of German crime fiction and set it apart from its international peers: 'Unlike the analytic detective story that dominated English, French, and American literature in the 1920s, the German crime story dispensed with the figure of the detective [...] and crossed

---

15 These efforts were nothing new. They began as early as in the late eighteenth century, but reached a climax in 1926 with the infamous 'Law to protect the Youth against Filth and Trash' ('Gesetz zur Bewahrung der Jugend vor Schund- und Schmutzschriften').

16 Cf. Hans-Otto Hügel, *Untersuchungsrichter, Diebsfänger, Detektive. Theorie und Geschichte der deutschen Detektiverzählung im 19. Jahrhundert* (Stuttgart: Metzler, 1978).

17 On German crime fiction from the turn of the century to the 1940s, cf. Knut Hickethier, 'Der Alte Deutsche Kriminalroman. Von vergessenen Traditionen', *Die Horen* 144 (1986), pp. 15–23.

over to a focus on the figure of the criminal [. . .].'[18] There was a palpable fascination with serial killers, pathological criminal masterminds and 'outsiders of society'[19] that manifested itself in crime fiction and in crime film during the years of the Weimar Republic. Iconic movies of the time, such as *Das Cabinet des Dr. Caligari* [1920, *The Cabinet of Dr. Caligari*] and Fritz Lang's films featuring criminal mastermind Dr. Mabuse [*Dr. Mabuse, der Spieler* [1922, *Dr. Mabuse, the Gambler*] and *Das Testament des Dr. Mabuse* [1933, *The Testament of Dr. Mabuse*] and *M – Eine Stadt sucht einen Mörder* [1931 *M – A City Looks for a Murderer*] reflected this fascination with the criminal.

Reading crime fiction was a favourite pastime in Nazi Germany. In 1939 alone, half a million detective novels were printed in Germany. The books of most of the famous Anglo-American authors were readily available in bookstores throughout the Third Reich, many of them even in their original language. It was only in early 1941 that book dealers were forbidden from selling detective novels by these authors and libraries were told to restrict their circulation.[20] The Nazis knew full well that crime fiction could be utilized as a means of distraction: crime fiction written by German authors had a function similar to that of film in the Third Reich: to entertain and thus divert its audience's attention from the increasingly brutal reality of the war.

German authors of crime fiction under Nazism still followed the established patterns and formulas of internationally successful crime fiction. They often wrote crime novels set in major American cities or in London and they wrote under English-sounding pseudonyms. Apparently, both critics of the genre and publishers were of the opinion that the English and American models remained unrivalled.[21] Crime stories written by German authors and set in Germany aimed above all to convey a positive picture of police work and to encourage their

---

18 Todd Herzog, *Crime Stories. Criminalistic Fantasy and the Culture of Crisis in Weimar Germany* (New York, Oxford: Berghahn Books, 2009).
19 *Außenseiter der Gesellschaft. Die Verbrechen der Gegenwart* [*Outsiders of Society. The Crimes of Contemporary Times**] was an imprint of the Berlin publishing house *Die Schmiede*. Edited by Rudolf Leonhard, a series of fourteen short novels was published in 1924 and 1925, written by authors such as Alfred Döblin, Egon Erwin Kisch, Ernst Weiß, and Theodor Lessing.
20 Walter T. Rix, 'Wesen und Wandel des Detektivromans im totalitären Staat', in Paul G. Buchloh, Jens P. Becker, *Der Detektivroman. Studien zur Geschichte und Form der englischen und amerikanischen Detektivliteratur* (Darmstadt: Wissenschaftliche Buchgesellschaft, 1989), pp. 121–134 (p. 123). On crime fiction in Nazi Germany, cf. Carsten Würmann, 'Zum Kriminalroman im Nationalsozialismus', in *Verbrechen als Passion. Neue Untersuchungen zum Kriminalgenre*, ed. by Bruno Franceschini and Carsten Würmann (Berlin: Weidler Buchverlag, 2004), pp. 143–186.
21 Würmann, 'Zum Kriminalroman im Nationalsozialismus', pp. 149–150.

readers to embrace vigilance and to cooperate with the police force, working together against 'internal enemies', be they criminals, political opponents or psychopathic serial killers.[22] Once the war began in 1939, the focus shifted to the type of spy novel that primarily dealt with protecting the 'homeland' from enemy spies. One of the motives frequently used was the supposedly nefarious stratagems of German-Americans returning to Germany to work against the new regime.

Crime fiction in Germany after 1945: The contributions in this volume

The only authors of crime fiction writing in German from the 1930s to the 1950s whose works are still read today are Friedrich Glauser (1896–1938) and Friedrich Dürrenmatt (1921–1990), both from Switzerland. Glauser was influenced by the enormously prolific and successful Belgian writer Georges Simenon (1903–1989), whose Inspector Jules Maigret is almost as well-known as Sherlock Holmes in Germany. *Syndikat*, the association of German crime writers, named its annual prize for the best crime novel written in German the Friedrich-Glauser-Prize in honour of the writer.[23] Friedrich Dürrenmatt is primarily known as a dramatist and writer of plays such as *Der Besuch der alten Dame* [1956, *The Visit*] and *Die Physiker* [1962, *The Physicists*]. He also wrote a number of detective novels, however, in which he critically explores the ontological and epistemological underpinnings of the genre. Glauser and Dürrenmatt were seminal for the development of contemporary crime fiction in German and are therefore the subject of chapter 2 of this volume.

Soon after World War II, there was tremendous demand in Germany for all of the cultural products that had been banned by the Nazis. Crime fiction by British and American authors was made available in translation and took the German market by storm. Readers had been well aware of the German detective novel as a genre in its own right before 1945, but there was then a complete 'break with tradition' and the readership became primarily interested in translations of Anglo-

---

22 Cf. Joachim Linder, 'Feinde im Innern. Mehrfachtäter in deutschen Kriminalromanen der Jahre 1943/44 und der "Mythos Serienkiller"', *Internationales Archiv für Sozialgeschichte der deutschen Literatur* 28.2 (2003), pp. 190–227.

23 Cf. the web page of the association: http://www.das-syndikat.com/. The various categories of the 'Glauser', as the prize is commonly called can be found under: http://www.das-syndikat .com/krimipreise/krimipreise-der-autoren/ehrenglauser.html.

American crime novels.[24] As a result, 'the German crime novel had to redefine itself in East and West [...] after 1945'.[25] Crime fiction written in West Germany in the 1940s and 1950s still by and large followed the model of the 'golden age' novels by the British and American masters. German-speaking authors preferred to set their novels in (for German readers) exotic and (for crime fiction) well-known locations such as London, Los Angeles and New York, as, for example, in the police procedurals by the Vienna-born Frank Arnau (the pseudonym of Heinrich Karl Schmitt, 1894–1976). There were certainly some initial, tentative attempts to gain a critical perspective on contemporary society and to create psychological depth in the novels' characters, but these and the generally more pronounced realism of the novels were mere precursors to a development that came into its own during the 1960s and 1970s with the arrival of the *Neuer Deutscher Kriminalroman* [New German Crime Novel], which will be covered in chapter 4 of this volume.

Like all cultural products, the development of the crime novel in the GDR had always been subject to the directives of the communist regime. The changing requirements of cultural policy pertaining to entertainment literature therefore determined what was possible in the realm of crime fiction and what was not. As a literary genre classified as 'Western',[26] the communist party had initially rejected the crime novel. It was only later that the party realized that they could use crime fiction as 'a tool to support the party's strategy on their way to a socialist political system'.[27] Because the GDR was avowedly a socialist society well on its way to communism, crime was supposed to be a by-product of capitalism. In the 'real socialism' of the GDR, capitalist property relations no longer existed, and crime was therefore impossible. If crimes were committed nonetheless, they were either committed by Western agents or by people with a fascist or capitalist agenda. In the first years of the GDR, the crime novel was therefore 'quasi-unpresentable'.[28] That changed in the 1950s, more specifically after 1953. After the attempted rebellion

---

24 Hügel, *Untersuchungsrichter, Diebsfänger, Detektive*, p. 207 (my trans.).

25 Thomas Wörtche, *Das Mörderische neben dem Leben. Ein Wegbegleiter durch die Welt der Kriminalliteratur* (Lengwil: Libelle, 2008), p. 21.

26 Manfred Jäger, 'Die Legitimierung der Unterhaltungsliteratur', in *Die Literatur der DDR*, ed. by Hans-Jürgen Schmitt, *Hansers Sozialgeschichte der deutschen Literatur vom 16. Jahrhundert bis zur Gegenwart*, vol. 11 (Munich: dtv 1983) pp. 229–260 (p. 246).

27 Reinhard Jahn, 'Jesus, Buddha, der Müll und der Tod. Spurensicherung in Sachen Soziokrimi', *Deutschsprachige Literatur der 70er und 80er Jahre. Autoren, Tendenzen, Gattungen*, ed. by Walter Delabar and Erhard Schütz (Darmstadt: Wissenschaftliche Buchgesellschaft, 1997), pp. 38–52, (p. 48).

28 Reinhard Hillich, 'Krimi in der DDR – DDR im Krimi', *Die DDR im Spiegel ihrer Literatur. Beiträge zu einer historischen Betrachtung der DDR-Literatur*, ed. by Franz Huberth (Berlin: Duncker & Humblot, 2005), pp. 105–116 (p. 106).

against the regime of June 17, crime stories were used as a means of indoctrination. The plot was always constructed in the same way: Western agents infiltrated the GDR, trying to sabotage the construction of the new state by stealing important inventions. These attempts were then thwarted by vigilant police officers and workers loyal to the regime.

By the 1960s, it had become clear that it was possible to utilize popular literature – and crime fiction as one part of popular literature – to keep the population in line. After 1968, crime novels and weekly *Heftromane*[29] [dime novels] appeared under several imprints: 'K-Series', 'NB-Novels', 'Yellow Series' or the popular 'DIE-Series' (Delikte, Indizien, Ermittlungen [Crimes, Evidence, Investigations]). With the relaxation of cultural policy in the early 1970s, there emerged a 'thriving production of crime fiction' that provided a view of the GDR that ran counter to the officially sanctioned image of the country and focused on corruption and petty crime as the norm of social and political reality.[30] At almost the same time, the GDR itself became the setting for fictional crime as a regular occurrence caused by home-grown problems.[31] Authors like Gert Prokop, Hartmut Mechtel, Barbara Neuhaus, Tom Wittgen and Klaus Möckel began exploring grievances within GDR society, such as the limited freedom of movement, the scarcity of luxury goods and a 'lack of self-determination and democracy',[32] and turned the population's general discontent into a catalyst for crime. During the 1980s, issues like prostitution, homosexuality and sectarianism became subjects of crime fiction, although they were not permitted as a topic of discussion in the media controlled by the regime.[33]

Although it was subject to extensive censorship,[34] crime fiction in the GDR was almost always *Bückware* (bottom-shelf goods). That meant that, due to its popularity and to limited print runs, you could only get your hands on it if you were on good terms with your bookseller, who would sell you the books under

---

29 *Heftromane* are still popular in Germany today. They appear weekly or bi-weekly, usually have 64 pages, and are printed on cheap paper. They are written by groups of authors who have to adhere to a general outline of settings and stock characters. One of the most popular (West) German *Heftroman* series is *Jerry Cotton*, which began in 1954 and features a fictional FBI agent fighting organized crime in New York.

30 Neuhaus, 'Die Schwierigkeiten der Deutschen', p. 13.

31 Walter T. Rix, 'Krimis in der DDR. Sozialistischer Seiltanz', *Die Horen* 144 (1986), pp. 71–77 (p. 76).

32 Hillich, 'Krimi in der DDR', p. 111.

33 Hillich, 'Krimi in der DDR', p. 105.

34 Rix, 'Krimis in der DDR, p. 73; Dorothea Germer, *Von Genossen und Gangstern. Zum Gesellschaftsbild in der Kriminalliteratur der DDR und Ostdeutschlands von 1974 bis 1994* (Essen: Die Blaue Eule, 1998), pp. 55–61.

the counter (and who would have to go out of his or her way to get them for you). In the 1970s and 1980s, crime fiction written in East Germany was tremendously popular, but the criticisms it contained never went beyond discussing the symptoms of political discontent. There was no tolerance for any critique of the political system itself or the regime.[35]

Crime fiction written by Austrian authors has become extremely popular among German-speaking readers since the 1990s. Writers such as Wolf Haas, Heinrich Steinfest, Edith Kneifl, Eva Rossmann, Alfred Komarek, Josef Haslinger, Manfred Wieninger and Paulus Hochgatter, to name just a few, have produced best-sellers, some of which even have been translated into other languages. Chapter 3 starts by providing a brief overview of the history of Austrian crime fiction and then looks at a number of specific features that allow us to define crime fiction written in Austria as a distinct literary entity. The chapter closes with a short discussion of two novels by Wolf Haas and Paulus Hochgatterer, *Auferstehung der Toten* [*Resurrection*] and *Das Matratzenhaus* [*The Mattress House*].

Chapter 4 is devoted to the West-German *Soziokrimi* or sociological crime novel. Although still indebted to the Anglo-American, Scandinavian and Western European traditions, the term *Soziokrimi* outlines the first step in the development of an autonomous literature of crime fiction in West Germany. It began around 1962 with the inception of the 'black' thriller series by the Rowohlt publishing house and ended in the 1980s, when a new generation of writers appeared on the scene. Important *Soziokrimi* authors include Hansjörg Martin (from 1965), Friedhelm Werremeier (from 1972), Irene Rodrian (from 1967), Michael Molsner (after 1968), '-ky' or Horst Bosetzky (from 1971) and Felix Huby (from 1977). What this group of authors – who preferred the designation *Neuer deutscher Kriminalroman* – have in common is a narrative perspective that views crime as socially determined, even produced by societal circumstances, and understands crime fiction as a form of social criticism. This view led to critical reassessments of institutions such as the police and the judiciary, but also the economy, the health care system and mass media. Crime scenes were often located in small towns in Germany, both fictional and real, imbuing many of these crime novels with a provincial atmosphere. For many authors, the books written by the Swedish writers Per Wahlöö and Maj Sjöwall between 1965 and 1975 were of tremendous importance, as was their connection to the most prominent German TV series *Tatort* (from 1970), for which many of the authors also wrote scripts.

---

35 Hillich, 'Krimi in der DDR', p. 115.

The regional crime story or Regionalkrimi is one of the most productive sub-genres in current crime fiction writing in German-speaking countries. On the one hand, it is heavily featured in the programs of certain publishing houses, such as Gmeiner, Grafit, Econ and Pendragon, and is written by authors who strive to spruce up their stories by adding a local touch. However, there is another group of writers who bring 'local knowledge' (Clifford Geertz) into play to create multiface-ted depictions of regional or urban spaces. These writers include Friedrich Ani, Jan Seghers, Oliver Bottini, Ulrich Ritzel, Uta-Maria Heim, Jörg Juretzka and Hansjörg Schneider. Chapter 5 explores how authors combine the conventions of, firstly, crime fiction writing and 'regionality' and, secondly, the 'poetics of murder' and 'local knowledge'. It will also pay attention to the question of how authors attempt to investigate issues of Germany's problematic past by focusing on local spaces.

Another subgenre of German crime fiction that has gained considerable pop-ularity and critical acclaim is the *Frauenkrimi* (crime fiction written by women). Taking its cue from the fact that female authors have played a significant role in the writing of crime fiction since the beginning, chapter 6 shows that crime fic-tion written by women tends to deploy comic strategies to cut male characters down to size while engendering female empowerment. This opens up new critical innovations for the genre, particularly when looking beyond the *Frauenkrimi* as a marketing label and understanding crime fiction in a broader sense as litera-ture about criminal behaviour, individuals and conquering criminality in a more comprehensive societal sense instead.

In recent German crime writing, revisiting German history has become a pop-ular and successful strategy. Authors such as Petra Oelker and Volker Kutscher write about detectives and police officers who have to negotiate the complex power structures of eighteenth-century and pre-Nazi Germany respectively as well as the ever-shifting contradictions of societies very much in flux. Chapter 7 looks at the contributions this kind of historical crime fiction has made to our un-derstanding of German history. Specifically, it looks at various types of historical crime fiction and the significant role played by paratexts before providing a brief overview of historical crime fiction written in Germany. The chapter concludes with short discussions of two popular novels by Frank Schätzing and Andrea Maria Schenkel.

As the reader will see in chapter 8, the genre of historical crime fiction is a significant component of *historical culture*, which Jörn Rüsen defines as an 'articulation of historical awareness in the life of a society'.[36] Critics usually

---

36 Jörn Rüsen, 'Geschichtskultur', *Geschichte in Wissenschaft und Unterricht* (46) 1995, pp. 513–521 (p. 513). 'Artikulation von Geschichtsbewusstsein im Leben einer Gesellschaft'.

distinguish between two subtypes: firstly, *historical crime novels* set entirely in a historical period that is depicted as an experienced present and, secondly, *retrospective historical crime novels* featuring present-day detectives whose enquiries lead the reader back into the historical past. However, this distinction can be redefined with regards to the different narrative strategies the novels employ in order to configure history in fiction and comment on 'canonized history'. Against the backdrop of Ansgar Nünning's typology of historical fiction (1995), chapter 9 examines the current tendency to rework the legacy of the Nazi past within the narrative framework of family history and discusses its manifold manifestations, varying from documentary recordings to metahistorical discourses.

As the genre's structure and its poetics of suspicion transform any given certainty into an – at best – plausible hypothesis, crime fiction explicitly displays culturally specific epistemological strategies to render the uncanny understandable and knowable. These strategies are now multiplying: in order to cope with the crimes of today's multicultural society, detective characters need to be able to read the clues against the backdrop of coexisting sign systems. Although this calls for an approach that (theoretically) opens up a 'third space', essentialist concepts of origin deriving from political debates on interculturality seem to sneak in through the backdoor. After providing a brief history of intercultural German crime fiction and a short discussion of the potential the genre's narrative pattern provides for intercultural reshufflings, chapter 9 begins by focussing on one specific aspect of detection strategies. It offers an analysis of strategies guided by concepts of origin, honour and terrorism discourses, and multicultural teamwork in Jakob Arjouni's *Kismet* [2001, *Kismet. A Kayankaya Thriller*], W.W. Domsky's *Ehre, wem Ehre . . .* [2009, *Honor To Whom Honor . . . **], Su Turhan's *Kommissar Pascha* [2013, *Detective Inspector Pascha**] and Ulrich Noller's and Gök Senin's *Çelik & Pelzer* [2010, *Çelik & Pelzer**]. In addition to taking a rather socio-critical perspective on these and other novels, the chapter then discusses the tendency in German-speaking crime fiction to somewhat whimsically enlighten multicultural society, paying special attention to narrative modifications and the ongoing play with the concept of probability in Osman Engin's *Tote essen keinen Döner* [2008, *Dead People Don't Eat Döner**], Hilal Sezgin's *Mihriban pfeift auf Gott* [2010, *Mihriban Doesn't Give a Damn about God**], Heinrich Steinfest's *Cheng* [1999/2007, *Cheng**] and *Die Haischwimmerin* [2011, *Swimming with Sharks**].

At least one third of the German book market comprises crime fiction, and its media extensions in television, cinema, cartoons, radio plays, etc. probably have a similar reach. In contrast to this quantitative dominance, many observers still – or once again – harbour reservations about this kind of 'trivial entertainment literature' for aesthetic, literary and political reasons. Interestingly enough, an over-supply, particularly of market-compatible, easily mass-produced German crime fiction, appears to confirm these misgivings. The intellectual and aesthetic emancipation of crime fiction which, on the whole, was believed to have been accomplished by the late 1990s, has given way to the incentives of 'the market' – as well as the competing discourse of 'serious' literature, which saw itself challenged by narratives that combined aesthetically challenging reading experiences with entertaining storylines. This over-supply, however, has also introduced a new dialectical moment: it has provoked a kind of *ennui* on the part of certain audiences, which, in turn, has triggered a more high-brow writing of crime fiction, which has been apparent for some time now. Chapter 10 analyses these developments in the literary field and illuminates their mutual interdependence vis-à-vis other narrative possibilities in crime fiction (in other media) and in comparison to other narrative strategies employed to produce either social consensus or dissent.

Some might view teaching (German) crime fiction at a college level as a dubious enterprise. Critics of the genre have pointed out its alleged shortcomings and questioned its suitability as an object of serious reading. In chapter 11, the authors take on this criticism – from Edmund Wilson to Franco Moretti – and show how these interventions, together with critical readings of crime fiction in the broadest sense, can be turned into a useful and satisfying pedagogical exercise. The chapter identifies three areas of instruction that teachers can cover using German crime fiction: basic narratological analysis, *Landeskunde* and social critique.

Chapter 12 introduces readers to authors and texts that are of special interest for contemporary German crime fiction and that the preceding chapters do not extensively comment upon. While chapters 2 to 11 are primarily concerned with broader developments in the genre and with providing overviews of certain trends in German crime fiction, the short portraits in this chapter will familiarize readers with some of the most interesting crime novelists writing today.

Since the 1980s, authors from Germany, Austria and Switzerland have been advancing innovative narrative strategies and techniques in crime fiction. They have negotiated modern and postmodern literary aesthetics and have also contributed to moving German literature towards 'readability'. In their books, they reflect on historical and contemporary social and political issues. Their works are informed by international crime fiction writing, and they are building a specific and multi-faceted oeuvre of crime fiction written in German. The contributions in this volume will explore the whole range of accomplishments that this exciting tradition has to offer.

Gonçalo Vilas-Boas

2 The Beginnings of Swiss Detective Literature: Glauser and Dürrenmatt

Detective fiction in Switzerland was a rather late phenomenon compared to the development of the genre in the Anglo-Saxon world. In nineteenth-century Switzerland, as in many other Europeans countries, there was great interest in protocols and reports on judicial cases. Some authors, such as Carl Albert Loosli (1877–1959), included some elements of this genre in their stories. But it was only in the 1930s that the genre fully entered the Swiss literary scene – first with Friedrich Glauser (1896–1938), followed by Friedrich Dürrenmatt (1921–1990). It was only in the 1980s that the genre, including the popular regional crime novel, began to play an important role in Swiss literature.

In this chapter, I will focus specifically on Glauser and Dürrenmatt, who represent the beginnings of detective fiction in German-speaking Switzerland. For the French-speaking part of the country, one would have to go back to 1904 and the works of Benjamin Valloton and his Commissaire Potterat, among others.[1] Even though the Anglo-American tradition was well known, Georges Simenon and his fictional detective, Maigret, played a major role in both parts of the country.

Glauser: Background and literary ideals

Friedrich Glauser lived a very troubled life. Since his work was intimately related to his life, I will explore his biography in some detail. I will begin with Glauser's own description in a letter he wrote to Joseph Halperin on 15 June 1937, one year before his death:

> Do you want facts? Right then: Born Vienna, 1896, Austrian mother and Swiss father. Grandfather on my father's side a gold-digger in California (*sans blague*), on my mother's side a senior civil servant (fantastic combination, don't you think?). Primary school, three years high school in Vienna. Then three years at the Glarisegg Reform School. Then three years at the Collège de Genève. Thrown out shortly before taking the school-leaving examination [...] took them in Zurich. Then Dadaism. My father wanted to have me locked away and placed under a legal guardian. Ran away to Geneva [...] detained in Münsingen for

---

1 Cf. Paul Ott, *Mord im Alpenglühen. Der Schweizer Kriminalroman. Geschichte und Gegenwart* (Essen: Nordpark, 2005).

https://doi.org/10.1515/9783110426601-002

a year (1919). Escaped from there. One year in Ascona. Arrested for morphine. Sent back. Three months Burghölzli (for a second opinion, because Geneva had declared me schizophrenic). 1921–23 Foreign Legion. Then Paris, washer-up. Belgium, coalmines. Later hospital orderly in Charleroi. Morphine again. Imprisoned in Belgium. Deported to Switzerland. Ordered to do one year at Witzwil. Afterwards one year labourer in a tree nursery. Analysis (one year) [...] To Basel as a gardener, then Winterthur. During that time (1928/29) wrote my Foreign Legion novel, '30/'31 one-year course at the Oeschberg tree nursery. July '31 follow-up analysis. January '32 to July '32, Paris as 'freelance writer' (as the saying goes). Went to visit my father in Mannheim. Arrested there for forged prescriptions. Deported to Switzerland. Imprisoned from July '32 – May '36. *Et puis voilà. Ce n'est pas très beau, mais on fait ce qu'on peut.*[2]

Then he went to France, together with his German girlfriend, Berthe Bendel, a nurse he had met in one of the many institutions he was placed in during his lifetime (Bürghölzli, Witzwil, Münsingen, Waldau and Prangins, among others), where he was diagnosed with 'moral insanity'. He then spent time in a clinic in Bale before going to Italy with Berthe. A few days before their wedding was set to take place, he died in Italy.

This brief text elucidates the main themes of Glauser's life: he was always escaping, always a marginal figure, prone to morphine abuse and to engaging in petty crime in order to obtain the drugs he needed, trying to make a living, but never in the conventional way. He attempted suicide five times. His mother died when he was four, his father was very hard on him, and his guardian did not always understand him.

---

2 Friedrich Glauser, *Thumbprint*, trans. by Kike Mitchell (London: Bitter Lemon Press, 2004), p. 199. 'Daten wollen Sie? Also: 1896 geboren in Wien von österreichischer Mutter und Schweizer Vater. Großvater väterlicherseits Goldgräber in Kalifornien (sans blague), mütterlicherseits Hofrat (schöne Mischung, wie?). Volksschule, 3 Klassen Gymnasium in Wien. Dann 3 Jahre Landerziehungsheim Glarisegg. Dann 3 Jahre Collège de Genève. Dort kurz vor der Matur hinausgeschmissen ... Kantonale Matur in Zürich. Dann Dadaismus. Vater wollte mich internieren lassen und unter Vormundschaft stellen. Flucht nach Genf ... 1 Jahr (1919) in Münsingen interniert. Flucht von dort. 1 Jahr Ascona. Verhaftung wegen Mo [Morphin]. Rücktransport. 3 Monate Burghölzli (Gegenexpertise, weil Genf mich für schizophren erklärt hatte). 1921–23 Fremdenlegion. Dann Paris Plongeur [Tellerwäscher]. Belgien Kohlengruben. Später in Charleroi Krankenwärter. Wieder Mo. Internierung in Belgien. Rücktransport in die Schweiz. 1 Jahr administrativ Witzwil. Nachher 1 Jahr Handlanger in einer Baumschule. Analyse (1 Jahr) ... Als Gärtner nach Basel, dann nach Winterthur. In dieser Zeit den Legionsroman geschrieben (1928/29), 30/31 Jahreskurs Gartenbaumschule Oeschberg. Juli 31 Nachanalyse. Jänner 32 bis Juli 32 Paris als ›freier Schriftsteller‹ (wie man so schön sagt). Zum Besuch meines Vaters nach Mannheim. Dort wegen falschen Rezepten arretiert. Rücktransport in die Schweiz. Von Juli 32 – Mai 36 interniert. Et puis voilà. Ce n'est pas très beau ... ' (*Briefe 2 (1935–38)*, ed. by Bernhard Echte. Zurich: Arche 1991, p. 623f).

Writing was his passion. He started with some poems, and between 1913 and 1916, while living in Geneva, he was already writing short stories and becoming acquainted with Dada writers at some of the meetings he attended. His first novel was entitled *Gourrama: Ein Roman aus der Fremdenlegion* [1940, *Gourrama: A Novel from the Foreign Legion**] and was followed by *Der Tee der drei alten Damen* [1941, *The Three Old Ladies' Tea*], his only detective novel that did not feature Sergeant (*Wachtmeister*) Studer, the protagonist of his other five crime novels, which were written in his last three years. These five novels were quite successful in his time, both serialized in newspapers and magazines, and later, when they were published as books. He also wrote a number of short stories, which he published in magazines. Some of their main themes are similar to the ones he explored in his novels – such as, for example, his experience in the Foreign Legion. Throughout his life and in his books, he was always trying to escape from the 'narrowest Switzerland' (*engste Schweiz*).[3]

Glauser was an avid reader of detective stories, and he wrote about his reading. He wrote a long letter to Stefan Brockhoff, who had published 'Zehn Gebote für den Kriminalroman' ['Ten Commandments for the Crime Novel'*] in the magazine *Zürcher Illustrierte* on 5 February 1937.[4] The magazine did not publish Glauser's response, written on 25 March 1937, in which he defended different points of view and questioned the necessity of Brockhoff's 'Ten Commandments'. He did not agree with Brockhoff that rules with the status of a set of commandments could be derived from the Anglo-American model, and he disliked the 'smart guy' detective, thinking and acting like a robot, using and abusing logical deduction. According to Glauser, suspense is not the main purpose of the novel; it should not hide what is important. He defended the idea of the protagonist as an imperfect detective, somebody with a wife or girlfriend, with everyday problems and feelings – a real person, not a schematic character. He wanted the great detective to be removed from his pedestal. Even the criminal, he said, should be a normal person, not a hero or an antihero, because anybody can become a murderer, depending on the circumstances.

---

3 Cf. Irmgard Wirtz, 'Verbrechen auf engstem Raum', *Quarto* 21/22 (2006) pp. 51–60 (p. 52).

4 This text was a response to Stefan Brockhoff's 'Zehn Gebote für den Kriminalroman', published in the *Zürcher Illustrierte* on 5 February 1937. 'Brockhoff' was a pseudonym used by three German writers in their detective novels. They postulated ten commandments following S. S. Van Dine's 'Twenty Rules for Writing Detective Stories' (1929) or 'Father Knox's Decalogue' (1929). The author must be fair to the reader; all cases must be solved; both the murderer and the detective must be presented as people – evil in the former case, clever in the latter; and other similar rules apply, some of them rather obvious, as Glauser points out in his reply.

Glauser questioned the classification of people as good or bad; he did not see any great '*Utilität*'[5] (utility) in such classifications. He wrote:

> The story of a detective novel can easily be told in one-and-a-half pages. The rest is stuffing. It depends on how you make use of it. [...] Not the criminal case as such, not the exposure of the perpetrator and the solution are important, but the people and especially the atmosphere in which they move.[6]

He did not like logical, deductive detectives like Poirot and Sherlock Holmes. As a model, he pointed to Georges Simenon and his great Inspector Maigret, who were much more interesting to him, even if Glauser himself did not follow all the rules of the French school,[7] especially the need to resolve the case at the end of the story. For example, Studer often says that he is not a judge; he refuses to judge others and instead tries to solve their problems and understand them. Glauser always wanted to show the truth about society through his fictional work.

He argued that detective novels should share the more general novelistic qualities of self-consciousness and reflectiveness, that they are not the poor relatives of the literary world. Instead, as Marle, a character in the novel *Der Tee der drei alten Damen*, says, 'Don't make fun of detective stories. They're the only medium today for popularizing reasonable ideas'.[8] The settings for Glauser's crime scenes, such as mental institutions and villages, are similar to locked-room scenarios.[9] This made it easier to convey the ambience – what Glauser called 'die Atmosphäre'.[10]

His characters are mainly ordinary people and are always the victims, even when they are the murderers. Sometimes he uses figures who abuse their power, such as Aeschbacher (in *Wachtmeister Studer* [1936, *Thumbprint*]) or Dr. Laduner (in *Matto regiert* [1936, *In Matto's Realm*]). The setting's atmosphere was essential

---

5 Cf. Patrick Bühler, *Die Leiche in der Bibliothek. Friedrich Glauser und der Detektiv-Roman* (Heidelberg: Winter, 2002), p. 105.

6 Friedrich Glauser, *Wachtmeister Studers erste Fälle*, ed. by Frank Göhre (Zurich: Arche, 1989), pp. 181–191, (p. 185 and 190), (my transl.). 'Die Handlung eines Kriminalromans läßt sich in anderthalb Seiten gut und gerne erzählen. Der Rest sind Füllsel. [...] Nicht der Kriminalfall an sich, nicht die Entlarvung des Täters und die Lösung ist Hauptthema, sondern die Menschen und besonders die Atmosphäre, in der sie sich bewegen'.

7 Cf.Bühler, *Die Leiche in der Bibliothek*, p. 146.

8 Friedrich Glauser, *The Three Old Ladies' Tea*, trans. by Peter Kalnin (Kindle edition, 2015). F. G., *Der Tee der drei alten Damen* (Zurich: Arche, 1989), p. 126–127. 'Spotten Sie nicht über Kriminalromane! Sie sind heutzutage das einzige Mittel, vernünftige Ideen zu popularisieren'.

9 Wirtz, 'Verbrechen auf engstem Raum', p. 52.

10 See note 6, 'the atmosphere' or, as Glauser's translator Mike Mitchell prefers, 'the locales'.

to him – it explained many things about the way people communicated and their dependence on each other. It was less important to solve the crime than to understand why it had occurred in the first place.

Glauser's Sergeant Studer: Questioning truth

Glauser wrote quite a few detective stories featuring Sergeant Studer. But in his first detective novel, *Der Tee der drei alten Damen*, Studer does not appear. Instead, a number of characters perform the detective role: Detective Inspector (*Kommissar*) Pillevuit, State Councillor (*Staatsrat*) Martinet, a district attorney (*Staatsanwalt*) who likes to write sonnets, the Irish journalist O'Key and two Soviet spies, Agent 72 (Baranoff) and Agent 83 (Natascha). Some other characters also take part in the action, such as Dr. Magde and Dr. Thievenoz from the Bel-Air insane asylum. The story is set in Geneva, which, as the seat of the League of Nations, is a centre of international affairs. It is about a series of poisonings in Geneva that involve a professor addicted to morphine and is a mixture of detective story and a spy novel. The narrator knows a lot about the characters, so he can be very ironic, bringing order to this large cast of characters and sometimes addressing the reader directly. Some commentators argue that it is not a very good novel when compared to his others.[11] However, as with all the others, it is based on many of the author's own life experiences, and the 'atmosphere' and suspense are well presented.

I will start by characterizing the protagonist, Studer, because it is mainly thanks to him that Glauser achieved renown. Saner writes about Glauser's main character: 'Studer is both a summary of the life of his creator and his ideal'.[12] He exhibits many of the characteristics of Glauser himself, but also represents some of his ideals, those that Glauser was unable to fulfil in his lifetime and could only realize in fiction. The author was both an anarchist and a defender of law and order – but the order he found was rather frightening. In his books, the author was the critical mouthpiece of the society he knew so well, but also collaborated with the police, defending that same society. This ambivalent position can be found in his texts. He prefers to follow a moral imperative rather than a social order. Glauser shows him more as a person than as an officer of the law.

---

11 Cf. Ott, *Mord im Alpenglühen*, p. 36.
12 Gerhard Saner, *Friedrich Glauser. Eine Biographie.* Vol. 1 (Zurich: Suhrkamp, 1981), p. 484. 'Studer ist die Summe der Lebenserfarung seines Schöpfers und zugleich dessen Ideal'.

At the same time, Glauser projects onto his character certain aspects that he would have liked to have seen in his own father. Studer does not believe in real justice, something he sees as impossible. He wants to help, but it is not up to him to judge; his task is to solve the case he is given. He does not believe in truth either – he questions its validity, just as he questions the idea of justice. Truth has nothing to do with social justice; these concepts are mere words and, as such, have no universal value. They are social, cultural, historical values. He would like to find some meaning in life, but this turns out to be a difficult quest. He feels like an outsider, and he believes in the 'imponderables' ('Unwägbares').[13] Even so, he is not a cynic; he has ideals worth fighting for, encapsulated in the battle against injustice and lies. Studer has no mercy when it comes to exposing lies; he tries to avoid injustice as much as he can, especially the injustice of the "Law"('die Ungerechtigkeit des "Rechts"').[14]

Saner characterizes Studer as a nihilist: he enjoys his work, but he tolerates a 'there is nothing else I can do' nihilism.[15] The criminals are often no worse than the other characters. People in general are selfish, angry and avaricious; not all of them are criminals, but each has the potential to become one.

Studer once had a case involving an influential banker in Vienna that went very badly, as a result of which he was demoted from the rank of detective inspector to that of sergeant and sent back to Bern. This case is mentioned in all the Studer novels, but we are never told what really happened. Studer is quite old and round, has a moustache and is always smoking a Brissago, a popular Swiss cigar. He is fond of alcoholic drinks, likes food, dresses rather conservatively and has a family he cares for – especially his wife, Hedy. Her husband's attraction to younger women, such as Marie in *Fever*, does not bother her.

Studer is a person with whom the reader easily sympathizes. As a sergeant, he wants to discharge his duties; he does not like to be in the limelight and prefers applying his knowledge of humankind to devising elaborate detective techniques. He dislikes men in power when he ascertains that there is deceit behind their words. He tends to sympathize with the simple people, those subjected to the arbitrary decisions of those in power. He is not exactly a friendly, kind person, but he is definitely not a 'tough guy'. Studer's judgement of character was not something he'd learnt from books, it was not based on physical appearance, handwriting analysis, psychological typologies or phrenology. He just allowed

---

13 Friedrich Glauser, *Fever*, trans. by Mike Mitchell (London: Bitter Lemon Press, 2006), p. 198; Glauser, *Fieberkurve* (Zurich: Arche, 1989), p.188.
14 Gerhard Saner, *Friedrich Glauser. Band I*, p. 488.
15 Idem, p. 490.

people to be themselves and relied on his instinct.[16] He does not like major police operations.[17] Glauser's writing is quite ironic, very well constructed and makes use of lively language, both on the part of the narrator and Studer himself. He also utilizes many Bernese dialect forms and French expressions, which reflect certain Swiss German language practices.

At the same time, Glauser concentrates his efforts on *intra*cultural differences. He carefully presents the seemingly idyllic places where Studer works as a sergeant in such a way that they can be extended to represent the whole world.[18] His first Studer text was the short story 'Der alte Zauberer' ['The Old Sorcerer'*],[19] in which the detective is still a *Polizeikommissär* (detective inspector), as he is in the novel *Knarrende Schuhe* [Squeaky Shoes*], one of Glauser's later Studer texts, which is set retrospectively in 1919. Some of the Studer novels were first printed in magazines and only later published in book form.

The first Studer novel was *Schlumpf Erwin Mord* [1936, The Murder of Schlumpf Erwin*], first published under the title *Wachtmeister Studer*, followed by his best-known novel, *Matto regiert*, as well as *Die Fieberkurve* [1938, Fever], *Der Chinese* [1939, The Chinaman] and *Krock & Co.* [1941, The Spoke]. At the same time, he wrote several short stories, published collectively as *Wachtmeister Studers erste Fälle: Kriminalgeschichten* [1936, Detective Studers's First Cases: Crime Stories*]. In each of these novels there is a reference to 'the big case' that he is always dreaming of, in contrast to the rather small cases that he is actually working on.

In the first novel, Studer tries to show that Erwin Schlumpf, an ex-convict and ex-child labourer, was not a murderer as the investigating magistrate was trying to prove. The setting is a village, which is home to a number of 'meeting places', including a gardening school, where some of the students have already been having problems with the magistrate and, of course, the local pub. Here, Studer demonstrates his sceptical view of language. He sees lies behind it; he is aware of true and false tones in it, refusing to accept that there is only one truth. Studer is presented polyphonically; most of the characters (as well as the

---

16 Glauser, *Fever*, p. 178; *Fieberkurve*, p. 170. '[...] ist ein Nihilismus des „Es bleibt mir ja nichts anderes übrig"'.

17 Glauser, *Wachtmeister Studers erste Fälle*, p. 53. 'Der Kommissär liebte keine großen Polizeiaktionen'. Cf. 'Das uneinige Paar' ['The Divided Couple'], in which Studer has just moved to another apartment in Bern.

18 Christa Baumberger, 'Glauser in Genf: Schauplatz literarischer Selbst(er)findung', *Quarto* 32 (2011), pp. 45–50 (p. 50).

19 First published on 1 March 1935 in the *Zürcher Zeitung*. Cf. Glauser, *Wachtmeister Studers erste Fälle*, pp. 9–28.

narrator) comment on his behaviour. For instance, the examining magistrate says, "'Sergeant Studer, I would like to ask you, in all politeness, what you think you are doing? Could you explain how you came to involve yourself without authorization – I repeat, without authorization – in a case which … ". The examining magistrate broke off, though he couldn't have said why himself'.[20] The sergeant shuttles back and forth between Thun and the small village of Gerzenstein.[21] He meets many people – a veritable network of possible murderers. He quotes a French police officer, who claims that it is much easier to detect a crime in a town than in a village, where everyone covers for everyone else. Studer usually talks to people in a polite way and tries to understand them, even when somebody is potentially perpetrating insurance fraud. In the end, he identifies the murderer, one of the most influential men in the village, who then commits suicide.

In this novel, Glauser provides a lot of information about Studer, whom the reader will meet again in four other novels: we learn about his past and a case involving a large bank in Vienna; about his wife, Hedy; about his Brissago cigars; about his taste for alcoholic beverages; about his questionable manners; about the way he behaves towards his superiors (in this novel, the magistrate fears him, while at other times, it is Studer himself who is in charge of the case); and about his friend, Münch the notary. He also gives thematic introductions – for example, a discussion of the importance of chance and truth. Chance is one of the most important instruments of detective work, and, Studer says, one must be open to it. Another interesting characteristic is that some minor characters in the novel compare their lives with those of the characters found in cheap novels by authors like Felicitas Rose and John Kling, which Glauser's characters read. Studer despises this type of literature, which only romanticizes the harsh realities of life,[22] and he makes fun of how easy it is to solve problems in books, as opposed to in real life – a theme that Dürrenmatt will further develop, as we will see. The reader follows Studer, since he is one

---

20 Glauser, *Thumbprint*, p. 15. 'Wachtmeister Studer, ich möcht Euch sehr höflich fragen, was Ihr Euch eigenmächtig – ich wiederhole: eigenmächtig! – in einen Fall einzumischen [...]'. (F.G., *Wachtmeister Studers erste Fälle*, p. 19).

21 Cf. Peter Rusterholz, 'Der Ausbruch aus dem Gefängnis. Wandlungen des Schweizer Kriminalromans, *Quarto* 21/22, 2006, pp. 29–39, (p. 32). One could argue that this novel is instead a regional detective story (*Regiokrimi*), a type of crime fiction that is very popular in Switzerland.

22 Cf. Glauser, *Thumbprint*, pp. 83, 151, 189, 105; *Wachtmeister Studer*, pp. 79, 141, 175, 180.

of the main focal points. Towards the end of the novel, when he is talking to the assassin, he says, 'I realize that the truth I find is not the real truth. However, I do know untruth very well'.[23]

Die Fieberkurve [*Fever*] was finished on 31 December 1935. It was first published in the *Zürcher Illustrierte* and appeared a few months later in book form, with the title *Wachtmeister Studers neuer Fall* [Sergeant Studers New Case*] It is a sort of 'adventure novel'[24] and involves an international plot, based on Glauser's own experiences in the Foreign Legion. It starts in Paris, where Studer is informed that two old ladies in Bale and Geneva are about to be murdered. The international dimension allows him to hope that this will be his 'great case', as he repeatedly calls it. And indeed, when Studer arrives at their homes, both have been killed in the same way: with gas. The matter seems to be connected to countries in North Africa, specifically near the Gurama Fortress of the Foreign Legion.[25] The motive is money, a common theme in literature, which is not very original. Studer travels to the fortress under a false name, and he has a complicated path to follow until the very end. Even then, the reader does not receive all the information for the simple reason that Studer shows no interest in handling some other minor cases, as he has solved his main case. The story is fast-paced, and it becomes quite complicated, but it is always fascinating.

Matto regiert, which is probably Glauser's best novel, is set in a mental asylum and deals with questions of power and psychiatry. Everything happens within an enclosed space, providing no opportunity for a great case. But Studer enjoys being there, since he does not have to run around, even when there is quite a lot going on. Dr. Laduner, an unconventional psychiatrist who knows Studer from the Vienna case, calls him in, even though he is not a conventional inspector, to investigate the disappearance of the director and of a patient, Pieterlein, a 'demonstration object', as Dr. Laduner calls him.The enclosed space gives the detective a lot of time to observe and to have long, self-reflexive conversations with the doctor. One very long chapter, 'Das Demonstrationssubjekt Pieterlein' ['Pieterlein: The Classic Case'], is based on a report Glauser had seen in Münsingen.[26] Studer

---

23 Glauser, *Thumbprint*, p. 185. 'Ich weiß auch ganz genau, daß die Wirklichkeit, die ich finde, nicht die wirkliche Wahrheit ist. Aber ich kenne sehr gut die Lüge'. (Glauser, *Wachtmeister Studer*, p. 170–171).

24 Gerhard Saner, *Friedrich Glauser. Eine Werkgeschichte*, vol. 2 (Zurich: Suhrkamp, 1981), p. 133.

25 In the novel he will use the spelling 'Gourrama'.

26 Cf. Hubert Thüring, 'Die Erfahrung der Psychiatrie. Friedrich Glausers *Matto regiert*' in *Es gibt kein größeres Verbrechen als die Unschuld'. Zu den Kriminalromanen von Glauser, Dürrenmatt, Highsmith und Schneider*, ed. by Peter Gasser, Ellio Pellin and Ulrich Weber (Göttingen, Zurich: Wallstein/ Cronos, 2009), pp. 13–37 (p. 24).

does not know much about psychology, but he is not stupid and does not like complicated ideas. We read about the potential for criminal behaviour, a theme Glauser often includes in his texts: we are all possible murders; it always depends on the 'imponderables' ('Imponderabilien') of life.[27]

The atmosphere in this novel is more important than the plot. At the same time, Glauser includes information about Switzerland and Europe during that period, meaning that the events are well contextualized and serve as a sort of mirror of society. The mental institution is in Randlingen, a fictional place with an interesting name: 'Rand' in German means 'border' or 'margin'. These people are on the margins for one reason or another; they have failed to function in normal society, to have normal social relationships in a harsh, patriarchal society, where people are often cruel to each other. The conversations are also situated at the margins of normality, questioning the very notion of 'normality' within a rather cruel society. Studer follows his instincts rather than preconceived ideas.[28] But by following them, he becomes morally responsible for some deaths. The ending seems to dilute the stress on criminality. Because we are in a mental institution, justice and the rule of law are suspended, which allows us to reflect on these concepts independently. The main focus is on 'ambivalence, indeterminacy and undecidability'.[29] In the end, the reader is not quite sure about the causes of the crimes or the real truth. Studer does not believe in truth; he believes it is always relative, and it is something he does not care much about as long as he manages to solve the specific problem he was tasked with. In this novel, reflecting on the complex motivations and interests of the characters seems to be much more important than the plot.

---

27 Friedrich Glauser, *In Matto's Realm*, trans. by Mike Mitchell (London: Bitter Lemon Press, 2005), p. 104; *Matto regiert* (Zürich: Arche 1989, p.101).
28 Cf. Glauser, *In Matto's Realm*, p. 145.
29 Thüring, 'Die Erfahrung der Psychiatrie', p. 35. As Ellio Pellin points out, the dialect films made in 1938 and 1947, both featuring the same actor playing Studer, contributed significantly to Studer's popularity. Everybody in German-speaking Switzerland knew Studer, but not everyone knew Glauser. In a 2007 film by Sabine Boss, Studer becomes a female detective! Cf. Elio Pellin, '*Matto regiert* – Eine Figur emanzipiert sich vom literarischen Text', in '*Es gibt kein größeres Verbrechen als die Unschuld*'. *Zu den Kriminalromanen von Glauser, Dürrenmatt, Highsmith und Schneider*, ed. by Peter Gasser, Ellio Pellin and Ulrich Weber (Göttingen, Zurich: Wallstein, Cronos, 2009), pp. 39–51.

In *Der Chinese*, the perpetrators are important personalities rather than common people. It is a 'story of the three locales' ('Geschichte der drei Atmosphären'),[30] by which the author means three important places: the village pub, a poorhouse and a horticultural college, each of which it is essential to understand if you want to solve a problem in a small village.[31] Chance and circumstantial evidence play a major role. Again, a small, rather enclosed space is evoked, which is open to minor intrigues and murders. The ambience is the most important element, and the murder is, of course, the driving force behind the action. However, the motive – money and an inheritance – is quite trivial in comparison. The murder victim, a man Studer refers to as 'the Chinaman' because of the slant of his eyes, was from a nearby village, had travelled all over the world and was quite wealthy. In his papers, the Chinaman had noted: 'If God wants to punish a man, He sends him relatives'.[32] He lived above the village pub and had a premonition that he was going to be murdered by one of the people who hoped to inherit his wealth, '[a]lthough one must never forget that reality was often more unbelievable than products of the imagination', as the narrator says.[33] At various times, Studer refers to other authors of detective stories, creating a link between reality and the literary genre. He once again shows sympathy for those who are less privileged – like Ludwig, one of the schoolboys he asks for help, who was an 'indentured child labourer' (*Verdingbub*).

In *Krock & Co.*, Studer goes to the Swiss canton of Appenzell, where his daughter is going to be married. However, things get complicated in the small village as one person after another is murdered. Studer is a Bernese police officer with no authority in other cantons, but they make an exception for him. This time the motives are money and blackmail. He sets out to get to know the suspects, who are from the village, to move among the villagers and the wedding guests and to observe them. These observations are what will lead him to the solution, calm and with no emotional investment on his part. We thus have a village setting that allows him to take a close look at the nature of the villagers. Dialects are stronger in this novel, which includes not only Bernese

---

30 Friedrich Glauser, *The Chinaman*, trans. by Mike Mitchell (London: Bitter Lemon Press, 2008). 'That is why I sometimes call it the story of the three locales.' 'Darum nenn' ich den Fall manchmal die Geschichte der drei Atmosphären'. (F.G., *Der Chinese*, Zurich: Arche, 1989), p. 56.

31 Cf. Wirtz, 'Verbrechen auf engstem Raum', p. 53.

32 Friedrich Glauser, *The Chinaman*, p. 32. 'Wen Gott strafen will, den schenkt er Verwandte'. (Glauser, *Der Chinese*, p. 32.)

33 Glauser, *The Chinaman*, p. 71. 'Die Wirklichkeit [ist] manchmal viel unglaubwürdiger als die Produkte der Phantasie'. (Glauser, *Der Chinese*, p. 68).

but also Appenzell expressions, one editor even added three pages of translations for these words and expressions, which a non-Swiss reader would hardly understand. This novel is the shortest of the Studer novels; it is as if Glauser was thinking about other projects rather than planning to continue with Studer.

Each Studer novel ends with a gathering of all the major characters – a device familiar to readers of Poirot novels – but something usually remains open. The cases are solved, but not everything is explained, and some lines of inquiry are simply abandoned, which causes the reader some astonishment. Patrick Bühler argues that Glauser discredits the idea of the grand finale that is so common to most detective stories.[34]

One characteristic of the Studer novels is their strong use of the vernacular Swiss dialect in dialogue as well as quite a few Helvetisms, which help to portray the Swiss context. Studer uses certain characteristic expressions in all the novels, such as 'nonsense' (*Chabis* in the Swiss dialect) or 'nothing special' (*nichts Apartiges*).

Another of Studer's characteristics is his scorn for trivial literature and its negative influence, particularly on female readers, who, Studer believes, mix up reality with the way life is presented in those books. In his opinion, men read detective and adventure stories in the same way, confounding literature and life. Studer sees himself as a 'liberator', freeing people from stereotypes and from those literary models.[35] Sometimes he behaves very paternally with young people facing various difficulties. It is interesting to note the complementarity of the voices and the focalization of both the narrator and Studer, who treat certain aspects of society, especially the ruling classes, with a great deal of irony. The narrator himself sometimes makes fun of Studer, although he clearly likes the detective, who does not always follow the rules and who demonstrates his humanity when faced with difficult situations.

Dürrenmatt: Background and literary ideals

Glauser published most of his novels as books in the 1940s, when Friedrich Dürrenmatt was searching for his niche as an artist, trying out both painting and theatre. His detective stories – *Der Richter und sein Henker* [1950/1951, *The Judge and His Hangman*], *Der Verdacht* [1951/1952, *Suspicion*] and *Das Versprechen*.

---

34 Bühler, *Die Leiche in der Bibliothek*, p. 147.
35 Cf. Bühler, *Die Leiche in der Bibliothek*, pp. 125–127.

Requiem auf den Kriminalroman [1958, *The Pledge. Requiem for the Detective Novel*] – were written and conceived of mainly in the 1950s. He did not finish *Der Pensionierte* [1997, *The Retiree*, finished by Urs Widmer]. Some of his other books involved crimes, but they were not detective stories, even if some detective work – a must in this genre – was present: *Die Panne* [1956, *Traps*], *Justiz* [1985, *The Execution of Justice*], *Der Auftrag oder Vom Beobachten des Beobachters der Beobachter* [1986, *The Assignment: Or, On the Observing of the Observer of the Observers. A Novella in Twenty-Four Sentences*]. I will discuss these books briefly at the end of this chapter.

In the early 1950s, Dürrenmatt badly needed money, so he agreed to write some detective novels. From the very beginning, he was sceptical of the traditional form of this genre, and none of his novels were really or only detective stories. Throughout his life, he treated other genres – for instance drama – in the same way. He was living near Lake Biel, on the border between the German and French languages, having fled from town life, which he disliked. Moving to this liminal place, he created distance for himself, which made his literary production possible; it was a distance he also needed to write his plays for the theatre.[36] One could argue that Dürrenmatt's main theme at this stage of his career was chance or accidents (*Zufall*), which made it impossible for logic to rule the worlds he created. He saw the world as a labyrinth, the result of the narrative connected with the Tower of Babel, as he points out in his book *Turmbau* [1990; *The Construction of the Tower*]. In 1962, in '21 Punkte zu den Physikern' ['21 Points on the Physicists'], he writes:

4. The worst possible turn is not foreseeable. It occurs by accident.
[. . .]
8. The more human beings proceed according to plan, the more effectively they may be affected by chance.
9. Human beings proceeding according to plan wish to reach a specific goal. They are most severely impacted by chance when, through it, they reach the opposite of their goal: the very thing they feared or sought to avoid (i.e. Oedipus).[37]

---

36 Peter Ruedi, *Dürrenmatt oder Die Ahnung vom Ganzen. Biographie* (Zurich: Diogenes, 2011), p. 321.
37 Friedrich Dürrenmatt, *Werkausgabe in 29 Bänden. Band 7*, Zürich: Arche 1980, pp. 91–92. '4. Die schlimmstmögliche Wendung ist nicht voraussehbar. Sie tritt durch Zufall ein. 8. Je planmäßiger die Menschen vorgehen, desto wirksamer vermag sie der Zufall zu treffen. 9. Planmäßig vorgehende Menschen wollen ein bestimmtes Ziel erreichen. Der Zufall trifft sie dann am schlimmsten, wenn sie durch ihn das Gegenteil ihres Zieles erreichen: Das, was sie befürchten, was sie zu vermeiden suchten'.

As Ulrich Weber puts it, Dürrenmatt saw 'the criminal story as an unsuitable model',[38] or as Wolfgang Pasche says, he understood 'the crime story as a provocation',[39] as he went against the grain of genre expectations. He refused to write a series of crime novels, because it implied the continued success of the detective. For him, detective stories have the same value as 'true' literature. They are by no means a less important genre, which is an idea he took from Glauser: writing detective fiction meant 'produc[ing] art where nobody suspects it'.[40] On 9 January 1949, he told Walter Muschg in a letter that he particularly enjoyed writing novels because it enabled him to engulf the whole region within a criminal framework.[41] It allowed him to see behind the apparent idyll.

He thought dramaturgically, as he writes in *Monstervortrag über Gerechtigkeit und Recht* [1969, *Monster Lecture on Justice and Law*] and applied this perspective to both his dramaturgical and his prose works:

> Ladies and gentlemen, I think dramaturgically. That is, my intellectual method as a dramatist consists in transforming the social reality of man into theater, and then using this transformed reality to investigate matters further. By playing out the world, I think the world through. The result of this thought process is not a new reality, but a comedic gestalt in which reality encounters itself in analyzed form, or more precisely, in which the audience encounters itself in analyzed form. This analysis is governed by imagination, by experimental thought, by playfulness; so it is not strictly scientific, it is in many ways frivolous, but useful precisely for that reason. [...] Dramaturgical thought examines reality by exploring its internal tensions. The more paradoxically reality can be depicted, the more suitable it is as dramatic material. Dramaturgical thought is dialectical, but not in the sense of political ideology.[42]

---

38 Ulrich Weber, *Friedrich Dürrenmatt. Von der Lust, die Welt nochmals zu erdenken* (Bern: Haupt, 2006), p.63. 'Der Krimi als untaugliches Modell'.

39 Cf. Wolfgang Pasche, *Friedrich Dürrenmatts Kriminalromane. Interpretationshilfen* (Stuttgart: Klett, 1997), p. 5 (my transl.). '[...] die etablierten Erwartungen an Literatur zu provozieren'.

40 Friedrich Dürrenmatt, 'Theaterprobleme' in *Werkausgabe in 29 Bänden, Band 24* (Zurich: Diogenes, 1980), pp. 71–2. 'Kunst da tut, wo sie niemand vermutet'.

41 Ruedi, *Dürrenmatt*, p. 324. 'Der Kriminalroman macht mir viel Spaß, besonderes Vergnügen finde ich darin, dass ich in ihm Gelegenheit habe, die ganze Bielerseegegend so en passant kriminalistisch auszuwerten'.

42 Friedrich Dürrenmatt, *Selected Writings, Volume 3: Essays*, ed. by Kenneth J. Northcott, trans. by Joel Agee (Chicago & London: The University of Chicago Press, 2006), p. 105. 'Meine Damen und Herren, ich denke dramaturgisch. Das heißt, meine Denktechnik als Dramatiker besteht darin, die gesellschaftliche Wirklichkeit des Menschen in Theater zu verwandeln und mit dieser verwandelten Wirklichkeit weiterzudenken. Ich denke die Welt durch, indem ich sie durchspiele. Das Resultat dieses Denkprozesses ist nicht eine neue Wirklichkeit, sondern ein komödiantisches Gebilde, in dem sich die Wirklichkeit analysiert wiederfindet, genauer, in dem sich der Zuschauer analysiert wiederfindet. Diese Analyse ist von der Einbildungskraft bestimmt, vom Gedankenexperiment, von der Spielfreude, sie ist darum nicht streng

He calls this lecture 'Eine kleine Dramaturgie der Politik' [1969, 'A Minor Dramaturgy of Politics']. He also uses the phrase 'dramaturgy of the labyrinth' when he writes about the labyrinth of Knossos and the Minotaur as a means of reflecting on society.

Dürrenmatt's detectives: Subverting convention

Dürrenmatt wrote only two novels featuring Kommissär Bärlach, a feared police detective who has cancer, lives alone in Bern and is not a very nice man. Bärlach is as conservative as Maigret and Studer. He does not make much use of the new scientific methods and is not very disciplined, but he is a cultivated person, as his library shows, and he loves food and drink. Dürrenmatt first wrote *Der Richter und sein Henker* and *Der Verdacht* for inclusion as serials in a magazine, the *Schweizerischer Beobachter*. Both were a sort of critique of the genre itself, and the author situates these stories at its margins.

Der Richter und sein Henker is set in a wine region near Biel, where the author himself lived. A police officer is found dead in his car. The book opens according to the rules of detective stories: a corpse sets the detective work in motion. However, even in the initial sequences, the detective has very strong suspicions about who the murderer is – he merely has to confirm them, without giving the reader any clues. A strange meeting takes place in a big, lonely house. The detective does just enough to confirm the final proof of his suspicions. Dürrenmatt takes this opportunity to voice strong criticism of Swiss politics and the role of the military in Switzerland using interludes in the story itself, which allows him to reflect upon the themes that interest him. We are informed of a bet that was made between Bärlach and his antagonist, Gastmann, in Istanbul forty years ago: in a rather drunken state, Bärlach argued that the perfect crime – one which leaves no circumstantial evidence – was not possible due to the role of the unforeseeable, of the accidental, of chance. Gastmann defends this possibility and proves it by committing a crime

---

wissenschaftlich, sie ist in vielem leichtfertig, doch gerade darum nützlich. [...] Das dramaturgische Denken untersucht die Wirklichkeit auf ihren Spannungsgehalt hin. Je paradoxer sie dargestellt werden kann, desto besser eignet sich die Wirklichkeit als theatralischer Stoff. Das dramaturgische Denken ist dialektisch, doch nicht in einem politisch-ideologischen Sinne'. (Dürrenmatt, 'Monstervortrag über Gerechtigkeit und Recht', *Werkausgabe in 29 Bänden. Band 27* [Zurich: Arche 1980] pp. 36–107, [p. 91]).

right before Bärlach's eyes. Their lives will be spent in pursuit of each other, with Gastmann improving his criminal techniques and Bärlach unable to catch him. It is a sort of game between law and freedom, but with many victims along the way. At the beginning of the novel, Bärlach has only one more year to live, so it becomes increasingly difficult to win the bet. He uses his fellow police officer, Tschanz – a telling name – as an instrument to kill Gastmann. Tschanz is a murderer without any plausible motives, apart from envy and the desire to emulate his more successful colleague, Ulrich Schmied.[43] Bärlach therefore takes on the role of judge and uses Tschanz as a hangman to kill Gastmann as a punishment for all of his crimes – except Schmied's murder, of which he was absolutely innocent. Thus, Gastmann is killed but wins the bet: Bärlach was not able to bring him to justice and himself commits a perfect crime, proving that Gastmann's theory was correct. Bärlach is a 'demon from Bern'.[44] He changes the rules, becoming a murderer himself.

One of the interludes is a discussion with a writer – who is a sort of detective himself – about literature and its role in clarifying the wrongs of society. At one point, the writer and Bärlach discuss the notion of nihilism, using Gastmann as an example: there is no morality, only the will. 'For [Gastmann] evil is not the expression of a philosophy or a biological drive, it is freedom: the freedom of nothingness.'[45]

The writer is only interested in creating an image of Gastmann, while Bärlach is after the real person.[46] The reader is guided through different confrontations: between political power and justice, justice and freedom, law and justice, logic and chance. The novel ends with a grotesque banquet where the policeman discloses all he knows about the murder of his colleague and the subsequent death of Tschanz, which can be seen as an accident (chance) or a suicide. The text does not provide a final answer; it is up to the reader to choose, though many critics champion the suicide hypothesis. While seemingly following the traditional

---

43 Ruedi sees Tschanz as an ironic variation of Oedipus, cf. Ruedi, *Dürrenmatt*, p. 378.

44 Ruedi, *Dürrenmatt*, p. 381.

45 Friedrich Dürrenmatt, *The Inspector Barlach Mysteries. The Judge and His Hangman and Suspicion*, trans. by Joel Agee (Chicago: The University of Chicago Press, 2006), p. 84. 'Bei ihm ist das Böse nicht der Ausdruck einer Philosophie, sondern seine Freiheit: der Freiheit des Nichts'. Friedrich Dürrenmatt, *Die Klassischen Kriminalromane* Der Richter und Sein Henker. Der Verdacht (Zurich/Cologne: Benziger 1953), p. 100.

46 Cf. Pasche, *Friedrich Dürrenmatts Kriminalromane*, p. 47.

scheme of the genre – crime, detection, punishment – Dürrenmatt actually subverts some aspects of detective fiction.[47]

His next novel, *Der Verdacht* (*The Suspicion*, also published under the title *The Quarry*), takes place in a completely different setting. At the beginning of November, Bärlach has had to be hospitalized after the feast at the end of the previous novel. At first, we find him in a hospital in Bern, where he sees a photo in a *Life* magazine and thinks he recognizes Dr. Nehle, who performed experimental operations without anaesthetic in Nazi Germany. Bärlach, who is close to retirement, wants to find out whether Dr. Emmenberger, a doctor at the Sonnenstein clinic in Zurich with a wealthy clientele, is in fact Nehle, who is supposed to be dead. The doctor finds out who Bärlach is as he is preparing to perform one of his inhumane operations on him. Bärlach thus finds himself in a rather hopeless situation. But he is saved *in extremis* by Gulliver, a sort of *deus ex machina*, 'a gigantic Jew in an old, spotty, and torn caftan'[48] – a Holocaust survivor and a representation of the Wandering Jew – in an ending which subverts the conventions of the genre. Just like Gastmann, Dr. Emmenberger is a defender of nihilism: 'Freedom is having the courage to commit a crime, because freedom itself is a crime.'[49] Evil is freedom itself, and he sees himself as an *Übermensch* in the Nietzschean sense.

This novel allows Dürrenmatt to raise the question of Switzerland's collusion with the Nazi regime. He argues for the universalization of evil: the Nazi regime rose to power in Germany, but under the right conditions, it could have happened anywhere. Instead of looking at specific countries, he stresses 'the difference between the tempted and the spared. That puts you and me, as Swiss citizens, among those who were spared the ordeal of temptation, which is a blessing and not a fault, as many say.'[50] Gulliver is a mouthpiece for Dürrenmatt's ideas. He says:

---

47 A film by Maximilian Schell was produced in 1957, in which Dürrenmatt himself plays the role of the writer.

48 Friedrich Dürrenmatt, *The Inspector Bärlach Mysteries. The Judge and His Hangman and Suspicion*, transl. Joel Agee (Chicago: University of Chicago Press, 2006), p. 154. '[...] im schwarzen Kaftan, der zerfetzt an den gewaltigen Gliedern herunterhing, der Jude Gulliver'. Friedrich Dürrenmatt, *Die Klassischen Kriminalromane* Der Richter und sein Henker. Der Verdacht (Zurich/Cologne: Benziger 1953), p. 324.

49 Dürrenmatt, *Suspicion* p. 268. 'Die Freiheit ist der Mut zum Verbrechen, weil sie selbst ein Verbrechen ist'. Dürrenmatt, *Die Klassischen Kriminalromane*, p. 315.

50 Dürrenmatt, *The Inspector Bärlach Mysteries*, p. 214. '[...] auch den Unterschied zwischen den Versuchten und den Verschonten. Da gehören denn wir Schweizer, Sie und ich zu den Verschonten, was eine Gnade ist und kein Fehler, wie viele sagen'. Dürrenmatt, *Die Klassischen Kriminalromane*, p. 251.

> We can't fight evil alone any more, like knights setting forth against some dragon [...]. We can't save the world as individuals, that would be a task as hopeless as that of poor Sisyphus [...]. Therefore, we should not try to save the world, but we must endure it. This is the only true adventure left to us at this late hour.[51]

Bärlach starts a conversation with Dr. Lutz, his superior, about the miserable state of justice in Switzerland and the way crime is prosecuted. Bärlach also provokes Dr. Emmenberger, telling him that he prosecutes war criminals. Another perspective is that of Dr. Malok, Emmenberger's girlfriend, a former communist who saved herself by becoming the doctor's mistress and is also a morphine addict. But she refuses to help Bärlach at all: 'The world is rotten, Inspector, it's decaying like a badly stored fruit.'[52] Gulliver kills Emmenberger, and Bärlach is saved. But the world stays the same.

The novel ends in ambiguity; there are no answers. It is the 'antitype of the detective novel', as Pasche argues.[53] There is almost no action, because the detective is confined to a hospital bed. Drinking vodka gives him strength again. He survives, but not as a result of his own efforts.

The novel explores a new means of social critique in a popular genre. The anti-Semitic tradition in Europe is nothing new; it is anchored in the Bible itself. Dürrenmatt thus uses this novel to criticize Christianity, especially the Catholic Church, for the way it has treated Jews since its very beginnings. Gulliver, a Jew who is persecuting all Nazis, follows his own law – just as Bärlach had done in a different way in the previous novel. Bärlach refuses to answer Emmenberger's question about the driving force behind life as an investigator. When confronted with a nihilist, there is no possible answer to such a question: the only possible defence is silence. By not providing an answer, Bärlach prevents Emmenberger from responding.

Dürrenmatt also uses another character, the fictional, critically minded writer Fortschig, who publishes his own magazine in a print run of just forty-five. Fortschig has a problem with the reality of life in Switzerland; he is not taken seriously and is eventually killed by Emmenberger's minions. This character thus calls into question the role of literature without providing an answer. Gulliver is

---

51 Dürrenmatt, *The Inspector Bärlach Mysteries*. p. 281. 'Wir können als Einzelne die Welt nicht retten, das wäre eine ebenso hoffnungslose Arbeit wie die des armen Sisyphos [...]. Wir können nur im Einzelnen helfen, nicht im gesamten [...]. So sollen wir die Welt nicht zu retten suchen, sondern zu bestehen, das einzige wahrhafte Abenteuer, das uns in dieser späten Zeit noch bleibt'. Dürrenmatt, *Die Klassischen Kriminalromane*, p. 331.
52 Dürrenmatt, *Suspicion*, p. 238. 'Die Welt ist faul, Kommissär, sie verwest wie eine schlecht gelagerte Frucht'. Dürrenmatt, *Die Klassischen Kriminalromane*, p. 280.
53 Pasche, *Friedrich Dürrenmatts Kriminalromane*, p. 77.

the driving force, not Bärlach: he has strong motives and a great capacity to act. He is a good example of not resigning oneself to one's fate: 'Farewell, my knight without fear or blemish, my Bärlach, Gulliver is moving on to the giants and the dwarfs, to other countries, other worlds, constantly, without cease'.[54] We therefore see that Bärlach diverges significantly from other classical detectives, especially in his role as a judge.[55]

Dürrenmatt moves further towards the margins of the genre with *Das Versprechen: Requiem auf den Kriminalroman*,[56] taking the detective and his use of logic to the extreme of failure and demonstrating 'the big lie of detection fiction'.[57] The definite article in the title points not to the genre itself, but rather to a certain type of detective novel and a certain type of detective. The original text was written for a film, *Es geschah am hellichten Tag* [1958, *It Happened in Broad Daylight*], about child sexual abuse. In the film, the murderer is caught. Dürrenmatt was not happy with this pedagogical ending and changed it in the novel, moving further away from the classical detective story. The plot is rather simple: Dr. H., the former chief of police in the canton of Zurich, offers a lift to a writer of detective stories who has given a talk in Chur. The writer is the narrator in this part of the novel. During the journey from Chur to Zurich, Dr. H. talks about a case that took place a few years ago, which he uses to show how misleading detective novels can be, as the detectives never allow chance to play a role in their work: 'You can't come to grips with reality by logic alone.'[58] He tells the story of a paedophile who killed a few young girls in the region they are passing through. Detective Inspector Matthäi, who had been scheduled to go to Jordan, promised the mother of one of the murdered girls

---

54 Dürrenmatt, *The Inspector Bärlach Mysteries*, p. 282. '"Leb wohl, mein Ritter ohne Furcht und Tadel, mein Bärlach" sagt er, „Gulliver zieht weiter zu den Riesen und zu den Zwergen in andere Länder, in andere Welten, immerfort, immerzu."' Dürrenmatt, *Die Klassischen Kriminalromane*, pp. 332–3.

55 Cf. Jochen Vogt. 'Krimis, Antikrimis, "Gedanken"-Krimis. Wie Friedrich Dürrenmatt sich in ein gering geschätztes Genre einschrieb', in *Dürrenmatt und die Weltliteratur. Dürrenmatt in der Weltliteratur*, ed. by Véronique Liard and Marion George (Pieterlen/CH: Martin Meidenbauer, Peter Lang, 2011), pp. 215–235 (p. 224.)

56 Some versions use the definite article 'den' instead of the indefinite 'einen': *Requiem auf den/einen Kriminalroman*.

57 Roger Crocket, *Understanding Friedrich Dürrenmatt* (Columbia/SC: University of South Carolina Press, 1998), p. 57.

58 Friedrich Dürrenmatt, *The Pledge*, transl. Joel Agee (Chicago: University of Chicago Press, 2006) p. 8. 'Der Wirklichkeit mit Logik nur zum Teil beizukommen ist'. Friedrich Dürrenmatt, *Das Versprechen. Requiem auf den Kriminalroman. Werkausgabe in 29 Bänden. Band 22* (Zurich: Arche 1980), p. 18.

that he would catch the killer. He devised a trap to catch him after talking to a psychiatrist: he took a former prostitute and her little daughter, who resembled the murdered girl, to a gas station. The plan was that the girl would play near the road to attract the murderer. Nothing happened, however, and Matthäi's life and state of mind started to deteriorate. Then, an old woman on her deathbed told the truth: the murderer, her husband, had been on his way to pick up the girl but had died in a car accident.

Therefore, Matthäi's logical approach was right, but unforeseeable events destroyed his plans. He is still waiting at the garage, senile and drunk: 'There is no greater cruelty than a genius stumbling over something idiotic.'[59] Matthäi is not an exemplary detective; in some respects, he is even incompetent. For instance, it should have been easy for him to find the American-made car with a licence plate from the canton of Graubünden, which the killer was driving.

This story enables Dr. H. to reflect upon the genre:

> I have never thought highly of detective novels. [...] No, what really bothers me about your novels is the story line, the plot. There the lying just takes over, it's shameless. You set up your stories logically, like a chess game: here's the criminal, there's the victim, here's an accomplice, there's a beneficiary; and all the detective needs to know is the rules, he replays the moves of the game, and checkmate, the criminal is caught and justice has triumphed. This fantasy drives me crazy.[60]

But who is Matthäi, compared to Bärlach? Ruedi characterizes Matthäi in the following words: 'He is blinded by his rationality, which he uses to stem the chaotic reality, a prisoner in the labyrinth of consistency.'[61] He is a competent detective, but he is not prepared for the intervention of the irrational; for him, man is like a machine or a chess piece. As a person, Matthäi is not very sensitive. He is 'emotionless, [...] stubborn, tireless, but when you [watch] him in action, he appear[s] to be bored; until one day he got embroiled in a case that

---

59 Dürrenmatt, *The Pledge*, p. 152. 'Nichts ist grausamer als ein Genie, das über etwas Idiotisches stolpert'. Friedrich Dürrenmatt, *Das Versprechen. Reqiem auf den Kriminalroman. Werkausgabe in 29 Bänden. Band 22*. Zurich: Arche 1980), p. 145.

60 Dürrenmatt, *The Pledge*, pp. 7–8. 'Um ehrlich zu sein, ich habe nie viel von Kriminalromanen gehalten [...] Nein, ich ärgere mich vielmehr über die Handlung in euren Romanen. Hier wird der Schwindel zu toll und zu unverschämt. Ihr baut eure Handlungen logisch auf; wie bei einem Schachspiel geht es zu, hier der Verbrecher, hier das Opfer, hier der Mitwisser, hier der Nutznießer; es genügt, daß der Detektiv die Regeln kennt und die Partie wiederholt, und schon hat er den Verbrecher gestellt, der Gerechtigkeit zum Siege geholfen. Diese Fiktion macht mich wütend'. Dürrenmatt, *Das Versprechen*, pp. 17–18.

61 'Er ist ein Verblendeter, in der Ratio, die er der chaotischen Realität entgegenstemmt, ein Gefangener im Labyrinth der Folgerichtigkeit'. Ruedi, *Dürrenmatt*, p. 616.

suddenly stirred him to passion.',[62] as Dr. H. puts it. He is not capable of having true relationships with others, and he abuses other people to fulfil his plans, although he is a brilliant detective. He will not be able to convince others of the innocence of von Gunten, the peddler who found the body of Gritli Moser, the last of the dead girls. Both the police and the villagers suspect von Gunten immediately, which leads to his suicide. The incompetence of the police force and the justice system is evident. Matthäi believes that he is responsible for von Gunten's suicide after an almost twenty-hour interrogation, during which methods were used that were not far from torture, but he oversteps his authority when he puts the child at risk:

> He wanted reality to conform to his calculations. Therefore, he had to deny reality. [...] Sometimes the worst possible thing *does* take place. We are men, we have to reckon with that, armor ourselves against it, and above all, we have to realize that the only way to avoid getting crushed by absurdity, which is bound to manifest itself more and more forcefully and clearly, and the only way to make a reasonably comfortable home for ourselves on this earth, is to humbly include the absurd in our calculations.[63]

The paradox of the world is that Dürrenmatt dismantles the exclusive importance attributed to rational planning.[64]

The Swiss author takes some ideas from Simenon's *Maigret tend un piège* [1955, *Maigret Sets a Trap*], but he further develops his critique of society and of powerful institutions. The chief of police defends order, but at the same time, he maintains that everyone should have a small island of disorder – not openly, but as a secret space of his or her own.[65] He uses self-irony in the character of Dr. H., who does not particularly like the works of the author in the text,

---

62 Dürrenmatt, *The Pledge*, p. 10. '[...] gefühlos geworden [...] So hartnäckig und unermüdlich er auch vorging, seine Tätigkeit schien ihm zu langweilen, bis er eben in einen Fall verwickelt wurde, der ihn plötzlich leidenschaftlich werden ließ'. Friedrich Dürrenmatt, *Das Versprechen. Reqiem auf den Kriminalroman. Werkausgabe in 29 Bänden. Band 22* (Zurich: Arche 1980), p. 17.

63 Dürrenmatt, *The Pledge*, pp. 152–153. 'Er wollte, daß seine Rechnunhg auch in der Wirklichkeit aufgehe [...] Das Schlimmste trifft *auch* manchmal zu. Wir sind Männer, haben damit zu rechnen, uns dagegen zu wappnen und uns vor allem klar darüber zu werden, daß wir am Absurden, welches sich notwendigerweise immer deutlicher und mächtiger zeigt, nur dann nicht scheitern und uns einigermaßen wohnlich auf dieser Erde einrichten werden, wenn wir es demütig in unser Denken einkalkulieren'. Friedrich Dürrenmatt, *Das Versprechen. Reqiem auf den Kriminalroman. Werkausgabe in 29 Bänden. Band 22* (Zurich: Arche 1980), p. 145.

64 Pasche, *Friedrich Dürrenmatts Kriminalromane*, p. 158.

65 Dürrenmatt, *The Pledge*, p. 48.

preferring those of Max Frisch![66] Here, again, Dürrenmatt plays with the idea of a trap, something that we can see in many of his texts.[67]

The novel has a parabolic structure, where the internal story is used to exemplify the ideas presented in the main text by Dr. H.'s narrative.[68] In both Bärlach novels, Dürrenmatt makes his critical views known through two fanatical villains who can materialize anywhere. And in both novels, Dürrenmatt includes discussions of philosophy and genre.

Dürrenmatt began writing another detective story, but did not finish it: *Der Pensionierte* [1995, *The Retiree**]. Kommissär Höchstettler, who is similar to Bärlach in many respects, is about to retire. He decides to start visiting the approximately two hundred people he was not able to bring to justice. Some of them think he is finally coming to put them behind bars, but he actually just wants to talk and drink with them. He knows that some of these petty criminals are not necessarily evil, and he lets them go. Thus, the author once again demonstrates the difference between what the law prescribes and justice. As he writes about the detective inspector visiting his former 'clients', the author revisits his former works and themes. Dürrenmatt continues to talk about this theme in a crescendo of grotesque forms in *Die Panne* [1956, *Traps*], *Justiz* [1985, *The Execution of Justice*] and *Der Auftrag* [1988, *The Assignment*]. He continuously revisits the dialectics of justice and law, crime and freedom.

Traps: A Still Possible Story[69] is not exactly a detective story. In fact, it is almost precisely the opposite: it is a 'disguised trial'.[70] First, we must take into account that there are three versions of this story, two of them with very different endings. The radio play ends realistically: The original title implies an accident or a car breakdown. The protagonist's name points to a trap. In the first part, the author reflects on possible stories, concluding with the following remarks:

> As we advance into this world of smash-ups and breakdowns, a few possible stories still take place by the dusty edge of the road, among billboards promoting shoes, cars, and ice cream, among tombs commemorating the victims of traffic; stories in which humanity gazes out from some dime-a-dozen face, and an ordinary mishap unintentionally widens

---

66 Dürrenmatt, *The Pledge*, p.151. The 2001 movie *The Pledge*, directed by Sean Penn, with Jack Nicholson playing the lead role, was also based on Dürrenmatt's novel.

67 Cf. Vogt. 'Krimis, Antikrimis, "Gedanken"- Krimis', p. 225.

68 Vogt, 'Krimis, Antikrimis, "Gedanken"- Krimis', p. 227.

69 Friedrich Dürrenmatt, '*Traps: A Still Possible Story*', in *Selected Writings, Volume 2. Fictions*, ed. by Theodore Ziolkowski, transl. by Joel Agee (Chicago & London: University of Chicago Press, 2006), pp. 195–229.

70 Ruedi, *Dürrenmatt*, p. 559.

into universality, and judgment and justice come into view, maybe grace as well, accidentally caught and reflected in the monocle of a drunken man.[71]

Traps is on a work trip, and his Studebaker[72] has broken down, so he has to stay
in the village. Since there are no available rooms, he is invited to dinner by
a nameless former judge, and the other guests are some very old people who were
formerly involved in legal activities: Zorn (meaning 'anger') assumes the role of
the prosecutor, Kummer (meaning 'sorrow') is the defence attorney, and Pilet is an
executioner. During dinner, they perform trial scenes, following the rule that everyone is guilty of some sort of crime. In their play, justice has no rulebook. As
they grow increasingly drunk during this grotesque dinner, they try to convict
Traps of the murder of his superior. He accepts his condemnation and commits
suicide, destroying the old people's game by confounding fiction and reality:
'Alfredo, my dear good Alfredo! For God's sake what were you thinking of? You've
ruined the most beautiful gathering we've ever had!.[73] Instead of solving the crime
after the corpse is found, here we have the reverse: something very Kafkaesque, if
we think of *The Trial*. Traps is not an intellectual; he is just an everyday man, reflecting Dürrenmatt's view of the general lack of thought among regular people.

This is a parody of detective fiction, but it does not include all the ingredients
of the genre. Moreover, rather than asking 'who' or 'how', it searches to find out
'what' has been done. Edgar Wallace's *The Four Just Men* (1905), in which the
characters decided to implement their own brand of justice,[74] may have had an
influence on the theme of justice in this book.

Dürrenmatt did not finish the novel *The Execution of Justice*, which he
started in 1957, until 1985. It is not exactly a detective novel, since there is no
detective work. It is a comedy about justice with a labyrinthine plot, a novel
'characterized by a postmodern playfulness. [...] This is rather a novel about
the elusive nature of truth.'[75]

---

71 Dürrenmatt, '*Traps*', p. 196. 'In der Welt der Pannen führt unser Weg, an dessen staubigem
Rande nebst Reklamwänden für Bally-Schuhe, Studebaker, Eiscreme und den Gedenksteinen der
Verunfallten sich noch einige mögliche Geschichten ergeben, indem aus einem Dutzendgesicht
die Menschheit blickt, Pech sich ohne Absicht ins Allgemeine weitet, Gericht und Gerechtigkeit
sichtbar werden, vielleicht auch Gnade, zufällig aufgefangen, widerspiegelt vom Monokel eines
Betrunkenen'. Friedrich Dürrenmatt, *Die Panne* (Zurich: Diogenes, 2007), p. 9.
72 In the latest, theatrical version from 1975, Traps drives a Jaguar as Studebakers no longer
exist and would be unknown to the audience.
73 Dürrenmatt, '*Traps*', p. 229. 'Alfredo, mein guter Alfredo! Was hast du dir denn um
Gotteswillen gedacht? Du verteufelst uns ja den schönsten Herrenabend!' Friedrich
Dürrenmatt, *Die Panne* (Zurich: Diogenes 1998), p. 80.
74 Pasche, *Friedrich Dürrenmatts Kriminalromane*, p. 136.
75 Crocket, *Understanding Friedrich Dürrenmatt*. p. 179.

The eminent Professor Winter is killed in a restaurant. The murderer, Dr. Isaak Kohler, a famous person himself, is immediately taken to prison. He hires a lawyer, Felix Spät, who is close to bankruptcy and on very good terms with alcohol. His job is to prove that Kohler did not commit the murder, since he did not have a motive and the murder weapon was never found. On the other hand, Dr. Benno was in the restaurant at the same time, and he had a good motive for killing the professor. Dr. Benno ends up committing suicide, which is seen as his confession. Ultimately, at the end of a convoluted story, the real murderer is set free. The detection of a crime that Dr. Kohler did in fact commit, but which is rendered fictional through a series of events, results in a grotesque distortion of the law. The truth – or one possible truth – is only revealed at the very end, by the narrator of the last fifth of the text, since most of the story is told by the drunken lawyer. In this novel, Dürrenmatt reflects on crime and detection, law and justice, the court system and the distortion of truth. He questions justice as such, by way of a parody, where the unthinkable becomes possible, where fiction turns into truth.

Dürrenmatt wrote another novel on the topic of justice *Der Auftrag oder Vom Beobachten des Beobachters der Beobachter* (*The Assigment; or, On the Observing of the Observer of the Observers*).[76] It is a novel that comprises only twenty-four long sentences, and its construction is modelled on the principle of chaos. The novel presents another variation on the idea of the labyrinth and the search for truth. All the elements of a detective novel are present: the wife of a famous psychiatrist is missing, and he asks a journalist to search for her and make a film about her murder. Shortly thereafter, she reappears at home, but the novel continues to follow the conventions of other genres, such as the spy thriller. Arms dealers are involved, and soon a corpse is indeed found, but it is that of a Danish girl, a journalist wearing a red coat just like the one the missing woman had been wearing. Other bodies are also discovered, and we find ourselves in a Maghrebin landscape, in the midst of internal political convulsions, where bombs go off and powerful nations make use of their spy satellites. The problem, as one of the minor characters, D., a professor of logic, puts it, is that people do not want to be observed, but at the same time, they suffer if they are not being watched, because then they feel that they are not important. It is not detection that is the important element here, but rather surveillance in this global world – observation in micro and macro spaces. The novel reflects on the dangers of a new technical order, in which the individual has almost no

---

76 This text is partially based on Ingeborg Bachmann's *Der Fall Franza* [1978, *The Franza Case*]. Cf. Crocket, *Understanding Friedrich Dürrenmatt*, p. 183.

influence. The world is a labyrinth, a recurrent theme in Dürrenmatt's works, even in his very early stories. At the same time, the author talks about identity and the necessity of individual memory, as seen in F., the journalist, one of the characters. Observation is a very important activity, especially when you know that you yourself are being observed.

Thus, Dürrenmatt uses his crime stories to reflect on major issues regarding the role of accident or chance in our societies, which we falsely assume are ruled mainly by logic. The philosophical subtexts of these stories are important to their success.[77] Dürrenmatt uses a popular genre, developing it into ever-more pronounced formal grotesqueness in order to show the deeper incongruences of our lives. As he points out in thesis 18 of the "21 Points": 'Each attempt made by an individual to solve for himself what affects everyone is doomed to fail.'[78] His detectives experience this as well: even when they solve their cases, they lose out in the end or have to be saved in some way.

Conclusion: Crime fiction and social critique

As Vogt puts it, Glauser observes reality and models it, while Dürrenmatt exceeds it, creating figures and circumstances that, in turn, generate grotesque situations with paradoxical and parabolic dimensions at the cost of reality itself. One could, as Vogt argues, speak of 'anti-crime novels'.[79] But in both cases, the authors speak of reality – in different ways, but always with a critical eye on society.

---

77 Vogt, 'Krimis, Antikrimis, "Gedanken"- Krimis', p. 217.

78 Dürrenmatt, '21 Points to the Physicists', http://pierfurcation.blogspot.pt/2005/12/durren matts-21-points-to-physicists.html. 'Jeder Versuch eines Einzelnen, für sich zu lösen, was alle angeht, muß scheitern'. (Dürrenmatt, *Werkausgabe in 29 Bänden. Band 7*, Zurich: Arche 1980), p. 93.

79 Vogt, 'Krimis, Antikrimis, "Gedanken"- Krimis', pp. 231, 233.

Thomas W. Kniesche

3 Modernity and Melancholia: Austrian Crime Fiction

The matter of whether there is such a thing as specifically Austrian crime fiction or whether we should understand it as a part of the wider realm of German crime fiction is open to debate. For the post-war period, Beatrix Kramlovsky states that there is 'a clear difference between the crime fiction of Germany and Austria'.[1] Thomas Wörtche, on the other hand, sounds a note of caution when he admits to feeling 'ein leises Unbehagen' [vaguely uneasy] when confronted with 'pseudo-concepts' such as 'Austrian crime fiction' and suspects them of having been invented as marketing ploys.[2] Most commentators, however, agree that Austrian crime fiction has grown out of its own, distinctive historical and cultural environment, just as Austrian literature in general has been shaped by factors genuine to that nation's history.[3] These differences consist in more than Austrian authors using dialects, vocabulary or even grammatical structures unique to Austrian German, relativizing the fact that they use the same language as their German colleagues. The common definition of 'Austrian' crime fiction is that it is written by an Austrian author and set in a location in Austria.[4] However, beyond language, nationality and setting, we should also ask: what is it that makes an author or a text belong to a distinctive category called 'Austrian crime fiction'? After a brief overview of the history of crime fiction from Austria, the second part of this chapter will discuss a number of formal and plot elements characteristic of contemporary Austrian crime fiction. In conclusion, two novels by Wolf Haas and Paulus Hochgatterer will be introduced as striking examples of crime fiction written in Austria.

---

1 Cf. Beatrix Kramlovsky, 'Show Your Face, oh Violence. Crime Fiction as Written by Austrian Woman Writers', *World Literature Today* 85.3 (2011), pp. 13–15 (p. 14).

2 Cf. Thomas Wörtche, 'Zivile Notwehr. Manfred Wieningers Marek-Miert-Romane', *Literatur und Kritik* 417/418 (2007), pp. 74–78 (pp. 74–75).

3 For more on the differences between German and Austrian literature from the perspective of cultural history, see Wolfgang Müller-Funk, *Komplex Österreich. Fragmente zu einer Geschichte der modernen österreichischen Literatur* (Vienna: Sonderzahl, 2009).

4 However, even the fact that an author was born in Austria (or not) is not always a distinguishing factor. Heinrich Steinfest, for instance, was born in Australia, grew up in Vienna and generally lives in the German city of Stuttgart. And yet, there can be little doubt that he is one of the most interesting representatives of contemporary Austrian crime fiction.

https://doi.org/10.1515/9783110426601-003

Landmarks of crime fiction from Austria

Between 1651 and 1654, the legal expert Matthias Abele von und zu Lilienberg (1616 or 1618–1677) published a four-volume collection of crime stories and case histories. Abele thus preceded François Gayot de Pitaval's famous *Causes célèbres et intéressantes* (1734–1743), the most prominent collection of its kind, by more than eight decades. Abele told real or imagined stories of crime and misdemeanour by seamlessly interweaving the discourses of literature and law to produce rhetorically sophisticated and entertaining texts.[5] During the 1860s, the Vienna-born journalist and writer Heinrich Ritter von Levitschnigg (1810–1862) wrote three crime novels with the sensationalist titles *Der Diebsfänger* [1860, *The Thief-Catcher**], *Der Gang zum Giftbaum* [1862, *The Walk to the Poison-Tree**] and *Die Leiche im Koffer* [1863, *The Corpse in the Suitcase**]. In *Der Gang zum Giftbaum*, which takes the reader to Java, Afghanistan, Vienna and India, he combines elements of the ethnographic novel and the historical novel with a crime fiction plot.[6]

In 1893, Auguste Groner's (1850–1929) detective Joseph Müller made his debut in the locked-room mystery 'Die goldene Kugel' ('The Golden Bullet').[7] In this case, as in the others that would follow, he not only demonstrates his analytical skills and his powers of observation, but also sympathizes with the perpetrators he has to hunt down when they are driven to their crimes by forces out of their control. Müller returned in at least another dozen novels and novellas and thus became the first serial detective in German-language crime fiction. Some of his adventures were translated into English and other languages, and enjoyed a fair amount of popularity in Great Britain and the US.[8] Groner also wrote crime fiction featuring other detectives, but all of her mysteries dealt

---

5 Cf. Eckhardt Meyer-Krentler, '"Geschichtserzählungen". Zur ›Poetik des Sachverhalts‹ im juristischen Schrifttum des 18. Jahrhunderts', in *Erzählte Kriminalität. Zur Typologie und Funktion von narrative Darstellungen in Strafrechtspflege, Publizistik und Literatur zwischen 1770 und 1920*, ed. by Jörg Schönert (Tübingen: Niemeyer, 1991), pp. 117–157 (pp. 121–125). On pp. 122–123, the case of the 'bratwurst murder' provides an example of Abele's treatment of crime stories.

6 Cf. Hans-Otto Hügel, *Untersuchungsrichter, Diebsfänger, Detektive. Theorie und Geschichte der deutschen Detektiverzählung im 19. Jahrhundert* (Stuttgart: J.B. Metzlersche Verlagsbuchhandlung, 1978), p. 66.

7 A slightly abridged English translation can be found in: *Early German and Austrian Detective Fiction. An Anthology*, trans. and ed. by Mary W. Tannert and Henry Kratz (Jefferson/NC and London: McFarland & Company, 1999), pp. 191–216.

8 The website 'Project Gutenberg' includes English translations of five stories featuring 'Joe Muller'.

with criminals faced with 'the Austro-Hungarian empire's rigid and oppressive social system'.[9] The Hungarian journalist and writer Adalbert Goldscheider (1848–1916) published numerous novels and novellas under his pseudonym Balduin Groller. In 1890, he created a Viennese version of Sherlock Holmes named Dagobert Trostler, whose case histories were published in six volumes between 1909 and 1912.[10]

The Viennese journalist Otto Soyka (1882–1955) was a prolific and well-known author who wrote a number of detective and crime novels between 1911 and 1936. Among them were *Die Söhne der Macht* [1911, *The Sons of the Power**], which combined crime fiction and science fiction, and the detective novel *Das Glück der Edith Hilge* [1913, *Edith Hilge's Happiness**], which was published accompanied by a competition. After the Nazi takeover of Austria, Soyka had to flee the country. He returned to Vienna in 1949 but died largely forgotten in 1955. One important event in the development of Austrian crime fiction was the publication of Hans Lebert's (1919–1993) *Die Wolfshaut [Wolf Skin**] in 1960. According to the crime writer Manfred Wieninger, the reissue of this novel in 1991 influenced many younger authors of crime fiction in Austria.[11] *Die Wolfshaut* tells the story of a sailor who returns to his native mountain village in 1952. The village is tellingly named 'Schweigen' [Silence], and that is exactly what he encounters on his quest to rediscover his personal past and the past of the village community. A number of villagers are soon killed under strange circumstances, and a wolf from the mountains is rumoured to be the cause. But as the sailor digs deeper into the recent history of the village, it becomes clear that an atrocity committed by the villagers during World War II is at the bottom of it all. Lebert's six-hundred-page novel was credited as being one of the first postwar novels in Austria to cast a critical gaze at the repression of the crimes committed during the Nazi period, making a major contribution to undermining the illusion of happiness and an idyllic world typical of the *Heimatroman* [homeland novel] of the 1950s and 1960s.

---

9 Tannert, Kratz, *Early German and Austrian Detective Fiction*, p. 191. On Auguste Groner, cf. Evelyne Polt-Heinzl, 'Frauenkrimis – Von der besonderen Dotation zu Detektion und Mord', in *Ich kannte den Mörder wußte nur nicht wer er war. Zum Kriminalroman der Gegenwart*, ed. by Friedbert Aspetsberger and Daniela Strigl (Innsbruck: Studien, 2004), pp. 144–170 (pp. 151–154).
10 The novella 'The Vault Break-In' [1909, 'Der Kasseneinbruch'] is printed in Tannert, Kratz, *Early German and Austrian Detective Fiction*, pp. 228–242.
11 Manfred Wieninger, 'Heimatliteratur ohne Kitsch', *Wiener Zeitung Online* September, 16 2011. (http://www.wienerzeitung.at/themen_channel/wz_reflexionen/kompendium/397240_Heimatliteratur-ohne-Kitsch.html).

Beginning in the 1980s, a heightened interest in 'literary' crime fiction manifested itself in Austria. A Viennese publisher came out with a seven-volume series of novels under the imprint 'Vienna School of Crime'. One of the novels in the series was *Internationale Zone* [*International Zone**] by Milo Dor and Reinhard Federmann, 'a cold-war thriller written like a Graham Greene novel'[12] that had been originally published back in 1951. The other volumes in the series included novels by Peter Matejka, Ernst Hinterberger, Werner Kofler, Ingrid Puganigg, Alfred Paul Schmidt and Helmut Eisendle, which were all written in the early 1980s and increasingly abandoned the conventions of crime fiction.

Characteristics of Austrian crime fiction

Austrian crime fiction demonstrates a number of features that may also be present in crime fiction from other countries but that are more prominent here than elsewhere. Taken together, these characteristics give Austrian crime fiction its special appeal. The first of them has been described as a noticeable inclination by 'established literary authors'[13] to use elements of crime fiction in their writing and to treat the *crime genre as a field of experimentation*. Robert Müller's *Camera Obscura* (1921) and Heimito von Doderer's *Ein Mord den jeder begeht* [1938, *Every Man a Murderer*] are early examples of novels that undermine the genre conventions of crime fiction and come close to the radical critique of knowledge, subjectivity and representation that we commonly associate with the postmodern anti-detective novel.[14] For example, in Peter Handke's 1967 novel *Der Hausierer* [*The Peddler**], each chapter begins with an analysis of the typical elements of a *Mordgeschichte* [murder story] and explores their implications for narrating a story. Examples include 'Order before the first disorder' (ch. 1), 'Pursuit' (ch. 5), 'Investigation' (ch. 6) or 'Exposure' (ch. 11). After each initial analysis (printed in italics), the remainder of the chapter provides one possible way of transforming the theoretical insights provided in the first part of the chapter into a story. The short sentences Handke uses in these narrative

---

12 Peter Plener, Michael Rohrwasser, '"Es war Mord". Zwischen Höhenkamm, Zentralfriedhof und Provinz: Österreichs Krimiszene', *Der Deutschunterricht*, 2 (2007), pp. 57–65 (p. 59).

13 Marieke Krajenbrink, 'Austrian Crime Fiction. Experimentation, Critical Memory and Humour', in *Crime Fiction in Germany. Der Krimi*, ed. by Katharina Hall (Cardiff: University of Wales Press, 2016), pp. 51–67 (p. 54).

14 Plener, Rohrwasser, 'Es war Mord', p. 57. On the anti-detective novel, see 'Postmodernism and the Anti-Detective Novel' in: John Scaggs, *Crime Fiction* (London and New York: Routledge, 2005), pp. 139–143.

passages should be understood as mere filler pieces that could easily be replaced by others. Thus, in Handke's novel, the conventions of crime fiction form the background for narrative experimentation and the exploration of various modes of storytelling. We find similar approaches in novels by Ingeborg Bachmann (*Malina; Der Fall Franza* [1978, *The Book of Franza*]), Albert Drach, Gerhard Fritsch, Gerhard Roth, Thomas Bernhard (*Watten*, 1969), Christoph Ransmayer (*Morbus Kithara*, 1995), Doron Rabinovici (*Suche nach M.* [1997, *The Search for M.*]) and Elfriede Jelinek (*Die Kinder der Toten* [1995, *The Children of the Dead**], *Gier* [2000, *Greed**]).[15] This list of authors suggests that the border between genre literature and sophisticated literature is more permeable than in Germany.[16]

Another noteworthy attribute that lends Austrian crime fiction a certain distinctive quality is how often the country's past and present become objects of highly critical accounts embedded in the plots of the novels. One of the founding myths of the 'Second Republic', the democratic Austrian state that was formed after the end of World War II, was that Austria had been a 'victim' of German aggression when it was taken over by the Nazi 'Anschluss' in 1938. The fact that Austria had been a fascist dictatorship in its own right between 1934 and 1938 and that many Austrians had welcomed the Nazi takeover of their country was largely repressed and did not become a subject of public discourse until much later. Instead, Austria created an image of itself as an ideal tourist destination, an idyllic realm untouched by the atrocities of the war and the destruction of nature.[17] To contradict this myth, contemporary Austrian crime fiction often paints a picture of *Austria as a dystopian wasteland*, full of crime and corruption, where the hero, or rather, the anti-hero leads a precarious life. The novels of Wolf Haas and Manfred Wieninger, featuring former police detectives and then amateur sleuths Simon Brenner and Marek Miert respectively, closely fit this paradigm.

Wieninger's *Der Mann mit dem goldenen Revolver* [2015, *The Man with the Golden Revolver**] is a case in point. The atmosphere of the novel is dominated by resignation and melancholia. Marek Miert is so down on his luck that at some point he even contemplates suicide. Miert lives in a neighborhood that

---

15 Cf. Krajenbrink, 'Austrian Crime Fiction', pp. 54–57 and Plener, Rohrwasser, 'Es war Mord', pp. 58–59, and Dagmar C.G. Lorenz, 'In Search of the Criminal – in Search of the Crime. Holocaust Literature and Films as Crime Fiction', *Modern Austrian Literature* 31.3/4 (1998), pp. 35–48.

16 Plener, Rohrwasser 'Es war Mord', p. 58.

17 Cf. Elke Sturm-Trigonatis, 'Der Wiener Privatdetektiv Markus Cheng – Charlie Chan in Österreich?' *Journal of Austrian Studies* 45.1/2 (2012), pp. 69–92 (p. 75).

resembles a post-apocalyptic landscape, consisting of run-down buildings and streets full of trash, inhabited by people who have no hope. His assessment of the situation is blunt: 'Nothing will ever get better here, no way'.[18] Compared to the mood the novel conveys, the crime plot is rather insignificant: a recently deceased former bank robber has hidden gold treasure, and both the police and a criminal, the eponymous man with the golden revolver, compete with the detective to find it. The allusion to the James Bond movie *The Man with the Golden Gun* (1974) is taken up later in the novel, when Miert buys a cheap used car with the license plate 'H*HH007'. The car is a wreck and the plate makes it clear that imagining Miert as a James-Bond-like character would be laughable (HHH = hahaha), thus confirming his status of anti-hero. As already mentioned, the mystery plot is not a detective story, but rather a quest for a hidden treasure, with an ending reminiscent of Poe's 'The Purloined Letter'. The mystery the detective has to solve does not consist in finding out 'whodunit', i.e. who the perpetrator of the crime was, but what the deceased bank robber did with his loot. As the first-person narrator, Miert frequently includes memories, stories and dreams in his account and thus digresses from the plot and undermines its importance. All of this shows that the dystopian ambiance of the novel is more important than the crime story. The detective and the stark environment he experiences on a daily basis are the focus of the novel. Wieninger combines elements of the American hard-boiled school of crime fiction with contemporary Scandinavian noir, but flavours this blend with a certain light-heartedness typical of the Austrian tradition of making fun of things when faced with the apocalypse.

Austrian crime fiction often conceives of crime as *the result of the return of the repressed*. The objects of repression in these cases are illustrations of Austria's fascist past. Crimes committed in the present have their roots in an earlier period that nobody wants to remember. This pattern can be found in novels such as Ernst Hinterberger's *Und über uns die Heldenahnen* [1992, *And Above us our Heroic Ancestors**], Alfred Komarek's *Blumen für Polt* [2000, *Flowers for Polt**] and Heinrich Steinfest's *Cheng: Sein erster Fall* [2000, *Cheng: His First Case**]. In Eva Rossmann's *Freudsche Verbrechen* [2001, *Freudian Crimes**],[19] it is the Nazi past and the repression of that past that are the reasons for crimes committed in the present. A young American woman is found strangled in the Freud Museum at Berggasse 19 in Vienna. 'Lifestyle journalist' Mira

---

18 Manfred Wieninger, *Der Mann mit dem goldenen Revolver* (Innsbruck, Vienna: Haymon, 2015), p. 117 (my trans).

19 Eva Rossmann (b. 1962) has published nineteen novels featuring Mira Valensky between 1999 and 2017.

Valensky receives a call from her former school friend Ulrike, who works at the museum and discovered the body. Ulrike is afraid the police will suspect her and, since Mira had been successful as amateur sleuth before, wants her to find the true killer. The location of the first murder in the novel, taken together with its title, suggests a link between some of the major ideas of Freudian psycho-analysis and the crimes committed, both in the present and in the past. This connection, although the reader cannot be aware of it at this time, is referred to at the very beginning of the narrative. After Mira has arrived at the museum, Ulrike tells her that she made the discovery of the body of the murder victim at '19 Uhr 44' (19:44 or 7:44 pm) and justifies her knowledge of the exact time by adding, 'I looked at my watch, I know that something like this is important'.[20] Noting the precise moment in time when the body is discovered is one of the principles of both police work and crime fiction. However, by simply leaving out one word ('Uhr'), that exact rendering of time in its German notation also refers to the year 1944, when the concentration-camp Auschwitz-Birkenau 'reached peak killing capacity'.[21] Thus, one designation of time (the year 1944) is hidden within another (the time of day 19:44); the murder in the present and the Holocaust, the mass-murder in the past, are linked by a reference to time. What is already indicated by a small detail at the beginning of the novel is mir-rored in the plot as a whole: it turns out that the young American woman, a college student from New York, was murdered because she had found out who benefited from the 'Aryanization', the forced sale of her Jewish family's home in 1938, after the 'Anschluss', when Austria became part of Nazi-Germany.[22] The murderer wanted to suppress this knowledge at all costs. The case is solved when Mira Valensky and her Slovenian cleaning woman and friend Vesna Krajner find out who the murdered woman was, that her Jewish family came from Vienna and that her grandparents had been killed in the Holocaust. What has greatly affected Austrian society since the end of World

---

20 Eva Rossmann, *Freudsche Verbrechen. Mira Valensky ermittelt in Wien* (Bergisch Gladbach: Bastei Lübbe, 2003), p. 9 (my trans.).

21 United States Holocaust Memorial Museum, 'Holocaust Encyclopedia', (https://www.ushmm.org/wlc/en/article.php?ModuleId=10007327).

22 1938 was also the year when the eighty-three-year-old, terminally ill Sigmund Freud left Austria for London, just before the Nazis could detain him. Mira Valensky, at the beginning of the novel, does not even know where the Freud Museum is located in Vienna. This exposes the repression of the inventor of psychoanalysis and the main theoretician of repression itself. Cf. Traci S. O'Brien, 'What's in Your Bag? "Freudian Crimes" and Austria's Nazi Past in Eva Rossmann's *Freudsche Verbrechen*', in *Tatort Germany. The Curious Case of German-Language Crime Fiction*, ed. by Lynn M. Kutch and Todd Herzog (Rochester/NY: Camden House, 2014), pp. 155–174 (p. 156).

War II to the present, namely the repression of the country's Nazi past, emerges as the hidden truth that the detective in Rossmann's novel has to uncover. The detective is doing the work of the historian or the psychoanalyst: finding out what happened in the past to determine the causes of human behaviour in the present.[23]

A further characteristic of sophisticated Austrian crime fiction is that is has *a penchant for reflecting on symbols, signs, and language and for critically exploring its own genre conventions*. This puts it in a close relationship with a long philosophical tradition of experimenting with language, scepticism about language's ability to serve as a reliable system of communication, and modern and postmodern literature. Hugo von Hofmannsthal's 'Ein Brief' [1901, 'A Letter'], for example, is one of the most renowned documents of early modernism in the German language. It presents a bleak view of language's potential as a means of communication. In the early twentieth century, Austrian thinkers like Fritz Mauthner (1849–1923) and Ludwig Wittgenstein (1889–1951) contributed groundbreaking work towards the philosophy of language. Experimenting with language became a prime concern in what is known as concrete poetry, such as in texts by Ernst Jandl (1925–2000) and Friederike Mayröcker (b. 1924). Literary groups like the Vienna School (late 1940s to 1964, when it was dissolved)[24] and the Graz Group (founded around 1958)[25] have continued to critically contemplate the philosophy of language and its influence on how members of society communicate with each other.

There are numerous indications that writers of contemporary Austrian crime fiction are thoroughly grounded in this tradition. To mention just two examples, Wolf Haas, one of the foremost authors of contemporary Austrian crime fiction (whose work will be discussed below), wrote a doctoral dissertation on the

---

23 On the parallels between detection and psychoanalysis and the psychoanalytic self-reflection of the detective in *Freudsche Verbrechen*, see Traci S. O'Brien, 'Note to Self? Postmodern Criminality and (Feminist) Consciousness in Eva Rossmann's *Freudsche Verbrechen*', *Woman in German Yearbook* 31 (2015), pp. 122–146.

24 Prominent members of the Vienna Group were, among others, H. C, Artmann, Friedrich Achleitner, Konrad Bayer, Oswald Wiener and Gerhard Rühm. They produced experimental literature in the tradition of Dada and Surrealism, with the aim of provoking the complacent middle class and disrupting the cultural establishment, thus continuing the pre-war and pre-fascist avant-garde and those factions of modernism that wanted to emancipate their audiences from the clutches of what Adorno and Horkheimer called 'the culture industry'.

25 The members of the Graz Group, among them Alfred Kolleritsch, Barbara Frischmuth, G. F. Jonke, Peter Handke and Elfriede Jelinek, shared many goals with the Vienna Group, but came together due to their deeply felt mistrust of the Viennese cultural establishment and its grip on cultural production.

theoretical foundations of concrete poetry before he started to write crime fiction.[26] Heinrich Steinfest's Chief Inspector Richard Lukastik, who makes an appearance in several of the author's novels, is an admirer of Wittgenstein's *Tractatus Logico-Philosophicus* (1921), in which Wittgenstein examines the relationship between language and knowledge. Lukastik has a personal mantra that is taken from the *Tractatus*: 'Das Rätsel gibt es nicht' [The riddle does not exist].[27] In a genre that is based on mysteries or riddles, such a maxim must seem paradoxical. Lukastik carries a copy of the *Tractatus* with him at all times. In the novel *Nervöse Fische* [2004, *Nervous Fish**], this actually saves the inspector's life.

Heinrich Steinfest's (b. 1961) critically acclaimed novels illustrate a tendency in contemporary Austrian crime fiction to engage in postmodern playfulness, black humour and a certain partiality to what is bizarre or grotesque. They are parodies of crime fiction formats such as the classical 'whodunit' or the more recent serial-killer novel. Their anti-realism is regularly furthered by including elements of the fantastic.[28] The fourth novel in Steinfest's Markus Cheng-series,[29] *Batmans Schönheit* [2010, *Batman's Beauty**] is a good illustration of Steinfest's style. Markus Cheng is a private detective of Chinese descent who resides in Vienna.[30] He does not speak Chinese and knows next to nothing about Chinese history or culture, but because of his features, everybody he meets takes him for an Asian. He is prone to all kinds of mishaps that result in permanent bodily harm. In the first novel *Cheng* (2000, rev. 2007) he loses an

---

26 Wolf Haas, *Sprachtheoretische Grundlagen der konkreten Poesie* (Stuttgart: Akademischer Verlag Stuttgart, 1990).

27 The full quotation from the *Tractatus* runs as follows: '6.5 For an answer which cannot be expressed the question too cannot/ be expressed./ *The riddle* does not exist./ If a question can be put at all, then it *can* also be answered'. Cf. Ludwig Wittgenstein, *Tractatus Logico-Philosophicus*, trans. C. K. Ogden (London: Kegan Paul, Trench, Trubner; New York: Harcourt, Brace & Company, 1922), p. 161.

28 Thomas Wörtche has described the second of the four Markus-Cheng-novels, *Ein sturer Hund* [2003, *A Stubborn Dog**] as a 'meta-novel' that does to the serial killer novel what the Italo-Westerns by Sergio Leone did to the classic Western movies: they destroyed a genre that had become obsolete. Cf. Thomas Wörtche, 'CrimeWatch No. 80', *Freitag* 52, December 19, 2003.

29 The other novels in the series are *Cheng* (2000, revised edition 2007*), *Ein dickes Fell* [2006, *A Thick Fur/Skin**]

30 The exception is *Ein sturer and Der schlaflose Cheng: Sein neuer Fall* [2019, *Sleepless Cheng: His new Case**] *Hund*, in which Cheng has moved to Stuttgart. Vienna and Stuttgart are also the cities in which Heinrich Steinfest grew up and where he lives today.

arm, his hearing is damaged and an injury to his leg forces him to limp.[31] His outward appearance and his battered body are his trademarks. In *Batmans Schönheit*, a serial killer is apparently haunting Vienna and murders male and female actors. The victims are all shot five times, and although their injuries are not immediately fatal, in each instance they are left to bleed to death. When they are found, they all have a rare postal stamp on their tongues. Everything points to ritual killings typical of a psychopath. Cheng becomes entangled in this affair rather by accident and, although he had crossed paths with two of the story's major characters earlier in his life, his contribution to solving the case remains marginal. As in all of Steinfest's novels, digressions from the plot in the form of short glosses, commentaries, ruminations, and literary and philosophical allusions continually interrupt the flow of the narrative. One example of this technique is the role of 'Batman', whose presumed beauty gives the novel its title. 'Batman' was the name of Cheng's cat, but in this novel, the new bearer of the name is a tiny salt-water crawfish from a science kit for children, whose antics in the small container of water where he survives all of the other members of his normally short-lived species are described in great detail.

One characteristic feature of Steinfest's novels is that he hints at how they can be read in the text. In *Batmans Schönheit*, the reader is hard pressed to find a fully-developed crime story. In one of the anonymous narrator's philosophical digressions, however, he asserts that, according to some people, 'the world is basically determined by a system of things and names and symbols'[32] that interact with each other. For the uninitiated, this system produces nothing but chance happenings or coincidences. In reality, though, the world and, by extension, the story of the novel are nothing but a 'pattern' that has no meaning beyond itself. Therefore, both in the novel and in the world at large, instead of stories or plots, there are only 'Muster' [patterns] without meaning or purpose.[33] Similarly, in a crime story, instead of clues, there are only 'signs'. When a young female detective seeks guidance from her mentor, she is told that she

---

31 In an afterword to the revised edition of *Cheng*, Steinfest notes that Markus Cheng was first conceived as a character in a comic. All of his 'accidents, bizarre blows of fate, his failures that occur as in an infinite loop' follow the logic of the comic, except that his injuries do not disappear, as in a comic, but stay with him. Cf. *Cheng* (Munich, Zurich: Piper, 2007), p. 263 (my trans.).

32 Heinrich Steinfest, *Batmans Schönheit* (Munich, Zurich: Piper, 2010), p. 94–95 (my trans.). '[...] daß die Welt im Grunde von einem Bezugssystem der Dinge und Namen und Symbole bestimmt wird'.

33 Steinfest, *Batmans Schönheit*, p. 95.

should always be on the lookout for 'Zeichen' [signs], and signs cannot be understood in the traditional sense of attributing meaning to them. Like an alien sign system that cannot be deciphered, 'like the writings of the Maya', they have to be 'translated', i.e. they have to be incorporated into a pattern.[34]

In the end, it transpires that it was not a serial killer who was responsible for the murders in *Batmans Schönheit*, but a conflict between angels. This is explained to Cheng by his therapist, who tells him that the explanation for this state of affairs can be found in 'a book' with the title 'Conjugal Love' published in Tübingen in 1845. What she tells Cheng is a summary of the Swedish mystic Emanuel Swedenborg's (1688–1772) book *Marriage Love* (1768), which did indeed appear in a German translation at the mentioned place and time.[35] The gist of Swedenborg's theory is that, under certain circumstances, angels can take over human beings and live their lives on Earth. Steinfest does not fail to mention Wim Wenders's well-known movie *Der Himmel über Berlin* [1987, *Wings of Desire*],[36] in which something similar happens, to make his idea of angels walking on Earth more palatable to his readers. Even more importantly, the name of Cheng's antagonist in the novel is Palle (Pál) Swedenborg, referring to the 'book' whose author was not named. These are just a few examples of a wealth of interwoven names, texts and ideas that are continually forming the 'patterns' that, according to the narrator, determine our existence. The point here is that the novel does not just claim that these patterns exist – it also produces them. This amounts to nothing less than a playful contribution to the long tradition of reflecting on the epistemological and ontological foundations of language and human existence so prominent in the Austrian cultural tradition.[37] In addition, the genre conventions of crime fiction are humorously undermined; the author teases his readers and their expectations of the genre and encourages them to reflect on the realism contemporary crime fiction supposedly upholds.

---

34 Steinfest, *Batmans Schönheit*, p. 220.

35 The full title of the German translation that was published in Tübingen in 1845 was: *Die Wonnen der Weisheit betreffend die eheliche Liebe dann die Wollüste der Thorheit betreffend die buhlerische Liebe.*

36 Steinfest, *Batmans Schönheit*, p. 250.

37 Steinfest also plays with the ontological foundations of narrative texts when he has his fictional characters interact with himself as a real person, even getting one character to argue that the Cheng-novels are 'written too badly' (Steinfest, *Batmans Schönheit*, p. 141). Narrative theory calls such overlapping between the fictional world of the text and the real world 'metalepsis'. For more on metalepsis, see John Pier, 'Metalepsis', *the living handbook of narratology* (http://www.lhn.uni-hamburg.de/article/metalepsis-revised-version-uploaded-13-july-2016).

A further peculiar quality of Austrian crime fiction consists in how frequently and enthusiastically writers employ *stylistic elements of playfulness, humour, irony and parody*.[38] Authors who are often mentioned in this context include Wolf Haas, Thomas Raab, the already discussed Heinrich Steinfest, Stefan Slupetzky, Günter Brödl and Kurt Palm. Female Austrian writers like Helga Anderle, Elfriede Semrau, Sabina Naber and others are credited with having mastered a specific form of 'Viennese black humor'.[39] A prime example of fictional representations of crime from Austria with a humorous twist is the TV series *Kottan ermittelt* [*Kottan Investigates**]. It was first conceived of by Helmut Zenker (1949–2003) as a short story for a crime fiction anthology in 1974. Zenker then developed a radio play from the material and, after that, a script for the production of (originally) only one movie for Austrian state television. The responses were so enthusiastic, however, that Zenker and Peter Patzak, the director of the original movie, received the go-ahead for expanding the concept into a TV series. Ultimately, nineteen episodes were produced between 1976 and 1983. Episodes 1–7 were ninety minutes long, whereas the following instalments of the series had a length of sixty minutes and were co-produced by the German broadcaster ZDF. From the beginning, the series was provocative and highly controversial. On the one hand, it had a solid fan base (and would later become a cult phenomenon[40]), while, on the other hand, government and police officials lodged vehement protests against the depiction of the police and police work in the episodes. One important element of *Kottan* was making fun of the police, making them look like idiots or bureaucrats mired in a fascist mind-set. The fact that Police Major Kottan's first name is 'Adolf' is no coincidence. The producers of the series would make fun of the official protests against *Kottan* by having the character Kottan watch an episode of *Kottan* and then call his local TV station to complain about the trash they were broadcasting.[41] Furthermore, a strong element of self-ironic or metafictional intertextuality

---

38 Russegger attributes '(self-) parody, an aesthetics of absurd nonsense, satire, persiflage, and travesty' to Austrian crime fiction, cf. Arno Russegger, 'Ortspiele. Wortspiele. Aspekte kriminalistischen Erzählens in der österreichischen Gegenwartsliteratur', in *Mord als kreativer Prozess. Zum Kriminalroman der Gegenwart in Deutschland, Österreich und der Schweiz*, ed. by Sandro M. Moraldo (Heidelberg: Universitätsverlag Winter, 2005), pp. 75–98, (p. 79, my trans.). The Austrian TV crime series that promote 'childish' humor, such as *Kommissar Rex* or *SOKO Kitzbühel*, will not be discussed here. These and other series often serve as advertising outlets for Austria's tourism industry, cf. Doris Priesching, 'Erfolgreich, werbewirksam, trivial. Anmerkungen zum österreichischen Fernsehkrimi', in *Ich kannte den Mörder*, pp. 221–239 (p. 227).

39 Cf. Kramlovsky, 'Show Your Face', p. 14.

40 See the website http://www.kottan.info/.

41 Cf. 'This is an absolute outrage' (my trans.) in episode 4 'Nachttankstelle', 36:40–37:77.

was part of the series. Characters would look or speak into the camera, or they would quote from other iconic pop cultural texts or crime shows, e.g. referring to Sergio Leone's classic Italian Western *Once Upon the Time in the West* (1968, in episode 5) or mimicking Telly Savalas in *Kojak* (1973–1978, in episode 3). In later episodes, more and more grotesque and slapstick elements were added to the satirical foundation of the series, developing *Kottan* into a constant provocation of the popular German TV crime series of the time. In a sense, *Kottan* was an 'anti-*Tatort*'.[42]

The image post-war Austria strived to project of itself consisted for the most part of that of a country that combined Vienna as a capital of world culture with the provinces as idyllic and picturesque realms of unspoiled nature and charming folk traditions. Contemporary Austrian crime writers have been using both *the political and cultural centre of Vienna and the provinces as settings* for their narratives. By digging out the hidden and forgotten skeletons in the closet of recent Austrian history, the investigators in novels by authors such as Alfred Komarek, Wolf Haas, Claudia Rossbacher, Kurt Lanthaler, Manfred Wieninger and Gerhard Roth have taken on the role of 'archaeologists of Austrian stories and histories'.[43] This *Regionalkrimi*[44] ['regional' or 'provincial' crime fiction] exposes the sordid underbelly of a society that takes pride in the charms of its unspoiled rural environments and markets them to tourists from around the world. Austrian *Regionalkrimis* 'use the conventions of the crime genre to challenge traditional local and international images of Austria and to subvert those preconceptions'.[45]

A good example of this kind of crime fiction that doubles as *Anti-Heimatliteratur* [anti-homeland literature] are the Simon-Polt novels by Alfred Komarek (b. 1945).[46] They are set in the 'Weinviertel' (the wine region in Lower Austria, north of Vienna, bordering on the Czech Republic) and represent a holdout for the pre-industrial means of producing wine and, by extension, for

---

42 On the German TV-series *Tatort* cf. chapter 6.

43 Cf. Plener, Rohrwasser 'Es war Mord', p. 65 (my trans.).

44 On regional crime fiction from Germany, cf. chapter 5.

45 Cf. Anita McChesney, 'The Case of the Austrian Regional Crime Novel', in *Tatort Germany*, pp. 81–98 (p. 81).

46 The series consists of the novels *Polt muss weinen* [1998, *Polt Has to Cry**], *Blumen für Polt* [2000, *Flowers for Polt**], *Himmel, Polt und Hölle* [2001, *Heaven, Polt and Hell**], *Polterabend* [2003, *Wedding Shower**], *Polt* (2009), *Alt, aber Polt* [2017, *Old But Polt**], and the collection of stories *Zwölf mal Polt* [2011, *Twelve Times Polt**]. For a discussion of these novels, cf. Thomas Kniesche, 'Gärgas: Die Kriminalromane von Alfred Komarek', *The German Quarterly* 79.2 (2006), pp. 211–233.

a communal lifestyle protected from the confusion, corruption and distractions of living in a big city. The differences to the not-too-distant metropolis Vienna are marked by the introduction of fictional Viennese characters who bring their emotional baggage, twisted desires and pathological fears – and often a criminal disposition as well – to the seemingly peaceful villages of the wine region, thus infecting this tranquil realm with the ills of modernity. The traditional way of life is also under pressure because the fall of the Iron Curtain, the border to the former communist countries, has opened it up to an influx of criminal activity from the East. The most dangerous developments, however, come from within. Time and again, the idyll is shown to be hollow, and the cases Inspector Simon Polt has to solve revolve around revenge, an unfulfilled desire for justice, obsolete concepts of honour and the unwillingness or inability to integrate individuals who – for one reason or another – do not conform to the standards of 'normal' life. In *Blumen für Polt* [2000, *Flowers for Polt**], for instance, a young intellectually disabled man is murdered by his father because he could not live with the shame of having engendered a disabled child. Komarek's Simon Polt novels insist that the quaint picture of provincial Austria is fake, a fantasy created for the sake of self-delusion and the needs of the tourist industry.

The Austrian capital of Vienna does not fare much better. In novels by writers such as Stefan Slupetzky, Ernst Hinterberger, Eva Rossmann, Günter Brödl and Elfriede Semrau it appears as 'the hub of an authoritarian, completely bureaucratized, inaccessible, downright Kafkaesque power'.[47] Following in the footsteps of Orson Well's character Harry Lime in Carol Reed's classic film noir *The Third Man* (1949), Vienna often appears as a realm whose exposed areas are tunnelled by subterranean spaces that are able to symbolically hide the secrets of the past and the neuroses of the present. These 'surface-subterranean tropes'[48] play a decisive role in such novels as Josef Haslinger's *Opernball* [1995, *Opera Ball**] and Heinrich Steinfest's *Nervöse Fische*.

---

47 Russegger, 'Ortspiele. Wortspiele', p. 78 (my trans.). 'Zentrum einer autoritativen, total verbürokratisierten, unzugänglichen, nachgerade kafkaesken Macht'.
48 Krajenbrink, 'Austrian Crime Fiction', p. 52.

Wolf Haas's *Auferstehung der Toten* and Paulus Hochgatterer's *Das Matratzenhaus*

Wolf Haas (b. 1960) is one of Austria's best-known contemporary authors of crime fiction. After studying psychology, literature and linguistics, he completed a doctoral dissertation on concrete poetry and taught for two years at the University of Swansea, Wales. He then had a successful career at an advertising agency in Vienna, before deciding to focus solely on writing. Between 1996 and 2014, he published eight novels featuring ex-cop and ex-private investigator Simon Brenner.[49] Haas received the Deutscher Krimi Preis [German Crime Fiction Prize] three times for his Brenner novels, four of which have been made into movies (with Haas participating as a scriptwriter). Moreover, several radio and theatre plays have been produced on the basis of the novels. With their critical assessment of contemporary Austrian affairs – from multiculturalism to the power of the tourist industry, from the role of the church to gender identity – they obliterate 'the official image and narrative of an idyllic Austria [. . .]'.[50]

Five of the novels start with a trademark sentence, 'Well, something's happened again',[51] that introduces the unique form of narration Haas employs in his Simon-Brenner series. The narrator is an anonymous[52] character, an average man from the streets, a John Doe or Joe the plumber who has known Simon Brenner for quite some time. He uses simple idioms, interspersed with expressions typically used in spoken language. The syntax of his narration is marked by inversions, repetition and ellipsis. Verbs are often missing.[53] The reader might imagine a man sitting next to him/her at a bar, telling a story and doing his very best to entertain – as if the reader were part of a (one-sided) conversation. This

---

49 They are: *Auferstehung der Toten* [1996, *Resurrection*], *Der Knochenmann* [1997, *The Bone Man*], *Komm, süßer Tod!* [1998, *Come, Sweet Death!*], *Silentium!* (1999, not translated), *Wie die Tiere* [2001, *Like Animals**], *Das ewige Leben* [2003, *Eternal Life**], *Der Brenner und der liebe Gott* [2009, *Brenner and God*], and *Brennerova* (2014, not translated).

50 Cf. Helga Schreckenberger, 'The Destruction of Idyllic Austria in Wolf Haas's Detective Novels', in *Crime and Madness in Modern Austria. Myth, Metaphor and Cultural Realities*, ed. by Rebecca S. Thomas (Newcastle: Cambridge Scholars Publishing, 2008), pp. 424–443 (p. 425).

51 Cf. Haas, *The Bone Man*, p. 9 and *Come, Sweet Death*, p. 3. The German original reads, 'Jetzt ist schon wieder was passiert'.

52 The identity of the narrator is revealed in the sixth novel in the series, *Das ewige Leben*. Haas had planned to end the series with this novel but, after an interlude of six years, came back to it.

53 A thorough linguistic analysis of Haas's narrative style is provided in: Sigrid Nindl, *Wolf Haas und sein kriminalliterarisches Sprachexperiment* (Berlin: Erich Schmidt, 2010). A shorter

form of 'fictional orality' or performed story-telling masquerades as a dialogue with the reader. The telling seems to be unstructured; the narrator constantly digresses or falls victim to associating the countless metonymic relationships between the circumstances of the case with his own memories. His manifold associations, the way he remembers seemingly unrelated events, people and circumstances are, however, part of a highly sophisticated narrative style. Delaying crucial information about the case and the use of frequent foreshadowing, especially at the end of a chapter, intensifies the foreboding and suspense, leaving the reader with the feeling that an unavoidable fate is taking its course.

Next to inventing a unique style of narration, Haas's other stroke of genius consisted in creating a distinctive fictional investigator: Simon Brenner is a drifter in Austrian society. If there is one thing that constantly eludes him, it is success. At the beginning of the first novel, he has a job as a police officer, he has an apartment, and he has a car. By the end of the last novel, he has none of these things. He aimlessly wanders from one Austrian city to the next, and from one low rung on the social ladder to the next (lower) one, and has stopped caring, except in certain situations, when, just like the hard-boiled detectives of the American tradition, he suddenly reveals himself to be the moralist he truly is at heart. Brenner has been compared to Jesus and has been called a 'man of suffering' and an 'incarnation of the martyr'.[54] He is a melancholic whose migraines and ever-deepening depression force him to increase the dosages of the drugs he is taking at an alarming rate. In spite of these handicaps, he always manages to solve the murders he is tasked with investigating. He relies on attention to small details, ponderous thought processes, taking detours and, most importantly of all, an uncanny ability to unconsciously arrive at the solution of the crime. As soon as he succeeds in deciphering the signs his unconscious is sending him, he can solve the case.

In *Auferstehung der Toten* [1996, *Resurrection*], the first Brenner novel, an elderly American couple is found frozen to death in a ski lift in the picturesque resort of Zell am See. In a plot that has many parallels to Friedrich Dürrenmatt's play *Der Besuch der alten Dame* [1956, *The Visit*], Brenner has to investigate a family in which incest and rape had driven away a young woman who returns after a long absence to take her revenge. At the end, after the killer has been identified, the narrator is reminded of a Greek tragedy. What makes Brenner's job so difficult in this case is that nobody wants to remember what

---

evaluation in English can be found in Jon Sherman, 'Plurality and Alternity in Wolf Haas's Detective Brenner Mysteries', in *Tatort Germany*, pp. 61–80 (pp. 67–71).

54 The terms used are 'Passionsfigur' and 'Inkarnation des Schmerzensmannes'. Cf, Plener, Rohrwasser, 'Es war Mord', p. 61.

had been done to the young woman before she was forced to leave. Whomever he asks and wherever he turns to, he is faced with a wall of silence. This unwillingness to remember the fate of one young woman is mirrored in the forgetting or repression of what happened in the area when Austria was part of Nazi Germany. The setting of the novel is crucial here. In the mountains above Zell am See, the Nazis had started to build a vast system of reservoirs:

> The dam's been up there for almost fifty years because the reservoir was opened right after the war, 'Symbol of the Republic', it said in the newspaper, that was 1951 when they opened it. [. . .] And a few years ago, that would be 1991, that was the forty-year anniversary. They even invited a few of the Ukrainian POWs because hundreds of them had died up there on the construction site during the War. It was the Americans, then, who finished building the reservoir.[55]

For forty years, the fates of the many victims of forced labour who perished during the mammoth building project had been forgotten and repressed. The 'Symbol of the Republic' was also a symbol of forgetting. By locating Simon Brenner's first case in this specific location and by making it a case about a 'ghost' from the past that haunts the family that had abused her, Haas connects the life of a traumatized individual with the past Austria and the Austrians had tried to cover up. In *Auferstehung der Toten*, the weather is ostensibly the reason why 'people will remember this year for a long time to come'.[56] Any attentive reader will know better, however.

Paulus Hochgatterer (b. 1961) is a writer and child psychiatrist and resides in Vienna. In his first crime novel, *Die Süße des Lebens* [2006, *The Sweetness of Life*], recipient of the 2009 European Literature Prize, a seven-year-old girl is spending an evening with her grandfather when he is brutally murdered. As a consequence of her traumatic experience, she refuses to speak. Psychiatrist Rafael Horn is asked to help her and thus becomes embroiled in the police investigation of the murder headed by detective inspector Ludwig Kovacs. The second novel in which Horn and Kovacs investigate is *Das Matratzenhaus* [2010, *The Mattress House*]. In many ways, *Das Matratzenhaus* subverts the expectations readers might have of a crime thriller. A prologue entitled 'How It Must Have Been' relates how an anonymous woman in a Third World country sells her daughter to a couple from Europe. The setting then shifts to a small town in Austria. The plot revolves around two mysteries: somebody is beating up young children with a stick, and a young man, the builder's apprentice

---

55 Wolf Haas, *Resurrection* (Brooklyn/NY, London: Melville House, 2014), p. 35.
56 Haas, *Resurrection*, p. 180.

Florian Weghaupt, falls to his death from some scaffolding. It is unclear whether it is suicide or somebody has pushed him. When the children are asked who beat them, all they reveal is that it was '[s]omething black'. Interspersed with these storylines are chapters in which a thirteen-year-old girl named Fanni interacts with a small girl Switi, who she calls her sister. During most of the novel, the focus is on the private and professional lives of Raffael Horn and Ludwig Kovacs. Horn is a department head in the psychiatric ward of the local hospital. He has a troubled relationship with his wife and becomes more and more estranged from his two sons. He is asked by the police to examine the children who were beaten but, to everybody's surprise, he is forced to admit that they do not appear to have been traumatized. Instead, they seem to have entered into some kind of contract with the abuser. Detective Inspector Kovacs is divorced and has an adolescent daughter who has become a punk. He has a new girlfriend with whom he tries to establish a closer relationship. Both Horn and Kovacs work in teams, and a lot of time is spent in the novel showing how the team members interact and how their private lives interfere with their work. The stories of a number of Horn's patients are told, for example that of Sabrina, a young woman who cuts herself with razors and was apparently the victim of sexual abuse committed by her father. Kovacs's cases, in turn, bring him into contact with drug dealers and their victims, child abusers, and the victims and survivors of violent crime.

In part a police procedural, in part a psychological novel, *Das Matratzenhaus* is set in Furth am See, a fictional provincial town in Austria that functions as a microcosm of the country as a whole. The story is narrated from four perspectives (first by elementary school teacher Stella Jurmann, then by Horn, then Kovacs, then Fanni) in the same exact order throughout the novel. Seemingly unrelated plots and sub-plots, such as, for example, the relationship between Stella Jurmann and the Benedictine monk Bauer – who reveres God as 'His Holy Bobness',[57] by which he means Bob Dylan, whose songs he sings and hums wherever he goes – combine to paint the picture of a society that is mired in violence, abuse and pathological behaviour. In the end, the identity of the person who beat the young children is revealed, but it turns out that the perpetrator did not act out of malice and that the beatings were a cry for help. Many questions remain unanswered though, and the reader's hope for closure is frustrated. *Das Matratzenhaus* tells a story of child abuse and child pornography, of the everyday violence committed against children and the problems of foster care,

---

57 Paulus Hochgatterer, *The Mattress House*, trans. Jamie Bulloch (London: MacLehose Press, 2012), p. 59.

xenophobia and how resentment against anybody who appears different is exploited for political purposes. With its complex narrative structure and its uncompromising social and psychological realism, it might exasperate readers who prefer more traditional mystery novels, but it also expands the scope of what crime fiction can accomplish today.

In their different approaches to crime fiction, both *Ressurection* and *Das Matratzenhaus* show contemporary Austrian crime fiction at its best. Their innovative narrative styles and the original way that they provide insights into the social and psychological underpinnings of present-day Austria demonstrate that Austrian crime fiction should be considered an area worthy of exploration by anyone interested in the genre.

Thomas W. Kniesche

4 The *Soziokrimi* or *Neuer Deutscher Kriminalroman*

After the end of World War II and the economic adversities of the immediate post-war years, German reading audiences were only slowly exposed to the international literary scene again. Before that, reading crime fiction had been a favourite pastime, even during the war, when literature from Western countries had been banned, but now the developing market for this genre was dominated by imports from England and the US, a situation that would not change again until the late 1960s. At this time, a new phenomenon began to register that first appeared under the label of the *Neuer Deutscher Kriminalroman* [New German Crime Novel] and was later called the *Soziokrimi*, from 'soziologischer Krimi' [sociological crime novel]. Both terms are largely interchangeable, but both need some initial clarification. After providing this clarification, some more general remarks in the first half of this chapter will be followed by specific examples of authors and texts in the second half.

'New' German crime fiction made use of the positive connotations of newness in modern and modernizing societies. To be new meant to be up to date, to leave behind older patterns of mystery writing such as the 'whodunit' and the cozy mystery of the English tradition and the hard-boiled school of American crime fiction. Coming up with a German alternative to Anglo-American imports served several purposes: it satisfied the urgent need to make a contribution to a genre that had been dominated by foreign writers, it showed that German writers, too, could write crime fiction, and it enabled German writers to at least tap into a share of the crime fiction market. The latter point was even more important since it opened up other media, such as radio and television, for these writers. The term 'sozio(logisch)' or sociological as a label for the *Neuer Deutscher Kriminalroman* was also used to mark this type of writing as something specifically German, thus employing the common stereotype of Germans as a people who have to add a feeling of religious, philosophical or – in the latest adaptation of 'being deep' – sociological profundity to everything they come into contact with, even in a form of entertainment such as crime fiction. The labels 'new' and 'sociological' were thus put into service to create the impression of an exciting and innovative variant of crime fiction appearing on the market: crime fiction made in Germany. It would be wrong, however, to view the *Soziokrimi* as nothing

https://doi.org/10.1515/9783110426601-004

more than just a marketing scheme (which it was!) and to argue that it only employed the narrative elements of traditional crime fiction.[1] As I will try to show later on, the *Soziokrimi* has made a significant contribution to German crime fiction, both as a subgenre that opened up new topics and as a way for writers to explore modern narrative techniques for crime fiction writing.

True to the meaning of 'sociological' as observing the structures and functioning of social groups and institutions, the *Soziokrimi* views crime not as the result of personal flaws or inherited defects, but as caused by societal relations and social structures. By default, sociological crime fiction is critical of societies that generate criminal behaviour in the very way in which they are organized. The *Soziokrimi* started in the mid to late 1960s with the publication of the first novels by writers such as Hansjörg Martin (1920–1999), Paul Henricks (pseudonym for Edward Hoop, 1925–2008), Michael Molsner (b. 1939), and others.[2] The editor Richard K. Flesch (1920–2008) was instrumental in establishing the work of these writers. In 1961, he started the imprint 'rororo thriller' at the *Rowohlt* publishing house, where most of the novels belonging to the new school of crime writing would be published.[3] Nicknamed 'Leichenflesch' [corpse Flesch], he not only served as series editor for the new imprint, but would also have a tremendous influence on German crime writing in the years to come. The *Soziokrimi* had its heydays in the 1970s and 1980s, but as a significant part of German crime fiction writing, it not only influenced generations of writers, but also taught them new ways of writing crime fiction. As a brief definition of the *Soziokrimi* we can formulate: the German *Soziokrimi* is closely related to the police novel, occasionally uses thriller elements and is written with a critical view

---

1 Reinhard Jahn, 'Jesus, Buddha, der Müll und der Tod. Spurensicherung in Sachen Soziokrimi', in *Deutschsprachige Literatur der 70er und 80er Jahre. Autoren, Tendenzen, Gattungen*, ed. by Walter Delabar and Erhard Schütz (Darmstadt: Wissenschaftliche Buchgesellschaft, 1997), pp. 38–52 (p. 38). Jahn starts out by provocatively claiming that '[t]he *Soziokrimi* probably never even existed' (my trans.), but later in his article acknowledges that the 'new' authors 'integrated societal circumstances as elements that developed the plot further and thus were successful in creating an equivalent to the international standard of crime fiction writing' (p. 44, my trans.).

2 A list of titles and authors, ordered chronologically, can be found at: http://www.bene-semper.de/Nummern.html.

3 More than one thousand novels were published under this imprint. Flesch served as series-editor until 1985. The imprint existed until April 2000, when the series was incorporated into the general program of the publishing house. The motto of the series, printed at the top of the second page of each volume, was: 'A Faint Cold Fear Thrills Trough My Veins' (from: *Romeo and Juliet* IV, 3).

of societal structures, demonstrating the detrimental effects of dysfunctional social milieus and the corruption of the elites on ordinary people who are forced into committing criminal acts. In many novels, this goes hand-in-hand with showing how members of the elites exploit economic and political structures to preserve their status.

Historical context and literary models

It is important to remember that *Soziokrimis* were first written during the 1960s, when German unification was still unimaginable and before socialism and communism were discredited after the fall of the Berlin Wall. The critique of capitalism carried out by left-wing intellectuals and political movements in West Germany was still based on a vast spectrum of Marxist theories, from orthodox Leninist theories to the more sophisticated teachings of the 'Frankfurt School', the scholars of the Institute for Social Research who gathered around Theodor W. Adorno (1903–1969) and Max Horkheimer (1895–1973). Leftist political and sociological theories were highly influential in the intellectual upbringing of many of the authors who would later write *Soziokrimis*, and even writers who were not exposed directly to those teachings lived in an intellectual climate that encouraged people to look at contemporary society through the lens of Marxist thinking. Furthermore, these authors were writing at a time when influential commentators and critics, such as Hans-Magnus Enzensberger, in *Kursbuch* 15 (1968), were demanding politically engaged literature, literature that would help to bring about real change in a society that was considered atrophied in its conservative mentality, controlled by intellectual, economic and political elites (the 'establishment') that were still caught up in their own Nazi past.

When the German authors who would be called the inventors of the *Soziokrimi* began writing their first novels, they took inspiration from a number of international trends in crime fiction. From the American school of hard-boiled writing, in particular Dashiell Hammett and Raymond Chandler, they adapted the idea of crime being the result of moral corruption based on perverted social structures and constellations. Also important was the impact of the work of the Belgian writer Georges Simenon (1903–1989), whose conception of fictional inspector Maigret rejected the fantasy of the all-powerful and self-assured detective and featured a middle-class investigator whose bourgeois mentality and behaviour put him on an equal social footing with the criminals he was supposed to apprehend. Instead of pulling off brilliant feats of detection like Dupin or

Sherlock Homes, or spine-tingling acts of physical exertion like Philip Marlowe or Sam Spade, Maigret would immerse himself in the psychological and social conditions of the crime he was investigating and would observe calmly and patiently everybody connected to a crime in order to understand why it was committed. At the end of this process, Maigret would be able to identify the perpetrators because he understood what drove them to commit the crime.

Even more important as a model for the crime fiction writing of the *Soziokrimi* was the work done by the Swedish writers Maj Sjöwall (b. 1935) and Per Wahlöö (1926–1975). Sjöwall and Wahlöö were the main Swedish translators of Ed McBain's *87th Precinct* novels and would adapt McBain's version of the police procedural for their own purposes. The novels of their ten-volume series featuring inspector Martin Beck were written between 1965 and 1975 and had been available in German translation since 1968 in Flesch's *rororo thriller* imprint. Writing from a decidedly Marxist point of view, Sjöwall and Wahlöö were interested in two things: looking at and reflecting upon the social conditions that turn ordinary people into criminals, and showing the unremarkable everyday work of the police. In their police procedurals, they follow a small group of politically enlightened police officers who do what they can to uphold the ideals of civilization in a society that is increasingly falling prey to capitalist alienation and fascist mentalities. They must resign themselves to the fact that the truly guilty are untouchable because of their elite status in society.[4] In the preface to the English translation of Sjöwall's and Wahlöö's first Martin-Beck novel *Roseanna*, Henning Mankell explains the couple's enormous impact on international crime fiction as being due to the way that they present 'meticulous and credible descriptions of various institutions and structures within Swedish society' and their inspiration 'to use crime and criminal investigations as a mirror of Swedish society'.[5] The German authors under consideration here followed their example.

---

4 The German title of the sixth novel in the series is programmatic for this. The Swedish original, published in 1970, was entitled *Polis, polis, potatismos!* Whereas the title of the English translation was coyly rendered *Murder at the Savoy*, the title of the German translation was *Und die Großen lässt man laufen* which in English could be translated as 'And the Big Fish Get Away with It'.

5 Henning Mankell, 'Introduction', in Maj Sjöwall, Per Wahlöö, *Roseanna*, trans. Lois Roth (New York: Vintage Crime/ Black Lizard, 2008), pp. vii–x (p. viii).

The poetics of the *Soziokrimi*

Paraphrasing John Dickson Carr's (1906–1977) fictional Dr Gideon Fell, the literary scholar Ulrich Schulz-Buschhaus has argued that, in the 'pointierter Rätselroman' (the traditional 'whodunit' or mystery novel), that which is highly unlikely, that which is physically all but impossible but happens nonetheless, takes precedence in the development of the plot by establishing the riddle the detective has to solve. In the *Neuer Deutscher Kriminalroman*, on the other hand, what is normal, what is psychologically and sociologically the norm, is the breeding ground for crime. This requires a kind of literary realism that enables writers to explore what is commonplace, quotidian – or, in other words: what constitutes everyday life. As a result, the suspense of having to solve a mystery or riddle is suspended; instead, what is typical and 'relevant' is the focus of the plot.[6] According to Schulz-Buschhaus, this 'Poetik der Alltäglichkeit'[7] embraces topics of contemporary interest and debate. During the 1970s in Germany, this included scandals involving fixed soccer matches,[8] alternative political movements, religious sects targeting young people and the German left-wing terrorism of the time. These poetics favour an attention to details that have nothing to do with the actual case. Comprehensive topographical information, particulars about certain professions, meticulous descriptions of the routines of police work: these details create an illusion of realness and authenticity precisely because they are not important to the plot. One example of the importance of topographic detail is the fictional town of Bramme, which will be discussed later in this chapter.

The poetics of the *Soziokrimi* assigns a new role to one of the central narrative components of crime fiction, the figure of the investigator. Solving the case is no longer the result of the dazzling intellectual feats of a brilliant detective but of tedious work. The investigator is not a dandy who escapes his *ennui* by catching killers (such as Poe's Dupin) or a private detective with a moral mission (such as Chandler's Philip Marlowe), but a paid professional in the service of the state. The *Kommissare* [detective inspectors] of the *Soziokrimi* have spouses and children who need their attention (and who sometimes become entangled in their investigations), they have to worry about schools and

---

6 Ulrich Schulz-Buschhaus, 'Die Ohnmacht des Detektivs. Literarhistorische Bemerkungen zum neuen deutschen Kriminalroman' in *Der neue deutsche Kriminalroman. Beiträge zu Darstellung, Interpretation und Kritik eines populären Genres*, ed. by Karl Ermert and Wolfgang Gast (Rehburg-Loccum: Evangelische Akademie Loccum, 1982), pp. 10–18 (p. 13).
7 Schulz-Buschhaus, 'Die Ohnmacht des Detektivs', p. 14. 'poetics of everyday life'.
8 Cf. Friedhelm Werremeier, *Platzverweis für Trimmel* [1972, *Red Card for Trimmel**].

mortgages, they are often struggling to balance the conflicting demands of their private lives and their professional obligations – in short: they lead normal middle-class lives – or at least they try to. Cutting down the figure of the investigator to a bourgeois character is a major element of the *Soziokrimi*. They are no longer people who live outside the restraints of bourgeois existence; they have private lives and their own political views, which can bring them into conflict with their duties as public servants. Michael Molsner's chief detective inspector Borowik, for example, is a police officer who reads the works of Theodor W. Adorno and Ludwig Marcuse, two of the Marxist philosophers of the Frankfurt School. Richard Hey's detective inspector Katharina Ledermacher sees herself more in the role of a social worker than in that of a crime investigator. For her, it is the job of the police to prevent crime, not to hunt down criminals. As a 'sympathizing observer', she personifies a 'vision of a progressive police work'[9] that stands in stark contrast to the police as a state agency that has to respond to the pressures it is put under by a manipulated public opinion or, as in the novels of Sjöwall and Wahlöö, it has to serve political interests.

Another traditional element of crime fiction that is assigned a new role in the *Soziokrimi* is the social setting or 'milieu' in which the characters interact. Milieus familiar to readers of crime fiction are aristocratic circles, the realms of academia, sports, the arts, the theatre and the world of horse racing in the novels of Dick Francis.[10] Various, painstakingly explored social milieus feature prominently in the novels of Dorothy Sayers (1893–1957). *Strong Poison* (1930) introduces readers to the world of artists and writers; in *Murder Must Advertise* (1933), it is the eponymous sphere of advertising that provides the background for the case; and *Gaudy Night* (1935) is set in the hallowed halls of Oxford University. In all of these and in her other novels, Sayers uses comprehensive descriptions of the social setting to develop the plot and motivate the crimes her hero, Lord Peter Whimsey, must solve. The *Soziokrimi* expands on the mere description of social milieus and launches a social *enquête*; it scrutinizes social and power structures and the role they play in causing crime. If they belong to the lower classes, the perpetrators of criminal behaviour are seen as victims of their social background or that which fosters alienation instead of (self-)fulfilment. Furthermore, in the *Soziokrimi*, the social setting or milieu not only becomes an integral element of the narrated world, the so-called *diegesis*; by providing a critical view of society, these novels also want to enlighten their audiences and

---

9 Peter Nusser, 'Kritik des neuen deutschen Kriminalromans', in Ermert and Gast, pp. 19–32 (p. 22 and 23). 'teilnehmende Beobachterin'; 'Entwurf einer progressiven Polizeiarbeit'.
10 Cf. John M. Reilly, 'Milieu' in *The Oxford Companion to Crime and Mystery Writing*, ed. by Rosemary Herbert (New York, Oxford: Oxford University Press, 1999), pp. 289–290.

to encourage them to actively seek change. Writers transformed crime fiction into social *enquêtes* or case studies with the goal of reaching a readership that would not under normal circumstances be concerned with the analysis of social structures and the critique of political institutions. Thus, in the *Soziokrimi*, a critical view of society and an emancipatory impetus are tightly interwoven with the plot of the novel.[11]

However, a word of caution is required within this context. Although the *Soziokrimi* followed the basic tenets of literary realism and subscribed to a poetics of everyday life, it is easy to forget that what we experience in these novels is not reality itself but a simulated version of it. We sometimes need to remind ourselves that literary realism is an aesthetic category. Literary texts that adhere to these conventions never present reality itself, but rather represent it as an aesthetic construct. It would be erroneous to read *Soziokrimis* as factual descriptions and scholarly analyses of (West) German society. As Horst Bosetzy, one of the foremost *Soziokrimi* writers and a sociologist by profession, stated about his novelistic *oeuvre*: 'It will always remain a phantasy world [...]'[12] As Andreas Blödorn has pointed out, someone like 'Prof. Horst Bosetzky' could just as well have clad his sociological insights in the form of factual writing to communicate directly with his audience.[13] In his *Soziokrimis*, Horst Bosetzky chose to use a different kind of writing, a form of expression that should be read and judged according to aesthetic categories, not as texts that mirror reality as it actually exists.

Finally, one crucial component of the poetics of the *Soziokrimi* relates to how it ends and what the reader takes away from such endings. In the Anglo-American 'golden age' mysteries of the interwar period, crime is understood as a disruption of the social order. With a murder, an element of chaos has penetrated the existence of the mostly upper middle-class cast of the novel.[14] It is the task of the detective to expose the killer and thus remove the threat of

---

11 Nusser, 'Kritik des neuen deutschen Kriminalromans', p. 19.

12 Interview with Horst Bosetzky in Jürg Brönnimann, *Der Soziokrimi: Ein neues Genre oder ein soziologisches Experiment? Eine Untersuchung des Sozialkriminalromans anhand der Werke der schwedischen Autoren Maj Sjöwall und Per Wahlöö und des deutschen Autors -ky* (Wuppertal: Nordpark, 2004), p. 275. 'Es bleibt ja immer eine Phantasiewelt [...]'.

13 Andreas Blödorn, '"Prodesse et delectare" oder Die Last mit der Lust. Der Soziokrimi als Experiment', Review of: Jürg Brönnimann, *Der Soziokrimi: Ein neues Genre oder ein soziologisches Experiment? Eine Untersuchung des Sozialkriminalromans anhand der Werke der schwedischen Autoren Maj Sjöwall und Per Wahlöö und des deutschen Autors -ky.* (Wuppertal: Nordpark 2004), *IASLonline* (March 19, 2005), (http://www.iaslonline.de/index.php?vorgang_id=1037), [32].

14 Cf. John Scaggs, *Crime Fiction* (London and New York: Routledge), pp. 46–49.

disorder and confusion. At the end of the traditional crime novel, the social and moral orders are restored.[15] The *Soziokrimi* rescinds the moral certainty gained by the guaranteed punishment of those who unhinge the social order by committing a crime. Although the immediate perpetrators are caught and punished, the manipulators – those who act in the background, pull the strings and are morally responsible for criminal behaviour – 'get away with it' as a rule, are not held hold responsible but, on the contrary, thrive because of the gains they have made by encouraging or supporting criminal acts. Among many other texts, this can be found in the novels by Horst Bosetzky set in the fictional small town of Bramme, in which the entrepreneur and building tycoon Buth, for example, is not held accountable for trying to kill a sociology student or for (albeit accidentally) shooting and killing the editor of the local newspaper (*Stör die feinen Leute nicht* [1973, *Don't Upset the Upper Crust**]).

The main authors of the *Soziokrimi*

Generally speaking, nine authors are considered to form the core group of writers associated with the *Soziokrimi*. They are (in chronological order of birth): Hansjörg Martin (1920–1999), Paul Henricks (Edward Hoop, 1925–2008), Richard Hey (1926–2004), Friedhelm Werremeier (b. 1930), Thomas Andresen (1934–1989), Irene Rodrian (b. 1937), Felix Huby (b. 1938), -ky (Horst Bosetzky, b. 1938), Michael Molsner (b. 1939) and Fred Breinersdorfer (b. 1946). The most important of them will be introduced briefly in this section.

Hansjörg Martin tried to make a living as a painter, circus clown, shop-window designer, stage designer and journalist, among other things, before he began focusing on writing crime fiction and novels for young readers. Martin was widely credited with having initiated the *Neuer Deutscher Kriminalroman*. His early crime novels feature German settings, middle-class milieus, straightforward plots, likable amateur investigators and simple mysteries. They were written in an easy to read, entertaining and ironic style. At the end of his first novel *Gefährliche Neugier* [1965, *Dangerous Curiosity**], for example, the

---

15 This is not true of the hard-boiled novel, though. Private eyes like the Continental Op or Philip Marlowe know that they cannot fundamentally change a corrupt society. In some cases, they are co-opted by the very system they wanted to fight. As Philip Marlowe admits at the end of *The Big Sleep* (1939), 'Me, I was part of the nastiness now'. Cf. Raymond Chandler, *The Big Sleep* (New York: Vintage Books, 1992), p. 230. The Hollywood movie adaptations of many of the classic hard-boiled thrillers countermand these disheartening conclusions, though, and replace them with happy endings.

protagonist justifies asking his inamorata to marry him by telling her: '[...] I tend to marry the women who save my life.'[16] The stress is on the interaction among the characters and how they are integrated into their social relationships. In his later novels, Martin was more interested in depicting the psyche of the perpetrator and what had driven him to commit a crime. According to Martin, this was a result of reading the novels of Patricia Highsmith and having learnt from her. He declared his sympathies for the 'underdog' and stated that he was more interested in the predicament of the perpetrator than in the hunt for the criminal. He saw the criminal as a victim of his personal circumstances, and this understanding of crime brought Martin close to the precepts of the *Soziokrimi*, as there, as we have seen, crime was generally understood as a result of being exposed to an unfavourable social environment.

Richard Hey did not finish his university studies and became a journalist, wrote radio and theatre plays and film scripts, and worked for several media and publishing companies. In three novels, written between 1973 and 1980, a female protagonist, Detective Inspector Katharina Ledermacher, investigates crime in West Berlin. Ledermacher is divorced and has a daughter, and her boyfriend is a leftist teacher. Because of her progressive mind-set and her strict upholding of the rights of suspects and criminals, she is in constant conflict with colleagues and superiors. The fact that she is a woman does not make professional life any easier for her in an environment that is ruled by male posturing and misogyny. Her first case pits her against a group of retirees who finance their golden years by committing bank robberies and then cover them up by committing a murder. In the second novel, the corpse of a young woman is found in the basement of a rundown mansion that had been used by squatters. It turns out that the young woman was the victim of a botched abortion, and the plot progresses as a twofold story of organized crime: the squatters were exploited by a ruthless group of real estate speculators who used them to degrade properties they wanted to buy cheaply and develop. The abortion was provided by a no less cold-blooded organization that specializes in such activities and knows no bounds when it comes to securing their profit margins. The third novel, *Ohne Geld singt der Blinde nicht* [1980, *The Blind Man Will Not Sing For Free**], starts out with the discovery of three corpses in Berlin and Italy. When it turns out that they are all somehow connected with international drug dealing, Katharina Ledermacher is sent incognito to Italy. She soon gets too close to the criminals who are behind the murders, who frame her, as a result of which she is put behind bars by the

---

16 Hansjörg Martin, *Gefährliche Neugier, Kein Schnaps für Tamara, Einer fehlt beim Kurkonzert*, omnibus edition (Reinbek: Rowohlt 1990), p. 208.

Italian police. Following a rebellion by the prison inmates and after her German superiors intervene, she is freed and can continue her investigations. Back in Berlin, she apprehends the mastermind behind the three killings. The culprit is the son of a man who runs a private clinic for drug addicts and who had gotten into financial difficulties. It turns out that drug money was being used to fund a clinic for addicts! However, that is not the end of the story. In the course of her investigations, Ledermacher also finds out that the West German political police are involved in international drug dealing. They are funnelling drugs to the leftist political scene and to suspected terrorists in Germany to hinder their activities and render them less dangerous. When Katharina Ledermacher exposes these machinations by a government agency, she decides she can no longer work for the police and quits her job. Hey is considered the most stylistically gifted author of the writers associated with the *Soziokrimi*. His three novels featuring Katharina Ledermacher have been called 'the best that the *Neuer Deutscher Kriminalroman* achieved in its early phase'.[17]

Friedhelm Werremeier was a journalist by training and worked as a courtroom reporter before he started writing books on true crime and then switched to crime fiction. His crime novels were inspired by the cases he reported on, and he also established a vast network of forensic experts, police officers, psychiatrists, lawyers and judges, on whose expertise he would later draw when he began writing his novels. His first two books were published under the pseudonym 'Jacob Wittenbourg'. All of his crime novels feature detective chief inspector Trimmel, who shares some character traits with Georges Simenon's Maigret. Trimmel is almost always in a bad mood. In many cases, he has his own ideas about justice. He is a fatherly type, solid (in both a psychological and a physical sense), with a deep, rumbling voice, bad manners and a deep sense of disrespect for authority. Trimmel habitually lulls his suspects into a false sense of security by appearing naïve and sympathetic, but only does so to mask his cleverness or even downright meanness when he confronts criminals. Werremeier had an almost uncanny instinct for contemporary issues that would dominate the news headlines (organ transplants, environmental concerns, bribery scandals) and organized his plots around those topics.

Michael Molsner started his professional career as a courtroom reporter and wrote dime novels on the side. He said that he had an epiphany reading

---

17 Jochen Schmidt, *Gangster, Opfer, Detektive. Eine Typengeschichte des Kriminalromans* (Hilleswheim: KBV, 1999), p. 946 (my trans.).

Raymond Chandler's *Farewell, My Lovely*, published in 1940, that gave him the self-assurance to start writing more sophisticated crime fiction.[18] Molsner's early novels feature a complex narrative structure with multiple points of view, a non-linear chronology and several parallel plots. In them, crime appears as 'a direct result of social dependences within a society based on material gain and intolerance'.[19] In 1985, Molsner shifted gears and started a series of novels based on two private detectives: *Die Euro-Ermittler* [*The Euro-Investigators**] appeared in seven novels written until 1990 and introduced new topics to German crime fiction – white collar crime, computer crime and drug dealing – highlighting the international scope of organized crime. At the end of the 1980s, Molsner created yet another series of novels. This time, the series, called 'Global-Agenten' [Global Agents] featured a team of German federal agents specializing in protecting politicians and foreign visitors. With these eight novels, published between 1989 and 1992 and highlighting contemporary international conflicts in Europe, the Balkans and the Middle East, Molsner shifted to political crime fiction or the Polit-Thriller [political thriller], as it is called in German.

A novel that provides a good impression of Molsner's early work is *Die rote Messe* [1973, *The Red Fair**]. The novel is set in the provincial town of Ährenfeld and recounts the murder of the Italian 'guest worker' Bracchi and the lynching of the young TV reporter Johanna ('Hanna') Kahmm by an angry mob of self-stylized vigilantes. Tensions have been running high since students at the local engineering college started protesting against an agricultural fair that was about to open in town. The students, most of whom are organized in Marxist groups, objected to the fact that an American chemical company that produced Napalm and defoliating agents for the war in Vietnam would have a stand at the fair. Their protest, called 'The Red Fair',[20] was intended to make the citizens of Ährenfeld aware of the atrocities of the Vietnam War and other issues. The story is told from the point of view of the journalist Jakob ('Jack') Nestor who reads a manuscript written by one of the students, Herrmann Marwitz, in which the latter tries to set the record straight, since the local newspaper had put forth a one-sided and politically convenient version of events.[21] When he reads this account, Jack is staying with detective inspector Erich Sommerfeld, who is

---

18 Jürgen Alberts, Frank Göhre, *Kreuzverhör. Zehn Krimiautoren sagen aus* (Hildesheim: Gerstenberg, 1999). p. 89.

19 Jürg Brönnimann, *Der Soziokrimi*, p. 71–72.

20 The title of the novel reverberates with Dashiell Hammett's first novel *Red Harvest* (1929).

21 Only one year after the publication of *Die rote Messe*, in 1974, Heinrich Böll's short novel *Die verlorene Ehre der Katharina Blum* [*The Lost Honor of Katharina Blum*] appeared, in which Böll exposes the consequences of one-sided and inflammatory reporting.

supervising the imminent arrest of Bracchi's killer. They talk about what happened and why Jack was fired from his job at the local newspaper. Jack is economically vulnerable because he depends on a steady job. His political and moral allegiance to the students and their demands puts him in jeopardy. Thus, narrative structure, plot elements, and sociological and political structures of the story world or *diegesis* are intricately linked.

In the end, it turns out that Bracchi was killed by the developer Tschaut. Bracchi had asked Tschaut to make improvements to the barracks the guest workers were living in. When Tschaut refused, Bracchi threatened to reveal publicly that Tschaut was using undocumented workers from Naples. Tschaut will not be held responsible, however, because he is too well connected in local politics and business organizations. Hanna's killers also get away with what they have done. Towards the end of the novel, Hermann Marwitz wants to know what led a group of 'normal' middle-class people to lynch Hanna. He wonders: 'what does this society do to its members?' and asks: 'which models of behaviour does society offer people to solve their problems?'[22]

Horst Bosetzky was born in Berlin. After completing an apprenticeship as an industrial management assistant at Siemens, he studied sociology, economics and psychology at the Free University. He was a professor of sociology at a university of applied sciences in Berlin from 1973 until his retirement in 2000. From 1971 to 1981, Bosetzky published his early crime fiction under the pseudonym '-ky' – initially, as he claims, to protect a potential career in local politics,[23] but later no doubt also to build up an air of mystery around his authorship that would help him to market his books. Bosetzky is a prolific author, who explains his enormous output by referring to his 'obsession' with or 'addiction' to writing.[24] His early novels are sociological 'case studies' of families, companies, social groups and small communities. Some of these novels are set in Berlin, but to get a better idea of Bosetzky's concept of the *Soziokrimi*, we should look at the novels that are set in the small fictional city of Bramme. Bosetzky invented Bramme to investigate the social milieus of the German upper middle class of the 1970s and 80s as if under a microscope. He laid out the topography of Bramme in great detail: it had about 80,000 inhabitants, and he named all the streets and marked the places where significant events took place on maps that Bosetzky

---

22 Michael Molsner, *Die Schattenrose, Wie eine reissende Bestie, Rote Messe*, omnibus edition (Munich: Heyne, 1987), p. 161 of *Die rote Messe*.
23 Alberts, Göhre, *Kreuzverhör*, p. 109. Bosetzky also relates that when his mother found out that he was '-ky' she wanted to disinherit him (p. 110).
24 Alberts, Göhre, *Kreuzverhör*, pp.116 and 110. Bosetzky's later oeuvre also includes historical crime fiction, cf. chapter 7 in this volume.

drew specifically for this purpose. He had lists of town inhabitants that he used for each new novel.[25] Bramme worked like a controlled experiment in which every parameter is known and can be changed. In this 'lab experiment', the author was able to 'expose the mechanisms of this [West German] society', 'the ossification of power structures' and 'how the establishment in such social systems utilizes power so that change is hardly possible at all'.[26] Using a term borrowed from the sociologist Max Weber, Bosetzky saw Bramme as 'idealtypisch' [as an ideal or pure type],[27] thus referring to it as a fictional construct that did not reflect all elements of reality, instead concentrating on those that were most common or characteristic.

Die Klette [1983, *The Burr**], co-authored by Bosetzky and the psychologist Peter Heinrich, is one of the novels set in Bramme. Hanns-Ulrich Lachmund, professor of law at the local college for public administration, inadvertently prevents a young woman, Ann-Kristin Angeleidt, from committing suicide. Lachmund's deed takes place due to sheer coincidence: he was at just the right place at the right time. Nonetheless, after a brief period of confusion and reorientation, the young woman is exceedingly grateful to the professor. She showers him with small gifts and tokens of her affection, follows him around wherever he goes and even enrols at the college where he teaches law courses for future civil servants. In short, she becomes his stalker or the eponymous 'burr' of the novel. Just before he inadvertently became a life saver, Lachmund's own life had seemingly reached its pinnacle: he was about to celebrate his 40th birthday as a successful academic, he had a wonderful family with a doting wife and two charming daughters, and he was about to set out on a career in local politics that could have taken him to new heights one day. Then, when Ann-Kristin's fixation takes its toll on his personal and his professional life, it all starts to fall apart. Interactions within the family become fraught with distrust, his academic career disintegrates as his students rebel against him, and his colleagues begin to distance themselves from him. His career is about to collapse. He loses the power to determine his own life and starts to feel like he is being controlled by strings, like a puppet. He thinks about ways to get rid of Ann-Kristin, from murdering her himself to hiring a hit man. Then, just when Lachmund is about to collapse under the strain, Ann-Kristin is murdered. Lachmund is arrested immediately but insists that he is innocent. The homicide investigation goes on for a while, but in the end, the serial killer Erwin Schultz, who had murdered three other women

---

25 Alberts, Göhre, *Kreuzverhör*, p. 107.
26 Alberts, Göhre, *Kreuzverhör*, p. 108 (my trans.).
27 Alberts, Göhre, *Kreuzverhör*, p. 109.

before, admits to killing Ann-Kirstin. However, it remains open whether Lachmund, his wife Uta or even his friend Hillermeier could be the real culprit. But Lachmund is exonerated and is able to re-establish himself as a successful academic.

Die Klette is written in the form of an epistolary novel. The authors act as fictional editors who have gathered a host of 'documents'[28] about the case. These include letters, but also newspaper articles, official statements, diary entries, transcripts of interrogations, the minutes of faculty meetings, memorandums and even a letter from the authors to the accused murderer Lachmund. This accumulation of private and public documents creates the impression of authenticity and verisimilitude. The linear succession in which the material is presented supports this kind of realism and creates suspense: the characters (and the readers) never know what will happen next. The characters write about their innermost fears and wishes. At one point, for example, Lachmund admits that he is attracted to the much younger and good-looking Ann-Kristin. He fantasizes about a new life with her, away from the constraints of marriage and parenthood. As an example of the Soziokrimi, Die Klette offers a number of striking features: the social milieu in which Lachmund and his friends and colleagues live – his middle-class existence and his academic life – is central to the plot. The motivations and actions of almost all characters in the novel are guided by their position within this milieu. Meeting the expectations and fulfilling the requirements that are characteristic of this milieu is constantly on everybody's mind. Moreover, in Die Klette, the roles of perpetrator and victim are fluid. Ann-Kristin is his stalker, but she is also Lachmund's potential victim. Lachmund, on the other hand, is the object of her obsession but he also plans to kill her. Finally, the end of the novel refuses to provide the kind of closure expected of a traditional crime thriller. The question of who really killed Ann-Kristin remains unclear. The typical middle-class existence of a useful member of society has been disrupted by desire and murder, but is re-established in the end. But this ending could very well be read as an ironic comment on the powers of a society that does not allow its members to change and break out of their routines.

---

28 -ky & Co., Die Klette (Reinbek: Rowohlt, 1983), p. 7.

Shortcomings and merits of the *Soziokrimi*: an attempt to gauge its impact on German crime fiction writing

By the early 1980s, the *Soziokrimi* had to a large extent exhausted itself as an innovative paradigm of crime fiction writing. Critical voices became more pronounced in pointing out the flaws of the model. One of the most disparaging critics of the *Soziokrimi* was Jörg Fauser (1944–1987), a young writer who had his own ideas about writing crime fiction.[29] According to Fauser, reading a *Soziokrimi* felt more like taking a sociology course at a community college than reading a crime novel.[30] He criticized the authors of the *Soziokrimi* for abandoning aesthetic considerations, what Fauser called 'style', in favour of expounding sociological theories.[31] Fauser condemned these authors because, as he said, instead of trying to elevate crime fiction to the status of true literature, like Hammett, Chandler and Himes had done, they tried to exploit it for their own political objectives, thus never attempting to free crime fiction from its reputation of being mere genre fiction or, as it is called in German, 'trivial' literature. Others agreed and saw the *Soziokrimi* as the generic term for an extensive list of German *Bindestrich-Krimis* [hyphenated crime fiction], such as the political thriller, the environmental thriller, the terrorism thriller or whatever topic happened to be in the news and promised to be profitable at the time. The derogatory term was supposed to indicate that the genre was being pressed into service to underline the importance of the content that dominated it; the concerns of the genre itself, its formal and aesthetic qualities were deemed a subordinate factor.

The *Soziokrimi* was also criticized for not meeting readers' expectations: focusing on sociological problems all too often meant that the element of suspense was neglected, that there was no real mystery and that the process of detection appeared truncated or artificially grafted on. With its critical view of society taking centre stage, the *Soziokrimi* had a fundamental problem from the beginning: readers expect suspense, an investigator they can identify with, a process of detection

---

29 See the section of Jörg Fauser in ch. 12.

30 Jörg Fauser, 'Leichenschmaus in Loccum', in *Der Strand der Städte – Blues für Blondinen. Essays* (Zurich: Diogenes, 2009), pp. 327–338 (p. 328). This essay was first published in *TransAtlantik* (3) 1983.

31 Fauser, 'Leichenschmaus', p. 331. Jürg Brönnimann has identified the underlying sociological theories of the *Soziokrimi* as those developed by Emile Durkheim and by the American sociologist Robert K. Merton, cf. Brönnimann, *Der Soziokrimi*, pp. 60–67.

that highlights the brilliance of the investigator or the teamwork of a group of police detectives and, by way of closure at the end, the reinstitution of the social
order. But this could only mean the affirmation of the existing social and political
order, as opposed to promoting a change in the structure of society. The constraints of the genre and the political aspirations of the authors collided, and there
was no way out of this dilemma. 'It was impossible to both articulate social critique and meet the requirements of a crime fiction plot while combining the two in
a meaningful way.'[32]

All this criticism notwithstanding, the *Soziokrimi* was important for the careers
of a number of authors of German crime fiction. This primarily related to their ability to combine writing for print publications with work for other media, such as
film, radio and television. Granted, they were not the first crime fiction authors to
do so. The famed Dr. Mabuse movies of the 1920s and 30s, for example, which
featured a criminal mastermind and were directed by Fritz Lang, were based on
the novels by Norbert Jacques (1880–1954).[33] However, the authors of the
Soziokrimi were able to work much more extensively with modern media than the
writers of the interwar period. Some of them, like Molsner, -ky and Rodrian,
started as writers of cheap, mass-produced dime novels, writing under the cover
of pseudonyms for series such as *John Drake, Secret Mission for John Drake* and
Jerry Cotton. Many (Huby, Werremeier, Hey, Martin, Molsner) began their writing
careers as journalists. More importantly, however, almost all of them, with the exception of Paul Henricks (Edward Hoop, who was a schoolteacher and local politician), did extensive work for radio and television. Richard Hey produced a vast
number of radio plays, among them a four-part adaptation of Umberto Eco's *The
Name of the Rose* (1986). Huby wrote scripts for the television series *Rosa Roth*,
and Rodrian for another series called *Hamburg Transit*. Molsner contributed radio
versions of his own novels, alongside other work for radio and television, and -ky
likewise adapted a number of his novels for radio. Two examples demonstrate
how German authors of crime fiction disseminated their work in a variety of
media,[34] thus maximizing their impact (and their earnings): Michael *Molsner's*

---

32 Jens Peter Becker, Paul Gerhard Buchloh, 'Ist der Kriminalroman im traditionellen englischen Sinn in Deutschland möglich?' in Ermert and Gast, pp. 50–57 (p. 55), (my trans.)
33 The first novel, *Dr. Mabuse, der Spieler* [*Dr. Mabuse, the Gambler*] appeared in 1921 and the
movie was released the following year. The second novel *Das Testament des Dr. Mabuse* [*The
Testament of Dr. Mabuse*] was published only after the movie was released in 1932. Other examples of crime fiction writers who had successful careers in the movie industry include Ernst
Reicher (1885–1936), Alfred Schirokauer (1880–1934) and Paul Rosenhayn (1877–1929). Cf.
Knut Hickethier, 'Der Alte Deutsche Kriminalroman. Von vergessenen Traditionen', *Die Horen*
144.31 (1986), pp. 15–23 (p.16).
34 Cf. Jahn, 'Jesus, Buddha, der Müll und der Tod', p. 51.

radio play Das zweite Geständnis des Leo Koczyk [*Leo Koczyk's Second Confession**] was broadcast in 1974. A *Tatort* episode entitled *The Second Confession* was aired in 1975 and a novel bearing the same title as the radio play was published in 1979. Or, to give another example, a book containing a collection of crime stories by -ky, entitled *Mitunter mörderisch* [*Murderous at Times**] appeared in 1976. The collection comprised stories adapted from four radio plays broadcast between 1973 and 1975.

The media outlet with the greatest reach and the broadest audience recognition for the writers of the *Neuer Deutscher Kriminalroman*, however, has been the television series *Tatort*. Broadcast since 1970 and having accumulated over one thousand episodes by the end of 2016, *Tatort* is an exceptional franchise.[35] An adaptation of Werremeier's second novel, *Taxi nach Leipzig* [1970, *Taxi to Leipzig**], starring Detective Inspector Trimmel, was the first episode in the series. Werremeier would go on to write Trimmel novels that were geared towards adaptation as *Tatort* episodes from the outset. In these novels, dialogue takes precedence over narrated segments, the settings change frequently, and action scenes provide additional suspense. Werremeier regularly worked on television scripts for a *Tatort* episode and on the manuscript for the printed version of a story that would be published as a novel at the same time. This explains the narrative structure of his novels, which appear cinematic or movie-like. Felix Huby was another author who was exceptionally successful at both writing novels and scripts for *Tatort*. Between 1977 and 2011, twenty-one such episodes were released featuring detective inspector Bienzle, another one on the long list of popular television detectives in Germany. Fred Breinersdorf also divided his time between writing novels, screen adaptations of his crime fiction and numerous episodes for *Tatort*.

In conclusion, one could argue that the *Soziokrimi* was an important step for German writers of crime fiction to prove themselves as competitive in the international arena of crime fiction writing – at least within their own country. By establishing the *Neuer Deutscher Kriminalroman*, they gained recognition among German-speaking audiences and demonstrated that crime fiction set in West Germany could attract a readership that was still familiar with the narrative structures of more traditional crime fiction. By adapting the poetics of crime fiction writing to suit their needs, these authors explored up-to-date topics and new ways of constructing plots and developing characters. The *Soziokrimi* was largely a reflection of the social and political upheavals of the 1960s and 70s in West Germany, and that, together with the shortcomings discussed above, may explain

---

35 On *Tatort*, see also ch. 5.

its relatively short-lived success. The novels did, however, bring awareness of social and political flashpoints to a genre that was generally not known for enlightening its audiences about such matters. In a broad sense, the *Soziokrimi* made German crime fiction more political.[36] Younger generations of authors were able to learn from the innovations and shortfalls of the (former) *Neuer Deutscher Kriminalroman* and develop the genre further.

---

36 Some of these authors were also active in political work. Michael Molsner, during the 1960s a self-confessed Marxist, was a member of the left-wing student organization *Sozialistischer Deutscher Studentenbund* [SDS, Socialist German Student Union] and the German Social Democratic Party (SPD). Like Molsner, Hansjörg Martin was also engaged in local politics. Fred Breinersdorfer was not only a founding member of Das Syndikat, an association of German-speaking crime fiction writers, he also was the chairman of the *Verband deutscher Schriftstellerinnen und Schriftsteller* [VS, Association of German Writers] from 2001 to 2005. The *Verband* has been part of the trade union representing people who work in the media (IG Medien) since 2001. Felix Huby has also been a longtime member of the SPD and was the Berlin chair of the VS.

Jochen Vogt
5 Regionalism and Modernism in Recent German Crime Fiction (1990–2015)

Since the early 1990s, crime writing in German has experienced an enormous increase, not just quantitatively in the volume of production, but in a marked rise in its literary quality as a genre. This development has affected not only post-reunification Germany, but Austria and the German-speaking part of Switzerland too. German crime writing has now come up to international standards. Inevitably, during this period, a range of different sub-genres, overall themes and individual writing styles had to struggle to establish themselves. Such competition can be found at all levels of the genre at any given time, and it has led to some strikingly different levels of commercial success.

In the process of such change, we cannot identify the rise of one single dominant type of crime writing. It is much harder to summarize this period than, for instance, the 1970s or the early 1980s, which were clearly marked by the emergence of what was referred to as the *Soziokrimi* [sociological crime novel]. In the following, I shall use the terms 'regionalism' and 'modernism' to give shape to recent developments and – without diminishing the diversity of the material – to identify important trends in the present.

Dear Professor Vogt . . .

In 2010, I – together with other writers on crime fiction – received a promotional letter from the publisher S. Fischer. The name Fischer is inseparable from the history of modern German literature, having published the works of authors such as Hofmannsthal, Kafka and Thomas Mann. This letter had a 'personal message' for me from one of Fischer's best-selling authors of the day, Klaus-Peter Wolf. It read:

> Just because Klaus-Peter Wolf's crime novels are set in a specific time and a specific place, and just because their titles contain the prefix *Ostfriesen-* [East Frisian], they are often written off as regional crime fiction. When you read them, however, you never have the feeling that you're reading a regional detective story. Instead, the reader gets an exact psychogram of a whole society on the edge of catastrophe.

Now, East Frisia is a quiet part of the country, geographically very much at the periphery. People appreciate its excellent tea blends, they keep dry in its sturdy

https://doi.org/10.1515/9783110426601-005

rain-gear, they enjoy what is probably the best beer in Germany, and they notice that the East Frisians never use two words when one would do. We should not forget to mention the famous jokes that everyone else likes to tell at the expense of the East Frisians, which are rather unkindly based on the idea that the East Frisians never say anything because they are stupid. On top of all that, the East Frisians now have their own detective stories, and Klaus-Peter Wolf has written a dozen of them, from *Ostfriesenkiller* [2007, *East Frisian Killer**] to *Ostfriesenschwur* [2016, *East Frisian Oath**] and *Ostfriesentod* [2017, *East Frisian Death**]. His total sales amount to some five million copies, mostly in paperback. When talking about them it is tempting to borrow the words that I saw on the wrapping paper in an East Frisian butcher's shop: 'Make local your first choice.' The publishers, however, prefer to shape the focus of their promotions by placing a life-size photo of the author in bookshops with the slogan: 'East Frisia's own Superstar.'

What is the significance of this? The idea of the region has taken off in the German language. It is not just used for sausages and other foodstuffs, but for literary works as well. As a label for books, it has a twofold function: on the one hand, it is a kind of trademark, a guarantee of quality, but, at the same time, it has (as Mr Wolf's letter made very plain) negative associations that have to be countered. The celebrated philosopher (and reader of detective stories) Ernst Bloch might well have remarked: 'Something's fishy here ... we've got to look into it. [...] This promises to be a good case, by the by.'[1]

What makes a region?

It was not until the 1950s that the idea of a region and the associated semantic field started to appear in German dictionaries. This indicates that the word was replacing more traditional concepts, concepts that had been so corrupted by the Nazis misusing them that they could never be used again: *Heimat*, *Volk* and *Nation* had gone that way, to say nothing of the *Gau* (as in *Gauleiter*) and *Lebensraum*. While this was certainly part of the explanation, shifts of this kind simply cannot account for the spectacular rise in regionalism, which is certainly not restricted to developments in the Federal Republic. Long before the

---

1 Ernst Bloch, Philosophische Ansicht des Detektivroman (1965), in *Der Kriminalroman. Poetik –Theorie – Geschichte,* ed. by Jochen Vogt (Munich: Fink 1998), pp. 38–51 (p. 38). 'Etwas ist nicht geheuer, damit fängt das an. [...] Der Fall selber muß etwas in sich haben, so ganz nebenbei'.

term 'globalization' had been coined, the idea of the 'region' had drawn support from various social and political movements in France and Spain, protesting against centralization and openly separatist. A key event in Germany was resistance to the building of a nuclear power station on the Upper Rhine at Wyhl: this protest movement was regional, but also international in character. It involved all classes of the population, and its most important feature was that it was successful: the power station was not built.

Regionalism is now a natural part of everyday speech and activity, but it has also become a keyword for 'top down' planning and strategies, especially in transport and infrastructure, energy, tourism and promotional advertising. Anyone getting into a tram in Freiburg, for instance, is well advised to do so with a *Regio* ticket in their hand, which will take them to and even across the French and Swiss borders. Tourism managers are putting together a publicity campaign to promote the Upper Rhine region – an area that comprises three separate nation states, bound by the three cathedral spires of Freiburg, Strasbourg and Basel. The point of this campaign is to attract wealthy visitors from the Far East and Russia (the USA is no longer a prime target) and from 'regional' neighbours in Italy and France.

Regionalism is a double-edged concept. On the one hand, it denotes protest and resistance to central planning, to the metropolis and to globalization. On the other hand, suitably adapted to modern ways of life and thought, it stands for an up-to-date way of influencing and manipulating citizens and consumers. Regionalism is reflected in the increasing merging of urban and rural life, which modernization and globalization are bringing about. The region thereby replaces the traditional idea of the province and blurs distinctions between itself and the metropolis.

The efforts of social geographers and urban sociologists to define the region as 'a medium-sized space' are hardly convincing. We can get a taste of such definitions from leading social geographers like Benno Werlen from the University of Jena in this account by Wilhelm Ammann, which reads:

> Regions integrate a heterogeneous population with scattered living spaces, multiple life-styles, migrant cultures and trans-nationalities, etc. They can be understood as flexible groups, which are built on the acceptance of the fact that there are no longer dominant traditional patterns of life rooted in particular places: such traditional patterns are at best one possibility among others [...]. They respond to a subjective need for belonging, which looks less to the past and is much more dependent on everyday routines. Such conditions presuppose that regions are interchangeable with one another.[2]

---

2 Wilhelm Ammann, '"Regionalität" in den Kulturwissenschaften', in *Periphere Zentren oder zentrale Peripherien? Kulturen und Regionen Europas zwischen Globalisierung und Regionalität*,

In the situation that Werlen and Ammann describe, collective discourses and collective symbols (including forms of popular culture, such as the detective story in book, film or TV) can take on an important function. Regrettably, present-day literary and media studies in Germany have completed their 'turn' to cultural studies, but have hardly begun to explore such issues or to uncover their implications.

Some preconditions for regional crime fiction . . .

It has long been recognized that – for both literary and historical reasons – the tradition of German-language crime writing has been weak and fragmented.[3] What the 1970s welcomed as the *Neuer Deutscher Kriminalroman* [New German Crime Novel] was the result of two separate developments. First, it was the product of the social liberalism of the period, in that it was above all concerned with the social causes of crime. Secondly, it was a sign of the much-delayed encounter with American and European classics in the genre – in print, film and TV. (Incidentally, the beginnings of a regionalization of the genre in the USA is usually dated to the early 1970s. To put this another way: without series such as *Rockford P.I.* and *The Streets of San Francisco*, there would probably never have been a German regional detective story at all.)

After a short phase of experimentation with fictional settings, virtually all German authors settled on crime scenes that actually existed and could be recognized and inspected in reality. It was at this time, in 1970, that the TV series *Tatort* [*Crime Scene**] started. *Tatort* is the most successful German TV programme, with nearly a thousand different episodes; indeed, we might call it the most significant achievement of West German popular culture.[4]

Tatort is particularly relevant to our theme, for both in its content and in its organization, it is regionally based. Nine different channels – under the umbrella organization of the ARD (usually known as the 'Erstes Programm' [the First

---

ed. by W.A., Georg Mein, Rolf Parr (Heidelberg: Synchron 2008), pp.13–30 (p. 19). Cf. Benno Werlen, *Sozialgeographie alltäglicher Regionalisierungen*, 3 vols. (Stuttgart: Steiner, 1995, 1997, 2007).

3 For a comprehensive survey see Thomas Kniesche, *Einführung in den Kriminalroman* (Darmstadt: Wissenschaftliche Buchgesellschaft, 2015).

4 For a list and details of all episodes see www.Tatort-Fundus.de; for a critical evaluation see Jochen Vogt, '"Tatort" – Der wahre deutsche Gesellschaftsroman', in *MedienMorde. Krimis intermedial*, ed. by J. V. (Munich: Fink, 2005); Christian Hißnauer, Stefan Scherer, Claudia Stockinger, *Föderalismus in Serie. Die Einheit der ARD-Reihe 'Tatort' im historischen Verlauf* (Munich: Fink, 2014).

Channel]) – currently put on their own series (sometimes more than one parallel series), set in various locations within the station's catchment area – from Kiel to Konstanz, from Saarbrücken to Leipzig. The resounding success of the programme over half a century has sparked a number of spin-offs and competing series, both on the ARD and the ZDF (the 'Zweites Programm' [Second Channel]) and on independent stations, which today form a nationwide week-long network. It is clear that the choice of a recognizable local or regional setting for these channels appeals to the feelings and expectations of many viewers, offering them some kind of reference point in life. One might regard this as compensation for the speed at which society is experiencing the increasing loss of certainties, as the globalized world becomes more and more completely networked.

Tatort was an important factor in the development of an independent German crime novel that could provide both literary quality and an intelligent analysis of society. Its importance was not restricted to the fact that it offered a TV outlet to those authors of an older generation who had been part of the *Neuer Deutscher Kriminalroman*: authors such as Felix Huby, who scripted more *Tatort* episodes than any other single author. In any case, the older generation had been replaced by a younger one, much more schooled in film and television. What is more important is that *Tatort*, despite inevitable and often serious variations in quality among individual seasons and episodes, has gotten readers and TV viewers and the authors themselves used to a professional level of craftsmanship in the genre. This has given the whole genre of crime writing in Germany a wide public and a certain standing. We might remember that even mainstream German literature – for instance, the authors of the Gruppe 47 – had strong regional tendencies. We think of Heinrich Böll's Rhineland, Martin Walser's Lake Constance, Günter Grass's Danzig or Uwe Johnson's Mecklenburg, not forgetting his Upper West Side in New York City.

. . . and a few early starters

By mentioning the Gruppe 47, I do not wish to argue that early regional crime novels consciously modelled themselves on these authors. However, it can be useful to observe how regional crime fiction evolved successfully from the mid-1980s, of which I would now like to provide some examples.

In 1986, Friedrich Hitzbleck, a clerk, founded his small private publishing house in Essen. Using the name Conny Lens, Hitzbleck published several detective stories in a rather stagey style. He called his series Steeler Straße. Steeler Straße was and is a busy narrow shopping street up by the water tower in Essen, marked by its contrasting social milieus and various ethnic groups. In 1923, during fierce fighting in the Ruhr district, Steeler Straße made it into the history books. Lens's stories stay in the present, combining realistic detail with authentic local dialect and elements of slapstick. His works appeared in the short-lived Haffmanns Press, before Hitzbleck established himself as a scriptwriter for early evening TV series. In 1984, Corinna Kawaters – at that time a student of sociology at the University of Bochum – published the short detective story *Zora Zobel findet die Leiche* [*Zora Zabel Finds the Body**]. With its mixture of anarchism and feminism, it became a cult book in the alternative scene, even though (or perhaps precisely because) the insider jargon of the scene barely manages to paper over the threadbare plot. At the time, it was only possible to buy *Zora Zobel* in left-wing bookshops or through the mail order firm *2001*. After the many years Kawaters spent in the South American 'underground', she staged a moderately successful comeback for her heroine Zora in 2010.

Werner Schmitz, a serving detective inspector from Bochum, brought a more down-to-earth way of writing to the table. His first novel was *Dienst nach Vorschuss* [1985, *Duty in Advance**] and his works have remained popular to this day, especially for use in school. They exploit – as Kawaters' early novel had begun to – one of the principal characteristics of the Ruhr district, its closely networked topography and infrastructure. This is because the Ruhr consists of a number of independent cities, linked together by motorways. This gives a particularly dynamic sense of space to the novel's action and to the narrative technique. This has been picked up by present-day writers of Ruhr crime novels such as Jörg Juretzka and Norbert Horst, even though – as we shall see – they use it to quite different narrative and stylistic effects.

At this point, we are obliged to turn our attention to one particular writer, even if to do so means interrupting the chronology of developments that I am trying to establish. As early as 1975, Jürgen Lodemann – an imaginative and influential programme-maker at the radio and TV station in Baden-Baden – produced a crime novel set in his home town of Essen. Since then Lodemann has found success in virtually all literary genres, but his first novel *Anita Drögmöller und Die Ruhe an der Ruhr* [*Anita Drögmöller and the Calm on the Ruhr**] was a major hit, extraordinarily witty and brilliantly successful at catching (as well as in sending up) the various clichés of the Ruhr district. His principal characters were Anita, a freelance sex-worker operating only in the best circles, endowed with a heart of gold and more than a little inclined towards loose talk, and Inspector Langensiepen. He has moved to Essen from Westphalia, initially suspects Anita, then falls for her and can ultimately do nothing to save her. The background to a titillating murder is provided by the stark contrasts between the south and north of Essen – geographically and socially the upper city and lower city. Lodemann has a good ear for how these contrasts are articulated at the various levels of the characters' language. (These of course were the years when international sociolinguistics devoted much of its energy to sorting out the various, socially determined codes in language.) Neither Jürgen Lodemann – who has never seen himself as an author writing a series in a single style – nor any other author has ever come up with a Ruhr crime novel that could compete with the unforgettable *Anita*, and no other author has ever challenged its pre-eminence.

Despite this flash of genius, we should stay with our original observation: that it was only in the mid-1980s that Germany saw a sizeable number of publications that are now customarily referred to as *Regionalkrimis* [regional crime novels]. This happened in several regions more or less at the same time; the novels were for the most part short and relatively unsophisticated detective stories by non-professional authors, partly self-published, partly in alternative or niche presses. The writing has to this day preserved the features of grassroots literature by self-taught writers, often members of hobby writing clubs. This type of writing can be found in every corner of Germany, even if much of its hardly vast readership is drawn from a narrow circle of regional enthusiasts and the books scarcely draw the attention of national book retail. Such publications amount to an entirely legitimate and probably very satisfying activity, one which lies somewhere between hobby and 'self-discovery', but it was partly this that led to the dismissive image of regional crime writing being 'grim' (as Thomas Wörtche's rather awful pun on the word Krimi as 'Grimmi' suggested). At that time, regional crime fiction had not yet established itself as a brand name in any professional or commercial sense, but it did not take long for mainstream publishers to recognize the potential market that such readers represented and to set out to exploit it.

Breakthrough in the Eifel

There is probably only one thing that German regional crime fiction has in common with the US Army, and that is that both of them achieved a breakthrough in the Eifel, even if those events were separated by forty-five years. For crime fiction, the decisive event was the national success of Jacques Berndorf's series of novels – thirteen titles in all – between 1989 and 2006. All of these novels bear the name of the region in the title, ranging from *Eifel-Blues* in 1989 and *Eifel-Schnee* [1995, *Eifel Snow**] to *Eifel-Müll* [2000, *Eifel Garbage**] and *Eifel-Kreuz* [2006, *Eifel Cross**] in 2006. To date, three million copies have been sold, together with ten other books. Behind the nom de plume is the investigative journalist Michael Preute (born 1936). He chose to set his conventionally constructed crime novels – by and by treating more complex and exciting cases – in the heavily wooded area located between the Catholic dioceses of Cologne, Aachen and Trier. Most Germans think of the area as being subject to continuous heavy rainfall, ruled by parochialism and Catholic piety, but one should also add that it is home to a high-quality German beer and one of the few remaining US Air Force bases in Germany. Berndorf combines intensive realism *en détail* with the somewhat improbable stylization of this area as a hotbed of criminality *en gros*. In doing so, he plays on two contradictory expectations, or moods, on behalf of his readers: their longing for the beautiful and romantic life of the countryside, and their certainty (which may be exaggerated, but is not entirely false) that, behind the idyllic facade of country life, there is as much lying and deception, murder and manslaughter as in the days of Sodom and Gomorrah or in the wicked metropolis. Ironically, it was in the cities that Berndorf found a publisher for his first series, Grafit-Verlag in Dortmund, a small left-wing press, whose financial stability Berndorf's success did much to build up, together with its reputation for regional and international crime fiction.

It was not just Grafit but a whole new type of publisher that defined and funded itself by means of the brand-name *Regionalkrimi*. Other examples are the Emons-Verlag in Cologne (where Friedrich Ani – now a highly renowned author – began his career). Emons promotes its titles with the tongue-in-cheek slogan: 'Neue deutsche Heimatliteratur' [New German Heimat Literature]. Then there is KBV in Hillesheim in the Eifel, whose owner, Rolf Kramp published not only Berndorf's later novels, but also his own series of Eifel crime novels: as a sideline he runs a hotel and bookshop, both with a crime theme. Finally, there is the Gmeiner Verlag from Upper Swabia, which has taken this business model to its logical conclusion. Publishing a huge number of relevant titles, listed according to their regional setting, Gmeiner's list resembles nothing so much as a thickly populated map of Germany.

That this business model pays off can be seen in the fact that high-class literary publishers such as Fischer, Suhrkamp, DTV and Hanser are not only cashing in on the general boom in crime fiction (publishing translations and the more ambitious of the German-language authors), but are not hesitating to enter the market for *Regionalkrimis*. At present, it is possible to identify a new sub-genre with the potential to be a best-seller.

The contemporary path to fame: Alpine crime

Let us start with a few names and facts. Firstly: Volker Klüpfel and Michael Kobr (both born in 1971), one a teacher, the other a journalist. *Der Spiegel* records them as being 'Germany's most successful author duo'. Together they created Inspector Kluftinger (aka 'Klufti'), from their hometown Kempten in the Allgäu, who has muddled his way through various, mostly comic personal crises and nearly ten cases, from *Milchgeld* [2003, *Milk Money**] to *Grimmbart* [2014, *Grim Beard**]. Having started with a small regional publisher, their books are now being published by the mainstream Piper Verlag. The print run starts at a quarter of a million (not including audio books), and their titles consistently feature in the upper ranks of the best-seller lists in the news magazines *Der Spiegel* and *Focus*. However, they have not yet managed to get a place on the 'KrimiZeit-Bestenliste' ['Best of Crime Writing List'; created by *Die Zeit*, now published in *Frankfurter Allgemeine Sonntagszeitung*], which seems to be too literary for them. In a characteristically innovative move, the duo now tour with a stage-show based on their latest title, with no less than eighty performances a summer, most of them in Bavaria, but occasionally venturing out into foreign territory, such as Cologne, Hamburg and Berlin. They once made a guest appearance at Circus Krone in Munich, a venue that (aside from other dubious leaders of the past) previously only the leader of the CSU and Prime Minister of Bavaria, Franz Josef Strauß, had been able to fill.

Secondly: Rita Falk (born 1964). Falk, married to a policeman, had no problem calling her first two high-calorie novels *Winterkartoffelknödel* [2010, *Winter Potato Dumplings**] and *Dampfnudelblues* [2011, *Steamed Noodle Blues**], and still fewer problems referring to her work as 'provincial crime fiction'. These stories are narrated in the first-person present tense by a certain Franz Eberhof, a duty policeman in (fictitious) Niederkaltenkirchen. They are about Franz's adventures, both personal and professional, some of them grotesque, others merely amusing. Franz is always ready to wash down a hearty Bavarian meal with a drink or two and does not forget about the erotic pleasures in life. The obvious inspiration for Falk's work – and in particular for the mixture of narration and monologue in a pastiche of dialect – comes from the Austrian Wolf Haas, but Falk makes little effort to reproduce the critical sting of Haas' work and settles for plodding populism instead. At the back of her novels, she includes a glossary of words in the Bavarian dialect and, as an extra, paratextual treat, some of 'Granny's recipes'. Both of Falk's titles – published in paperback by the high-quality publisher DTV – stayed in the bestseller lists for many months and have since been joined by other fresh delicacies of home-baking and crime, most recently *Zwetschgendatschikomplott* [2015, *Damson Tart in*

Distress*], *Leberkäsjunkie* [2016, *Meat Loaf Junkie**] and *Weißwurstconnection* [2017, *The Veal Sausage Connection**].

Much further down the list, we come to our third example, Jörg Maurer, with (to date) ten alpine crime novels, from *Föhnlage* [2009, *The Föhn is Blowing**]) to *Am Abgrund lässt man gern den Vortritt* [2018, *At the Abyss One Likes to Defer to Someone Else**], *Im Schnee wird nur dem Tod nicht kalt* [2018, *In the Snow, Only Death Doesn't Get Cold**]and *Am Tatort bleibt man ungern liegen* [2019, *Nobody Likes to Remain Lying at the Crime Scene**]. His hero is Inspector Jennerwein, who conducts his investigations at high altitudes, even on the sheer rock faces above Garmisch. Maurer makes his intertextual approach clear in his choice of names. Jennerwein Girgl was the most famous poacher in Bavaria until he was shot down in the forest by a rival in 1877, but he remains a legend to this day. Maurer's novels (around 350 pages in length) include countless mottos and quotes, yodellers, vignettes of chamois standing around on Alpine crags, musical excerpts, quiz questions and pieces of a jigsaw puzzle – we should also mention that some obscenities are blacked out in the text and left to the readers' creativity – while the whole thing is rounded off with an exchange of letters between the author and people who helped him to put the text together. The message could not be clearer: postmodern attitudes are mixed with a virtuoso arrangement of Bavarian mountain scenery, and clichés are particularly welcome. Aside from his alpine detective stories, Maurer started out as a teacher of German, theatre director and radio presenter, and he is still active on the regional circuit with a quality programme of musical cabaret.

Alpine crime fiction comes down to sea level rather more often than the chamois, but it is still not easy to get in our sights, i.e. to arrive at a fair critical assessment of it, for there are fundamental historical aspects to its success. Bavaria – once a kingdom in its own right, now a Free State – is far more conscious of its special features than any other state in Germany. It is home to towns and natural features that, for generations, have been popular tourist spots. We need only think of the Hofbräuhaus in Munich, the fairy-tale castle of Neuschwanstein or Germany's highest mountain, the Zugspitze, up and down whose slopes Inspector Jennerwein conducts his enquiries. Moreover, despite their high-tech image, the majority of the Bavarians are proud to cultivate their folklore, even down to Munich's Oktoberfest beer festival – something that most other Germans regard as being halfway between the exotic and the unacceptable. It was Strauß who initiated this development and one of his successors, Edmund Stoiber, who coined the slogan 'laptop and Lederhosen'. It cannot be denied that this approach has modernized a once agricultural part of Germany, but the hybrid culture that its transformation into a high-tech region produced still awaits serious academic analysis.

Maurer's novels present this culture in a humorous light, as his books mix crime fiction and comedy, not to mention farce. Rita Falk's stories could easily be adapted to the stage – as a sort of update to *Komödienstadel* [Bavarian dialect for 'Comedy Barn'], which for decades presented popular theatre on the public broadcasting channels. That programme has disappeared now, but Falks' 'crimedies' have still made it to prime time. Kobr/Klüpfel and Maurer as cabaret artists have – as we said – long since completed their *performative turn* to the stage. The danger is that the crime novel as such gets left behind. The 'whodunit' serves as a mere device on to which a series of slapstick scenes are fixed, and each time the investigation itself becomes more threadbare still. Entertainment and event culture swallow up the literary genre. The crime novel becomes a universal narrative style, but only at the expense of its own self-destruction. Fortunately, there are alternatives.

You win some . . .

Berndorf's Eifel classics were criticized for not being specific enough in their settings. It was claimed that, if you changed the place names, the plots could easily be taking place somewhere else. That is not necessarily the case, but this discussion touched on what was, for those who are interested in crime fiction *as literature*, the real point. It is precisely because regional elements can be used in different functions and on different literary levels that the central issue in deciding the quality of a text as a crime novel is whether and in what way regional elements, especially when foregrounded in the novel, contribute to the essentials of the plot, i.e. to the case and to its investigation. Are there plausible connections with the investigations? Do those connections make the investigation distinctive? Or are they just props, a bit of local colour or just padding? We are taking only slight liberties with a famous remark made by Walter Benjamin when we say: 'The aunt was murdered on this sofa, and she couldn't have been murdered *anywhere else than on this sofa*'.[5]

If this is so, we need to consider *which* regions, even *what kinds of* regions satisfy particular reader expectations. For readers, recognizing familiar places has a pleasant effect, but, despite the vast increase in readers' personal mobility, it remains only a limited one. Looking forward to one's next holiday

---

5 Walter Benjamin had written, 'On this sofa, the aunt can only be murdered'. ['Auf diesem Sofa kann die Tante nur ermordet werden!'] Walter Benjamin, *Einbahnstraße. Gesammelte Schriften*, Vol. IV/1 (Frankfurt a.M.: Suhrkamp Taschenbuch Verlag, 1991), p. 89.

destination may be a factor in choosing the next book to buy, and publishers certainly exploit this, look beyond frontiers and go through foreign crime writing to find suitable novels to translate into German because they are set in Provence or Brittany. They foster a kind of international regionalism, French, British or German style. But the most important thing seems to be – at least as far as the German regions are concerned – that, while there are obvious stereotypical features (e.g. in the Eifel: pouring rain, Catholic, but with decent beer), they leave both reader and author enough space for flights of imagination, whether or not they are plausible. This is useful if the author is familiar with the region, but is not from there and has two views of it. While Berndorf comes from Osnabrück and Wolf from the Ruhr, the ratings queen of the moment, Nele Neuhaus, comes from Paderborn, though her novels are all set in the Taunus near Frankfurt.

With these considerations we are obviously avoiding the most important question: what has a regional slant got to do with literary quality? Regional novels of a different kind – *Buddenbrooks*, for instance, or *Ulysses* – clearly show that there must be a connection, or at least there had to be a century ago. But we should stay in our local league – which in German football is referred to as the Regional League. What we call regionalism, even if we cannot entirely define it – let us say traditions, mentalities and the given facts of a particular place – all this should have an effect on crime fiction, like the effect that yeast has on dough: it should make it rise.

There is a positive, if rather simple example of this in a crime novel by Felix Huby (we mentioned him earlier: a work-a-day crime novelist, real name Eberhard Hungerbühler, born 1936). The book is *Bienzle und das Narrenspiel* [1988, *Bienzle and the Game of Fools**]. The setting is the provincial town of Venningen, but behind this fictitious name, it is easy to recognize Rottweil in Württemberg, a town famous for its traditional annual 'game of fools'. The town combines a number of small thriving industries with a strong sense of tradition. This is where a murder takes place, and, what is more, right in the middle of the 'Fasnet', i.e. the carnival that has been celebrated in same way for centuries. Inspector Bienzle has to solve this murder. He comes from Stuttgart and happens to be in Venningen simply to enjoy the carnival, especially the 'game of fools' – a parade of figures wearing heavy wooden masks. This novel and the excellent dramatization of it for *Tatort* in 1994 (which, after public protests in Rottweil, had to be filmed in Ravensburg instead) was built around the opportunity provided to hide the murderer among the many innocent characters who are unrecognizable behind their masks. At the same time, the story is constructed around a number of conflicts within a high-tech family business (typical of Swabia, by the way, and typically prosperous), appropriately, at a time when globalization was starting to make itself felt – which was certainly an effective context for a murder.

A counter example is offered by the work of Nele Neuhaus (real name Cornelia Löwenberg, born 1967). Her series has now grown to comprise nine titles and sales of five million. Particular audience favourites have been *Schneewittchen muss sterben* [2010, *Snow White Must Die*] and, more recently, *Die Lebenden und die Toten* [2014, *I am Your Judge*], *Im Wald* [2016, *In the Woods**], and *Muttertag* [2018, *Mother's Day**]. All the novels are set – like their individual subtitles, indeed as the title of the whole series indicates – in the Taunus, the hilly hinterland of Frankfurt am Main, a city that remains the centre of German finance and air transport. Neuhaus provides a telling portrait of the region, with its exclusive small towns like Bad Homburg and Kronberg, where the desirable residences of Frankfurt's leading citizens are crowded together, and other places, where villas and modern offices rub shoulders with traditional village structures and where the local dialect still thrives, even in a heady mix with Serbo-Croat and other more exotic tones. Such circumstances are the source of pleasant, occasionally comic intercultural scenes and effects. Neuhaus' work is more strongly marked, however, by a looser connection between the setting and the various criminal cases, any of which could have happened elsewhere. It follows that the author takes pains to link in as many modern social and political, ecological and above all human conflicts and problems as possible within the framework of the crime and its regional setting, even when they have precious little to do with the case itself. The crime is a conveyor belt for the issues of the day, which Neuhaus enjoys presenting in an explanatory and often didactic fashion. Alongside her crime novels, Neuhaus was and remains the author of popular horse books and girls' fiction. Perhaps this has helped to increase the extraordinarily wide appeal of the Taunus novels. None of this has prevented Neuhaus' work – especially in the versions faithfully filmed by ZDF – from being the target of regular sarcastic attacks, not least from the ranks of the FAZ, whose TV reviews are generally regarded as authoritative.

Closing the gap: New conditions for German crime fiction

Up until now, we have looked at the *Regionalkrimis* produced by amateur and semi-professional writers and at some of the best-selling authors. But there is a third group, for whose crime writing the concept of a 'regional crime novel' is too narrow and certainly misleading – despite (or indeed because of) the fact that they use regional and local differences in their settings, not just as the framework for the plots, but as places of topographical, social and historically cultural action, places that possess their own logic. Before I turn to these writers in the concluding section, it would be useful to reflect on some of the changes in the organization of German literature that have affected these authors and the nature of their contribution to crime writing.

The idea of cities possessing their own 'logic' was introduced from urban studies to literary studies by Julika Griem, a professor of English literature. She applies it to crime novels, films and TV series (notably to *Tatort* itself).[6] In order to allow a particular space to 'speak' or (as the historian Karl Schlögel elegantly puts it) to be able 'to read time in a particular space'[7] – in order for this to happen, a far larger repertoire of narrative forms and strategies is required than the pioneers of the *Neuer Deutscher Kriminalroman* had at their disposal. The more recent authors whom we have been discussing, coming from an in-between generation, have participated in and benefited from a process that – in the context of a similar observation by Pierre Bourdieu – I once called 'modernism catching up'.[8] I was referring to the fact that, from the end of the nineteenth century, crime writing was regarded as part of the literature of social modernity. Its authors shared this understanding, and yet – on account of the conventions that they were quick to establish in their writing – they failed to exploit the technical and narrative innovations that avant-gardist and modernist literature developed after 1900 and more strongly after 1920. This has meant that the crime novel (just like the spy novel) constitutes a type of modern

---

6 Cf. Julika Griem, 'Beweisaufnahme. Zur medialen Topographie des "Tatort,"' in *Tatort Stadt. Mediale Topographien eines Fernsehklassikers*, ed. by J. G., Sebastian Scholz (Frankfurt a.M., New York: Campus, 2010), pp. 9–28 (p. 20–23).

7 Cf. Karl Schlögel, *In Space We Read Time: On the History of Civilization and Geopolitics*, trans. by Gerrit Jackson (New York: Bard Graduate Center, 2016) [K.S., *Im Raume lesen wir die Zeit. Über Zivilisationsgeschichte und Geopolitik* (Munich: Hanser 2003)].

8 Cf. Pierre Bourdieu, 'The Market of Symbolic Goods', in P.B., *The Field of Cultural Production. Essays on Art and Literature,* ed. by Randal Johnson (New York: Columbia University Press, 1993), pp. 112–141 (p. 120–131) and Jochen Vogt, 'Der deutsche Schäferhund und sein Innerer Monolog. Einige Bemerkungen zur nachholenden Modernisierung des Erzählens im neueren Kriminalroman', in *Literatur als Interdiskurs. Realismus und Normalismus, Interkulturalität und Intermedialität von der Moderne bis zur Gegenwart. Eine Festschrift für Rolf Parr zum 60. Geburtstag,* ed. by Thomas Ernst and Georg Mein (Munich: Fink 2016), pp. 511–520.

literature that relies on pre-modern techniques. It is, in short, 'modernity without modernism'.[9]

This observation applies to the genre internationally – one must only compare the novels of Virginia Woolfe and the early novels of Agatha Christie, which were published more or less simultaneously in the 1920s. In Germany there were particular historical reasons for the considerable delay in taking up modernist techniques such as non-linear, multi-perspective narration, stream of consciousness, explicit inter-textuality and self-referentiality as well as the hybridization of genres, to name but a few. Leading members of Gruppe 47 worked strenuously to get mainstream literature to catch up in the 1950s and 1960s, but in German crime fiction – traditionally somewhat behind the international genre – this process began a whole generation later. It looked, on the one hand, to the state of the art as established by Anglo-American, West European and Scandinavian crime fiction, while, on the other, the global success of more or less postmodern 'nearly crime novels' (in Sigrid Thielking's phrase) in the 1980s – such as Umberto Eco's *The Name of the Rose*, Paul Auster's *New York Trilogy* and Patrick Süskind's *Perfume* – played an important role in developments.[10] By now, all these titles lie a generation back in time, and with regard to the generation of authors writing today, we might say that they have enabled German language crime writing to hold its own in international comparisons. Moreover, they have achieved this without sacrificing any specifically German (Austrian or Swiss-German) features – i.e. regionalism – to a globalized or standardized best-seller model.

Influences of this kind were literary symptoms of the gradual overcoming, even closing of the legendary gap between high and lowbrow culture – a metaphor that American usage rescued from phrenologists and to which Leslie Fiedler dedicated a seminal article in 1969.[11] But they were more than symptoms: they accelerated these processes. Everyone knows that this gap was particularly wide and long lasting in German literature – its origins can be found in Weimar Classicism. It led to a categorical downgrading and massive,

---

9 Jochen Vogt, 'Modern? Vormodern? Oder Postmodern? Zur Poetik des Kriminalromans und seinem Ort im literarischen Feld', in *Verbrechen und Gesellschaft im Spiegel von Literatur und Kunst*, ed. by Véronique Liard (Munich: Meidenbauer, 2006), pp. 17–29 (p. 23); see for a similar argument Peter von Matt, *Die Intrige. Theorie und Praxis der Hinterlist* (Munich: Hanser, 2006), pp. 453–465.

10 Sigrid Thielking, [Introduction], in *'Beinahekrimis' – Beinahe Krimis?* ed. by S. T., Jochen Vogt (Bielefeld: Aisthesis 2014), pp. 7–19.

11 Leslie Fiedler, 'Cross the Border, Close the Gap', in *A New Fiedler Reader* (Amherst, New York: Prometheus Books, 1999) pp. 270–294.

in part malevolent denigration of the genre of crime fiction on behalf of the law-making powers-that-be in the literary system. By 'law-making', I mean a number of forces: teaching at secondary school, literary studies at university, book reviewers in the so-called quality press, the juries responsible for awarding literary prizes and, last but not least, public libraries and library associations. None of these bodies changed their position an inch during the 1950s and 1960s, and only very slowly in the 1970s did their attitudes begin to relax.

All this may or may not particularly matter. After all, the greater the hostility towards crime writing and the more complete the marginalization of crime fiction (and at best the demonstrative lack of interest in it), the greater freedom is left for readers to follow their own individual preferences and tastes, regardless of what anyone else said. Of course, that is still true today, and it is only through the market place and through book promotions – in other words via *commercial* channels – that these preferences and tastes can be satisfied. You do not need the whole apparatus of literary criticism to make that choice. The question of my favourite detective story or favourite author is my own business; I do not have to justify my choice to anyone.

The situation has been changing, if in fits and starts, since the 1970s. Even the authorities who rule over the literary system are cautiously beginning to revise their hostility towards crime writing. If they did not stock books of that kind, public libraries would soon be out of business. Since then, the sub-genres in crime fiction – the radio play for children, or prescribed reading-lists in high school – have found a place in schools; crime novels with a regional slant are particularly popular; and creative writing classes will often encourage students to write crime fiction themselves. University courses in 'language and literature' have changed too. Classes on crime fiction are both possible and in fact quite common, particularly so in English and American Studies, and in the Romance languages; in German they are less common. Crime fiction is still regarded patronizingly as little more than a hobby for a few faculty members – it certainly does not further one's career to conduct research in this field. There is a double bind on crime fiction: it is too sociological for literary scholars and too literary for experts in cultural studies. Everyone is talking about the fashionable cultural turn in literary studies, but – in Germany at least – mass literature and crime writing are not included in it. It has been more fashionable since the cultural turn to use the new methods to reconsider for the nth time the canonical products of high culture than to include new materials.

Perhaps, however, a situation of this kind is not in itself particularly important. Today, no one believes that the classic cultural institutions have that much influence over the consumption of literature and other media: it is the media themselves and the advertising industry that have the power – in particular television. It is TV that, since the 1980s, has been promoting crime writing in every type of format and length (from thirty to ninety minutes), and series producers ensure that, quantitatively speaking, they are the dominant form of non-documentary TV programme.[12] These figures hold true for the 'dual system' of German TV, that is, both for the public service and for private stations; for locally produced programmes in various formats; and for standard US-American series, such as *Law and Order* or *CSI*. It also applies to high-quality series and serials, especially those from Great Britain and Scandinavia. The average weekly programme offered by the public service stations contains a jam-packed network of TV crime programs, from early evening (where 'crime comedies' are especially favoured) through prime time (the classic slot for *Tatort*, its spin-offs and competitors) to late evening (the time of choice for repeats of *Tatort* on the regional stations and for popular imported series). Even on high days and holy days, like Christmas, Easter and Whitsun – days which were once kept free of sex and crime *by law* – are packed with crime series.

Crime fiction, crime films and TV crime series are occupying increasing space in the print media. *Bild-Zeitung* – with the largest circulation of any of the popular newspapers – likes to run stories about controversial episodes of *Tatort* and is, of course, full of the details of TV stars' private lives. Seriously minded regional newspapers like the *Tagesspiegel* in Berlin, the *Westdeutsche Allgemeine Zeitung* in Essen and the *Stuttgarter Zeitung* follow closely the interests and viewing preferences of the majority of their readers and run reports on new titles, TV programmes, well-known authors and actors, readings and every kind of 'crime writing event'. Even the national newspapers – *Frankfurter Allgemeine Zeitung, Die Welt* and *Süddeutsche Zeitung* – and weeklies such as *Die Zeit* and the much smaller, left-of-centre *Freitag* have for years now run monthly full-page features, sometimes even entire supplements, on crime fiction. In addition, *Die Zeit* once published a monthly 'KrimiZeit-Bestenliste', put together by twenty critics specializing in the field and discussed, in less technical terms, by the responsible editor, Tobias Gohlis.[13] The *Frankfurter Allgemeine Sonntagszeitung* recently took over this regular feature.

All these developments are both symptomatic of a gradual revaluation of crime fiction and a response to the reading and purchasing habits of the broader population. Bookshops and promotional materials have long displayed

---

12 See Reinhold Viehoff, 'Der Krimi im Fernsehen. Überlegungen zur Genre- und Programmgeschichte', in *MedienMorde*, pp. 89–110.
13 www.zeit.de/krimizeit-bestenliste.

the bulky hardcover crime novels of German and, in particular, international authors alongside highbrow literary novels. What is more, they take liberties to charge just as much for both types of literature, i.e. somewhere between 19 and 29 Euro. But it does seem that, for the public – both in their opinions, their tastes and their buying habits – there is much less of a gap between highbrow and lowbrow literature, or – to use the shorthand of the book retail managers – between E (for earnest) and U (for entertainment). Indeed, one might get the impression that the gap had now been all but bridged.

These are very positive changes, but it still holds that a professional under-standing of crime writing lacks any kind of academic or institutional basis. This has always been a feature of this field – look, for instance, at the massive scale of amateur research into Sherlock Holmes – and is in fact true of all hobby-style activities. In the digital age, this means that expert knowledge can over-whelmingly be found on the internet, where it is easy enough to find suitable portals, archives and discussion forums.[14]

The most recent German crime writing: Richness and depth

I will conclude this survey of the field by mentioning some of those authors who, in their own individual way, combine regionalism and modernism, and who have thereby brought the German-language crime novel to a level where it can compete internationally. This section is both a series of recommendations and, of course, a very personal selection, even if my judgements are backed up by reviewers and by the juries responsible for awarding numerous book prizes in recent years. Most of the authors in this section are the subject of individual portraits in other parts of the volume. Because of this, I need do hardly more than a little name-dropping.

As I attempt my roundtrip of the German speaking regions, I will try to sug-gest what – quoting Julika Griem – the last section called the individual 'logic' that these regions possess, and it makes sense to start in the Ruhr. The various aspects of this industrial heartland of the federal state of North Rhine-Westphalia (and of the 'old' Federal Republic before unification as well), its

---

14 See www.krimilexikon.de (German-language authors); www.bokas.de (bibliography); www.krimi-couch (general information); www.culturmag/crimemag; www.kaliber38.com (most competent and critical discussions).

historical ruptures and social conditions – all of this features in the novels of Jörg Juretzka (born in 1955). To date, there are twelve novels, from *Prickel* (1998) to *Trailer Park* (2015), most of them set in the Ruhr. Their principal character is a rather shady personality, the part-time detective Kristof Kryszinski. A characteristic feature of these novels is that Juretzka subtly overplays both the regional and the social reality of his setting, as well as the distinctive 'Ruhr German' dialect, and achieves a kind of deconstruction of that world by means of surrealistic humour.

In direct contrast to Juretzka's work are the crime novels of Norbert Horst. Some of these – starting with *Leichensache* [2004, *A Matter of Corpse**] are set in the eastern part of Westphalia, others – up to and including *Mädchenware* [2014, *Girls for Sale**] and, most recently, *Kaltes Land* [2017, *A Cold Country**] – are set in Dortmund, Germany's tenth largest city. The Dortmund novels are clearly in the tradition of the (American) police novel. Horst's realism consists of an authentic and detailed portrayal of the city, and its special feature is that Horst uses elements and stories taken from real police investigations. This is hardly surprising, given that, for dozens of years, Horst has been and still is himself a full-time police inspector in Bielefeld. His realism also involves a very deliberate concentration on the language of his narratives. They combine multiple perspectives and are often similar to newspaper reports, but they achieve psychological depth as they focus on the personal viewpoint of the investigating officer.

If the Ruhr District sees its detectives eating up the miles on the region's motorways, Robert Marthaler, Chief Inspector of the murder squad in Frankfurt am Main, is more often on his bicycle. It is well known that his creator, Jan Seghers – born in 1958 and known in real life as Matthias Altenburg – is a fanatical cyclist. Moreover, his six novels to date – the first *Ein allzu schönes Mädchen* [2006, *The Girl is Too Pretty**], and the most recent *Die Sterntaler-Verschwörung* [2014, *The Star Money Conspiracy**] and *Menschenfischer* [2017, *Catcher of People**] – very successfully convey on two wheels the topography of the city and the heavily populated Rhine-Main region that surrounds it. Seghers points out the striking contrasts between metropolitan life – the global city that is the financial centre and a major hub of European air-travel – and the many parts of the city that have remained more down to earth, more provincial, but also much more ethnically diverse.

A change of scene: Friedrich Ani (born 1959) is regarded by many critics as the most important German crime writer. His loyal readers have enjoyed twenty-one volumes of his Inspector Tabor Süden novels, which began in 1998 with *Die Erfindung des Abschieds* [*The Invention of Farewell**] and continued up to *Der Narr und seine Maschine* [2018, *The Fool and His Machine**]. Süden solves missing persons cases in modest and sometimes deprived areas of Munich, Germany's third largest city, which likes to bask in its provincial glamour. Not every missing person turns out to have been the victim of a crime, but each case opens up stories of human suffering and wretchedness.[15]

Ani's novels can be read with a city map in one hand, but for Wolf Haas (born 1960) and his eight novels, you need a map of the whole of Austria. His series – running from *Auferstehung der Toten* [1996, *Resurrection of the Dead**] to *Brennerova* (2014) – features the one-time policeman Simon Brenner, now only occasionally involved in detective work, and enjoys a unique cult status, having been extravagantly praised by the reading public, by devotees of the crime novel and by mainstream critics. It is not simply that these novels take their readers around choice Vienna locations and tourist hot spots like Salzburg and Kitzbühel, but rather that Haas (a trained linguist) has given his narrator a highly personal, artificial language, to which his readers appear to have become addicted.

Haas takes a panoramic view of Austria, but Alfred Komarek (born 1945) stays within very local confines. His six novels and one collection of short stories move off the slopes down into the lower levels, not only geographically as they move among the wine presses of the valleys of Lower Austria – but psychologically, socially and morally, descending into the depths of human misery which, it seems, can be found anywhere one is prepared to dig deep enough. The digging is done by Simon Polt, an Inspector of Gendarmerie who is now retired – a man whose comfortable joviality is highly deceptive. There is no avant-garde or surrealistic techniques at work in Komarek's work, but a rather anachronistic narrative style reminiscent of the village tales of the nineteenth century.

Continuing our round trip across frontiers, we find the nine crime novels of Hansjörg Schneider (born in 1938): the first *Silberkiesel* [1993, *Silver Gravel**] and the most recent *Hunkelers Geheimnis* [2015, *Hunkeler's Secret**]. They too are conventionally narrated. The investigating officer is Inspector Hunkeler and, like others, he retires during the course of the series. His patch is the historic frontier town of Basel, part of the 'region' on the Upper Rhine to which we referred earlier. The frontiers between Switzerland, France and Germany may be open and flexible, but not the bureaucracy nor the mentalities of the three states. Schneider's themes come from borders and their crossing, from their

---

15 Cf. Thomas Kniesche, "'Der Kommissar für die, die weg sind". Friedrich Anis Tabor-Süden-Romane und die Topographie des Traumas', in *andererseits. Yearbook of Transatlanic German Studies 3* (2013), pp. 125–145. Online version: http://andererseits.library.duke.edu/article/view/14941/6119. For a portrait of Friedrich Ani, see p. 251–254.

historical ruptures and the regional contrasts. Schneider's work is at times elegiac, at times satirical (with the Swiss banking system a regular target), but for all the ironic sophistication of the narration, the crimes themselves remain relatively straightforward.

Across the Rhine, Hunkeler often has to deal with the Black Forest and other parts of southwest Germany, where Uta-Maria Heim (born 1963) has her hunting ground. Her early crime novels received book prizes in the early 1990s. There are now some twenty novels in all, although it is not easy to separate them from her ten other 'non-crime' novels. Between *Das Rattenprinzip* [1991, *Rats Too Have Principles**] and *Wem sonst als Dir* [2014, *To Whom but You**] her work displays two consistent features: the author's critical, almost anarchistic attitude to political, social and literary conventions, and she often takes pleasure in turning these on their head; and, secondly, the breadth of detailed historical and literary knowledge at her disposal. Her use of this knowledge puts her work far above that of many of her fellow-writers.[16]

There is a group of writers, most of them members of a younger generation, whose work we might describe as regionalism *sans frontières*. In this category, I should mention Veit Heinichen (born 1957), who, as a German, has settled into his adopted home of Trieste and has built important historical and political themes into his novels. There are nine of these to date, from *Gib jedem seinen eigenen Tod* [2001, *To Each His Own Death**] to *Im eigenen Schatten* [2013, *In His Own Shadow**] and, with them, Heinichen has created a conventional regional crime novel based in a different country.[17] But by 'regionalism *sans frontières*', I primarily mean a type of story that, staying close to the big issues of the day, creates a dialectic between the local and the foreign, the present and the past, regionalism and globalization.

Ulrich Ritzel (born 1940), for many years a journalist specializing in crime and legal reporting, began writing crime novels set in southwest Germany. His novels then shifted to Berlin, Germany's new and former capital city, but Berlin is more than a new local setting for his work. Instead, Ritzel's plots focus on the long shadow cast by the Balkan wars of the 1990s in *Schlangenkopf* [2011, *Snake's Head**] and on the globalization of infrastructure across Europe in *Trotzkis Narr* [2013, *Trotzki's Fool**].[18]

Oliver Bottini (born 1965) belongs to a younger generation. In 2005, his novels focussing on Louise Boní, a police detective in Freiburg, began

---

16 For a portrait of this author, see p. 276-281.
17 For a portrait of this author, see p. 281–285.
18 For a portrait of this author, see p. 298–301.

attracting attention. The most recent titles are *Im weißen Kreis* [2015, *In the White Circle**] and *Der Tod im stillen Winkel des Lebens* [2017, *Death in the Quiet Corners of Life**]. In *Der kalte Traum* [2013, *The Cold Dream**], the focus is on the southwest provinces, but also Berlin and Serbia, showing how the crimes of the present can be traced back to the wars of the 1990s. More strongly even than Ritzel, Bottini's work switches genre from crime fiction to the spy novel and the political thriller – a development particularly evident in Bottini's next text, *Ein paar Tage Licht* [2014, *A Few Days' Light**], which takes as its context the theme of the Arab Spring and Islamic terror.[19]

In a similar fashion, Merle Kröger (born 1967) uses authentic events to structure *Grenzfall* [2013, *Frontier Incident**]. There is also a regional crime scene – the German-Polish frontier in Mecklenburg/Pomerania, but the problems that come to a head there are shown to have their origins elsewhere – in this case in Romania. Kröger's most recent novel, *Havarie* [2014, *Collision*], tackles the issue of the stream of refugees crossing from North Africa to Europe. The novel is set in 2014 on a cruise liner in the Mediterranean. It is there that a wide range of interwoven personal and national problems are concentrated: the liner becomes the stage on which globalization is seen to play out its larger and smaller dramas.[20]

Finally, in this group, we should mention Zoë Beck (born 1975), whose two most recent crime novels – *Brixton Hill* (2014*) and *Schwarzblende* [2015, *Fade to Black*] – are not set in Germany at all, but in London. This is not the foggy London of Conan Doyle and Edgar Wallace, however, but today's megalopolis, the epicentre of global networking and conflict a dangerous mixture of foreign capital, ethnic diversity, virtual reality and Islamist terror.[21]

Whether the genre of crime writing will prove capable, within the framework of a literary genre, of coming to terms with these types of themes and situations, and what material and structural changes it will have to make to do so, is one of the most interesting issues of the day. As in the best crime novel, the outcome is anything but certain.

And where is Berlin in all this?

This is an important issue, not least for American readers. One might object that there is more to Germany than Berlin, or – to put it less aggressively – point out

---

19 For a portrait of this author, see p. 258–262.
20 For a portrait of this author. see p. 290–293.
21 For a portrait of this author, see p. 254–258.

that Germany's largest city, restored as the capital of a united Germany, presents the crime writer not only with a whole range of distinctive features in terms of its economy, politics, social structures and the atmospherics of the city, but also with distinctive difficulties. As far as I can see, no crime writer has yet managed to paint a convincing picture of the regional complexities and contradictions of the city. Berlin certainly qualifies as a region, but continues to misunderstand itself as a metropolis. No other region or city in Germany is more obviously scarred by the huge fractures of twentieth century history (1945, 1949, 1961, 1989). But Berlin is at present in the midst of a process of dynamic change, which makes the city particularly attractive for German and international tourists, for young people from across the globe and for the so-called creative economy – art and culture, new media, fashion and design, entertainment. On the other hand, the city is not yet able to stand on its own two feet: it is racked by local politics in their most parochial and pernicious form, as well as by social problems, not least the integration of new migrants. To get hold of all this in a literary work – to say nothing of a crime novel – is an undertaking that is easier said than done It does not help that anyone attempting that task would immediately find him- or herself standing in the shadow of Alfred Döblin's epoch-making novel *Berlin Alexanderplatz* of 1929.

Of course, there is no shortage of Berlin crime novels, but none so far which has broken through to the inner logic of the place itself. It seems possible that this will be achieved – initially at least – only by taking a historical angle on the topic, something that promises to trigger interesting hybrid forms and variants of the present forms of crime writing. When it is hard to grasp the present, the past – perhaps even the future – seems like a good option. That, at least, is the approach taken by the last two authors whom I would like to recommend. One of these authors is Volker Kutscher from Cologne. In his seven volumes, from *Der nasse Fisch* [2007, *Babylon Berlin*] to *Marlow* [2018*], we see the fruits of Kutscher's scrupulous historical research into the final years and days of the Weimar Republic and the first weeks of the Nazi regime respectively. The other writer is Simon Urban, whose novel *Plan D* appeared in September 2011 and is set in October of the same year. The action takes place in East Berlin, in a resuscitated GDR, making the book a cross between a contra-factual historical novel, a crime novel and a futuristic novel. Quite apart from being a very exciting criminal-investigation-cum-spy-story, Urban's novel manages a witty, grotesque but devastating critique of the old system and of the Stasi in particular. Urban possesses, like the young Günter Grass, a great storytelling imagination and linguistic inventiveness, and the resulting texts are a delight to read.

Translated by Hugh Ridley

Gaby Pailer
6 Female Empowerment: Women's Crime Fiction in German

We undergo our life experiences in catastrophic form. We have to infer from catastrophes the way in which our societal coexistence works. We have to think to work out the 'inside story' behind crises, depressions, revolutions and wars [. . .]. Behind the events that are reported, we suspect other events that are not reported. Those are the *real* events [. . .]. Only history can instruct us about these real events [. . .]. History is written *after* catastrophes.

This basic situation in which intellectuals find themselves according to which they are the objects and not the subjects of history, trains the type of thinking that they can pleasurably set to work in crime novels.[1]

Since Bertolt Brecht wrote these lines in 1938, the 'crises, depressions, revolutions and wars' have significantly changed, as has the genre of the *Kriminalroman* [crime novel].[2] Looking for progenitors, Edgar Allen Poe and Arthur Conan Doyle readily come to mind, yet earlier forms, such as police reports, crime novellas and detective stories, have been found within the British, French and German literary traditions,[3] some reaching back into the 1700s, for example the Pitaval stories,

---

1 Bertolt Brecht, 'The Crime Novel', in *Brecht on Art and Politics*, ed. by Tom Kuhn and Steve Giles, London 2003, pp. 263–269 (p. 268–269). German original: Bertolt Brecht, 'Über die Popularität des Kriminalromans', in *Werke. Große kommentierte Berliner und Frankfurter Ausgabe*, ed. by Werner Hecht, Jan Knopf, Werner Mittenzwei and Klaus-Detlef Müller (Frankfurt a.M.: Suhrkamp, 1993), vol. 22, pp. 504–510 (p. 509–510). "*Wir machen unsere Erfahrungen im Leben in katastrophaler Form.* Aus Katastrophen haben wir die Art und Weise, wie unser gesellschaftliches Zusammensein funktioniert, zu erschließen. Zu den Krisen, Depressionen, Revolutionen und Kriegen müssen wir, denkend, die 'inside story' erschließen [. . .]. Hinter den Ereignissen, die uns gemeldet werden, vermuten wir andere Geschehnisse, die uns nicht gemeldet werden. Es sind dies die *eigentlichen* Geschehnisse [. . .]. Nur die Geschichte kann uns belehren über diese eigentlichen Geschehnisse [. . .]. Die Geschichte wird *nach* den Katastrophen geschrieben. Diese Grundsituation, in der die Intellektuellen sich befinden, daß sie Objekte und nicht Subjekte der Geschichte sind, bildet das Denken aus, das sie im Kriminalroman genußvoll betätigen können".
2 I wish to acknowledge my colleague Jason Lieblang's thoughtful contributions, especially to the English version of this paper.
3 Cf. Ulrich Broich, 'Von Inspektor Field zu Sherlock Holmes. Die englische Detektivliteratur nach 1850 und die historische Realität', in *Literatur und Kriminalität. Die gesellschaftliche Erfahrung von Verbrechen und Strafverfolgung als Gegenstand des Erzählens. Deutschland, England und Frankreich 1850–1880*, ed. by Jörg Schönert (Tübingen: Niemeyer, 1983), pp. 135–154. Elisabeth Schulz-Witzenrath, 'Emile Gaboriau und die Entstehung des roman

https://doi.org/10.1515/9783110426601-006

which Friedrich Schiller popularized in Germany.[4] Considering the variety of forms, it seems useful to re-consider 'Kriminalliteratur' [crime literature], as Jörg Schönert suggests, in the broader sense of 'literature about deviant criminal behaviour, about criminal individuals [...] and about the defeat of criminality'.[5]

In German crime fiction from the 1970s onward, it has almost become the rule to break with the 'golden rules' of the genre, for example that the culprit must never be a syndicate and that the crime must never reach uncontrollable social or political dimensions. Instead, it is now rather typical to address a wide range of current and controversial themes – the sex and drug trades, child abuse, forced migration, religious conflict, ecological crisis, animal cruelty and technical disaster, to name just a few. This turn to current thematic complexity renders protagonists ultimately unable to unravel all of a case's details, let alone bring the chief perpetrators to justice. This shift in thematic scope has also changed the ways in which reality – i.e. the deployment of true names and places, cases and events – comes into play. In his survey study, Peter Nusser determined two opposite poles between which crime fiction tends to navigate: either the investigators are 'unreal' (or 'idealized') but operate within a 'real' (or 'realistic') setting, in which case we have the form of the detective novel; or it is the other way around, in which case we have the form of the thriller.[6] This binary model, however, needs to be rethought, especially in light of crime novels referring to concrete historical and contemporary catastrophic events, interweaving aspects of the detective and thriller modes.[7]

---

policier', in *Literatur und Kriminalität*, ed. by Jörg Schönert, pp. 155–183. Hans-Otto Hügel, *Untersuchungsrichter, Diebsfänger und Detektive. Theorie und Geschichte der deutschen Detektiverzählung im 19. Jahrhundert* (Stuttgart: Metzler, 1978).

4 Cf. *Kriminalfallgeschichten*, ed. by Alexander Košenina, *Text & Kritik. Zeitschrift für Literatur. Sonderband*, 5 (2014). *Schillers Pitaval. Merkwürdige Rechtsfälle als ein Beitrag zur Geschichte der Menschheit, verfaßt, bearbeitet und herausgegeben von Friedrich Schiller*, ed. by Oliver Tekolf (Frankfurt a. M.: Die Andere Bibliothek/Eichborn, 2005). Further, Schiller's novella *Der Verbrecher aus verlorener Ehre* [*The Criminal of Lost Homour*], the first version of which appeared in 1786 and the second version in 1792, served as an early paradigm in German literature. Cf. Friedrich Schiller, *Der Verbrecher aus verlorener Ehre. Studienausgabe*, ed. by Alexander Košenina (Stuttgart: Reclam, 2014).

5 *Literatur und Kriminalität. Die gesellschaftliche Erfahrung von Verbrechen und Strafverfolgung als Gegenstand des Erzählens. Deutschland, England und Frankreich 1850–1880*, ed. by Jörg Schönert (Tübingen: Niemeyer, 1983), p. 7. German original: 'Literatur über abweichendes, kriminelles Verhalten, über Kriminelle [...] und über die Bekämpfung von Kriminalität'.

6 Cf. Peter Nusser, *Der Kriminalroman*. 2nd amended edn. (Stuttgart: Metzler, 1992), p. 11.

7 In earlier studies, the two terms, 'Detektivroman' and 'Kriminalroman', were discussed as either two genre paradigms, one more focused on detection, the other more focused on crime (cf. Richard Alewyn, 'Anatomie des Detektivromans', in *Der Kriminalroman. Zur Theorie und*

From the beginning, the genre appealed strongly to women. Again, we tend to think of the Anglo-American tradition first, with writers such as Agatha Christie, Dorothy Sayers or Patricia Highsmith. But in German literature, we find even earlier examples of crime stories, for example by Annette von Droste-Hülshoff, and detective stories by the relatively unknown Auguste Groner.[8] Female writers around 1800 tend to combine crime and persecution plots with aspects of the historical novel bordering on the gothic genre – notably by Sophia Lee in Great Britain, and Sophie Albrecht and Benedikte Naubert in Germany. In spatial terms, castles, vaults and turrets often symbolize the captivity of females within patriarchal heteronormativity, while the metaphor of burial (premature or as a pretence for escape) signifies civil death.[9] Research on women's crime fiction in contemporary German literature tends to diverge widely in its conclusions. Cornelia Behrens, for instance, posits that the detective plot and resolution of the criminal case ultimately function to affirm the same societal order the novels set out to question,[10] whereas Sabine Wilke instead deems the 'Frauenkrimi' a suitable means by which to deconstruct everyday gender biases and myths.[11]

One needs to be mindful, though, that, in epistemological terms, there is no such thing as 'women's crime fiction' in the sense that female authors do anything specifically different from males. Over the long course of western literary history, women have partaken of the same genre traditions, narrative modes and motives, and thus should be considered and included in all aspects of historical and present developments in German crime fiction. In this article, speaking of 'female authors' merely means to look at writers whose gender is

---

Geschichte der Gattung, ed. by Jochen Vogt, vol. 2 [Munich: Fink, 1992], pp. 372–404), or using the latter as an umbrella term for all narrative fiction dealing with criminal acts as such, in which the detective mode would form a subgenre (cf. Richard Gerber, 'Verbrechensdichtung und Kriminalroman', in *Der Kriminalroman*, ed. by Jochen Vogt, vol. 2, pp. 404–820).

8 Silke Arnold, '"Ermordet?" Eine Kriminalnovelle von Auguste Groner', *Script. Frau Literatur Wissenschaft im alpen-adriatischen Raum*, 6 (1994), pp. 3–7.

9 Cf. Diana Wallace, '"The Haunting Idea". Female Gothic Metaphors and Feminist Theory', in *The Female Gothic. New Directions*, ed. by Diana Wallace and Andrew Smith (Basingstoke: Palgrave McMillan, 2009), pp. 26–41. Silke Arnold-de Simine, *Leichen im Keller. Zu Fragen des Gender in Angstinszenierungen der Schauer- und Kriminalliteratur (1790–1830)* (St. Ingbert: Röhrig Universitätsverlag, 2000).

10 Cornelia Behrens, 'Verwischte Spuren. Die Detektivin als literarische Wunschfigur in Kriminalromanen von Frauen', in *Weiblichkeit und Tod in der Literatur*, ed. by Renate Berger and Inge Stephan (Cologne, Vienna: Böhlau, 1987), pp. 177–197 (p. 197).

11 Sabine Wilke, 'Wilde Weiber und dominante Damen. Der Frauenkrimi als postfeministischer Verhandlungsort von Weiblichkeitsmythen', *Literatur für Leser*, 3 (1995), pp. 151–163 (p. 163).

perceived or labelled as such, for instance by literary marketing practices evoking the notion of women as a subspecies by coining terms like 'Frauenkimi'. Female writers, historical and present, work within heteronormative societal orders in which the 'male' gender represents the norm and the 'female' is defined – more implicitly than consciously – as deviant, opposite or deficient, notions which pertain to the gender of authors and heroes alike.[12]

Due to their principal disposition as 'relative creatures' within a principally male order of discourse (in culture, society, politics, economy, law etc.), female authors of crime novels tend to link current socio-political issues with overturning traditional gender and power relations.[13] They do this by deploying narrative strategies that have typically been named for the comic as a principle and comedy as a form ('das Komische').[14] While, on the one hand, exposing those characters adherent to the male norm to 'comic failure' (a term coined by Karlheinz Stierle[15]) and turning them into 'objects' of derision, on the other,

---

12 Of Judith Butler's gender theoretical works, her study *Antigone's Claim. Kinship Between Life and Death* (New York: Columbia University Press, 2000) is particularly useful here. She analyses the ancient Antigone myth, juxtaposing gender and kinship relations to societal rules of law and crime, and in a Lacanian re-reading produces a counter-narrative to the Freudian Oedipus myth.

13 Some major publications in chronological order: Jessica Mann, *Deadlier than the Male. An Investigation into Feminine Crime Writing* (London: David & Charles, 1981). Maureen T. Reddy, *Detektivinnen. Frauen im modernen Kriminalroman* (Mühlheim: Guthmann-Petersen, 1990). Sally R. Munt, *Murder by the Book? Feminism and the Crime Novel* (London, New York: Routledge, 1994). Evelyne Keitel, 'Der weibliche Blick im amerikanischen Kriminalroman', *Das Argument* 37 (1995), pp. 35–51. Gabriele Dietze, 'Die verlorenen Schlachten der Männer und die Metamorphose der Privatdetektive', *Das Argument* 37.1 (1995), pp. 19–33. Kathleen Gregory Klein, *The Woman Detective. Gender and Genre* (Urbana, Chicago, IL: University of Illinois Press, 1995). Gabriele Dietze, *Hardboiled Woman. Geschlechterkrieg im amerikanischen Kriminalroman.* (Hamburg: Europäische Verlagsanstalt 1997). Kathleen Gregory Klein, *Diversity and Detective Fiction* (Bowling Green, OH: Bowling Green State University Popular Press, 1999). Gaby Pailer, '"Weibliche" Körper im "männlichen" Raum. Zur Interdependenz von Gender und Genre in deutschsprachigen Kriminalromanen von Autorinnen', *Weimarer Beiträge* 4 (2000), pp. 264–581. Faye Stewart, 'Girls in the Gay Bar. Performing and Policing Identity in Crime Fiction', in *Tatort Germany. The Curious Case of German-Language Crime Fiction*, ed. by Lynn M. Kutch and Todd Herzog (Rochester, NY: Camden House, 2014), pp. 200–222.

14 A number of groundbreaking studies I am referring to in this article appeared in *Das Komische*, ed. by Wolfgang Preisendanz and Rainer Warning (Munich: Fink, 1976).

15 Building on earlier theories by Henri Bergson, Sigmund Freud, Helmut Plessner and Michail Bachtin, Karlheinz Stierle developed a concept of 'comic failure' concerning act and speech act theory. The most simple form is the so-called 'Tücke des Objekts' [vice of the object] when a human is turned into an object by a non-human item, such as the infamous banana

they emphasize female empowerment by creating gender-aware or queer pro-tagonists gaining agency as 'subjects' of action.[16] Referring back to the opening quote, women's crime fiction tends to provide intellectual pleasure in a world where issues of gender, violence and in/justice are experienced in catastrophic form, and where traditional heteronormative concepts of male author/hero are diminished at the same time, empowering women and other 'others'.

Rather than presenting an exhaustive typology of crime novels by German fe-male authors in recent decades, I prefer to discuss the hypothesis outlined above for the three narrative modes, choosing two examples for each: the detective mode (Doris Gercke; Pieke Biermann), the thriller mode (Dagmar Scharsich; Ingrid Noll) and the crime and catastrophe mode (Sabine Weigand; Alina Bronsky).

The detective mode

> I stood there and realized they were laughing at me and would brag the first chance they got that they had taken me for a ride. I hated them so much it made me throw up again. [...]. I'll kill them, I thought over and over again.
> Until it sunk in that this really was the only solution.[17]

Thus ends the first chapter of Doris Gercke's *Weinschröter, du mußt hängen* [*Wine Porter, You Must Hang**] from 1988. A woman has been brutally abused and

---

peel; a more complex structure of vice occurs, when in a literary text or film a character tries to render another the object of his/her actions, which might be turned over by his or her target. Karlheinz Stierle, 'Komik der Handlung, Komik der Sprachhandlung, Komik der Komödie', in *Das Komische*, ed. Preisendanz/Warning, pp. 237–268.

16 Regarding interrelations of gender, laughter and crime fiction, cf. Gaby Pailer, 'Das komische Scheitern der Wiedervereinigung: Zum Verhältnis von Komik und Kriminalroman am Beispiel zweier deutschsprachiger Frauenkrimis der 90er Jahre', in *Gelegentlich: Brecht. Jubiläumsschrift für Jan Knopf zum 15jährigen Bestehen der Arbeitsstelle Bertolt Brecht (ABB)*, ed. by Birte Giesler, Eva Kormann, Ana Kugli and Gaby Pailer (Heidelberg: Winter, 2004), pp. 197–227. Gloria A. Biamonthe, 'Funny, Isn't It? Testing the Boundaries of Gender and Genre in Women's Detective Fiction', in *Look Who's Laughing. Gender and Comedy*, ed. by Gail Finney (Amsterdam: Gordon and Breach, 1994), pp. 231–254. Lizabeth Paravasini and Carlos Yorio, 'Is It or Isn't It? The Duality of Parodic Detective Fiction', in *Comic Crime*, ed. by Earl F. Bargainnier (Bowling Green: Bowling Green State University Popular Press, 1987), pp. 181–193.

17 Doris Gercke, *Weinschröter, du mußt hängen* (Hamburg: Galgenberg, 1988), p. 14. German original: 'Ich stand da und begriff, daß sie über mich lachten und bei der erstbesten Gelegenheit damit angeben würden, wie sie mich reingelegt hatten. Ich haßte sie so, daß ich mich von neuem übergab. [...] Ich bring' sie um, dachte ich immer wieder. / Bis mir klar wurde, daß das wirklich die einzige Lösung war'.

resolves to take revenge. As the plot develops, she kills all three people involved in the crime. An interwoven plotline concerns police inspector Bella Block's travels to the small rural town in which two homicides, masked as suicides, have already occurred. Block determines who the perpetrator is, but rather than turning her in, lets her commit a third murder, then quits her job right after. In contrast to the abused woman, Bella is sexually and emotionally independent and stable, in spite of the fact that she operates within a traditionally male institution: the German Police. For example, she recalls a field trip to a crime museum together with her squad, where they saw photographs from a sodomitic rape scene. Her male colleagues, rather than expressing disgust at the act and empathy with the victim, show an attitude of brutality and contempt for humans in general and women in particular.[18]

For Bella, the police apparatus represents a reactionary and male-dominated societal system, which re-manifests itself in the functionalisation and exploitation of the female body. She experiences this via the numerous attempts by her colleagues to turn her into the object of their sexual desire. Block's body and mind, however, claim their space within and at the same time against the patriarchal system. In her early fifties already, she is neither naïve nor dainty – five feet nine in height, she weighs 165 pounds. The female investigator is 'idealized' in that she denies any form of compliance with the system and thus expresses herself through her lifestyle, which involves the frequent changing of both flats and lovers. Other female characters in the novel are depicted as collaborators, for example the police office staff and the townswomen. The abused woman herself has to be completely destroyed before she is able to realize the need to strike back. All spaces, societal and personal, are occupied by the patriarchal system, leaving Bella Block no secure realm other than that of her own body.

Considering comic strategies, Gercke's novel works with subject-object switches, especially by turning the rape victim into a triple murderess, and this under the eyes of the female police investigator, who, by the same token, takes her revenge on the police apparatus for coercing her into complying with the cultural norm of male supremacy. Hans-Robert Jauß distinguishes three principal types of comic heroes: the 'anti-heroes' (laughed *at* and thus turned into an object), the 'humoresque' (laughing *with* from a position of subject) and the 'grotesque' (subverting societal norms by conflict between body and language).[19] In *Weinschröter*, Bella Block represents the 'humoresque', the male

---

18 Gercke, *Weinschröter*, p. 50.
19 Hans Robert Jauß, 'Über den Grund des Vergnügens an komischen Helden', in *Das Komische*, ed. by Preisendanz/Warning, pp. 103–132.

objects of revenge the 'anti-heroes' and the abused woman the 'grotesque'. The laughter evoked by Gercke's novel is a bitter one; the mode of narration is sarcasm. Poking fun at gender and power relations is a sensitive matter and perhaps, as this novel at least seems to suggest, no laughing matter at all.[20]

After the success of *Weinschröter*, Gercke continued to produce novels with Bella Block as a private investigator who becomes increasingly frustrated and depressed. Her protagonist was also turned into a TV detective, with the first episode, 'Die Kommissarin' [The Detective Inspector*], appearing in 1993 under the direction of Max Fährböck and starring Hannelore Hoger. In contrast to her literary counterpart, the filmic Bella Block remains in the police service, and the plotline's comedic aspects come more to the fore on screen. The dual structure of alternating crime story and detective work derives from the subgenre of the *Soziokrimi* [sociological crime fiction][21] that emerged during the 1960s, both in literary and televised form. The longest lasting TV series *Tatort* [*Crime Scene**] seems prototypical and has been quite influential in terms of the literary development of the German crime genre.[22] Over the past two decades, this crime franchise, which rotates between various German cities and focuses on different police teams, has increasingly featured female investigators, most of them 'idealized', albeit lonely, heroines like Bella Block, operating within heteronormatively contaminated landscapes of Federal German 'reality'.

Pieke Biermann's *Herzrasen*[23] [*Racing Heart**], from 1993, takes place shortly after German reunification. It starts with a disaster scene: a house is on

---

20 Regarding the question of gender and laughter more generally, a number of excellent studies have been provided: Cf. Helga Kotthoff, 'Vom Lächeln der Mona Lisa zum Lachen der Hyänen', in *Das Gelächter der Geschlechter. Humor und Macht in Gesprächen von Frauen und Männern*, ed. by Helga Kotthoff (Konstanz: Universitätsverlag, 1995), pp. 121–163. Rose Laub Coser, 'Lachen in der Fakultät', in *Das Gelächter der Geschlechter*, ed. by Kotthoff, pp. 97–120. Judy Little, *Comedy and the Woman Writer. Woolf, Spark, and Feminism* (Lincoln: University of Nebraska Press, 1983). *Look Who's Laughing. Gender and Comedy*, ed. by Gail Finney (Amsterdam: Gordon and Breach, 1994).

21 For more on the *Soziokrimi*, see chapter 4.

22 *Zwischen Serie und Werk. Fernseh- und Gesellschaftsgeschichte im 'Tatort'*, ed. by Christian Hißnauer, Stefan Scherer and Claudia Stockinger (Bielefeld: Transcript, 2014). Another new volume dealing with the media history of the German crime genre is: *Tatort Germany. The Curious Case of German-Language Crime Fiction*, ed. by Lynn M. Kutch and Todd Herzog (Rochester, NY: Camden House, 2014).

23 Biermann, Pieke, *Herzrasen* (Berlin: Rotbuch, 1993).

fire, a little boy has been mutilated, a woman tries to shelter a little girl under her coat, and neo-fascists are brutally entering a building. It is suddenly revealed that police chief Karin Lietze is only dreaming. She gets up, takes a shower and faces reality. This opening scene, entitled 'Ouvertüre' [overture], immediately marks the difference between the novel's good and evil figures. According to the awakening policewoman: 'The heartless heroes crumbled like stardust.'[24] Following this pattern, the evil party in the story is reduced to failing acts that lead to comic relief. The baby-killer turns out to be the child's own father, Christian Eube, a neo-fascist pimp, who gets delicately injured in his 'private parts' during a fight with a prostitute. Calling his comrades to help, they beat him nearly to death, and the police team can only take his shattered body to the hospital. Obviously, his own acts turn against him, changing him from the subject to the object of brutality.[25] Another comic character is Heinz Klaus Jähder, a Saxon businessman who deals in human organs and is in particular need of a new heart himself. When he meets thirty-year-old Karin Hall, who is weary of life, he hopes to drive her to suicide in order to gain a new pump. Unbeknownst to him, she also has heart problems and finally ends her life jumping from the tower at the Alexanderplatz.

The 'heartless' heroes are all from East Berlin. The novel plays with their names: Jähder, for example, mimics the sound of the word 'jeder' [everyman] in the Saxon vernacular. The infant's mother, who complies with the killer, has the last name Wolter, a Germanized version of the French Enlightenment philosopher Voltaire. Characters like these are typical anti-heroes: their failures invite us to laugh *at* them, which means, on the one hand, to feel psychic relief and, on the other, to morally protest against their criminal activities. Further, the East is portrayed as a world with a very distinct gender hierarchy. The criminals are all males; women are either their collaborators or victims. By contrast, the characters involved in crime detection are all people 'with heart': the team of police for precinct Berlin-Mitte, with Karin Lietze as its head, represents an ideal range of gender identities: Detlev Roboldt is gay, Sonja Schade is lesbian, and Lothar Fritz is heterosexual but certainly not 'macho'. Similarly, the prostitutes of the West-Berlin Tiergarten area are depicted as self-conscious and politically responsible characters; they run their own business and fight the new pimps who are coercing women from Eastern Europe into prostitution. In terms

---

24 Biermann, *Herzrasen*, p. 11. German original: 'Die herzlosen Helden fielen in sich zusammen wie Sternenstaub'.
25 Cf. Biermann, *Herzrasen*, pp. 207–210.

of the comic, East Berlin is represented by anti-heroes, West Berlin by humoresque characters, and Karin Hall, we might conclude, represents the grotesque.

Regarding the detective mode, Gercke and Biermann share a critique of female acquiescence to the patriarchal system while at the same time exposing public and private spaces as occupied by traditional notions of male supremacy. In Gercke's *Weinschröter*, a utopian perspective arises through Bella Block's awareness of her own body as the only site from which she can draw the strength to stand up to and – as her apt name suggests – form a 'lovely bloc' against the system. In Biermann's *Herzrasen*, the utopian perspective arises from new forms of social interaction based on a multiplicity of gender identities and orientations that break with the heteronormative model of two distinct and definable 'sexes'.

The thriller mode

Dagmar Scharsich's *Die gefrorene Charlotte*[26] [*The Frozen Charlotte*], also from 1993, takes place during the last months of the German Democratic Republic, from August to November 1989. It tells the story of a naïve young woman, Cora Ost, who works as a hospital librarian in East Berlin. Her aunt, her last living relative, bequeaths her a valuable doll collection that is soon to become an object of desire for two people: Dr. Brendel, a representative of the state-supported company Trade-Unimex, which confiscates antiques and sells them to the West; and Markus Behnesch, a Stasi collaborator who hunts Dr. Brendel for revenge. They both make Cora believe that they are partial to her and want to work to her benefit. A hospital professor and a policeman from the Volkspolizei help Cora to unravel their real motives.

The protagonist is a typical comic character of the grotesque kind, a fact marked both by her apt name, Cora Ost [Cora East] and by a certain tic: her mouth is always open, which she only realizes when reminded by others to close her mouth. The tic symbolizes Cora's frozen status, a result of having lived for thirty years in the GDR. She resembles the set of seven puppets, the 'gefrorene Charlotten' [frozen Charlottes] from her aunt's collection, paralyzed in the act of speaking. Though the narrative is told from Cora's point of view, she never seems to be in a subject position but rather the object of others, especially men. Only in the end does she learn to use her tic as a means by which to trick others and thus save her own life. Through most of the novel, she is

---

26 Scharsich, Dagmar, *Die gefrorene Charlotte* (Hamburg: Ariadne, 1993).

completely oblivious to the entanglement of personal and political affairs around her, and especially to the fact that *she* is the key to the story. To name just two examples of her 'comic failures': after Brendel has invited her to a chic Western-style hotel, offering original French cognac to drink, she dreams of sitting with him on her old sofa watching TV and drinking the GDR liqueur Goldbrand. Moreover, when Behnesch, who pretends to be partial to her, gives her a black party dress and high heels as presents, she wears them to work the next day.

Brendel and Behnesch are GDR officials who work for their own profit, selling out East German goods and legacies to the West. The confrontation between the criminals and the supposed victim is thus more of an East-East confrontation than an East-West one. Whereas the protagonist is female, her pursuers or helpers are all male. Other women either die, like her aunt, or flee to the West, like her colleague Marion. The East-West confrontation only comes into play indirectly in that the proto-Western invasion takes place in the form of sexual seduction and deception. Laughter functions in this novel as social protest against the corrupt GDR system, however, without suggesting that the West is a better world.

Ingrid Noll's *Der Hahn ist tot*[27] [*The Rooster is Dead**] from 1991 presents a protagonist who breaks out of her ordinary life by turning into a serial murderess: fifty-two-year-old Rosemarie Hirte has a crush on her 'Volkshochschuldozent' [continuing education lecturer] and becomes obsessed with the idea of having him. Working as a facilitator for an insurance company, she is surrounded by a hierarchical system dominated by men. While she works neatly, does exactly as ordered and takes meticulous care of her outer appearance, she has never received much recognition:

> I earn a decent income, I keep up fine. At fifty-two I look better than in my youth. God, when I look at the pictures from back then! A good twenty pounds too heavy, those unbecoming glasses, the ungainly lace-up shoes and that folklore skirt [...]. Why didn't anyone tell me there are other options! [...] Today I am slim and well-groomed, my dresses, my perfume and more than anything my shoes are expensive. Has it gotten me anywhere?[28]

---

27 Noll, Ingrid, *Der Hahn ist tot. Roman* (Zurich: Diogenes, 1993) [first 1991].
28 Noll, *Der Hahn ist tot*, p. 7. German original: 'Ich verdiene gut, ich halte mich gut. Mit meinen zweiundfünfzig Jahren sehe ich besser aus als in meiner Jugend. Mein Gott, wenn ich die Fotos von damals sehe! Gute zwanzig Pfund zuviel, eine unvorteilhafte Brille, diese plumpen Schnürschuhe und der Bordürenrock [...]. Warum hat mir damals keiner gesagt, daß es auch anders geht! [...] Heute bin ich schlank und gepflegt, meine Kleider, mein Parfum und erst recht meine Schuhe sind teuer. Hat es was gebracht?'

Of course, this is a rhetorical question. Clearly, her professional skills, flawless work ethic and perfect appearance have not brought her what she deems most important: a man. While other women her age have or had families, and have raised children, she laments that she has not even had a miscarriage. Her deficient concept of self is mirrored in her apartment: adhering to every possible norm of homey ambience, it is the precise opposite of the kind of place that others would like to visit, let alone stay. Her self-awareness remains on the body's surface.

The plot turns macabre, when Rosemarie starts killing women attached to or interested in her male object of desire, the lecturer Rainer Witold Engstern. She starts snooping around his house at night, eliminating his wife first, next her own friend Scarlett and then another competitor, Vivian.[29] With her apparently ordinary, petit bourgeois lifestyle, Rosemarie manages for a long time to fool the police, which allows her to lead a murderous double existence à la Jekyll/Hyde. For her, it is not about love, but about her obsession with her desired object, whom she calls 'Witold', reserving his middle name for herself alone. Rosemarie is a grotesque character, an over-achiever both professionally and personally; she perfectly plays the social role of a woman her age and her single status. Ultimately, Witolt ends up under her control, however with the bitter irony that he is paralyzed. An accident that she caused, at least partially, renders him deprived of his physical and mental health; he is taken care of in a sanatorium, where she visits him:

> They put his wind jacket on, a strong nurse heaves him into the wheelchair. I kneel in front of him and close his zipper. Then I start pushing him. Sometimes I tell him that I was once very much in love with him.[30]

Rosemarie Hirte is a dangerous character, yet not powerful. Her notion of empowerment is based on the over-fulfilment of patriarchal norms and a deficient concept of self. In contrast to Rosemarie, her three female victims have a partner or husband, but define themselves less as 'relative creatures'

---

29 The choice of the names Scarlett and Vivian clearly hints at the protagonist and actress of the movie *Gone with the Wind*, Scarlett O'Hara and Vivian Leigh signifying the spectacularly ruthless enchantress who marries three men in order to keep the one she is really after as close as possible.

30 Noll, p. 266. German original: 'Man zieht ihm die Windjacke über, eine starke Schwester hievt ihn in den Rollstuhl. Ich knie vor ihm und mache ihm den Reißverschluß zu. Dann schiebe ich mit ihm los. Manchmal erzähle ich ihm, daß ich ihn einmal sehr geliebt habe'.

within the patriarchal norms than she does. After killing three women, she boasts of killing a man – a policeman suspicious of her – as a new level of achievement.[31] Turning herself from an object of societal norms to the subject of her own actions, she has turned her desired man into an object of medical care. Yet, the more she kills, the more her own body suffers and is gradually eaten up by cancer. The novel centres on a woman who switches from being the victim of societal expectations to being a perpetrator. Male supremacy is ridiculed, as quoted in the title, which refers to the children's song 'Der Hahn ist tot … ' [the rooster is dead, deriving from the French 'Le coq est mort'], however, there is no positive vision of new gender identities beyond hetero-normative traditions of thought, and a single existence becomes the object of derision rather than being idealized.[32]

Differently from the novels in the detective mode, in those following the thriller mode, the protagonists appear rather 'grotesque' and do not represent any new utopian place of identity. Scharsich's Cora Ost is oblivious to her own role as the key to a series of crimes. It is, ironically, precisely on account of her naïve compliance with the cultural codes that she learned in the GDR that she is able to render her male adversaries objects of derision.[33] Noll's Rosemarie Hirte forms a remarkable Western counterpart to Cora Ost, a woman who sys-tematically miscomprehends her own desires; consumed as she is by her exag-gerated efforts to climb the pedestal of societal recognition by gaining herself a man, she destroys her desired object along with herself.

The crime and catastrophe mode

Sabine Weigand's historical novel *Die Markgräfin*[34] [*The Marquise**] from 2004 combines a contemporary detective plot with the recounting of the life of

---

31 Cf. Noll, *Der Hahn ist tot*, p. 241.
32 The leitmotif of female criminal possession of a male is reminiscent of Stephen King's *Misery* (New York: Viking Press, 1987), and the film comedy *Serial Mom*, dir. John Waters (USA 1994) also comes to mind. Another novel in German to consider for comparison is Ulla Hahn's *Ein Mann im Haus* (Stuttgart: DVA, 1991), in which a rape victim seeks revenge on the rapist.
33 Scharsich tries to continue this pattern with her next crime novel, however, the emplot-ment of everyday gender issues with a protagonist who suffers mainly from migraines trying to unravel events of the GDR past does not carry much suspense. Cf. Dagmar Scharsich, *Verbotene Stadt* (Hamburg: Ariadne, 2002).
34 Weigand, Sabine, *Die Markgräfin. Roman*, 2nd edn. (Frankfurt a.M.: Fischer Taschenbuch, 2010). [first Frankfurt a.M.: Krüger, 2004].

a sixteenth-century noblewoman, Barbara von Brandenburg-Ansbach, which increasingly turns into a thriller. The detective plot stretches from December 2001 to January 2003; the historical plot unfolds between 1526 and 1546. Both alternating narrative strands share the same main location, the fortress Plassenburg near Bayreuth. The novel is subdivided into three books, chapters are titled with dates and places, and both narratives interweave 'documentary' materials such as letters, bills and certificates.

The contemporary action opens with the discovery of an infant's corpse in the basement of the Plassenburg during renovation work. Curator Gregor Haubold immediately calls a meeting of his group of four hobby researchers, the 'Forschenden Vier', the other three members being a priest, an archivist and a teacher. The archival search to solve the riddle of the sixteenth-century child murder turns into Haubold's pastime project, during which he not only discovers a secret escape tunnel, but also another skeleton, this time an adult missing a leg. About midway into the novel, the group grows to six members, now including the young curator of a small ethnological museum, Thomas Fleischmann, and the archival assistant Geli Hufnagel, who grow partial to each other over the course of the investigation.

The historical action unfolds chronologically: at the age of ten, Marquise Barbara is married to the Duke of Glogau, who dies two years later. Her next suitor is the King of Poland who, however, never takes the bride home; the nuptials are merely a paper transaction and only targeted at territorial gain. Now in her twenties, Barbara takes her next marriage into her own hands and appeals to the Pope to annul her Polish marriage. Her two brothers, Georg and Albrecht, both now Dukes of Brandenburg-Ansbach, are outraged over this, especially the younger Albrecht, the 'Bavarian Alcibiades', a fierce warlord, who locks up his sister in the Plassenburg. The captive Marquise-Duchess-Queen Barbara, who denies her brother the signature required to dissolve the new betrothal, becomes physically and mentally ill. Only after two young girls are recruited as chambermaids does Barbara regain her strength and health, even growing into a mature beauty. The leitmotif and leading clue for the detectives in the contemporary action is a panoramic mural in the Plassenburg, which depicts a war scene and, interestingly, a female figure standing on a turret; her mark of distinction is a broken finger.[35] The narrative's final section stages

---

35 This injured finger forms the main link for her identification between the contemporary and historical action: it is first noticed by Haubold on the mural (Weigand, p. 162f.); then on the smaller portrait (p. 210). In the historical action, Barbara has an altercation with her brother Albrecht; he slams the door in wrath, impinging her finger (p. 332). Finally, it is mentioned during the Italian artist's work on both the mural and the portrait (p. 537f.).

a love story. The new priest Jakob Tiefenthalter and Barbara fall for each other; she gives birth to twins, of whom she can only rescue one. The other infant is condemned to death by her brother Albrecht, the executioner being his and Barbara's childhood friend Georg von Leuchtenberg who, after losing a leg in combat, has been installed as commander-in-chief at the fortress. Upon Barbara and her friends' escape through the secret tunnel during the 'Bundesständischen Krieg' (a regional feudal war in 1554), they run into Georg, who is horrified to see that the baby he thought he killed is alive and well again, and Barbara, enraged to recognize in him the murderer of her baby, stabs him to death. Hence, the riddles of the infant corpse and the one-legged skeleton are revealed to the reader and ultimately solved by the hobby detectives.

Both the contemporary detective plot and the historical action play together to reveal ever more contours in the maturing heroine and her female empowerment. Barbara is indeed characterized by quite modern notions of class and gender: for example, she treats her bourgeois maids as peers and, furthermore, identifies (and tolerates) Albrecht's homosexuality. Her intellectual curiosity and general openness stem from her first marriage to the elderly Duke of Glogau, an alchemist possessed of a passionate thirst for knowledge, who also playfully introduced the young princess to sexuality. Anachronisms in the depiction of mentalities are fairly typical for the historical genre: in Weigand's novel, the historical heroine and her allies – that is, her chambermaids, her lover Tiefenthalter, the painter Neri and another priest – are all characterized by a 'modern' mentality, while her adversaries, especially Albrecht and Georg, are depicted as rather 'atavistic' in both their behaviour and thought.

Weigand alters historical facts, notably by making Barbara Albrecht's sister, as opposed to his aunt, which she really was. She justifies this (in her afterword) with the lack of knowledge about historical women and the need to re-imagine plausible characters. In research on the historical novel– as in research on crime fiction – women authors tend to be treated differently to men.[36] What often gets overlooked is that *all* historical novels, and not only those by women, are 're-writing history', some by inventing alternate histories, others by combining historical fiction with crime and detection plots. In Weigand's *Die Markgräfin*, the

---

36 For more genre context on women's historical novels cf. Gaby Pailer, 'Frauen im Turm. Geschichtserzählung und Geschlechterverhältnis bei Felicitas Hoppe, Viola Roggenkamp und Sabine Weigand', in *Vergegenwärtigte Vergangenheiten. Romanhaftes Geschichtserzählen im beginnenden 21. Jahrhundert*, ed. by Daniel Fulda and Stephan Jaeger, in collaboration with Elena Agazzi. Berlin: De Gruyter, 2019 (forthcoming).

dual structure of contemporary detection and historical plot seems fairly unusual. Whereas the action in the historical thriller is increasingly suspenseful, the detection plot contains more comic aspects, with the hobby detectives serving as humoresque characters. Interestingly, the gender critique is more to be found in the historical action, while the contemporary detective plot remains fairly affirmative of existing gender and power structures.

Alina Bronsky's acclaimed bestseller *Baba Dunjas letzte Liebe* [*Baba Dunja's Last Love*],[37] from 2015, may not at first sight appear to be a work of 'crime fiction', but I would like to consider it as such, especially in light of an intertextual reference to Dostoevsky, Fyodor Mikhailovich. The novel deploys the motifs of murder, investigation and trial within the setting of the aftermath of the April 1986 Chernobyl disaster, taking place in the village of Tschernowo. The protagonist and first-person narrator is a lady in her eighties, whose full name, Evdokija Anatoljewna,[38] the reader only learns towards the end. For most of the novel, she is addressed as 'Baba Dunja', the commonly accepted leader of the contaminated township.[39]

The novel begins with Baba Dunja's annoyance at her neighbour Marja's rooster Konstantin, whom Marja treats – and who consequently behaves – like a surrogate husband bossing the entire village around. Despite Baba Dunja's history as a caregiver – she used to be a nurse – she 'has today decided to become a murderer. Konstantin is a stupid creature, always making such a racket for no reason.'[40] Konstantin's murder proves unnecessary, though, since he suddenly dies at the very moment she is about to grab him. This mock murder scene precedes a real homicide, or casualty, the event that forms the peak and turning point of the story: Baba Dunja has assigned a new settler with his little daughter an empty house. She later talks with Marja about the girl, wondering why the stranger would bring a healthy child into the death zone. Rather upset, the old woman challenges the irresponsible father, which leads to an altercation and, ultimately, to his death:

---

37 Bronsky, Alina, *Baba Dunjas letzte Liebe. Roman*, 11th edn. (Cologne: Kiepenheuer & Witsch, 2016). [first 2015; audiobook: *Sophie Rois liest Baba Dunjas letzte Liebe* (Bochum: tacheles! Roof Music GmbH, 2015)]. English translation: Bronsky, Alina, *Baba Dunja's Last Love*. Translated by Tim Mohr (Kindle Edition) 2016.
38 Bronsky, *Baba Dunjas letzte Liebe*, p. 133.
39 Bronsky, *Baba Dunjas letzte Liebe*, p. 49.
40 Bronsky, *Baba Dunja's Last Love*, pos. 28. German original, p. 7: 'beschließt, eine Mörderin zu werden'.

He kicks me with in the side with all his weight, his face looks distorted. His fingers close around my throat. I hear myself wheezing. How quiet two people can be when one is in the process of killing the other.

Jegor stands behind him, crying.

What happens next I don't understand at first. A dry snap out of nowhere. The man, who never introduced himself by name, stands up straight and lurches. For a second he stands there in a contorted, unnatural position. Then he falls to the ground, right next to me.

Against my will I suddenly start to moan. When a strong man just falls over like that it's always a fright. My first imperative is to stand up. I roll onto my left side and then onto my stomach. Next I get to my knees and brace myself with my hands. I crawl over to the fallen man.

'Sir, what is with you, sir?'

His face is lying in a pool of blood. There's a hatchet stuck in his skull. I look over at Jegor, who is holding his hands up as if to say: You can see for yourself that I'm unarmed. I kneel there groaning with pain and my gaze wanders slowly through the dark, against which a figure slowly starts to form.

'Petrow,' I say. 'You swine'[41]

The manner of narration of this episode is Baba Dunja's personal perspective communicated in the present tense and in real time.[42] The small axe creates a link to Dostoevsky's novel *Crime and Punishment*,[43] in which the Petersburg student Raskolnikov murders the elderly pawnshop dealer Aljona Ivanovna (and her sister) with a hatchet. The crime triggers a game of cat-and-mouse

---

41 Bronsky, *Baba Dunja's Last Love*, pos. 688–700. German original, p. 68f.: 'Er tritt mir mit voller Wucht in die linke Seite, sein Gesicht ist verzerrt. Seine Finger schließen sich um meinen Hals. Ich höre mich röcheln. Dass zwei so leise sein können, wenn einer von ihnen den anderen gerade umbringt. / Jegor steht hinter ihm und weint. / Was dann passiert, verstehe ich zuerst nicht. Ein trockenes Knacken aus dem Nichts. Der Mann, der sich mir nicht mit Namen vorgestellt hat, richtet sich auf und taumelt. Einen Augenblick steht er in einer verrenkten, widernatürlichen Haltung da. Dann stürzt er zu Boden, und zwar nur knapp neben mich. / Ganz gegen meinen Willen beginne ich plötzlich zu jammern. Wenn ein starker Mann einfach so hinfällt, dann ist das immer ein Schreck. Es gilt aber erst einmal selbst aufzustehen. Ich rolle mich auf die linke Seite und dann auf den Bauch. Als Nächstes gehe ich auf die Knie und stütze mich mit den Händen ab. Ich krieche zu dem Mann, der umgefallen ist. / 'Herr, was ist mit dir, Herr?' / Sein Kopf liegt mit dem Gesicht in einer Blutlache. In seinem Schädel steckt eine kleine Axt. Ich sehe zu Jegor rüber, der die Hände hebt, als wollte er sagen: Du siehst doch, ich bin unbewaffnet. Ich knie mich stöhnend hin, und mein Blick wandert langsam durch die Dunkelheit, aus der sich ein Umriss löst. / 'Petrow', sage ich, 'Petrow, du Schwein.' Paragraph breaks are marked by slash.

42 Notably, there is some similarity to Friedrich Schiller's *Der Verbrecher aus verlorener Ehre* (*The Criminal of Lost Honour*) (cf. endnote 4). The protagonist switches to first-person narrator and real-time motion, when recounting the scene of his first and only homicide.

43 Fyodor Dostoevsky, *Crime and Punishment*, transl. by Constance Garnett with an introduction by Joseph Frank (New York: Bantam Dell, 2003).

between him and the police investigator Porify, who is always just one step behind. Meanwhile, Raskolnikov makes the acquaintance of the Marmeladov family, especially the daughter Sonja, whom her alcoholic father forces into prostitution. Another girl in need of protection from male aggressors is Raskolnikov's sister Avdotya. In the end, Raskolnikov atones for his trespasses: he is sent to the labour camps of Siberia, where Sonya follows him.

Bronsky's novel toys with the motif of a murder plot (of the rooster Konstantin) and the actual murder scene (Petrow coming to Baba Dunja's rescue) in reference to *Crime and Punishment*. In addition, it makes reference to another work by Dostoevsky, *The Idiot*, by means of the daughter's first name, 'Aglaia', which leads Baba Dunja to reason as to why 'they name little girls like ancient women in the capitals these days'.[44] As in *Crime and Punishment*, there are two girls in distress in *Baba Dunja*: not only the little girl Aglaia, but also the protagonist's granddaughter Laura, whom she only knows through her daughter Irina's letters from Germany (where the latter works as a physician). Laura, who must be in her teenage years, has run away from home, writing Baba Dunja a letter in English, which she carries about, unable to read it. It is in jail – where Baba Dunja finds herself after taking responsibility for the manslaughter so that her fellow villagers can go free – that she learns the basics of the English language from a fellow inmate. She makes the letter's full translation her project, returning to Tschernowo once released from jail rather than accepting medical treatment in Germany as her daughter has arranged. Her return to the death zone compares to Raskolnikov's atonement in Siberia, with the ironic twist that the old woman is not the murderess she claims to be, has nothing to atone for and chose jail over freedom, at least temporarily.

The murder episode also shows Baba Dunja's perception of her fellow humans in Tschernowo: fluid boundaries exist between those who are 'still alive' (like Baba Dunja and Marja); others with translucent skin, who are 'nearly dead' (such as Petrow), and an increasing number of 'living dead' (apparitions of deceased ones, such as her husband Jegor). Time frames oscillate between the present, the time 'before the reactor'[45] (i.e. before 1986) and Baba Dunja's youth. Her perspective is grotesque, since her female empowerment and dignity as the leader of the village community comes only in old age, amidst the post-disaster reality of the Chernobyl reactor accident. By switching between times, Bronsky interweaves a critical view of gender and power relations in the public

---

44 Bronsky, *Baba Dunja's Last Love*, pos. 605. German original, p. 60: 'dass kleine Mädchen in den Hauptstädten heutzutage wie uralte Leute heißen'.
45 Bronsky, *Baba Dunja's Last Love*, pos. 236 et passim. German original, p. 25 et passim: 'vor dem Reaktor'.

as well as the private sphere in the longer term. It is with wry laughter that one reads her account of the flourishing flora and fauna triggered by nuclear radiation, rendering all her attempts at sustainable living and the preservation of natural resources – for example, she gains juice from the bark of birch trees without harming the trunks – entirely futile. Remarkably, the novel's cover shows a middle-aged woman in worker's attire standing next to a birch tree against a deceptively peaceful turquois background.

Both Weigand and Bronsky combine crime and catastrophe plots with aspects of detection and thrill, presenting a narrative upheaval of heteronormative gender expectations and biases. Weigand revitalizes a historical war zone, amidst which a sixteenth-century noblewoman is able to create for herself and her circle of friends a new identity (focused on modern values of tolerance, diversity and solidarity), which is set against the historical 'normality' of male supremacy. Remarkably, the contemporary detective plot has more comedic, yet less gender-critical aspects. Alina Bronsky combines the catastrophe theme with questions of crime and justice under the new preconditions of life and death in the Chernobyl disaster zone. Her witty and grotesque heroine Baba Dunja actually puts the boasting and self-righteous 'cock' to rest twice – a farewell to all the 'nearly dead' or 'living dead' males haunting the contaminated landscape, in which she, in her mid-eighties, experiences the time of her life.

Thomas W. Kniesche
7 Crime Fiction as Memory Discourse: Historical Crime Fiction from Germany

Mystery novels set in a more or less distant past have been enjoying tremendous popularity. This is true of historical crime fiction written in English[1] as well as for such texts by German-speaking authors. As the bibliographies by Palmer and Burgess/Vassilakos[2] show, by the beginning of the twenty-first century, historical crime fiction covered historical epochs from ancient Egypt to the early decades of the previous century. Although some of the writers belonging to the 'golden age' of crime fiction writing from the 1920s to the 1950s, such as Agatha Christie, John Dickson Carr and Josephine Tey, had already contributed to the sub-genre, historical crime fiction really took off at the beginning of the 1980s, after the international success of Umberto Eco's medieval bestseller *The Name of the Rose* (Italian original 1980, translated into English 1983). The reasons for this kind of popularity are manifold and will be discussed briefly later on, when we delve into historical crime fiction by German-speaking authors.

As is the case with historical novels, historical crime fiction forms a wide and differentiated field, from mass produced entertainment that uses historical background merely as ornamentation to sophisticated texts that probe the breadth and reliability of historiography or even question the very possibility of historical knowledge itself. The similarities between detective and historian have now been under discussion for some time.[3] Both want to know what really happened or, to quote the nineteenth-century historian Leopold von Ranke's

---

1 For overviews of historical crime fiction by English-speaking authors, see: Chapter 9 'Historical Mysteries' in Hans Bertens, Theo D'haen, *Contemporary American Crime Fiction* (Houndmills/Hampshire, New York: Palgrave, 2001), pp. 146–159 and Ray B. Browne, 'Historical Crime and Detection', in *A Companion to Crime Fiction*, ed. by Charles J. Rzepka and Lee Horsley (Chichester: Wiley-Blackwell, 2010), pp. 222–232. A brief introduction to the theoretical aspects of historical crime fiction can be found in chapter 6 of John Scaggs, *Crime Fiction* (London and New York: Routledge, 2005), pp. 122–143.

2 Jennifer S. Palmer, 'Mysteries of the Ages. Four Millenia of Murder and Mayhem in Historical Mysteries', *The Armchair Detective*, (30) 1997, pp. 156–164; *Murder in Retrospect. A Selective Guide to Historical Mystery Fiction*, ed. by Michael Burgess and Jill H. Vassilakos (Westport: Libraries Unlimited, 2005).

3 Cf. *The Historian as Detective. Essays on Evidence*, ed. by Robin W. Winks (New York et. al.: Harper & Row, 1968); *The Detective as Historian. History and Art in Historical Crime Fiction*, ed. by Ray B. Browne and Laurence A. Kreiser (Bowling Green: Bowling Green State University Popular Press, 2000).

https://doi.org/10.1515/9783110426601-007

famous ambition, to know 'wie es eigentlich gewesen'.[4] Ranke's objective for the historian might be considered outdated in light of recent debates regarding the limitations to historical knowledge, the challenges historians are facing and the opportunities that result from a new understanding of historiography,[5] but the fictional detective's ultimate goal is still to find out 'whodunit' or what really happened.[6] Both crime fiction and historiography are based on the desire to find out about the past, and both (re-)construct a narrative of the past to fulfil that desire.

Before we delve deeper into the intricacies of historical crime fiction, we should come to an understanding of what it is we are looking at. Historical crime fiction is a combination of historical fact and criminal fiction. Or, to be more precise: historical crime fiction is a narrative that embeds fictional crime and fictional characters within a framework of circumstances, characters and events that are recognized and accepted as historically authentic and accurate. The historically accepted framework of a 'true' environment might be more or less fully developed in historical crime fiction, but it will always proceed from generally accepted historical knowledge and exploit the fact that this kind of knowledge is always incomplete and leaves open a multitude of options. We might know, for example, who ruled a certain country during a specific part of the thirteenth century and we might even have a pretty good idea of the people surrounding this ruler and what the social and cultural life of that epoch looked like. We do not know, however, who else was around during that time: who were the common people, those whom the history books do not mention? What did they do? How did they live their lives? What motivated them? Here, there is much room for invention and imagination, and this is where historical crime fiction comes into its own. Similar to the historical novel, historical crime fiction is therefore based in part on what (we think) really happened and in part on what might have happened, thereby, as the hybrid genre that it is, once again bringing together the history and literature that Aristotle separated in his *Poetics*.[7]

---

4 Leopold von Ranke, *Geschichte der romanischen und germanischen Völker von 1494–1514*, *Sämtliche Werke* vol. 33/34 (Leipzig: Duncker und Humblot, 1885), p. 7. 'how it really was'.

5 The 'linguistic turn' in the philosophy of history was largely responsible for this rethinking, most notably in the work of Hayden White and Louis O. Mink in the 1970s and 80s. More recently, deconstructionist historians such as Robert A. Rosenstone, Alun Munslow, Simon Schama and Jonathan Spence have continued this line of work.

6 However, this claim has become an object of critical challenges, mostly in so-called 'metaphysical', 'postmodern' or 'anti' detective stories. A good example is Umberto Eco's already mentioned novel *The Name of the Rose*, in which the very possibility of ultimately arriving at 'the truth' is rejected by the detective-figure in the end.

7 *Poetics* 1451b; Aristotle, *Poetics*, trans. by Anthony Kenny (Oxford: Oxford University Press, 2013), p. 28.

Types of historical crime fiction

Historical crime fiction can be divided into two large groups: historical crime fiction proper and 'retrospective' or 'trans-historical' crime fiction. John Scaggs defines the two groups thusly: 'The first is crime fiction that is set in some distinct historical period, but which was not written in that period. The second is crime fiction that has a detective in the present investigating a crime in the remote, rather than recent, past.'[8] A more precise distinction between the two types is offered by Achim Saupe: differentiating between the 'story of the crime' and the 'story of the investigation (of the crime)' – a structural distinction or 'duality'[9] that is 'at the base' of every detective story – Saupe defines a historical crime novel as one in which both the story of the crime and the story of the investigation belong to the same temporal or historical register: both are set in the past.[10] In the 'retrospective' (or trans-historical) crime novel, on the other hand, the story of the investigation is set in the present time, the present of the author and the reader, whereas the story of the crime is set in a more or less distant past. Saupe stresses that the retrospective/trans-historical crime novel is much closer to (post)modern 'meta-historic' fiction, in which the very processes of remembering, of exploring the past, of mediating history themselves undergo critical scrutiny.[11]

Whereas historical crime fiction is popular both in Anglophone countries and in Germany, trans-historical crime fiction enjoys a much higher grade of popularity in Germany than in the English-speaking world, where novels such

---

8 Scaggs, *Crime Fiction*, pp. 145–146. Scaggs's 'trans-historical' follows Murphy's terminology, cf. Bruce F. Murphy, *The Encyclopedia of Murder and Mystery* (New York: St. Martin's Press, 1999), p. 247.

9 It was Tzvetan Todorov who discussed the duality of these two stories as 'the story of the crime and the story of the investigation' or a 'first story' and a 'second story'. See his 'The Typology of Detective Fiction', in *The Poetics of Prose*, trans. by Richard Howard (Ithaca/NY: Cornell University Press, 1977), pp. 42–52 (pp. 44). Scaggs rightly pointed out that in a sense, 'all crime fiction is trans-historical', it just depends on the time that has elapsed between the crime and the investigation (*Crime Fiction*, p. 125).

10 Achim Saupe, *Der Historiker als Detektiv – der Detektiv als Historiker. Historik, Kriminalistik und der Nationalsozialismus als Kriminalroman* (Bielefeld: transcript, 2009), pp. 267–268.

11 Saupe, *Der Historiker als Detektiv.* p. 268. Saupe also mentions two other categories of historical crime fiction, counter-factual crime fiction (Philip K. Dick, *The Man in the High Castle* [1962] or Robert Harris, *Fatherland* [1992], to give just two examples) and documentary crime fiction. Whereas counter-factual crime fiction enjoys some considerable popularity among English-speaking readers, neither group is very important in Germany.

as Josephine Tey's *The Daughter of Time* (1951) or Collin Dexter's *The Wench is Dead* (1989) remain relatively rare exceptions. In contrast, German-speaking authors have written a number of internationally successful trans-historical crime novels that are merely one part of a larger trend in Germany.[12] Bernhard Schlink's *Selb* trilogy belongs to this group (*Selbs Justiz* [1987, *Self's Punishment*], *Selbs Betrug* [1992, *Self's Deception*], *Selbs Mord* [2001, *Self's Murder*]), but also Thomas Hettche's *Der Fall Arbogast* [2001, *The Arbogast Case: A Novel*], the *Stachelmann*-series by Christian von Ditfurth (with *Mann ohne Makel* [2002, *A Paragon of Virtue*] as the first novel in the series), Ferdinand von Schirach's *Der Fall Collini* [2011, *The Collini Case: A Novel*] and Mechthild Borrmann's *Trümmerkind* [2016, *Child of the Rubble**]. With the exception of the last title, all the novels just mentioned have been translated into English. As this list of authors and texts demonstrates, trans-historical crime fiction from Germany is often considered more than just genre literature: it is seen as 'true' literature that is defined by its aesthetic and formal subtleties, rather than by its mere entertainment value. This is especially true of authors like Schlink and Hettche, whose other work is perceived as belonging to the realm of 'high culture'.

There are multiple reasons for contemporary Germany's penchant for trans-historical crime fiction and historical crime fiction in general. According to Michael Braun, memory, remembering and *Erinnerungsliteratur* [memory literature] have become a new paradigm of contemporary German literature.[13] Faced with the fact that the eyewitnesses to the Holocaust and other atrocities are dying out, the work of memory and recording memory takes on a new urgency. Furthermore, after the fall of communism, differing versions of history in the West and in the East compete and, as a result, memory discourse intensifies. Thirdly, memory and historical discourse have become subject to increased mediatization and critical scrutiny. Given these circumstances, crime fiction – with its double narrative of the story of the crime and the story of the investigation – is

---

12 In a quite different context and at a different time, trans-historical crime fiction had become a staple of cultural production long before the texts discussed here. Although not known under that name, trans-historical crime fiction was formulaic in a branch of GDR crime fiction. In these novels, the very existence of crime in a socialist society – that, as a classless society, had supposedly abolished all reasons for committing crimes – could be explained as the result of the actions of former Nazis who either wanted to sabotage the new political system or cover up their Nazi past.

13 Michael Braun, *Die deutsche Gegenwartsliteratur* (Cologne, Weimar, Vienna: Böhlau, 2010), p. 110.

structurally predetermined to delve into the past to explain events in the present. Such a genre and particularly trans-historical crime fiction that has its point of departure in the present but that finds reasons for present crimes in the past must appeal to a desire to elucidate the present by going back into the past. In addition, in the German (and Austrian) crime fiction of the 1980s and 90s, the detective figure was potentially always subject to the question: what did you do during the war? Whether the answer to this question was known or not did not matter. '*Any* German-speaking detective automatically raises the memory of the past.'[14] Bernhard Schlink's private detective Gerhard Selb is a prime example of this dictum. As a former Nazi prosecutor who has distanced himself from his erstwhile beliefs, Selb is ceaselessly confronted with present events that have their roots in Germany's Nazi past.

The function of paratexts in historical crime fiction

Paratexts play an important role in historical crime fiction. Not every historical crime novel uses them, but when they are used, they suggest historical accuracy, veracity and reliability and thus create the impression that what we read is the historical truth. Paratexts come in a variety of forms and media.[15] The kind of paratexts we are concerned with here are organized around the text of the novel itself and consist mostly of dedications, prefaces, postscripts, acknowledgments, footnotes, glossaries and bibliographies. Karl-Heinz Göttert, for example, dedicates his novel *Anschlag auf den Telegraphen* [2004, *Attack on the Telegraph**] to the contributors of the *Kölnische Zeitung* [*Cologne Newspaper*] for their wonderful reporting from January to March 1848, thus revealing one of the primary sources of his historical crime novel. In an afterword, Göttert reviews the historiographical sources he consulted when writing his novel. The use of footnotes and bibliographies is unusual for a fictional text, as we expect these formats to belong to scholarly discourse. When they do occur in a novel, they

---

14 Bruce B. Campbell, 'Justice and Genre: The *Krimi* as a Site of Memory in Contemporary Germany', in *Detectives, Dystopias, and Poplit. Studies in Modern German Genre Fiction*, ed. by Bruce B. Campbell, Alison Guenther-Pal and Vibeke Rützou Petersen (Rochester/NY: Camden House, 2014), pp. 133–151 (p. 133).
15 Cf. Gerard Genette, *Paratexts. Thresholds of Interpretation*, trans. by Jane E. Lewin (Cambridge: Cambridge University Press, 1997).

suggest to us that what we read is based on historical truth, that the story unfolding before us while we read, although it is a fictional account, might have happened exactly as it is told and that we are learning something about history by reading a historical (crime) novel. Another example shows other aspects of how paratexts are put into service to determine the status of the text they surround. In his novel *Unter dem Schatten des Todes* [2012, *Under the Shadow of Death**], Robert Brack provides a glossary of abbreviations for political parties and organizations and for contemporary newspapers of the historical period in which his novel is set, the early 1930s. He also includes a postscript in which he levels harsh criticism against the historians who have written about the burning of the German Reichstag in February of 1933. Brack denounces these historians as mere 'storytellers' and positions his own text, a historical crime novel, in the context of historiographic writing, claiming that his novel is a contribution in its own right to a complex and puzzling debate that has not produced any final verdict on what really happened that night.[16]

The paratexts we have discussed so far are called 'peritexts'. They are part of the book that we are reading. Gérard Genette has identified another type of paratexts, which he called 'epitexts'.[17] Epitexts are texts that 'surround' a text but are not printed together with it, such as interviews, conversations, letters and diaries. A good example of how these epitexts can shape the reading of historical crime fiction is Volker Kutscher's series of novels starring detective inspector Gereon Rath. The series is set in Germany during the late 1920s and early 30s. Kutscher provides a host of epitexts to his novels on the internet site 'Kriminalkommissar Gereon Rath'.[18] The site provides photographic material, information about the books of the series, short descriptions of a whole host of characters that appear in the novels, a short biographical essay about and a lengthy interview with the author, a list of relevant web links and an extensive bibliography on the historical period the novels use as their background, among other things. These epitexts make it possible for the readers of the novels to do their own research on the historical period of the novels and to compare what they read there with documentary material, biographies, contemporary novels and movies, and scholarly work on the period. Kutscher thus positions his

---

16 For a recent scholarly account, cf. Benjamin Carter Hett, *Burning the Reichstag. An Investigation into the Third Reich's Enduring Mystery* (Oxford: Oxford University Press, 2014). Notice the terms 'investigation' and 'mystery' in the title of the book. Although it was written by a historian, these terms place the book in the proximity of crime fiction.

17 Cf. Gerard Genette, *Paratexts: Thresholds of Interpretation*, trans. by Jane E. Lewin (Cambridge, New York: Cambridge University Press, 1997). p. 5.

18 Cf. http://gereonrath.de/.

novels within a larger framework of texts – scholarly and otherwise – that all have a common subject matter: Germany just before and after the Nazis come to power. His novels appear to be the outcome of extensive and meticulous work on the historical intricacies of pre-Nazi Germany. Readers are given the feeling that the novels can be trusted as historically accurate and that they are on an equal footing with scholarly historiography.

A brief overview of historical crime fiction by German-speaking authors

This section will attempt to show which authors and texts have been enjoying a greater degree of popularity among German-speaking readers.[19] The focus is on providing a comprehensive outline of what has been written by German-speaking authors. Questions of literary quality will take a back seat, unless they are specifically addressed. The vast majority of texts listed here do not aspire to literary excellence or philosophical depth; they were written for audiences who want to be entertained. Some authors have written novels set in different historical periods, their names will therefore be mentioned more than once. Many of the authors mentioned here have either studied history at university or, as amateur historians, have gained in-depth knowledge of the history of the region in which they grew up or reside. In many cases, historical crime fiction in German is also regional crime fiction.[20] It must be kept in mind that the novels written by the major Anglo-American authors mentioned in the following paragraphs have all been translated into German and are widely read.

Greek and Roman antiquity receive some coverage in German historical crime fiction but nowhere near as much as readers of Steven Saylor, Lindsey Davis, John Maddox Roberts or David Wishart – to name just a few – are used to. Only a few authors, such as Franziska Franke, Robert Gordian (whose names will come up again in quite different contexts), Ingo Gach and Bernhard Hennen have written novels set in ancient Rome or Greece. There are two writ-

---

19 A shorter overview which focusses on the twentieth century only can be found in: Katharina Hall, 'Historical Crime Fiction in German: The Turbulent Twentieth Century', in *Crime Fiction in German. Der Krimi*, ed. by Katharina Hall (Cardiff: University of Wales Press, 2016), pp. 115–131.
20 On regional crime fiction, see chapter 5.

ers, however, who have contributed more significantly to this sub-genre, although in different ways: Hans Dieter Stöver and Gisbert Haefs. Stöver, a former history teacher, is best known for his series of ten novels featuring 'C.V.T.' (Gaius Volcatius Tullus), written between 1982 and 1986, and his young adult novels, also set in ancient Rome. Gisbert Haefs has written a number of novels set during the conflict between Rome and Carthage in the third and second centuries BC. What makes Haefs's novels noteworthy is that they are narrated from the perspective of a Carthaginian protagonist, thus providing the point of view of a culture that had been largely wiped out by the Romans.[21]

The Middle Ages are a favourite of German-speaking crime fiction writers and readers. Just as English-speaking audiences have Ellis Peters, Margaret Frazer, Peter Tremayne and Paul C. Doherty, German readers have a number of native authors who set their novels in medieval times, although they do not enjoy the international recognition that their English counterparts do. One of these authors, Frank Schätzing, will be discussed in some detail later in this chapter.

Chronologically speaking, the first fictional historical detectives from Germany are Robert Gordian's (b. 1938) Odo and Lupus, who work for Charlemagne. In seven novels published between 1995 and 2016, this team of knight and monk strive to uphold the emperor's laws in eighth-century Francia. Gordian has also written other historical mysteries set during the reign of the Merovingians and the Carolingians (in the fifth to ninth centuries).

Cologne in the thirteenth and fourteenth centuries, with its conflicts between the ruling clergy, patrician merchant families and powerful artisan guilds, is the backdrop for corruption and crime not only in one of Frank Schätzing's novels, but also in books by Stefan Blankertz (b. 1956), Dennis Vlaminck (b. 1970) and Richard Dübell (b. 1962). Dübell, an enormously prolific writer, is best known internationally for his thriller trilogy (published 2007–2010) featuring the 'Codex Gigax' or the 'Devil's Bible', a mysterious, but factually extant manuscript, said to bestow ultimate power.

Strong independent, intelligent and educated women in the fourteenth and fifteenth centuries are the protagonists of the novels by Astrid Fritz (b. 1959), Andrea Schacht (b. 1956) and Petra Schier (b. 1978). All three authors portray these women as members of religious communities that granted their female members, referred to as the 'Beguines', a considerable measure of personal freedom. Medieval crime fiction that deals with women who were denounced as witches can be found in novels by Astrid Fritz (*Die Hexe von Freiburg* [2003, *The*

---

21 See also the section on Gisbert Haefs in chapter 12.

Witch of Freiburg*], Die Tochter der Hexe [2005, The Witch's Daughter*], Die Gauklerin [2005, The Female Juggler*]) and Kathrin Lange (b. 1969; Seraphim 2008, Cherubim 2010, Madonna 2012). In her trilogy, Lange also highlights medieval anti-Semitism and the machinations of the Holy Inquisition.

The history of the Hanseatic League, a formidable economic and military alliance that yielded much power in Northern Europe from the fourteenth to seventeenth centuries, is a favourite playground for crime writers from Germany. Frank Goyke (b. 1961) has written a series of crime novels exploring the economic, political and cultural impact of the league. Waldtraut Lewin's (b. 1937) tremendous output includes, alongside historical crime fiction for younger readers, two novels (written with her daughter Miriam Margraf) set in the world of the Hanse. Derek Meister's (b. 1973) series featuring Lübeck merchant Rungholt also incorporates fictional crime into the historical framework of global trade in the fourteenth century.

Uwe Klausner's series of novels featuring Brother Hilpert of Maulbronn is set in the early fifteenth century. Parallels and similarities to Eco's The Name of the Rose, particularly in the first novel of the series, Die Pforten der Hölle [2007, The Gates of Hell*] are clearly discernible.

The British historian and writer Paul C. Doherty is one of the most prolific authors of historical mysteries. In addition to crime fiction set in ancient Egypt and medieval England, he has also contributed to historical crime fiction covering the period between the sixteenth and the eighteenth centuries under both his real name and various pseudonyms (Michael Clynes, Ann Dukthas). No German-speaking writer interested in this period even comes close to Doherty's breadth of coverage and writerly output, but there are a number of authors who have been highlighting interesting aspects of the early modern age. Writers like Ursula Neeb (b. 1957) have continued the theme of strong independent women as protagonists. Her 'Hurenkönigin' (Queen of Whores) series introduces an unusual detective figure, the female principal of the local prostitute guild in early sixteenth-century Frankfurt. This motherly sleuth not only has to deal with prejudiced and bigoted townspeople, but also with the personal problems of her wards as well as with religious fanatics and political intrigue against the background of the rising influence of Protestantism in Germany and the conflicts this generated in all walks of life. The highly successful series centred on the professional actress and amateur detective Rosina, written by Petra Oelker (b. 1947), also falls within the category of historical crime fiction with a determined and resourceful female lead character. The series, launched in 1997 with Tod am Zollhaus [Death at the Customs House*] had grown to comprise ten volumes by 2010.

Karl-Heinz Göttert (b. 1943), professor emeritus of German Literature at the University of Cologne, published four novels between 2003 and 2005 that construct fictional crime stories within the historical context of phenomena such as secret codes (*Entschlüsselte Geheimnisse* [*Decoded Secrets**], set in 1590), voice analysis (*Die Stimme des Mörders* [*The Voice of the Murderer**] set in 1610), acoustics and architecture (*Das Ohr des Teufels* [*The Ear of the Devil**], set in 1652) and – set in a later historical epoch – telegraphy (*Anschlag auf den Telegraphen* [*Strike Against the Telegraph**], set in 1847). All four novels are set in Cologne and are based on Göttert's scholarly book *Geschichte der Stimme* [1998, *History of the Voice**].

Oliver Pötzsch (b. 1970) is an internationally renowned author of historical novels for children and adults. In six of his novels, published between 2008 and 2016, the daughter of the executioner in the Bavarian town of Schongau teams up with her father and a young physician to solve crime in the period after the end of the Thirty Years' War (1618–1648). The profession of executioner was considered unclean and dishonourable, and the social stigma associated with this occupation is not only an important part of Pötzsch's novels, but also reflects his family's history: the author is himself a descendant of a dynasty of executioners that lived in Bavaria from the sixteenth to nineteenth centuries.

Sandra Lessmann (b. 1969) studied the history of England and is also an expert on the history of medical science. Her series featuring the Catholic priest and physician Jeremy Blackshaw is set in seventeenth-century London, after the end of the civil war. Most of the novels written by Wolf Serno (b. 1944) are set in either the sixteenth or eighteenth century. They often introduce detective figures who work as physicians or apothecaries, or who command some kind of medical knowledge. One of his heroes is a Jewish puppeteer and ventriloquist who, together with his female companion, a professional mourner, journey through Prussia in the 1780s. Prussia in the eighteenth century is also the stage for Tom Wolf's (b. 1964) series of novels starring Honoré Langustier, an Alsatian cook brought to Berlin by Fredrick II (King of Prussia from 1740 to 1786). In thirteen novels, published between 2001 and 2013, the cook acts as the king's crime solver and explores the secret underbelly of the Prussian court and eighteenth-century Berlin in general. Wolf has complemented the series by writing a number of novels in which Langustier's descendant Gerardine de Lalande takes over as investigator in the 1790s and in the early years of the eighteenth century.

Historical crime fiction that gives a picture of the nineteenth century often describes life in the big cities. This is true of Anne Perry's William Monk series and of her Charlotte and Thomas Pitt series, both set in Victorian London.

Together, these two series had grown to comprise more than fifty novels by 2019. A similar metropolitan focus can be found in a series of novels initiated by Horst Bosetzky (b. 1938). In the 'Es geschah in Preußen' [It happened in Prussia] chain novel, written by a group of three authors (Bosetzky, Jan Eik, Uwe Schimunek),[22] each title refers to a neighbourhood, a street or a landmark in the city of Berlin.[23] The series begins in 1840, and each subsequent volume is set two years after the previous one. Another metropolis, Vienna, is the setting for the novels of the Austrian writer Edith Kneifl (b. 1954). Kneifl is a practicing psychoanalyst and an author whose novels have been translated into several languages, although English is not one of them. The first in her series of historical crime novels, *Der Tod fährt Riesenrad* [2012, *Death Rides the Ferris Wheel**], introduces the private detective Gustav von Karoly, whose investigations in 1897 lead him to uncover a family tragedy within the declining nobility that is being replaced by a rising bourgeoisie, while clinging to its status with sometimes murderous determination. In his subsequent cases, he faces a serial killer murdering young women, an architect who falls from the scaffolding of the Vienna cathedral and a death at the opera. Vienna landmarks are a staple in these cases and the suspects are always found in aristocratic circles. Another major city is the scene of crimes committed in Boris Meyn's (b. 1962) novels. Meyn is an expert on the history of art and architecture and confronts his detective with conflicting visions of urban architecture, rivalries between famous architects, corruption and destructive real estate speculation in nineteenth-century Hamburg.

Writing stories about canonical nineteenth-century authors investigating crime in fictional settings has become quite popular in post-2000 Germany. Stephanie Barron paved the way with her crime novels starring Jane Austen (1775–1817) as the detective figure. In Dieter Hirschberg's (b. 1949) three novels, published between 2004 and 2006, it is the writer and judge E.T.A. Hoffmann (1776–1822) who has to solve murders in Eastern Prussia and Berlin. Frank Goyke has written a series of crime novels starring Theodor Fontane (1819–1898) and two novels with the lesser-known Fritz Reuter (1810–1874) as investigators, and Tilman Spreckelsen (b. 1967) has contributed two novels featuring Theodor

---

22 The same group of authors are also writing the series 'Es geschah in Sachsen' [It happened in Saxony], with the first volume set in 1918. A larger group of authors are busy with the series 'Es geschah in Berlin' [It happened in Berlin], with the first volume set in 1910. This series has reached the year 1970 by now (April 2019).

23 This system mirrors Perry's method of designating the Charlotte and Thomas Pitt series, where the individual volumes have titles such as *The Cater Street Hangman, Callander Square,* or *Paragon Walk*.

Storm (1817–1888). More recently, even the two heroes of classical German literature, Johann Wolfgang Goethe (1749–1832) and Friedrich Schiller (1759–1805) have assumed the roles of Sherlock Holmes and Dr Watson respectively, in a novel by Stefan Lehnberg (b. 1964) entitled *Durch Nacht und Wind: Die criminalistischen Werke des Johann Wolfgang Goethe* [2017, *Through Night and Wind: The Criminalistic Works of Johann Wolfgang Goethe**].

The desire to read more about the world's most famous fictional detective than his creator Arthur Conan Doyle was able to provide has motivated numerous writers, such as Nicholas Meyer, Caleb Carr, Laurie R. King, Anthony Horowitz, Charles Veley to add to Sherlock Holmes's case book. German authors have participated in this vogue and have brought the legendary sleuth to Germany and beyond. In this way, in the final years of the nineteenth and the beginning of the twentieth century, Holmes comes to Cologne and journeys from Cairo to Cologne in novels by Stefan Winges (b. 1957); solves mysteries in Leipzig, Berlin, Dresden and in the Balkans; and travels on the Lusitania in books by Wolfgang Schüler (b. 1952). In one of three Holmes novels, Klaus-Peter Walter (b. 1955) takes him to Prague, where he meets Franz Kafka, who thinks he has seen a golem, and becomes involved in espionage just before the outbreak of WWI (*Sherlock Holmes und der Golem von Prag* [2016, *Sherlock Holmes and the Golem of Prague**]). In Franziska Franke's version of events, Holmes is travelling in Italy in 1891 when he discovers that his arch-enemy, Professor Moriarty, has survived their infamous encounter at the Reichenbach Falls. Trying to escape the clutches of his nemesis, Holmes takes on his old pseudonym Sigerson, after the Norwegian explorer, and tours the world solving crime from Florence to Paris and then on to Belgium, Germany, Malta, Egypt and India – in eleven volumes so far, published between 2009 and 2019.

Just like the novels of Frank Tallis and J. Sydney Jones, Austria's Gerhard Loiblsberger's (b. 1957) books depict Vienna at the beginning of the twentieth century. However, whereas Tallis and Jones focus on turn-of-the-century Vienna, with their detectives collaborating with Sigmund Freud and Hans Gross respectively,[24] Loiblsberger has his police investigator and gourmet Joseph Maria Nechyba prowl, not so much the streets, but the restaurants and coffee houses of Vienna between 1903 and 1916.

In terms of both quantity and quality, the twentieth century marks the focal point for historical crime fiction from Germany. Specifically, the decades from the 1920s to the 1940s, the period of the rise of fascism in Germany, have

---

24 Hans Gross (1847–1915) was an eminent criminologist whose scholarly compendiums were used widely and well into the twentieth century.

spurred the imagination of a number of writers.[25] In this, they share a common interest with Anglo-American authors such as Philip Kerr, David Downing, Alan Furst, Paul Grossmann and J. Robert Janes, and with the Polish writer Marek Krajewski (b. 1966), whose six-novel series is set in Breslau and spans the years 1919 to 1945.[26]

The 1920s were an economically and politically highly volatile time in German history. Writers of crime fiction use this period of social instability to highlight some of the infamous historical events that are still part of collective memory today, sometimes in the service of remembrance, sometimes with the more or less outspoken goal of uncovering the true motivations and perpetrators. The 'Golden Twenties' – which, for many contemporaries, were anything but 'golden' in reality – form the backdrop for novels by Susanne Goga, Robert Hültner, Gunnar Kunz and Uwe Schimunek. Goga's (b. 1967) Leo Wechsler series begins in Berlin in 1922 during a period when inflation was increasingly curbing economic activity and ruining the middle class. In subsequent novels in the series, Detective Inspector Wechsler investigates right-wing secret societies, the burgeoning movie industry and the fashion industry. Robert Hültner (b. 1950) chose his native Bavaria as the location for his acclaimed six-volume 'Inspektor Kajetan' series, which spans the period from 1919 to the end of the 1920s. Munich is the capital of the budding Nazi movement, and Kajetan becomes entangled in the collusion taking place between the police and right-wing organizations, forcing him to leave the police force. However, even as a private detective, he cannot escape the machinations that render politics in Bavaria and Germany more and more unstable. With the novels of Gunnar Kunz (b. 1961), we return to 1920s Berlin, where an unlikely trio comprising a male professor of philosophy, his brother, who is a detective inspector, and a young female physics student have to negotiate uncertain times and undoubtedly dead bodies. The series begins in 1920, during the right-wing Kapp Putsch, and covers inflation, black markets and the French-occupied Ruhr district in the west of Germany, even offering a classic closed-world mystery: a murder on

---

25 Chapter 8 will provide a closer look at writers such as Mechthild Borrmann, Horst Bosetzky, Christian von Ditfurth, Susanne Goga, Reiner Gross, Volker Kutscher, Ferdinand von Schirach and Jan Zweyer. Historical crime fiction set during Nazi rule (1933–1945) comprises, according to Katharina Hall, 'a substantial subgenre containing over 150 transnational crime novels' (cf. Katharina Hall, 'The "Nazi Detective" as Provider of Justice in post-1990 British and German Crime Fiction. Philip Kerr's *The Pale Criminal*, Robert Harris's *Fatherland* and Richard Birkefeld and Göran Hachmeisters's *Wer übrig bleibt, hat recht*', *Comparative Literature Studies* 50 [2013], pp. 282–313).
26 This series has been translated into German and is also available in English.

a zeppelin. Uwe Schimunek (b. 1969), besides contributing to the 'Es geschah in Preußen' series and writing other historical Leipzig mysteries, is another one of several authors (Franziska Steinhauer, Jan Eik, Horst Bosetzky and Katrin Ulbrecht) who wrote the 'Katzmann' chain novel 'Es geschach in Sachsen' [It happened in Saxony], whose instalments cover the years from 1918 to 1932 and are set in various locations in Saxony. Schimunek wrote the three Leipzig novels in the series, in which the series detective, journalist Konrad Katzmann, investigates against the background of class struggle and the Kapp Putsch (1920), counterfeit money and the Leipzig spring fair (1926), and the Schreber movement (owners of allotment gardens) during the economic crisis caused by the Great Depression (1930).

The 1930s have attracted a lot of attention from German writers of historical crime fiction. Probably the most celebrated among them is Volker Kutscher (b. 1962), whose Gereon Rath series covers the period from 1929 to 1938. Seven of the planned ten volumes appeared between 2008 and 2018; the first four novels in the series have been translated into English. The first novel *Der nasse Fisch* is available as *Babylon Berlin* and as a graphic novel (in German) as well. A TV series based on the novel, directed by Tom Tykwer, was launched in 2017. Kutscher's Detective Inspector Gereon Rath has transferred from Cologne to Berlin and experiences first-hand the social and political changes the 1930s bring to Germany. In great detail and with his fictional hero interacting with countless historical personalities from the Berlin police force and the political establishment, Kutscher captures the atmosphere of this crucial and troubled period in German history.

Robert Brack, whose real name is Robert Gutberlet (b. 1959), has authored numerous historical crime novels. Under the pseudonym Virginia Doyle, he has written a series starring master cook Jacques Pistoux, who travels late nineteenth-century Europe solving whatever cases present themselves. His latest novels are set during the 1920s in St Pauli, the notorious red-light district in Hamburg, but a trio of novels written between 2008 and 2012 are set in the early 1930s (*Und das Meer gab seine Toten wieder* [*And the Ocean Released its Dead**]; *Blutsonntag* [*Bloody Sunday**], *Unter dem Schatten des Todes* [*Beneath the Shadow of Death**]). They are all based on authentic cases and involve, among other things, police corruption and the female police force, a mass killing during a Nazi demonstration in a proletarian neighbourhood in Hamburg and the burning of the Berlin Reichstag in 1933.[27] Another author who has his

---

27 The burning of the Reichstag on February 27/27, 1933 is also the background for Volker Kutscher's fifth Gereon Rath novel *Märzgefallene* [2014, *March Casualties of War**].

detective inspector solving crimes in early 1930s Berlin is Martin Keune (b. 1959). His protagonist Sándor Lehmann is not only a police officer but also a semi-professional Jazz musician. In the first novel in the series, *Black Bottom* (2013*), he investigates undercover as a member of a Jazz band, amidst Nazi attacks on modern Western music and against the backdrop of economic crisis and street battles between the unemployed and the police. Like Kutscher, Keune also has his fictional hero report to historical police officials, such as Ernst Gennat (1880–1939), director of the Berlin criminal police, and Dr Bernhard Weiß (1880–1951), Vice President of the Berlin police. Subsequent Sándor Lehmann novels explore the schemes of the numerous occult movements in early 1930s Berlin (*Die Blender*, [2014, *The Dazzlers**]) and the Berlin boxing scene in 1932 (*Knockout*, 2015*), where notorious boxing fan Bertolt Brecht (1898–1956) makes an appearance. Bernward Schneider (b. 1956) is a lawyer by profession, and it is therefore no surprise that his investigator is an attorney in a series of novels that span the years 1932 to 1936. In the first novel, *Spittelmarkt*, [2010*], the protagonist Eugen Goltz has to deal with occultists and racists who support the Nazi party and its leader. In the sequel *Flammenteufel* [2011, *Firedevil**], the trial of the burning of the Reichstag takes centre stage; while the plot of *Berlin Potsdamer Platz* [2013*], set in June 1934, unfolds as the confrontation between the SA and other elements of the Nazi movement moves towards its climax, known as the 'Night of the Long Knives', when members of the SA leadership were assassinated by members of the SS and the military. Schneider has also written a novel that is set in April 1945. In *Endstation Reichskanzlei* [2015, *Last Stop Reich Chancellery**], Greta Jenski, who is a Gestapo informant but actually works as a double agent, roams the streets of Berlin during the last chaotic days of the Third Reich.

The final months of the Third Reich are another period that has attracted the interest of German crime fiction writers. In Harald Gilbers's (b. 1969) novels, Berlin between the summer of 1944 and April 1945 provides a dark and eerie setting, with its frequent and ever more deadly and destructive air raids, black market activities and rivalries between various Nazi organizations. Similar to the St Cyr/Kohler mysteries by J. Robert Janes, where a French police officer and a Gestapo agent team up to solve crime in occupied France, Gilbers's Kommissar Oppenheimer series features a former Jewish detective inspector of the Berlin police with an SS officer as his partner. In three novels that appeared between 2013 and 2017, Oppenheimer must walk a fine line between pleasing his Nazi superiors so that they will let him live a while longer and not becoming too successful and therefore creating envy. Sebastian Thiel's (b. 1983) Nikolas Brandenburg series features another detective inspector who serves the Third Reich during the last months of its existence. During the first novel in the series, *Wunderwaffe*

[2012, *Wonder Weapon**], however, this police officer becomes a member of the French resistance when he investigates crimes associated with the notorious IG Farben conglomerate in 1944 Paris. His subsequent adventures see him in the race to develop a nuclear weapon (*Uranprojekt* [2014, *Project Uranium**]) and searching for another secret weapon (*Geheimprojekt Flugscheibe* [2015, *Secret Project Flying Saucer**]). Thiel has written another novel, *Das Adenauer-Komplott* [2017, *The Adenauer Conspiracy**], which also begins in 1944, but is not connected to the Nikolas Brandenburg series and extends into the post-war era. In this novel, the fictional protagonist helps Konrad Adenauer (1876–1967), the first Chancellor of the Federal Republic of Germany, escape from an SS prison and then becomes one of his closest advisors during Adenauer's initial rise to power.

The immediate post-war era is also the setting for three novels by Harald Pflug (b. 1967), in which John Edwards, a captain in the Seventh United States Army and commanding officer of a scout patrol, fights crime in Germany in the summer of 1945. Cay Rademacher (b. 1965) is an erudite author of historical crime fiction who has published novels set in ancient Egypt, ancient Rome and Cologne, in medieval Paris and in the late 1930s. He has also written three novels depicting Hamburg in 1947 and 1948. This series features a detective inspector who is helped by a lieutenant of the British occupying forces. In their first case, they hunt a serial killer in the winter of 1947 while people are dying of hunger and starving to death. They are then faced with gangs of feral children whose parents died during the war and who have fled from occupied territories in the East. Their third case develops against the background of the black market, counterfeit money and the upcoming monetary reform of June 1948. Jan Zweyer (the pseudonym of Rüdiger Richartz, b. 1953) has written medieval mysteries portraying conflicts between secular and religious powers, between nation states and the Hanse, and between the Inquisition and regional rulers. He has also written a trilogy featuring a police officer who has to negotiate the challenging times from the 1920s to the 1950s in Germany. In the first novel of the trilogy, *Franzosenliebchen* [2007, *The Girl Who Fraternized with the French**], detective inspector Peter Goldstein is sent to the French-occupied Ruhr area in 1923 to find the killer of a young woman who is said to have had affairs with French soldiers. In the sequel (*Goldfasan*, [2009, *Golden Pheasant*[28]]), however, it is the year 1943, and Goldstein has not only changed his name to the less Jewish-sounding Golsten, but has also become a member of the Nazi party and the SS. Zweyer is not the only one who has his protagonist investigate crimes in Nazi

---

28 This was a nickname for members in the higher echelons of the Nazi party and the military who were notorious for decking themselves out with golden medals and other ornaments.

Germany, but Goldstein/Golsten is a thoroughly ambivalent figure, a conformist and fellow traveller, who does whatever is necessary to get ahead in life. In the third novel in the trilogy, *Persilschein* [2011, *Persil Certificate**[29]], set in 1950, Golsten has reverted to calling himself Goldstein, because a more Jewish-sounding name is no longer a threat to him. On the contrary: now it might further his career in post-Nazi democratic West Germany.

German historical crime fiction and how to find it

The overview of historical crime fiction by German-speaking authors above might be somewhat extensive, but it is by no means complete. Historical crime fiction is a burgeoning industry: new titles are being published as you read this. The large and wide-ranging number of authors and texts raises the question of how to best negotiate this wealth of material. How can a reader find out what is available and what is worth reading? Due to the relatively few titles that are translated from German to English, this is less of a problem when one is restricted to reading in English, but for those who read German, this can be a real challenge. One way of finding out what has been published is to check the programmes of publishers who offer a separate list for historical crime fiction, such as Random House, Rowohlt and Emons.[30] There are also a number of smaller publishers that maintain historical crime fiction lists: Gmeiner, Sutton, grafit, Pendragon, KBV, Edition Nautilus and Jaron (for the 'Es geschah in Berlin' [It happened in Berlin] chain novel).[31] These smaller publishing houses print the novels of authors such as Robert Brack, Bernward Schneider, Uwe Klausner, Horst Bosetzky, Gunnar Kunz

---

29 A 'Persilschein' in postwar Germany was a certificate issued by the Allied occupying forces confirming that the holder had not committed any atrocities and was not guilty of having sympathized with the Nazis. 'Persil' was (and still is) a laundry detergent. The certificate that bore its name was supposed to give the holder a 'clean' bill of (moral) health.
30 The lists for Random House can be found at: https://www.randomhouse.de/Webtags/ Historischer-Kriminalroman/9050.rhd and at: https://www.randomhouse.de/Kategorien/ Literatur-&-Unterhaltung/Krimi-&-Thriller/LITUKRIMI.rhd?&level4CategoryId= KRIMHISTOR&kindOfCover=&publisherId=&sortOrder=titel&language=de&level3CategoryId= LITUKRIMI&sortOrderDetail=titelABisZ&monthOfPublication=01.05.2017. Rowohlt's list is here: https://www.rowohlt.de/themen/belletristik-und-verwandte-gebiete/kriminalromane-und-mys tery/historische-kriminalromane.
31 Emons Verlag: https://www.emons-verlag.de/programm/krimis/historischer-krimi; Gmeiner: http://www.gmeiner-verlag.de/zeitgeschichtliche-krimis.html; Sutton: https://verlag shaus24.de/krimis-und-romane/historische-romane/?paf=1; KBV: http://www.kbv-verlag.de/ 18.html.

and many others. In particular, authors who are not yet well known or whose work might appeal only to a limited audience often find a home with these publishers first, before, in some cases, they move on to bigger publishers.

Another way to find historical crime fiction in German is to consult specialized websites maintained by non-professional or professional readers. One such site, 'Lovelybooks', where readers recommend books to other readers, works like a social network for readers and has a sub-category with the title 'Bücher mit dem Tag "historischer Kriminalroman"' [books with the tag 'historical crime novel'].[32] The online magazine 'Histo-Couch' features reviews by semi-professional and professional readers (as well as by non-professional readers who communicate their impressions after reading a novel) under subheadings for the historical periods antiquity, medieval, early modern, nineteenth century and twentieth century. Under each historical period, a number of subcategories are available, one of which is 'Kriminalromane' [crime novels].[33] The site 'Krimi-Couch' has a category called 'Krimi-Berater' [crime fiction advisor] that lets users filter results according to a number of parameters, one of which is the historical period in which the novel is set.[34] In addition, caliber38.de is a website authored by Thomas Wörtche, one of the leading experts on crime fiction in Germany, which also has a sub-category for historical crime fiction, which lists what is available in or has been translated into German.[35]

Three sample texts: Frank Schätzing's *Tod und Teufel*, Maria Andrea Schenkel's *Tannöd* and Uta-Maria Heim's *Feierabend*

To conclude this chapter, I would like to discuss briefly three historical crime novels. Frank Schätzing's *Tod und Teufel* [1995, *Death and the Devil*] is a historical thriller and an eminently readable novel with a medieval backdrop. It gives the reader the feeling that he or she is learning something about

---

32 This site is at: https://www.lovelybooks.de/stoebern/empfehlung/historischer%20kriminal roman/. Readers should be aware that this site is maintained by the Georg von Holtzbrinck Group, one of the leading publishing conglomerates worldwide.
33 Historical crime fiction set during the Middle Ages can be found at: http://www.histo-couch.de/historische-kriminalromane-ueber-das-mittelalter.html etc.
34 Cf. http://www.krimi-couch.de/krimis/dr-watson.html.
35 www.kaliber38.de/navigator/Geschichte.

a distant historical epoch while being entertained by a story of suspense that provides the additional bonus of having a philosophical touch. The reader can enjoy a 'good yarn' without having to feel guilty about it.

With *Tannöd* [2006, *The Murder Farm*], Andrea Maria Schenkel takes readers back to the post-war period after World War II in West Germany. Her novel is set in a remote rural area and uses elements of a historical crime that was never solved. Schenkel manages to create an atmosphere of horror and anticipation by structuring the text of her novel in such a way that her readers paradoxically assume the simultaneous roles of distant observers, victims of the crime and the role of the perpetrator himself, thus creating a unique reading experience.

Uta-Maria Heim's[36] *Feierabend* [2011, *After Hours**] is one example of the many German trans-historical crime novels in which investigators expose the forgotten and repressed deeds of the older generations that were linked to Nazi atrocities. Heim's novel can also be read as a critical reflection on what is referred to as *Heimatliteratur* [literature of the homeland or native country],[37] in which the very notion of *Heimat* is scrutinized and put into the context of a problematical usage of memory and history. The impact of *Feierabend* on the concept of historiography or historical knowledge will be the focus of the discussion.

Frank Schätzing's *Tod und Teufel* and the fascination of the Middle Ages

English-speaking readers have been familiar with Frank Schätzing since the translation of his international bestseller *Der Schwarm* [2004, *The Swarm*] was published in 2007. *Der Schwarm* is a science-fiction thriller in which ocean-dwelling collective intelligence threatens humanity. In the aftermath of this book's success, attention was also directed towards Schätzing's earlier work. His first novel, *Tod und Teufel* (1995), was translated into English as *Death and*

---

36 For more on Heim and her work, see the section on her in chapter 12.

37 *Heimatliteratur* has a long tradition in German-speaking countries, going back to the nineteenth century. For a brief introduction to traditional regional literature cf. James P. Sandrock, 'Understanding Heimatliteratur: An Approach to Traditional Regional Literature', *Die Unterrichtspraxis* 14.1 (1981), pp. 2–8.

the Devil in 2007.[38] *Tod und Teufel* is a medieval thriller and tries to ride the wave of the favourable reception of Ellis Peters's Cadfael novels (1977–1994) and Umberto Eco's *Il nome della rosa* [1980, *The Name of the Rose*], although it never reaches the historical breadth of Peters' twenty-one-book corpus, nor does it compete with the philosophical depth of Eco's novel.

Tod und Teufel is set in the city of Cologne in the year 1260. It tells the story of a young man called Jacob the Fox (after his unruly mop of red hair), who tries to make a living by stealing whatever he needs to survive. When fleeing from an angry mob after being caught stealing food in one of the local markets, Jacob stumbles on a murder crime scene. He witnesses Gerhart Morart, the architect of the colossal new cathedral that is being erected in Cologne, plunging to his death from the scaffolding of the new building. But Jacob also sees that Gerhard did not slip before he fell to his death: the master builder was pushed. And whoever the shadowy figure was who caused Gerhard's untimely demise, that killer also saw that Jacob saw him, which means: the hunt is on. Two of the friends to whom Jacob tells his story are killed in short order, and Jacob knows that he will be next. What he does not know is the reason for Gerhard's killing, which comes to light only gradually after Jacob makes the acquaintance of Richmodis, her father Goddert and her uncle Jaspar, who is a physician, professor of canon law and dean of one of the numerous local churches. It transpires that Gerhard's murder is part of a conspiracy that pits different members of the ruling elites against each other. The conspirators were afraid that Gerhard would reveal their machinations and had him killed to silence him. To do so, they secured the services of the mysterious and deadly Urquhart, a trained assassin with a troubled past. The plot of the novel unfolds as a game of who can best whom between the conspirators and Urquhart on one side, and Jacob and Jaspar on the other.

Cologne Cathedral, construction on which began in 1248, although it was officially completed only in 1880, shapes the historical and cultural setting of the novel. This Gothic cathedral, built to house the remains of the Three Kings and to provide a place of worship for the Holy Roman Emperor, has several functions in the novel. Firstly, it demonstrates the importance of religion throughout all walks of life in the medieval European world. This enormous building project shows how scarce resources were committed to an undertaking that represented the cultural identity of an entire society and determined the

---

38 Frank Schätzing, *Death and the Devil.* trans. by Mike Mitchell (New York: William Morrow, 2007). Quotations with page numbers in brackets are from this edition. The German paperback edition had forty print runs by 2003.

daily lives of a multitude of people who were in one way or another involved in the building process. Secondly, the building site of the cathedral is the location where the murder at the beginning of the novel takes place and where the showdown between the main characters happens at the end, thus connecting the historical setting and the plot of the fictional crime. Here, the author employs an often-used element of historical crime fiction: the murder victim Meister Gerhard (Gerhard von Rile, aka Meister Gerardus) was the first architect (*Dombaumeister* or master architect) of the Cologne Cathedral and died under mysterious circumstances by falling to his death from the scaffold. Schätzing, in typical form for a writer of historical crime fiction, uses the opening provided by the unknown reason for Gerhard's death to construct a crime story around it, although he changes the date from April 1271 (when the historical Meister Gerhard died) to September 1260 (when the novel is set). Thirdly, the cathedral is also part of the period detail the novel uses to create the historical 'text world' or diegesis, the specific background and setting in front of which the plot develops and which is presented to the reader as a specimen of the genre 'historical thriller'. Other period details that contribute to making this particular backdrop come alive include clothing, certain foodstuffs, the houses of the rich and the hovels of the poor. Various locations within the city, such as market squares, streets and buildings, are identified by the historic names that many of them still carry today.[39] The original German novel even provides a map of thirteenth-century Cologne (although this is not included in the English translation).

The novel features a narrative structure that has become increasingly popular since the 1990s, when authors such as Henning Mankell helped to make it the most widely used narrative pattern in crime fiction. Before the story starts, a prologue, in which a lone, roaming wolf comes close to the city gates, sets the tone. Not only does it serve to foreshadow the arrival of the assassin Urquhart in the city, it is also intended to show that wilderness and civilization are not separated from each other by a clear-cut border. As the implied parallel between beast and man indicates, this is also true of the actions of human beings: *homo hominis lupus est*, as the novel makes abundantly clear.

---

39 The novel thus participates in the by now well-known phenomenon of crime fiction tourism that invites readers to visit the settings of crime fiction and retrace the stories they have read in the real world. This is a particularly popular leisure activity for fans of historical crime fiction. An example for how readers of Ellis Peters' novels are targeted thus can be found at: https://www.visitengland.com/experience/visit-shrewsbury-abbey-fictional-home-brother-cadfael. Potential visitors are lured with the invitation: 'Visit Shrewsbury Abbey and follow in the footsteps of Cadfael, the monastic sleuth, where the books and TV series were set'.

Tod und Teufel combines a number of plot types that are typical in crime fiction. Firstly, a process of detection is set in motion after Jacob witnesses the death of Master Gerhard. To protect himself from the killer, who knows that Jacob saw him, Jacob has to uncover the assassin's identity. From early on in the novel, Jacob will be helped in this endeavour by Jaspar, who is not only much more knowledgeable, but can also move much more freely around the city because he has not been made a suspect in the murder case by the conspirators.

Secondly, the thriller element is introduced by the assassin trying to hunt down and silence the witness to the initial murder. Jacob is on the run from the very beginning, at first only because he stole some meat from the market, but soon because he knows that Gerhard's fall was not an accident. The danger he finds himself in soon spreads to everybody who is in contact with him and then specifically to those who try to help him, such as Richmodis and Jaspar. Innocent bystanders and others connected to the first killing are murdered, and bodies begin to pile up.

As a third element of the plot, the detectives are also on a quest to uncover the conspiracy that is behind all the killings, although it never becomes quite clear *why* they want to derail the conspiracy, except to save their own lives. This quest also introduces a race against time, since it is the conspiracy's goal to murder a certain dignitary on a certain occasion. At the same time, the killer comes ever closer to the detectives, until they have to face him in a final showdown.

As has become common in thrillers, the story is told from various perspectives and the point of view switches back and forth rapidly between the perpetrators/conspirators and the detectives, the hunter (Urquhart) and the hunted (Jacob, Jaspar, Richmodis). In the beginning, Jacob is presented as a mere bystander who is drawn into machinations that he cannot possibly understand. As the story unfolds, Jaspar takes over more and more as the leader of the investigation and thus becomes the true detective figure, whereas Jacob becomes a mere sidekick or Watson figure.

As discussed earlier, the specific use of paratextual material indicates what role historical knowledge or 'truth' plays in historical crime fiction. *Tod und Teufel* begins with a quote by Peter Abelard (Petrus Abealardus, 1079–1142): 'Language does not veil reality, but expresses it.' The wider implications of this motto for the novel will be discussed later, but even at first glance, such a maxim at the beginning of a historical novel seems to indicate that reality or truth can be accessed through language and that the relation between language and truth is not problematical.

Other relevant paratexts include the aforementioned map of Cologne, a glossary of names, concepts and quotations, and a note of thanks from the author. All of this material is missing in the English translation, and this influences the way in which the text of the novel is framed and presented to the reader. The glossary or explanation of names, concepts and quotations in the German original not only provides translations of numerous Latin words and phrases, but also offers important background information on local history. The ongoing contest for political and economic power between the archbishops of Cologne and the leading merchant clans of the city, which forms the historical backdrop to the conspiracy in the novel, appears in several places in the glossary. This particular kind of information concerns the contact point where fictional narrative elements are injected into factual history. It bolsters the impression of historical accuracy, even for elements of the texts that are clearly fictional.

The note of thanks from the author at the end of the German original of *Tod und Teufel* serves a similar purpose. The author expresses his thanks to, among others, the staff of the Historical Archive of the City of Cologne, a tour guide who showed him even 'the highest and breeziest corners'[40] of the Cologne Cathedral and the author of a doctoral dissertation on the earliest phase of the construction of the Cologne cathedral. He also thanks the authors of the 'numerous scholarly books'[41] he used while writing the novel. By thanking all of these people, the author of the novel demonstrates that he has immersed himself in historical research about the place and period he is writing about, that the historical knowledge that he presents in the novel is reliable, and that the reader can therefore safely assume that he or she will learn something while reading the novel.

An 'epilogue' tells the story of how the conflict between Cologne's patricians and the archbishops transpired and how it eventually ended, with Cologne becoming 'a free imperial city'.[42] In the English translation, this chapter is called 'Author's Note', and this heading captures much better the status of the chapter as a paratext. Just as the prologue, the author's note is printed in italics, but unlike the prologue, in the note, the author is speaking, addressing the reader directly. The impression that the reader takes away from reading the author's note is unmistakable: the conflicts among the rich and powerful, which are always fought out on the backs of the common people, are frivolous and pointless. They are invariably caused by greed and vanity, and lead to nothing good. This may not be an original insight, but the point here is

---

40 Frank Schätzing, *Tod und Teufel* (Munich: Goldmann, 2003), p. 509. 'bis in seine luftigsten Höhen und Winkel'.
41 Schätzing, *Tod und Teufel*. p. 509. 'vielen Fachbüchern'.
42 Schätzing, *Death and the Devil*, p. 391.

something else: the implications thus put forth are that historical knowledge is freely available, that it can be transmitted by crime fiction, and that reading this kind of fiction has an added bonus (in addition to being entertaining): not only can we learn *about* history, but we can also learn *from* history.

Both of these implied claims, that we can learn about and from history, are also incorporated into the narrative itself. At several points throughout the novel, historiographic digressions interrupt the flow of the narrative. In some instances towards the beginning of the novel, the omniscient[43] narrator speaks directly to the reader (13–14, 22, 27–29). Much more interesting, however, are those occasions when Jaspar explains to Jacob the historical background of present events (157–163, 309–314, 320–325). By making Jacob stand in for the reader, this narrative technique avoids making the impression that the reader is being subjected to a 'history lecture'.[44] Jacob is an ideal target for historical explanations because he is so ignorant but at the same time so eager to learn about history. At one point, Schätzing even offers a small dose of self-ironic metafiction: when Jacob fervently requests that Jaspar tell him about the Crusades, Jaspar warns him: 'A history lesson. Might be a little dry.'[45] But Jacob's response is unequivocal: 'Doesn't matter' (156). For Jacob as a historically challenged *ignoramus*, learning about history has become a desire that he cannot resist.

As mentioned above, learning *from* history is also part of the narrative. When Jaspar enlightens Jacob about the history of the Crusades, it takes the form of a debunking of the supposedly idealistic motivations behind the movement and its seemingly glorious results. In Jaspers version, the Crusades were nothing but economically motivated mass murders and xenophobically induced mass hysteria, with religious fanaticism serving as a useful tool to manipulate the people. Again, the message is clear: history must be read critically or against the grain, and if we do so, we can learn from it. In the German context, the parallels

---

43 'Omniscient' in the present context means that the narrator has extensive historical knowledge about medieval times. He could be imagined as a history teacher.

44 Peter Lovesey states: 'All we ask of the historical mystery is that it tell a story consistent with known facts and that those facts arise naturally from the plot. If we want a history lecture, we can go to college'. The latter seems to be a rather onerous proposition in Lovesey's estimation. ('The Historian, Once upon a Crime', in *Murder Ink. The Mystery Reader's Companion*, ed. by Dillys Winn [New York: Workman Publishing, 1977], p. 476).

45 The German original has: 'Nachhilfe in Geschichte. Vorsicht, das wird trocken!' 'Nachhilfe' refers to the help weak students receive from a private tutor when they are in danger of failing a class and is not a thirteenth-century concept. This is a good illustration for the dilemma every author of historical fiction must face: the strangeness of temporarily distant cultures can only be explained by taking recourse to present-day concepts and ideas. 'Nachhilfe' has a host of connotations that have nothing to do with medieval society.

with the Holocaust cannot be overlooked. Although as historical events, the Crusades and the Holocaust differ in many respects, Jaspar's critical attitude towards mass violence and the manipulation of vast segments of a population serve as a model of how to write and learn from history.

Learning from history, however, also takes place on another, quite different level in *Tod und Teufel*, namely in the form of overcoming a traumatic experience. Both Jacob and the assassin Urquhart have been traumatized: Jacob as a child when his family was brutally murdered, and Urquhart after he joined the Crusades as an idealistic young man and then witnessed atrocities committed by his fellow crusaders. Urquhart is in some respects the most interesting character in the novel: with his total disregard for the value of human life, the casual nonchalance with which he kills, his total lack of feeling and compassion, his cynical view of human affairs and politics, and his cold analysis of the motivations of his employers, he fills the role of mercenary and cold-blooded killer, a medieval hit man. Both Urquhart and Jacob cannot act according to their free will because their lives are determined by their traumatic experiences in the past. Urquhart is condemned to lead the existence of a shadowy figure of death, a demon-like creature that is mistaken for the devil by those who witness his slayings. Jacob is unable to settle down in any form of domestic life and compulsively moves on from town to town whenever a situation requires some kind of decision-making or commitment.

As opposed to Urquhart, who is locked into endlessly repeating his trauma by negating the value of human life, Jacob is able to overcome his trauma by learning from his own personal history. In his case and with the help of Jaspar, historical and political knowledge is imparted by way of a process of education that is at the same time a process of healing and leads him to becoming a useful member of society. His development in the novel is thus reminiscent both of a successful psychoanalysis and of the Bildungsroman. A prominent role in this process is given to the philosopher Peter Abelard and his ideas. Jaspar 'model[s] himself on him' (354) because, among other things, his insistence on man's ability to exercise his free will. According to Jaspar, Abelard never despaired about what happened to him in his life, he was never stuck in the past, or, in other words, he was immune to traumatic experiences and their symptoms. Whereas Jacob and Urquhart are being remote-controlled by horrific events from their pasts, Abelard upholds the principle of free will and always having a choice throughout his life. Given the importance of this philosopher and his teachings for the main character, it is only fitting that 'Abelard' is the final word of the novel.

Andrea Maria Schenkel's *Tannöd* and the destructiveness of male desire

With her first book *Tannöd*, Andrea Maria Schenkel (b. 1962) exploded onto the German crime fiction scene with a bestselling success.[46] Although the initial response was rather reserved, a year after its release in Germany, *Tannöd* had already sold 300,000 copies; by 2009, one million copies had been sold. The author received a number of prizes for her novel, among them the prestigious Deutscher Krimi Preis [German Crime Fiction Prize]. Several theatrical adaptations were staged, and a movie version of the novel was released in 2009. Today, *Tannöd* is standard reading in German high schools. The short novel is based on a true crime, the murder of six people on a lonely farm in Upper Bavaria in the spring of 1922. The perpetrator was never identified, and the case fires the imagination of local historians, journalists, documentary moviemakers and writers of crime fiction to this day. After the tremendous success of her novel, Schenkel was accused of plagiarism, but she was later cleared of those charges. Since her first book, Schenkel has authored a number of novels that, like *Tannöd*, combine historical events with fictional re-workings of true crime.[47]

In contrast to the actual historical crime that *Tannöd* is based on, the novel is set during the mid-1950s. It starts with a short prologue in which an anonymous first-person narrator reminisces about her happy life in the countryside immediately after the end of World War II and the happy memories she has about this place. A number of years later, however, news has reached her that a horrendous crime has been committed in her former refuge, and the erstwhile 'island of peace' is now known as 'the murder farm'.[48] The narrator then goes back to the village that is home to the murder farm and asks a number of villagers about what has happened. According to the narrator, the residents talk freely with her because she is not a complete stranger, but also because she is not one of them and will leave again after the conversations have been concluded.

Readers who expect a linear account of the story of the crime and the investigation will be disappointed. The story is presented as an assortment of

---

46 This section is a shortened version of the chapter on *Tannöd* in my *Einführung in den Kriminalroman* (Darmstadt: Wissenschaftliche Buchgesellschaft, 2015), pp. 147–152.
47 Her later crime novels include *Kalteis* (2007, Ice Cold [2010]), *Bunker* (2009, Bunker [2011]), *Finsterau* (2012, The Dard Meadow [2014]) and *Täuscher* (2013*).
48 Andrea Maria Schenkel, *The Murder Farm*, trans. by Anthea Bell (New York, London: Quercus, 2014), p. 1.

fragments that follow no chronological order, instead jumping back and forth between various points of view. It is the task of the reader to combine these fragments and arrive at a meaningful whole. The text of the novel consists of transcripts of fictional interviews (with only the responses of the villagers, but not the questions of the narrator) and short chapters narrated mostly in free indirect speech, following the characters in their movements before the murder. These passages are interspersed with segments from 'The Litany for the Comfort of Poor Souls', which has been taken from a spiritual guide for young women that was published in 1922.[49] The structure of the novel creates the impression of experiencing the horrific murder from the point of view of the perpetrator and the victims at the same time, but also of being an unfathomable and terrifying event that the community somehow has to cope with.

The novel tells the story of the murder victims Hermann and Theresia Danner, their daughter Barbara and Barbara's two children, eight-year-old Marianne and two-year-old Joseph. They and the servant girl Maria, who has just arrived at the farm, are all slaughtered like animals in the barn of their farm one night. Only towards the end of the novel does the reader learn that Hermann Danner had abused his daughter Barbara since she was twelve years old and that Barbara's two children were fathered by him. To cover up this incest, Barbara married when her first child was born and had a brief relationship with another man when she had her second child. There were rumours in the village about the incestuous relationship Hermann Danner had with his daughter, but nobody wanted to know about what was going on, nobody wanted to know the truth, and the Danner family was ostracized and left alone on their lonely farm off the beaten track. This is the background to the murder of the entire family and the servant girl who just happened to be in the wrong place at the wrong time.

The first-person narrator, who comes to the village to find out what happened to her place of refuge after the war, and the responses to the questions she asks there introduce an almost ethnographic view to the story from the beginning. What the responses of the villagers reveal can be described as a dysfunctional rural community that has lost all sense of unity, identity and spirit of kinship. The crime in their midst lays bare resentment, antipathies and repressed guilt that go back decades. The social isolation of the Danner family – reflected in the geographical remoteness of the family farm – is a result of Hermann Danner's egoism, his stinginess, his opportunism and his

---

49 The English translation marks the three different kinds of texts by using different font. In the German original, only the passages from the litany are printed differently.

delusions of grandeur. He saw himself as 'Lord God Almighty'[50] on his farm, as an absolute ruler with limitless power over the members of his family. The rural community, in turn, regarded Danner as a 'suspicious curmudgeon'[51] and his entire family as 'loners'.[52]

The ethnographic view also exposes the moral corruption of the rural dignitaries, who represent the religious and secular authorities. The village teacher had only recently arrived in the village and betrays his indifference towards the children he teaches by admitting that he did not really know Marianne all that well. The mayor first talks about having been 'liberated' by the Americans in April 1945, but then complains that they 'acted like vandals' and that the village suffered 'severe damage'.[53] When he then talks about the 'fall of the regime'[54] instead of 'liberation', it seems likely that he was a former Nazi himself. His grumbling about the losses *he* and *his community* have suffered as a result of the war shows that he is confusing cause and effect, a strategy many Germans employed to repress their responsibility and their feelings of guilt after the war. Furthermore, he does not want to talk about the death of a foreign female worker who had been forced to work on the Danner farm during the war and supposedly hanged herself. He adamantly opposes any 'attempt to revive old stories' and wants to 'lay those stories to rest once and for all',[55] thus subscribing to a classic stratagem of the German culture of repression after the war. The village priest also denies any possible connection between the killings and what happened during the war. He bemoans that, '[c]ommunity life has ceased to exist. Everyone distrusts his neighbor'.[56] Like the mayor, he cannot fathom that the murder might be the belated outcome of a state of mind shaped by outdated gender roles and wartime traumas.

This, however, is precisely how the mass murder at the lonely farm came about. The perpetrator had come home from the war as a deeply disturbed person. He was suffering from nightmares from which he woke up screaming: 'There is nothing human about the scream, he screams in despair like a wounded animal'.[57] Being

---

50 Schenkel, *The Murder Farm*, p. 84.
51 Schenkel, *The Murder Farm*, p. 44.
52 Schenkel, *The Murder Farm*, p. 49.
53 Schenkel, *The Murder Farm*, p. 114.
54 In the German original, the mayor uses the word 'Zusammenbruch' or 'total breakdown', which indicates more clearly that he experienced the end of the Nazi regime as a loss and not as a liberation.
55 Schenkel, *The Murder Farm*, p. 115.
56 Schenkel, *The Murder Farm*, p. 145.
57 Schenkel, *The Murder Farm*, p. 104.

reduced to the state of a wounded animal mirrors his twofold narcissistic mortification: as the soldier of a defeated and disgraced army and as a male who has been rejected and ridiculed by a woman he desired. The latter occurred when he had a brief sexual relationship with Barbara, who had then abandoned him and treated him 'like a stray dog'. She '[l]aughed at him, mocked him', told him that he was 'a stinking alcoholic sissy'.[58] At this point, he lost control of himself, killed her first and then the other inhabitants of the farm in a 'frenzy of bloodlust', acting under a compulsion that made him feel as 'Lord of life and death' that night.[59] By killing everybody in reach, he experienced a feeling of omnipotence that compensated for his sexual frustration and degradation.

Tannöd tells the stories of a number of women who have been systematically oppressed, violated and forced into the position of mere sexual objects by the men who control them. It starts with Theresia Danner, who has been degraded and abused by her husband Hermann since her wedding. Amelie, the Polish foreign worker who was forced into a kind of slavery on the Danner farm, was also sexually abused by Hermann Danner and committed suicide as the only way out. When the mayor disregards what happened to her with the casual remark that the suicide of a half-Jewish Polish woman was hardly worth all this fuss, he betrays the fascist mentality to which the villagers still adhere.

The central character in the novel is Barbara. It was she who tried to break out of the circle of violence and submission under male domination. Shortly before she was murdered, she had managed to convince her father to turn the farm over to her. That would have meant economic and sexual independence for her, but it never came to that. Her attempt to free herself from her traditional role as a woman in a patriarchal society triggers a pathological response in a murderer who cannot accept that she is rejecting him because she no longer needs him. *Tannöd* is a historical crime novel that illustrates how a rural community suffers a total breakdown as a result of sticking to a centuries-old mentality, exacerbated by the collapse of civilized behaviour during the Nazi regime. Old patriarchal structures have become obsolete in a modernizing society in which women demand their due, both in economic and sexual terms. The violence against women that had been an essential part of these old structures only demonstrates its utter defeat and helplessness when it erupts into a mass killing that punishes the guilty, the victims and the innocent.

---

58 Schenkel, *The Murder Farm*, p. 165.
59 Schenkel, *The Murder Farm*, p. 166.

Uta-Maria Heim's *Feierabend* and the trans-historical German crime novel

From January to December 1940, 10,654 people whose lives were deemed 'unworthy' were killed at the former hospital for the mentally ill in Grafeneck, southeast of Stuttgart, as part of the Nazi euthanasia programme. Nazi atrocities have been a favourite object of trans-historical crime fiction from Germany, and so it is no surprise that the murder of intellectually disabled people at Grafeneck has become another focus for this subgenre. Rainer Gross's novel *Grafeneck* (2007*) features an elderly elementary school teacher who gradually finds out about his family's involvement with what happened at Grafeneck and a murder connected to it more than half a century earlier. Gross's novel was awarded the prestigious Friedrich Glauser prize for the best crime novel in 2007, has become a bestseller and is recommended reading for high school students in Germany. *Grafeneck* makes it easy for the reader to identify with its protagonist and to follow him on his voyage back in time to unearth what transpired in 1940, who was responsible for it and what became of the perpetrators. At the end, the characters in the novel know almost everything about what happened, how it happened and why it happened. Although the protagonist Hermann Mauser has to live with the ambivalence of his father's actions in 1940, his questions have been answered, he has been liberated from the torturous uncertainty, in short: closure has been granted to the characters in the story and to the reader.

The exact opposite is the case in Uta-Maria Heim's *Feierabend*, although Heim's *Kriminalroman* is also concerned with Grafeneck and written in the form of a trans-historical crime novel. In the last sentence of *Feierabend*, the protagonist Helene Spitznagel realizes: 'I will investigate (against) myself. It is time',[60] thus recognizing that the true work of uncovering the past has only just begun and that any kind of closure is at best a still distant goal. Helene's intention to make herself the object of an investigation into an event that happened before she was even born can be understood as the answer to a short text that precedes the novel and is entitled: 'We have hushed it up for too long'.[61] In this preface, the author briefly states the known facts about Grafeneck and then asserts that the 'industrialized murder in Grafeneck' had been 'repressed and tabooed for too long' and that her novel will tell 'a fictional but

---

60 Uta-Maria Heim, *Feierabend* (Meßkirch: Gmeiner-Verlag, 2011), p. 327. 'Ich ermittle gegen mich selbst. Es ist Zeit.'
61 Heim, *Feierabend*, p. 7. 'Wir haben es zu lange totgeschwiegen.'

nonetheless possible story' in the place of 'hushing up and forgetting'. This is followed by another paratext consisting of extended quotations from a letter written by a protestant bishop in 1940, in which he condemns the Nazi euthanasia programme (although he starts his letter by thanking God, the 'Führer' and the German military).[62]

Although most of the story is set in the present, the causes and origins of what happens in the present lie in the past or, more specifically, in the year 1940. The novel starts with a short chapter set in that year. A young woman named Hildegard discovers the corpse of another young woman floating in the Neckar River. Subsequent chapters are set '70 years later' and are interrupted twice more with short chapters entitled '1940'. The chapters set in the present are always structured in the same pattern, and they are narrated from the point of view of three women: Helene, Susanne and Una, who is also called Milena at times. Helene is a freelance translator and Hildegard's daughter; Susanne is a teenager and Helene's daughter; and Una is a homeless person at the beginning of the novel, but later works as a cleaner in Helene's office and as a part-time secretary at Susanne's school. As is turns out later, she is also Helene's cousin. A 'family secret' shapes the lives of all the female characters in the novel, their relationships to each other and to the male characters they interact with. This family secret is somehow connected to what happened at Grafeneck, but since it has been repressed as a traumatic experience of those living at the time, it produces more and more symptoms in the lives of the descendants. The psychoanalytic context is stressed by Helene's notion that her office is haunted by the ghost of Jakob Silberzahn, a Jewish psychoanalyst who had worked in her office before he was forced to emigrate before the start of World War II. The symptoms created by Helene and Una's inability to mourn include depression, panic attacks, repetition compulsion, *mémoire involontaire* and delusions.

Their suffering is compounded by the fact that they do not know what really happened. The complicated family secret that is at the bottom of all is revealed in bits and pieces as the story unfolds, but there are different versions about who was responsible for what. Helene's mother Hildegard not only discovered the body in the river, but also worked as a nurse at Grafeneck and was involved in the murder of the inmates of mental institutions who were bussed there from other mental asylums in the infamous grey buses, whose windows were darkened with paint. One of the victims who was supposed to

---

62 Heim, *Feierabend*, pp. 8–10.

be killed at Grafeneck was her twin sister Brunhilde, who was intellectually disabled. It was Brunhilde whose corpse Hildegard had seen in the river, but what exactly happened to Brunhilde remains unclear, as there are several versions of what occurred in 1940. Henriette, an old 'school foe' of Helene who is a historian and has done research on the Nazi period, calls her and tells her that she believes that Brunhilde is still alive. There are other indications that this might indeed be the case. However, at the end of the novel Henriette retracts her previous assertion, claiming that Brunhilde was killed by Hildegard to save her from being gassed. This is only a 'theory' she has,[63] though. What all of the family members believe is that Brunhilde was killed at Grafeneck together with all the other patients who were inmates or transported there.

There is, however, another, third version of what happened to Brunhilde. This version is told in a series of footnotes in the second short chapter entitled '1940'.[64] This chapter ends with: 'The family secret was shared by only a few, the wound never healed'.[65] The wound that never healed is a common metaphor for an evil deed, a guilty conscience, a moral debt that has not been paid, or for repression and the inability to mourn.[66] In *Feierabend*, this wound was opened up when Brunhilde was killed, and this deed became the object of a process of mythologizing that extends to the present day. The aforementioned footnotes quote a letter from an 'uncle Hermann', in which he tells his version of what happened when Brunhilde was taken away from her home and brought to Grafeneck. Hermann, who had been Brunhilde's godfather, was one of the drivers of the busses that transported the patients to Grafeneck and thus to their deaths. However, Hermann could not bring himself to deliver Brunhilde to her killers. He confesses to having shot Brunhilde with his gun in a cornfield during a break when he was driving to Grafeneck. Then, after he was done with his shift for the day (after 'Feierabend'), he came back and put her in the river.[67] He accuses Brunhilde's parents and indeed his whole extended family of surrendering her to the authorities even though they knew what was going on at Grafeneck and what would happen to

---

63 Heim, *Feierabend*, p. 314.
64 Heim, *Feierabend*, pp. 221–223.
65 Heim, *Feierabend*, p. 223. 'Das Familiengeheimnis teilten nur wenige, die Wunde heilte nie.'
66 Well-known examples are King Amfortas in the various adaptations of *Parzival* or Theodor W. Adorno's essay on Heinrich Heine with the title 'Die Wunde Heine' from 1956.
67 Heim, *Feierabend*, p. 222.

her. 'Everybody knew', he claims in his letter. If her parents had only kept her in the house and hidden her, 'all of this would never have happened'.[68]

We will come back to what 'all of this' refers to in the novel, but first it must be pointed out that this letter, which seems to reveal the family secret, was never received by the family and was perhaps never even written. Hermann supposedly wrote it while serving on the Eastern front during World War II. The footnote first says that he was killed in action before he could send the letter.[69] At the end of the footnote, however, an 'Anmerkung' [note] says: 'This letter is only a hypothesis ["These"]. One among many. Nobody knows anything specific'.[70] This move is typical of the novel in its entirety: whenever certain facts are revealed about the past, different versions of the event pop up and take back what the characters and the readers of the novel think they know. Nothing is confirmed in the end; nothing is certain. Instead, everything is in flux: everything remains open to another account of what happened. This uncertainty can be read as an equivalent of the symptoms the characters suffer from because they have repressed the past. To the readers of the novel, this symptom manifests itself as the inability to know what really happened, as the impossibility of ever finding closure when reading or interpreting the past. The last footnote states laconically: 'Thus, all that remained was a hollow uncertainty. For it could never be proven that she [Brunhilde] in fact arrived at Graveneck and died there'.[71]

Although there is no way of knowing what really happened to Brunhilde, one thing is real, and that is the suffering of the female descendants of her twin sister Hildegard: 'A chain of female births [i.e. births of female children] created misfortune and nothing but misfortune.' This is the outcome of Brunhilde's death, which results in 'damage for generations'. Without the corpse in the water, Hildegard and her husband Heinrich would never have met, and all this suffering would never have happened. Under these circumstances, the misfortune, damage and suffering resulting from Brunhilde's death take on tragic or even mythic proportions. Hermann's killing of Brunhilde, committed out of compassion and to save her from the indignity of being corralled like cattle into the

---

68 Heim, *Feierabend*, p. 222. '[. . .] dann wär alles nicht passiert.'

69 The footnote text says that he was 'verschüttet' [buried alive], but elsewhere in the novel it is said that he ran into enemy fire to get killed because he could not bear his guilt over having murdered Brunhilde anymore.

70 Heim, *Feierabend*, p. 222. 'Genaues weiß kein Mensch.'

71 Heim, *Feierabend*, p. 223. 'So blieb eine dumpfe Ungewissheit. Denn dass sie tatsächlich in Grafeneck an- und dort umkam, ließ sich nie belegen.'

gas chamber at Grafeneck, becomes a 'family secret' that might never even have happened, but that will haunt the female descendants of the family for generations to come. This is the meaning of 'all of this' referred to by Hermann in his apocryphal letter. Even the death of Una's daughter Jessica at the age of sixteen is attributed by her mother to a repetitive compulsion she could not escape from: 'I adopted the pattern I had grown into, exaggerated it in a perfidious way, and brought it to its end'.[72] Una will be haunted by her responsibility for her daughter's death for the rest of her life. Although it is only alluded to, it seems that Una commits suicide at the end of the novel. It means 'Feierabend' for her, as she calls it herself.[73]

The mythological dimension of the plot in *Feierabend* is reinforced by Helene's final words, according to which she has to investigate herself. This refers to one of the first investigators or detectives in word literature, Oedipus. He also had a family secret, a repressed guilt that has haunted him, and he also investigates himself, although he does so unknowingly. What is crucial in Uta-Maria Heim's *Feierabend*, which is subtitled 'Kriminalroman' [crime novel], is that the truth of the family secret is never really discovered. Since *Feierabend* is a trans-historical crime novel, in which an investigation in the present is supposed to determine what happened in the past, this has ramifications for both the notion of historical knowledge and for the subgenre itself. The very feasibility of historical knowledge is put into question when, instead of finding out what really happened, at the end of the novel, all that can be discerned from the story is that the characters are caught up in a vicious circle of guilt and repetition or, in short: historiography is replaced by mythology. In this kind of crime fiction, secure knowledge about the past is no longer guaranteed. What is revealed in trans-historical crime writing like Heim's is just another part of the tragedy of history. This might sound as if history can only be understood as an impersonal unfolding of predetermined events that are outside of anybody's sphere of influence. The concept of individual responsibility is not abrogated, however. When the protagonist realizes with the last sentence of the novel that her investigation is only just commencing, she

---

72 Heim, *Feierabend*, p. 303. 'Ich habe das Muster, in das ich hineinwuchs, übernommen und auf perfide Weise überhöht und zu Ende geführt.'
73 Heim, *Feierabend*, p. 322. 'Für mich ist Feierabend'. In German, 'Feierabend' can be used metaphorically to pronounce that something is coming to an end. Even life itself can be the object of 'Feierabend'.

proceeds on both the moral and the epistemological front: she accepts her own accountability and she understands that history is not just a story with a beginning, a middle and an end,[74] but a construct that has to be renegotiated again and again. In the trans-historical investigation of her family's involvement with Grafeneck, the end is not the end, but only the beginning.

---

74 Cf. Aristotle's definition of a story as a 'whole' in: *Poetics*, p. 26.

Sandra Beck

8 The Legacy of the 'Third Reich': Reworking the Nazi Past in contemporary German Crime Fiction

Behind the 'Heimat-Krimi', the next big marketing-driven trend is already lurking: the historical crime novel (combining historical fiction and modern crimes in the anachronistic costumes of bygone eras). No time period will be spared, and luckily, historical epochs can still be subdivided – regional, sexual, with cats, without cooks, with hairdressers. [...] Great.[1]

Instead of praising the hybrid nature of crime fiction like some scholars do, Thomas Wörtche blames marketing ploys for the proliferation of preposterous subgenres. But his scorching criticism ignores the increasing interest in history since the 1980s, an interest aroused by cultural, historical and political issues that go well beyond marketing campaigns.[2] In fact, historical crime novels seem to be a significant component of historical culture, which Jörn Rüsen defines as the 'practical and effective articulation of historical consciousness in the life of a society'.[3] Compared to other types of stories circulating in public discourse, this (sub)genre stands out because it not only represents history, but also presents the process of its making. Specializing in the 'reconstruction of the untold',[4] crime fiction performs a detection process in which readers can observe how '[a]us einzelnen Fakten [...] eine Geschichte wird'[5] [single facts (...) are turned into history]. While making sense of clues and evidence by transforming subjective and fragmentary knowledge into a consistent, finalized, causal narrative, the pattern of the genre calls for definite answers to the questions of 'whodunit' and 'whydunit' – questions that constitute the cornerstones of post-war debates about the 'Third Reich'.

---

1 Thomas Wörtche, 'Krimis zwischen Dessous und Jägerzaun. Die Dialektik des Marketing' [2003], *kaliber.38: krimis im internet* (http://www.kaliber38.de/woertche/einzelteile/jaeger zaun.htm).

2 For an in-depth discussion, see chapter 7 of this volume.

3 Jörn Rüsen, 'Was ist Geschichtskultur? Überlegungen zu einer neuen Art, über Geschichte nachzudenken', in *Historische Faszination: Geschichtskultur heute*, ed. by Klaus Füßmann, Heinrich Theodor Grütter and Jörn Rüsen (Köln/Weimar/Wien: Böhlau, 1994), pp. 3–26 (p. 5).

4 Ernst Bloch, 'Philosophische Ansicht des Detektivromans' [1960/1965], in *Der Kriminalroman: Poetik – Theorie – Geschichte*, ed. by Jochen Vogt (München: Fink, 1998), pp. 38–51 (p. 41).

5 Krystyna Kuhn, *Wintermörder* (München: Goldmann, 2007), p. 390.

https://doi.org/10.1515/9783110426601-008

In today's historical culture, the genre accounts for a twofold 'historical enlightenment': it offers images of a historical era as 'it might have been', and it reveals the presence of the past in contemporary society. Consequently, critics distinguish between two subtypes.[6] Historical crime fiction proper embeds the story of the investigation and the story of the crime within a specific historical period, which is depicted as lived experience on the diegetic level. Retrospective historical crime novels, on the other hand, feature present-day detective characters whose investigations lead them back into the past. Predictably, novels frequently combine elements of both types. The retrospective subtype also explores the narrative possibilities of envisioning the past as lived (through) history – for instance, by expanding the narrative formula of eyewitness testimony to a 'mimesis of memory'.[7] This formal innovation is linked to a broad shift in the politics of representation of the Nazi period. The tendency to include the private memories of contemporaries in later generations' methodical investigations of the past reveals a gap between lived history and its distant, retrospective appropriation, and yet it also often seeks to bridge this very gap. Hence, on the one hand, the novels challenge the idea that detecting yet another atrocity is futile. On the other hand, they tend to emphasize 'German wartime suffering'[8] as well as the agony of the second and third generations in the face of their families' guilt.[9] While they do not deny the crimes perpetrated by the Nazis on any level, the narratives of these novels still display a certain propensity to obscure and marginalize them.[10]

In the following, I will discuss the frameworks that historical crime novels currently employ to represent and understand the Nazi past and its perpetrators –

---

6 See *Geschichte im Krimi. Beiträge aus den Kulturwissenschaften*, ed. by Barbara Korte and Sylvia Paletschek (Köln/Weimar/Wien: Böhlau, 2009); Dagmar Dappert, 'Der historische Kriminalroman als hybrides Genre', in *Crimina. Die Antike im modernen Kriminalroman*, ed. by Kai Brodersen (Frankfurt a. M.: Antike, 2004), pp. 127–142.

7 Michael Basseler and Dorothee Birke, 'Mimesis des Erinnerns', in *Gedächtniskonzepte der Literaturwissenschaft. Theoretische Grundlegung und Anwendungsperspektiven*, ed. by Astrid Erll and Ansgar Nünning (Berlin/New York: De Gruyter, 2005), pp. 123–147.

8 Helmut Schmitz, 'Representations of the Nazi Past II. German Wartime Suffering', in *Contemporary German Fiction. Writing in the Berlin Republic*, ed. by Stuart Taberner (Cambridge: Cambridge University Press, 2007), pp. 142–158.

9 See Erin McGlothlin, *Second-Generation Holocaust Literature. Legacies of Survival and Perpetration* (Rochester, NY: Camden House, 2006); and Caroline Schaumann, *Memory Matters. Generational Responses to Germany's Nazi Past in Recent Women's Literature* (Berlin/New York: De Gruyter, 2008).

10 See William Collins Donahue, *Holocaust as Fiction. Bernhard Schlink's 'Nazi' Novels and Their Films* (New York: Palgrave Macmillan, 2011).

both then and now. This chapter focuses on the different forms of diachronic contextualization of the 'Third Reich' and discusses the trend of accounting for the Nazi past from the perspectives of later generations. Because the 'Third Reich' is predominantly presented within the narrative framework of family history, the respective narratives detail the agony of the descendants when they are confronted with the suspicion of their (grand)parents' complicity in Nazi policy. Thus the novels derive their narrative energy from the dichotomy demonstrated by Welzer et al., according to whom there are two conflicting registers in which to narrate the history of the 'Third Reich': the 'album' of family memory, preserving images of victimhood and heroic resistance; and the 'lexicon' of distant historical knowledge, informed by academic studies.[11] In the narrative arrangement of contemporary German crime fiction, this critical distinction threatens to collapse: by narrating detection processes that illustrate the angst that comes with wondering whether complicity in and responsibility for the crimes of the 'Third Reich' might be a dark secret in one's own family album, crime novels both scrutinize and ward off the Nazi atrocities on the new level of mediated personal dismay.

Documenting the privileges of fiction

Reconsidering the relationship between literature and history as a poetic construction of the past, scholars such as Ansgar Nünning and Astrid Erll have discarded assessments of 'authenticity' in favour of narrative and topical examinations. Accordingly, their focus on the different modes of representation presumes that literature presents fictional worlds in their own right, but is nevertheless linked to extratextual appropriations of the past. Consequently, most authors – like Rose Gerdts in *Morgengrauen* [2013, *Dawn**] – discern between fact and fiction in a foreword or afterword:

> Die Beteiligung zweier Bremer Polizeibataillone nach 1939 am Völkermord im Osten sowie in den Niederlanden ist historisch belegt. Der Roman ist jedoch fiktiv. Ähnlichkeiten mit lebenden oder verstorbenen Personen sind rein zufällig.[12]

> [The involvement of two police battalions from Bremen in the genocide in the east after 1939, as well as in the Netherlands, is historically accurate. The novel, however, is fictional. Any resemblance to real persons, living or dead, is purely coincidental.]

---

11 See Harald Welzer, Sabine Moller and Karoline Tschuggnall, *'Opa war kein Nazi'. Nationalsozialismus und Holocaust im Familiengedächtnis*, 2nd edn (Frankfurt a. M.: Fischer-Taschenbuch, 2002).
12 Rose Gerdts, *Morgengrauen* (Reinbek bei Hamburg: Rowohlt, 2013).

In documentary novels, the line drawn between the verifiable story of historical events, documented and evidenced by historians, and their symbolic concentration in fictional narratives seems to be blurred on purpose. By interweaving factual and fictional discourses, documentary re-narrations of authentic cases present fiction as history. A closer look, however, reveals the poetic strategies that these novels utilize to construct a meaningful story and to comment on canonized history.

Since the documentary pattern addresses verifiable and knowable historical events, 'whodunit' suspense is usually set aside. Instead, the text focuses on the task of providing an explanatory model in which a mixture of psychological, social, historiographical and political aspects is intended to elucidate the crime and the context that enabled it. Echoing the criminal case histories of the eighteenth and nineteenth centuries, Horst Bosetzky's *Wie ein Tier: Der S-Bahn-Mörder* [1995, *Like an Animal: The S-Bahn Murderer**] subjects the case of a sexual predator in Berlin in 1940, who rapes and kills women beside the tracks of a commuter train, to a general psycho-historical interpretation of the 'Third Reich', which 'Prof. Dr. Horst Bosetzky' clearly spells out in the epilogue:

> Ich [...] verstehe dieses Buch [...] als Plädoyer gegen alle Männerbünde militärischer und paramilitärischer Art, denn Paul Ogorzow war kein Einzeltäter, sondern nur einer, der, abgesprengt [...] vom Heere derer, die die wahren Massenmörder waren, seine Verbrechen beging. Er wurde enthauptet, die meisten anderen durften mithelfen, das neue Deutschland zu bauen.[13]

> [I (...) understand this book (...) as a plea against all men's military and paramilitary organizations, because Paul Ogorzow was not a lone perpetrator, but rather just someone who, split off (...) from the army of those who were the true mass murderers, committed his crimes. He was decapitated, while most of the others were allowed to help build the new Germany.]

Bosetzky's reading of the story jumps abruptly to the explicit assignation of its exemplary historiographic meaning. The author's note defines a context of references in which the case story of a *Lustmörder* metonymically vouches for a general interpretation of the 'Third Reich' as, in Freudian terms, the reign of the unleashed *id* that waits for its time to come in every man. Although the text discloses its contents as derived from and bound to knowable and verifiable historical facts, the specific emplotment of these facts conveys a pre-shaped image of the National Socialist regime, for which Ogorzow serves as a case

---

13 Horst Bosetzky, *Wie ein Tier. Der S-Bahn-Mörder* (München: dtv, [1995] 2009), p. 324.

study. Accordingly, the author frankly states that he has supplemented and adjusted the material to fit his view:

> Zugleich aber ist mein S-Bahn-Mörderbuch auch ein Roman [. . .] und Ergebnis diverser Kunstgriffe aus dem Spannungsschreibergewerbe. Da war auf cliffhanger hinzuarbeiten, und thrill und suspense waren ebenso einzuweben wie die Muster des klassischen Polizeiromans, vor allem aber Figuren zu erfinden, die nötig sind, um Paul Ogorzow [. . .] "historische Tiefenschärfe" zu verleihen, das heißt deutlich zu machen, was hier passiert ist: Ein Mensch mit einer bestimmten genetischen und sozialisationsbedingten "Programmierung" gerät in ein Milieu und eine Zeit, den nationalsozialistischen Mörderstaat und die Verdunkelung Berlins, die seine Taten in ihrer einmaligen Konstellation [. . .] regelrecht provozieren.[14]

> [At the same time, however, my S-Bahn murder book is also a novel (. . .) and a result of diverse tricks of the suspense writer's trade. Cliffhangers were required, and likewise thrill and suspense had to be woven in, just like the patterns of the classic police novel, but above all, characters who were necessary to (. . .) lend Paul Ogorzow 'historical depth' had to be invented, which means making clear what has happened here: a man with specific genetic and socialization-dependent 'programming' finds himself in a setting and a time – the National Socialist murder state and the Berlin blackout – which, in their unique constellation, (. . .) blatantly provoke his crimes.]

This epilogue damages the narrative facade of objectivity and authenticity by pointing out the narrative arrangement of the documented facts and the intention upon which it is based. Therefore, the 'true' historical meaning of the case is both stated and staged. In accordance with the statements of its fictional characters and the assessment of the epilogue, the novel mirrors the aetiology of Ogorzow's pathologically morbid sexuality in Gerhard Baronna's development from a representative of law and order to a mass murderer in the East. By naming the exact dates, times and places, the novel signals a documentary mode of representation, thus giving a striking example of the crucial role narrativization plays in the production of meaning, inasmuch as the dating of Ogorzow's crimes suggests a reading that equates the increasing brutality of the perpetrator with the 'cumulative radicalization' of Nazi politics.[15] Even though Bosetzky's novel creates the illusion of documenting an authentic criminal case, the narration makes sure to point beyond the solving of Ogorzow's crimes. It highlights the facilitative function of the historical background and mediates the image of

---

14 Ibid., pp. 320–321.
15 See Irina Gradinari, *Genre, Gender und Lustmord. Mörderische Geschlechterfantasien in der deutschsprachigen Gegenwartsliteratur* (Bielefeld: Aisthesis, 2011).

a murderous male society, in which 'the path to genocide'[16] and sexually motivated murder are equivalent options through which to act out innate drives.

Playing on the threshold between factual and fictional discourses, the documentary pattern creates the illusion of simply chronicling a past historical reality while actually designing a diegetic world in its own right. The epilogue of Bosetzky's novel unmistakably reveals an *arranger les faits* political poetics and instructs its readers to focus on the image sketched of Nazi Germany, condensed in a serial-killer narrative. However, both the mode of representation and the image of German perpetrators seem outdated. While Rolf Hochhuth's *Der Stellvertreter* [1963, *The Deputy*] and Peter Weiss's *Die Ermittlung* [1965, *The Investigation*] constitute the peaks in a period of documentary and critical literary visions of the 'Third Reich' and its aftermath in the 1960s and 1970s, the majority of crime novels today take a realist approach and tend to replace the distant notion of inhuman evil with recognizably human motives, such as opportunism, greed, corruptibility and revenge. Instead of pathologizing the perpetrators, current novels testify to the kind of 'banality of evil' that Hannah Arendt did not have in mind.[17]

Family histories

If one revisits the history of retrospective crime fiction since the 1970s, a subtle yet significant change in topics and narrative patterns becomes apparent. Instead of addressing the continuity of the 'Third Reich' and the denial of its atrocities, the genre currently reworks the Nazi past as a sensitive, intergenerational family matter. According to Welzer and Lenz, there is a remarkable gap between the official culture of remembrance and the reproduction of the 'Third Reich' in family memory: private and public versions of history are drifting apart.[18] Investigations in the archives of family history consequently dwell on feelings of fear and shock nurtured by a reasonable suspicion that complicity in Nazi policy must not be confined to the 'lexicon' but is equally part of the private 'album' of family memory.

---

16 Christopher R. Browning, *The Path to Genocide. Essays on Launching the Final Solution* (Cambridge: Cambridge University Press, 1992).

17 See Hannah Arendt, *Eichmann in Jerusalem. A Report on the Banality of Evil* (London: Faber and Faber, 1963).

18 See Harald Welzer and Claudia Lenz, 'Opa in Europa. Erste Befunde einer vergleichenden Täterforschung', in *Der Krieg der Erinnerung. Holocaust, Kollaboration und Widerstand im europäischen Gedächtnis*, ed. by Harald Welzer (Frankfurt a. M.: S. Fischer, 2007), pp. 7–40.

Realism in series

Realist historical crime novels set exclusively in the 'Third Reich' are clearly outnumbered by texts that investigate either the Weimar Republic or the post-war period. In accordance with well-known historiographical patterns – 'crisis and decline' for the Weimar Republic, 'rise and fall' for the 'Third Reich' – these series of novels concentrate on historical questions of cause and effect. As a result, first of all, one encounters serial detective characters who begin their careers in the Weimar Republic and witness its doom. The most prominent among these characters are surely Philip Kerr's Bernie Gunther and Volker Kutscher's Gereon Rath.[19] Acclaimed as the best historical crime fiction series in the German language, the adaptation of Kutscher's novels under the direction of Tom Tykwer, Achim von Borries and Hendrik Handloegten 'is widely predicted to become an international television sensation'.[20] The filming of the first novel of the series, *Der nasse Fisch* [*Babylon Berlin*], in two seasons consisting of eight episodes each, has been identified from the start as comparing favourably with the finest US television series, such as *The Wire, Breaking Bad* and *Boardwalk Empire*.[21] According to Christian Buß in *Der Spiegel*, this goal has been achieved, given that, 'as a conspiracy scenario, the series unwinds smoothly, like the best US series – while being completely in line with the cinematic tradition of essentially German angst'.[22]

In addition to these historiographic literary projects that link the 'reconstruction of the untold' on the diegetic level to the reconstruction of historical causation, the subgenre also concentrates on the final years of Nazi terror.[23] Both the Allied bombings that heralded in Germany's 'total defeat' and the

---

19 Kerr has published thirteen Bernie Gunther novels. Kutscher plans to cover the years 1929 to 1936, which leaves one novel still to be written. For further examples, see the series written by Susanne Goga, Robert Hültner and Bernward Schneider, or the Hermann Kappe series, with the telling title *Es geschah in Berlin*.

20 See Siobhán Dowling, 'Sex, Drugs and Crime in the Gritty Drama "Babylon Berlin"', *New York Times*, 7 November 2017 (https://www.nytimes.com/2017/11/07/arts/television/sex-drugs-and-crime-in-the-gritty-drama-babylon-berlin.html).

21 See 'Wegweisende Produktion. "Babylon Berlin" mit Tom Tykwer', *Das* (http://www.daserste.de/specials/ueber-uns/serie-babylon-berlin-tom-tykwer-100.html)Erste.

22 See Christian Buß, 'Weltmeister der Angst', *Der Spiegel*, 10 October 2017 (http://www.spiegel.de/kultur/tv/babylon-berlin-von-tom-tykwer-serienmeisterwerk-ueber-die-weimarer-republik-a-1170044.html).

23 The same holds true for retrospective historical crime novels, such as Wiedergrün's *Blutmadonna* (2013 [*Madonna of Blood**]), Neuhaus's *Tiefe Wunden* (2009 [*Deep Wounds**]), Gross's *Grafeneck* (2007) and Schorlau's *Das dunkle Schweigen* (2005 [*The Dark Silence**]).

suffering of civilians form the background against which processes of self-reflection are staged, displaying inner conflicts between the mandated Nazi worldview and antagonistic personal beliefs, which are still concealed in public: '"Wir verteidigen Europa gegen den Bolschewismus. Wir verteidigen unsere Frauen und Kinder. Unsere Heimat". Standardparolen. An denen hielt er sich fest'[24] ['We defend Europe against Bolshevism. We defend our women and children. Our homeland'. Standard slogans. He clung to them].

Both tendencies converge in Jan Zweyer's *Goldfasan* [2009, *Golden Pheasant**], the second novel in his Peter Goldstein series. This novel is set in Herne in 1943, and the case of a missing forced labourer forms the angle for a 'social enquête'.[25] In contrast to the propaganda image of a committed *Volksgemeinschaft* [national community], the narrator presents conflicting behavioural patterns with regard to the regime, varying from resistance and anxious obedience to personal gain cloaked in steadfast adherence to the *Führer*. In Zweyer's portrayal of Nazi society, the polycratic power structure is murderous but, first and foremost, corrupt. While *Sturmbannführer* [major] and *Kriminalrat* [detective superintendent] Wilfried Saborski is ordered to get rid of Walter Munder – the deputy *Kreisleiter* [county leader] of the NSDAP, whose Polish forced labourer is missing – influential circles provide cover for the murderer of Marta Slowacki in exchange for a considerable share in the illegal profit that Munder's father-in-law Wieland Trasse makes from the genocide. Confronted with the true meaning of the incriminating Nazi phrase *Sonderbehandlung* [special treatment], Trasse is shocked for a moment, but instantly recovers when he sees the Jewish belongings stored by the SS:

> Ohne ein weiteres Wort öffnete Müller sein Pistolenhalfter, zog die Waffe heraus, entsicherte sie und schoss dem Mann in den Kopf. / Trasse packte das blanke Entsetzen, als er den Juden in seinem Blut vor sich liegen sah. [...] Aber er folgte Müller und Lahmer zum nächsten Regal, bestaunte goldene Uhren, Bilder niederländischer Meister, Ringe aus Silber und Platin. // Als Trasse am Abend in einem Militärzug Richtung Westen saß, hatte er den Vorfall mit dem Juden schon wieder völlig vergessen.[26]

> [Without another word, Müller opened his holster, pulled out the gun, took off the safety and shot the man in the head. / Trasse was horrified, as he saw the Jew lying in his own blood right in front of him. (...) But he followed Müller and Lahmer to the next shelf, marvelled at gold watches, paintings by Dutch masters, rings of silver and

---

24 Richard Birkefeld and Göran Hachmeister, *Wer übrig bleibt, hat recht* (Frankfurt a. M.: dtv, [2002] 2004), p. 125.
25 Stefanie Abt, *Soziale Enquête im aktuellen Kriminalroman. Am Beispiel von Henning Mankell, Ulrich Ritzel und Pieke Biermann* (Wiesbaden: Deutscher Universitätsverlag, 2004).
26 Jan Zweyer, *Goldfasan* (Dortmund: grafit, 2009), pp. 146–147.

platinum. // As Trasse sat in a military train heading west that evening, he had already completely forgotten the incident with the Jew.]

Whereas the pattern of the genre characteristically reserves the right to discover the truth for the detective character, Golsten[27] only glimpses the conspiracy and the planned crimes with which the reader is already familiar due to the constant switching of viewpoints. In this regard, the novel makes it clear that truth, justice and the rightful punishment of murderers were beyond the reach of a low-level official in 1943, unless he wanted to embark on a suicide mission. Consequently, the text abandons the 'whodunit' suspense in favour of a thorough observation of the investigator's personal struggle between his ethics and his official duties. As a member of the SS and the criminal investigative forces, Golsten represents law and order as well as its distortion in Nazi Germany. The subsequent question of whether 'it was even possible to behave like a real detective in a world that was owned and run by criminals'[28] doubles as the choice between resistance and complicity arises in both his private and work life. Golsten is confronted by Heinz Rosen, a Jewish communist who has been hiding in his father-in-law's rabbit hutch. Even though his wife and her father dissuade him from denouncing Rosen to the Gestapo, Golsten still insists that Rosen has to leave for the sake of his family's safety and, in doing so, is responsible for his capture a few days later. Anticipating this unexpected opportunity, Golsten's superior, Saborski, presents Rosen as the murderer of Marta and her child. The confession Saborski submits bears a signature Golsten knows to be forged, but which he nonetheless authenticates with his own altered name. As a result, the two signatures on this 'confession' stand for the murder conviction of an innocent and the opportunism of a *Mitläufer* (follower).

The allegedly minor detail of an altered surname metaphorically indicates, on the one hand, the police officer's willingness to set personal beliefs aside for the sake of his career. On the other, it foreshadows the myriad name changes and contorted identities in the post-war period, which are depicted in the subsequent novel *Persilschein* [2011, *Persil Certificate**] that reads in both form and content like a repetition of the *Goldfasan* case. Although

---

27 Goldstein changes his Jewish sounding name into Golsten in 1939, at the suggestion of his superior, who tells him that '[d]iese Entscheidung sei sein Bekenntnis für die Tätigkeit im Reichssicherheitshauptamt, für den nationalsozialistischen Staat und für Deutschland und seiner Karriere nur förderlich' [this decision is a commitment to his function in the Reich Security Main Office, for the National Socialist state and for Germany, and only beneficial for his career]. Ibid., p. 23.

28 Philip Kerr, *Prague Fatale. A Bernie Gunther Thriller* (London: Quercus, [2011] 2012), p. 431.

Goldstein is now able to uncover the conspiracy that benefitted from the genocide, he once more offers false promises and, in the end, is forced to conceal the truth and to sign another document – this time his resignation. With this repetitive structure, the series parallels the failures of its central character in both Nazi and post-war Germany.

Iconography versus banality

Compared to the extraordinary attention paid to the Eichmann trial in Jerusalem in 1961/1962,[29] the media's response to recent revelations indicating that the German intelligence service BND had known precisely where to find the chief organizer of the Holocaust since 1952 was minimal. This lack of public interest suggests a general acceptance of Germany's handling of the legacy of the 'Third Reich' in the 1950s. In this respect, Uwe Klausner's *Eichmann-Syndikat* (2012), set in Berlin in 1962, challenges the historiographical normalization[30] of the allegedly bygone 'politics of amnesty and integration'.[31] By means of the thriller's narrative structure – typically depicting a lethal contest between good and evil – the Eichmann case is reviewed as a fight between the former victims of National Socialism and the merciless, powerful post-war conspiracy of all the 'many little "Eichmanns"'.[32] However, the novel seems to put later generations and their self-righteousness to the test by emphasizing their corruptibility and failure in a scenario that is best described as a resurgence of the 'Third Reich'.

Illustrated with a picture of Eichmann's left handprint taped to a file card labelled with Hebrew lettering, the novel invokes an authentic, yet (undis)-closed historical background. Depicting what might have happened if a whistle-blower had handed over the incriminating BND file to the press in 1962, Klausner adds two counterfactual storylines to his representation of Eichmann's capture and execution: the story of tabloid reporter David Rosenzweig, alias Theodor

---

29 See Marc von Miquel, 'Explanation, Dissociation, Apologia. The Debate over the Criminal Prosecution of Nazi Crimes in the 1960s', in *Coping with the Nazi Past. West German Debates on Nazism and Generational Conflict, 1955–1975*, ed. by Philipp Gassert and Alan E. Steinweis (New York/Oxford: Berghahn, 2006), pp. 50–63.

30 See Gavriel D. Rosenfeld, *Hi Hitler! How the Nazi Past is Being Normalized in Contemporary Culture* (Cambridge: Cambridge University Press, 2015).

31 See Norbert Frei, *Vergangenheitspolitik. Die Anfänge der Bundesrepublik und die NS-Vergangenheit* (München: Beck, 1996), Engl. transl. *Adenauer's Germany and the Nazi Past. The Politics of Amnesty and Integration* (New York: Columbia University Press, 2002).

32 Peter Krause, *Der Eichmann-Prozeß in der deutschen Presse* (Frankfurt a. M./New York: Campus, 2002), p. 54.

Morell, to whom the incriminating evidence is leaked; and that of Thomas von Sydow, who is trying to protect him against a murderous alliance of 'Gestapo, BKA oder BND – [diese] Typen [sind] doch alle gleich'[33] [Gestapo, BKA or BND – (these) guys (are) all the same]. Even though readers are provided with a strict distinction between real and fictional characters in the first pages, it is misleading to define the counterfactual storylines 'by an "estranging" [...] relationship to historical reality'.[34] In fact, the novel claims to visualize historiographic findings concerning Germany's *Vergangenheitspolitik* ('policy for the past'[35]) and its aftermath, for which Adolf Eichmann serves as a paradigmatic case study.[36]

The novel's intent to spell out historiographical assessments in a fictional storyline for readers who are not proficient in history becomes apparent in the use of (sometimes obtrusive) footnotes and references to secondary sources. Together with the narrator's heterodiegetic overview of what is going to happen, all of the paratexts cut across 'the illusion of glimpsing the past'.[37] By referring to historical knowledge beyond the characters' points of view, Klausner's novel not only offers an imaginary depiction of the past, but also provides the frame for its interpretation. In this regard, quotations from eyewitness reports, (auto)biographies and historical works attest to the historiographical probability of the *what-if* scenario from today's point of view, instead of documenting a mimetic relationship to *real* history. Consequently, the interpretative horizon rests upon present-day evaluations of Germany's 'policy for the past', as summed up in the motto: 'Lieber ein untergetauchter SS-Obersturmbannführer als ein geständiger Massenmörder'[38] [Better an *SS-Obersturmbannführer* (lieutenant colonel) in hiding than a mass murderer admitting his guilt].

---

33 Uwe Klausner, *Eichmann-Syndikat* (Meßkirch: Gmeiner, 2012), pp. 247–248.

34 Gavriel D. Rosenfeld, *The World Hitler Never Made. Alternate History and the Memory of Nazism* (Cambridge/New York: Cambridge University Press, 2005), p. 5.

35 Frei, *Adenauer's Germany*, p. xii. With this phrase, Frei 'refer[s] to the sum total of [...] political-legal measures', which aimed at the 'vitiation' of the Allied 'policy of purging'. 'The basic elements of the policy for the past [...] are thus amnesty, integration, and demarcation' (ibid).

36 See *Interessen um Eichmann. Israelische Justiz, deutsche Strafverfolgung und alte Kameradschaften*, ed. by Werner Renz (Frankfurt a. M.: Campus, 2012); Bettina Stangneth, *Eichmann vor Jerusalem. Das unbehelligte Leben eines Massenmörders*, 2nd edn (Hamburg/Zürich: Arche, 2011), Engl. transl. *Eichmann Before Jerusalem. The Unexamined Life of a Mass Murderer* (New York: Alfred A. Knopf, 2014).

37 Astrid Erll, 'Literature, Film, and the Mediality of Cultural Memory', in *Cultural Memory Studies. An International and Interdisciplinary Handbook*, ed. by Astrid Erll and Ansgar Nünning, in collaboration with Sara B. Young (Berlin/New York: De Gruyter, 2008), pp. 389–398 (p. 391).

38 Klausner, *Eichmann-Syndikat*, p. 204.

Even though it offers conflicting assessments of the political situation, the variable focalization of the novel adds up to a consistent picture. All three main figures agree that they are witnessing old Nazi cliques rising to power again. Agnes von Sydow, Eichmann's former mistress and a camp guard in Theresienstadt, praises this development, while David and Tom fear it and fight it in vain. Most interestingly, Agnes personifies the topical resurrection of Nazism. Presumably killed during a US air strike in February 1945, Agnes managed to escape prosecution and now returns to Berlin. Presented as an alluring, demonic and cold-blooded femme fatale, she is intended to embody the Nazi past, which consequently appears as a haunting ghost walking behind the *Wirtschaftswunder* cover-up. While portraying adherence to Nazism as a result of seduction and seductiveness, the novel stages the revival of a formerly abandoned Jewish identity:

> Bei Kriegsende war er [d.i. David Rosenzwei] noch voller Hoffnung gewesen [...]. Er hatte geglaubt, dass sich alles zum Besseren wenden würde. Beharrlich, hartnäckig, felsenfest. Und war eines Schlechteren belehrt worden. / Die Peiniger von einst, all die Menschenschinder, Schreibtischtäter und Henkersknechte – sie waren wieder da. Jeder wusste es, aber niemand sprach darüber. Sie waren wieder salonfähig geworden, jene, an deren Händen Blut klebte, an die man nicht erinnert werden wollte.[39]

> [At the end of the war, he (i.e., David Rosenzweig) had still been full of hope (...). He had believed that everything would take a turn for the better. Tenaciously, stubbornly, unwaveringly. And he had been wrong. / The erstwhile tormenters, all the oppressors of men, the bureaucratic perpetrators and executioner's servants – they were back. Everyone knew, but no one spoke about it. They had once again become presentable, those whose hands were stained with blood, of which one did not wish to be reminded.]

The denunciation of the lack of political will to prosecute Hitler's 'ordinary men' entails the reidentification process of the Jewish tabloid reporter. Pursued once more, Rosenzweig abandons his pen name and commits suicide in the same arbour where he had hidden for the last two years of the 'Third Reich', with the yellow star pinned on his chest – 'ein Relikt aus den Tagen, die er für immer überwunden zu haben glaubte'[40] [a relic from the days that he thought he had overcome for good].

Echoing Timothy Naftali's remark that '[t]he Eichmann capture had yanked several skeletons out of the closet',[41] Klausner's counterfactual *what-if* scenario

---

39 Ibid., p. 293.
40 Ibid., p. 295.
41 Timothy Naftali, 'The CIA and Eichmann's Associates', in *U.S. Intelligence and the Nazis*, ed. by Richard Breitman and others (Cambridge: Cambridge University Press, 2005), pp. 337–374 (p. 340).

reviews the complex issue of Germany's 'policy for the past' as a family matter. Mediated by its characters and their paradigmatic lives, the political climate of the 1960s is portrayed as a silent revival of the 'Third Reich'. The case of Adolf Eichmann serves as a narrative frame to display the symbol of Holocaust evil against Hitler's 'ordinary men', who still define German society, and hence to juxtapose Germany's 'first' and 'second guilt'.[42] With Agnes, the hysterical and fanatical 'vamp',[43] the novel personifies the popular narrative of a seduced German majority, while David's symbolic suicide accounts for the failure of later generations to cope with the moral, political and judicial aspects of the Nazi past in a society infiltrated by the 'Eichmann-Syndikat'. Instead of popularizing the iconographic image of the so-called 'desk murderer' Eichmann, the novel emphasizes shared responsibility for the Nazi crimes and their concealment after 1945. The detailed depiction of Tom von Sydow sacrificing David and the truth for the sake of his family's well-being, however, shifts the focus from entanglement in the Nazi years to entanglement in the post-war years, which see the death of those who escaped the extermination camps by sheer chance.

The legacy of Nazi biopolitics

The idea of a purified and healthy *Volkskörper* [body politic] was one of the cornerstones of Nazi ideology. While propagating, in brief, a male body as hard as steel and a fertile female womb to produce the desired 'Aryan' children for the *Führer*, the Nazis inversely set in motion the extinction of 'life unworthy of life'.[44] Two of those biopolitical efforts at racial purification were the SS projects of *Lebensborn* [the Fount of Life] and *Euthanasia*, which Henry Friedlander considers 'the first chapter of Nazi genocide'.[45] Studies on racial cleansing and these attempts to breed an 'Aryan race' therefore focus on the families targeted by the Nazi policy of procreation and annihilation. Rainer Gross' novel

---

42 Ralph Giordano, *Die zweite Schuld oder Von der Last Deutscher zu sein* (Hamburg: Rasch und Röhring, 1987).

43 Klausner, *Eichmann-Syndikat*, p. 283.

44 See *Rasse, Blut und Gene. Geschichte der Eugenik und Rassenhygiene in Deutschland*, ed. by Peter Weingart, Jürgen Kroll and Kurt Bayertz (Frankfurt a. M.: Suhrkamp, 1988); Hans-Walter Schmuhl, *Rassenhygiene, Nationalsozialismus, Euthanasie. Von der Verhütung zur Vernichtung 'lebensunwerten Lebens' 1890–1945* (Göttingen: Vandenhoeck & Ruprecht, 1987).

45 Henry Friedlander, *The Origins of Nazi Genocide. From Euthanasia to the Final Solution* (Chapel Hill, NC/London: University of North Carolina Press, 1995), p. xii.

Grafeneck (2007) and its sequel, *Kettenacker* (2011), and Jörg S. Gustmann's *Rassenwahn* [2012, *Racial Fanaticism**] attest to the fatal effects of Nazi policy on German families and the suffering of *Lebensborn* children. Given that gene-alogy and descent help to define individual self-understanding, this topical var-iation of 'privatization' reconsiders the personal implications of those crimes that have been scrutinized and subsequently restored in the darkened areas of collective memory:

> Irgendeinen Nazi-Greuel aufzudecken, nach fünfzig Jahren, das ergibt keinen Sinn, denkt er [d.i. Kommissar Greving]. Nichts, was man davon nicht schon wüßte. Wahrsc-heinlich lebt der Täter gar nicht mehr, und die genauen Umstände lassen sich auch nicht rekonstruieren.[46]

> [To disclose some Nazi atrocity, after fifty years, that makes no sense, he (i.e., Commissar Greving) thought. There is nothing that wasn't already known. The culprit was probably not even alive any more, and the specific circumstances can't be reconstructed either.]

The gap between the alleged meaninglessness of yet another Nazi crime and the realization of personal involvement is the crucial topic here. The amateur histo-rian Hermann Mauser, whose sister was murdered in Grafeneck in 1944,[47] liter-ally excavates a mummified body in a hermetically sealed cave. While exploring the untouched scene, Mauser instantly senses the presence of his father and feels a personal obligation to the dead man and his history. This vision sets the tone for the subsequent story of investigation. By cross-fading presentiment and knowledge, the novel focuses on the emotional implications beyond the scope of legal prosecution and thus turns Officer Greving into a bystander in Mauser's pri-vate investigation. Declaring the case a family affair, Mauser's story points to the crucial question of 'wie unsereiner mit den entdeckten Geschichten lebt'[48] [how people like us get along with the discovered stories]. This privatization is spelled out by means of transforming the story of the investigation into an identity crisis. In this context, the sequence of conflicting images of his father, whom Mauser suspects to be the murderer, is bound to the assumed identity of the dead. When it turns out that the mortal remains are the body of Dr Jürgen Schumacher, for-mer leader of the institute in Grafeneck, Mauser is relieved:

---

46 Rainer Gross, *Grafeneck*, 11th edn (München: Goldmann, 2010), p. 167.
47 According to the trend in contemporary crime fiction of setting the story of the crime in the final years of the 'Third Reich', Gross's novel extends the period of the killings until 1944, whereas Aly specifies that the killings in Grafeneck took place from January to December 1940. See Götz Aly, *Die Belasteten. 'Euthanasie' 1939–1945: Eine Gesellschaftsgeschichte* (Frankfurt a. M.: S. Fischer, 2013), p. 48.
48 Gross, *Grafeneck*, p. 115.

Der Alptraum ist vorüber: Er muß seinen Vater nicht mehr für einen Nazi und einen Behindertenmörder halten. Stattdessen sieht er ihn vor sich, in seiner Uniform, [...] wütend und hilflos und bereit, sein Ideal zu verraten. Ratlos, weil sich Recht und Unrecht nicht mehr scheiden lassen.[49]

[The nightmare is over: he does not have to think of his father as a Nazi and a killer of the disabled anymore. Instead, he sees him before his eyes, wearing his uniform (...) angry and helpless and ready to betray his ideals. Baffled, because right and wrong can no longer be distinguished.]

In the beginning, the Nazi past is portrayed as a time 'in der der Vater gekämpft, gelitten, standgehalten hat'[50] [during which the father fought, suffered, withstood], but this view is increasingly blurred, and the formerly clear distinction between right and wrong vanishes with it.

This 'privatization' of the Nazi past characterized by shame, atonement and mercy is sealed by the confessional secret and entombed in autobiographic memory. This theme is continued and broadened in the subsequent novel, *Kettenacker*, in which Mauser investigates the life and case history of his sister. Although the background of the so-called *Aktion T4* [T4 Program] points to the core of Nazi ideology, the novel only touches the surface of the motives of race fanatics. The confrontation with secular and religious notions of good and evil establishes a broader, rather ahistorical framework, in which the identification of the perpetrators seems to be of subordinate importance. It is the feeling of an obligation to commemorate the story of the victims that drives the investigation:

Mauser geht es nicht mehr um die Bestrafung des Täters, er geht davon aus, dass er tot ist. Aber er braucht ihn für Mutz' Geschichte. Er muss wissen, wo sie ihren Anfang nahm, wo aus einem stillen, aber gesunden Kind ein Traumaopfer, eine Schwachsinnige und schließlich ein 'unwertes Leben' geworden ist.[51]

[Mauser is no longer interested in the punishment of the perpetrator; he assumes that he is dead. But he needs him for Mutz's story. He must know where it started, how a quiet but healthy child became a victim of trauma, an imbecile and lastly a 'worthless life'.]

In contrast to Gross's melancholic novels that rework bleak family secrets, Gustmann's multi-perspective thriller *Rassenwahn* relies on a familiar formula. It links exhaustive reviews of the historical background to the story of a troubled police officer hunting down a psychopathic serial killer who has been hired to 'prevent' *Lebensborn* children from suing for their rights. Although the book details

---

49 Ibid., p. 190.
50 Ibid., p. 14.
51 Rainer Gross, *Kettenacker* (Bielefeld: Pendragon, 2011), p. 248.

how these children cope with their origins and the knowledge of their anonymous fathers' complicity in Nazi policy, the logic of the plot presents them as a living threat: they are the genetic evidence of their fathers' devotion to the biopolitics of Heinrich Himmler, as well as unwelcome co-heirs in the eyes of their half-siblings. Consequently, the novel ends with a sour compromise: while the mild sentences of Nazi perpetrators and their descendants' loss of wealth and career prospects are noted in detail, former *Lebensborn* infant Emilie Braun becomes the sole heir to her biological father's fortune and engages Officer Martin Pohlmann to manage her assets, enabling him and his family to enjoy a life of luxury:

> Seine Zuneigung war zu Liebe geworden, erst recht, nachdem sie ihm eröffnet hatte, dass er bald Vater sein würde. [...] Er hatte längst das Traumschloss für sich und seine Familie gefunden, ein Penthouse über den Dächern von Lüneburg. Mit einem Fahrstuhl von der Tiefgarage direkt bis in die Wohnung, davon hatte er schon immer geträumt.[52]
>
> [His affection had become love; more so after she told him that he would be a father soon. (...) He had found the dream home for himself and his family long ago, a penthouse over the rooftops of Lüneburg. With an elevator going from the underground garage straight into the apartment. He had always dreamt of that.]

By contrasting private happiness, which culminates in humane and loving reproduction, with public notions of justice, the novel stages another variation on the 'privatization' of the Nazi past: it reworks the personal question of a burdensome legacy into that of the fair distribution of wealth, emphasizing instead the recognition of identity as the recognition of inheritance claims. On the other hand, dealing with the *Lebensborn* paints a picture of SS men as ideologically perverted caricatures of father figures, whose devotion to 'positive eugenics' merely echoes their ruthless eagerness to contribute to the regime's murderous program of racial 'cleansing'. This imagery of depraved fathers is supplemented with the detection of false motherhood in Nele Neuhaus's *Tiefe Wunden* [2009, *Deep Wounds**] and Krystyna Kuhn's *Wintermörder* [2007, *Winter Murderer**]. In this regard, the 'Third Reich' and its implications are presented as the destruction and disintegration of (German) families bound to the strictly gendered crimes of ruthless fathers and demonized mothers.

---

52 Jörg S. Gustmann, *Rassenwahn* (Meßkirch: Gmeiner, 2012), p. 561.

The phantasm of revenge

In his study *Ordinary Men*, Christopher Browning quotes Major Wilhelm Trapp, commander of Reserve Police Battalion 101: 'If this Jewish business is ever avenged on earth, then have mercy on us Germans.'[53] These words, spoken by a perpetrator, attest to a pervasive fear fuelled by Nazi propaganda: the phantasm of Jewish revenge. Accordingly, Hermann Göring's speech on 4 October 1942 in the *Berliner Sportpalast* ties attendants to a racially coded national community, bound to a common destiny by the crimes of the regime:

> There is one thing I would like to tell the German people, so that it is hammered home in your brains and engraved in your hearts: [. . .] German people, you must know, you will be exterminated if the war is lost. The Jew, with his infinite hatred, stands behind these ideas of extermination. [. . .] And no one should deceive himself and come along afterwards and say: I was always a good democrat, under these vulgar Nazis I just barely . . . [. . .] Ha! Then the Jew will give you the right answer. No matter if you whine to him that you have been the greatest Jew-lover or Jew-hater, he will treat both equally, because he will take vengeance on the entire German people.[54]

In his notorious Posen speech on 6 October 1943, Himmler presented his 'absolutely clear solution' to this matter: 'I did not feel I had the right to exterminate [. . .] the [Jewish] men, while allowing the avengers on our sons and grandsons, in form of their children, to grow up.'[55] The declining chances of an Axis victory obviously gave rise to the trope of Jewish revenge, in which anti-Semitic beliefs, justifications of 'total war' and projections of guilt are inextricably intertwined. This distorted amalgamation of exculpation and confession, rationalization and denial still prevailed in post-war Germany, as becomes apparent in the controversy over Rainer Werner Fassbinder's play *Der Müll, die Stadt und der Tod* [1975, *Garbage, the City, and Death*].[56] For German post-war society, the trope seemed alluring

---

53 Christopher R. Browning, *Ordinary Men. Reserve Police Batallion 101 and the Final Solution in Poland* (New York: Harper Collins, 1992), p. 58.

54 Hermann Göring, 'Görings Erntedankrede von 1942', in *Volkes Stimme. Skepsis und Führervertrauen im Nationalsozialismus*, ed. by Götz Aly (Frankfurt a. M.: S. Fischer, 2006), pp. 149–194 (pp. 191–192). The speech is edited according to the wording of the sound recording made by Großdeutscher Rundfunk.

55 'Ich hielt mich nämlich nicht für berechtigt, die Männer auszurotten [. . .] und die Rächer in Gestalt der Kinder für unsere Söhne und Enkel groß werden zu lassen'. Heinrich Himmler, 'Rede vor den Reichs- und Gauleitern in Posen am 06.10.1943', in *Heinrich Himmler. Geheimreden 1933 bis 1945*, ed. by Bradley F. Smith and Agnes F. Peterson (Frankfurt a. M./Berlin/Wien: Propyläen, 1974), pp. 162–183 (p. 169).

56 See Janusz Bodek, 'Ein "Geflecht aus Schuld und Rache"? Die Kontroversen um Fassbinders *Der Müll, die Stadt und der Tod*', in *Deutsche Nachkriegsliteratur und der Holocaust*, ed. by Stephan Braese et al. (Frankfurt a. M./New York: Campus, 1998), pp. 351–384.

because it was – and still is – bound to an imaginary reversal of victim and perpetrator. Portraying the descendants of former victims of persecution as today's perpetrators in a motive-driven genre like crime fiction therefore results in a profoundly probable storyline, with a Janus-faced villain and/or hero who may just as well shape the anti-Semitic fear of having to ward off a 'Jewish threat'.

The politics of representation in contemporary German crime fiction, however, is not dominated by the trope of 'Jewish vengeance', nor is it comparable with Quentin Tarantino's blood-soaked, anti-historical revenge fantasy *Inglourious Basterds* (2009). In contrast, revenge-driven plots set in the 'Third Reich' primarily display personal vendettas of individual *Volksgenossen* [German nationals]. In Richard Birkefeld and Göran Hachmeister's *Wer übrig bleibt, hat recht* [2002, *Who Remains, is Right**] or Jörg Isringhaus's counterfactual thrillers *Unter Mördern* [2010, *Among Murderers**] and *Ein fremder Feind* [2013, *A Foreign Foe**], we come across determined male figures who kill for private vengeance in an attempt to settle the score with the regime. Taking into account the limited scope of post-war legal prosecution, the authors of retrospective crime fiction also use the motive of revenge to review the 'policy for the past'. Consequently, all the novels that feature a revenge plot demonstrate a twofold reason for the action: the actual crime and the failure of the post-war legal system to prosecute Nazi perpetrators.

The interplay between insufficient impersonal legal action and the private vengeance this triggers is plainly presented in Ferdinand von Schirach's *Der Fall Collini* [2011, *The Collini Case*]. Having shot a former SS-*Sturmbannführer* [major] and major industrialist in post-war Germany, Fabrizio Collini turns himself in but refuses to disclose his motives. During the trial, his attorney – who had known the victim only as a caring, grandfatherly mentor and had been unaware of his past involvement with the SS – reveals that Collini was seeking retribution for the killing of his father in 1944 that the law had denied him. Even though Collini pressed charges in 1969, the implementation of the *Einführungsgesetz zum Gesetz über Ordnungswidrigkeiten* [Introductory Act to Administrative Offences] on 1 October 1968, which enacted nothing but a 'kalte Amnestie für fast alle'[57] [a cold amnesty for almost everyone], closed the proceedings.[58] In addition to addressing this politically calculated

---

57 Ferdinand von Schirach, *Der Fall Collini*, 2nd edn (München/Zürich: Piper, 2011), p. 182, Engl. transl. *The Collini Case*, trans. by Anthea Bell (New York: Viking, 2012).
58 In 1968, the Introductory Act to Administrative Offences created a legal loophole from which Nazi perpetrators benefitted immensely, as Rebecca Wittmann explains: 'According to the old version of § 50 of the German Criminal Code, anyone who was convicted as an accomplice to a crime was subject to the same penalty as the perpetrator. This meant, ostensibly, that a Nazi defendant who was convicted as an accomplice to murder could be sentenced to

inefficacy of the legal system, the novel reopens the gap between justice served in courtrooms and the elementary sense of justness, inasmuch as it considers the murder of Collini's father, a partisan, to be justified by international law. The novel itself offers Collini's suicide as the only solution to the conflicting legal and moral implications of the 'Third Reich'.

In this regard, the shift from justice to retribution sets the stage for a tragic mode – a mode with which crime fiction has been associated for some time and with which it is currently obsessed – brothers killing brothers (Isringhaus: *Unter Mördern*), sons killing unknown fathers (Wiedergrün: *Blutmadonna* [*Madonna of Blood**]), sisters killing to cover up for their brothers (Borrmann: *Wer das Schweigen bricht* [*Those Who Break the Silence**]), mothers killing to avenge the murder of their families and the kidnapping of their sons (Neuhaus: *Tiefe Wunden*), as well as sons killing and kidnapping in order to force perpetrators and their descendants to reveal their families' crimes (Kuhn: *Wintermörder*). The evident dramatization and privatization that shapes these novels is caused by the narrative framework of family history, because it compels the characters involved to incorporate the profound yet distant historical knowledge of Nazi atrocities into their family memory as one of its undeniable parts. In this regard, the lack of 'Jewish revenge' is striking, but it corresponds to the findings of Welzer et al., according to whom, 'in Gentile families, the past of the Jewish Germans who were killed appears only as the history of their disappearance, not even as the history of the dead, let alone as living history'.[59] Only two novels, Christian von Ditfurth's *Mann ohne Makel* [2002, *A Paragon of Virtue*] and Rose Gerdts's *Morgengrauen*, present plots in which the working hypothesis of Jewish revenge is combined with reasonable suspicion regarding the role of the respective father figures in the mass murder of European Jewry.[60]

---

life in prison.' After the amendment, 'in order to sentence a convicted accomplice to life in prison, the prosecution had to show that the defendant possessed "base motives". Otherwise, the defendant had to be given a shorter sentence, which would be 15 years or less. [...] The problem here lies with the statute of limitation [...]: all crimes carrying sentences of 15 years or less were no longer prosecutable after 1960, because they became statute barred 15 years after the crime was committed.' Rebecca Wittmann, 'The Normalization of Nazi Crime in Postwar German Trials', in *The Nuremberg Trials: International Criminal Law since 1945 / Die Nürnberger Prozesse: Völkerstrafrecht seit 1945*, ed. by Herbert R. Reginbogin and Christoph J.M. Safferling (München: Saur, 2006), pp. 209–215 (pp. 211–212).

59 Welzer, Moller and Tschuggnall, *'Opa war kein Nazi'*, p. 210.

60 For a further discussion of the trope of Jewish vengeance in German crime fiction see Magdalena Waligórska, '"Darkness at the Beginning". The Holocaust in Contemporary German Crime Fiction', in *Tatort Germany. The Curious Case of German-Language Crime Fiction*, ed. by Lynn Kutch and Todd Herzog (Rochester, NY: Camden House, 2014), pp. 101–119.

In Gerdts's novel, the plausibility of a serial murderer retaliating against the slaughter of his father's family in 1941 is used to lead readers astray. Antanas Kurdika, who is blackmailing the former members of Police Battalion 105 to pay for his father's treatment, indirectly causes the murders, since one of the members refuses to pay and kills the others to prevent his own exposure. Due to this framework, the formal interrogation of Karl Mollenhauer, the murderer of both Kurdika's family and the 'old comrades', is followed by a private conversation with Kurdika. The antagonistic framing of the interviews in terms of subject, topographical setting, the participants and their reaction sets the stage to present a considerable division of responsibility. While interrogating Mollenhauer, the officers agree to concentrate on the present in order to prosecute him; testifying to the crimes of the 'Third Reich' is left to the victim's son. The subsequent shift from an examination in legal terms to a matter of ethics culminates in a twisted scene in which the investigating officer, Steenhoff – who suspects his foster father of having worked as a camp guard in Westerbork, 'the symbol of the Holocaust in the Netherlands'[61] – attempts to shatter 'Kurdikas selbstgerechte Sichtweise auf die Dinge, die geschehen sind'[62] [Kurdika's self-righteous perspective on the things that have happened] with a blatant lie. Steenhoff shows him a photograph of the Wailing Wall and tells him that Max, the grandson of the former police battalion member Erich Wessel, was deeply moved by Yad Vashem, stating: 'Bei Ihrer Wahrheit [. . .] hätten erst die Enkel von Max wieder ein Recht auf ein Leben ohne Schuld'[63] [Adhering to your truth (. . .) would mean that only Max's grandsons would have the right to a life without guilt]. According to this rationale, a (fabricated) gesture of emotion compensates for the genocide.

Remarkably, Steenhoff is the only one who persistently brings up the terms 'guilt' and 'revenge', while Kurdika refers to the children's and grandchildren's responsibility to face the past – an obligation Steenhoff, preoccupied with his own suffering, is obviously not capable of fulfilling. Instead, he dreams of forgiveness and even envisions a tacky scene in which he meets with Antanas's father, '[gibt] ihm zum Abschied die Hand [. . .] und dieser [zieht] ihn plötzlich an sich'[64] [reaches out to shake his hand to say goodbye, and the other suddenly pulls him in close]. But Antanas's father is dead, and forcing the gesture

---

61 Pim Griffioen, 'Westerbork', in *Enzyklopädie jüdischer Geschichte und Kultur. Bd. 6*, ed. by Dan Diner (Stuttgart/Weimar: Metzler, 2015), p. 397.
62 Gerdts, *Morgengrauen*, p. 310.
63 Ibid.
64 Ibid., p. 307.

of reconciliation on his son does not console Steenhoff, so, in his dreams, he usurps the biography of the child saved from the genocide:

> In der Nacht träumte er, dass er in eine alte Kastanie hinter dem Wohnhaus seiner Tante Else und seines Onkel Willi kletterte. Kaum hatte er es sich auf seinem Lieblingsast bequem gemacht, sah er, wie Flammen aus den Fenstern des Hauses schlugen. Er wollte schreien, um seinen Halbbruder Peter, seine Mutter und seine Tante zu warnen, [...] aber er brachte keinen Ton hervor. Als das Dach mit lautem Getöse in sich zusammenstürzte, wachte Frank Steenhoff schweißgebadet in seinem Hotelbett auf.[65]

> [That night, he dreamed that he was climbing an old chestnut tree behind the home of his Aunt Else and Uncle Willi. He had barely made himself comfortable on his favourite branch when he saw the flames billowing out of the windows of the house. He wanted to scream, to warn his half-brother Peter, his mother and his aunt, (...) but he could not make a sound. As the roof collapsed with a loud crash, Frank Steenhoff woke up in his hotel bed, drenched in sweat.]

Reading these last few pages is quite an imposition on the reader on many levels. The imaginary victim-perpetrator reversal, which emphasizes Steenhoff's agony, nevertheless sketches the probable profile of a character who fears being a 'schuldlos schuldige[s] Täterkind'[66] [innocently guilty child of perpetrators]. The minute this suspicion is proven baseless, the novel relieves its protagonist of his obligation to face the past and allows Steenhoff to return to normal.

Von Ditfurth's novel uses comparable motifs – a child saved from the Holocaust and a German father figure involved in the deportation of Jews – but in contrast to Steenhoff, the historian and amateur detective Josef Maria Stachelmann is trained to think in terms of historical causation:

> 'Leopold Kohn war kein Mörder im üblichen Sinn. Er war einer, der aus Verzweiflung tötete. Was immer Herrmann Holler im Einzelnen in der NS-Zeit angerichtet hat, wie groß immer sein Beitrag gewesen sein mag zur Ausrottung der Familie Kohn und anderer, wir werden es wahrscheinlich nicht herausfinden. Aber ich weiß, dass Herrmann Holler Leopold Kohn erst zerstört und schließlich ermordet hat. [...] Kohn ist zuerst ein Opfer. Herrmann Holler ist ein Killer'.[67]

> ['Leopold Kohn was not a murderer in the regular sense. He was someone who killed out of despair. What Herrmann Holler did during the Nazi regime, how large his contribution to the eradication of the Kohn family and others might have been, we will probably never

65 Ibid., p. 311.
66 Christoph Ernst, *Dunkle Schatten* (Bielefeld: Pendragon, 2012), p. 294.
67 Christian von Ditfurth, *Mann ohne Makel. Stachelmanns erster Fall*, 22nd edn (Köln: Kiepenheuer & Witsch, [2002] 2012), p. 371.

> find out. But I know that Herrmann Holler first destroyed and finally murdered Leopold Kohn. (...) Kohn is foremost a victim. Herrmann Holler is a killer'.]

The connection Stachelmann emphatically establishes between the mass murder of European Jewry and the serial killings is echoed in the passages in which Kohn's motive is detailed in psycho-narration. Kohn commits premeditated murder in order to put Maximilian Holler in his situation; he too should be the only remaining survivor of his family and have nothing left to do but mourn the dead: 'Erst wenn Holler so allein war wie Leopold Kohn, herrschte Gerechtigkeit'[68] [Not until Holler was as alone as Leopold Kohn would there be justice].

In its multi-perspective narration, the novel confronts this understanding of justice – inspired by the Old Testament concept of revenge – with Stachelmann's disclosure of an 'SS Mafia',[69] the expert advice of a profiler pathologizing the perpetrator's state of mind and the police officers' focus on the fraudulent aspects of Holler's real-estate business. A thorough study of sources and daily routines as well as psychological evaluations may yield partial answers to the 'whydunit', but will ultimately fail in the light of the 'Final Solution':

> 'Warum haben Sie die Kinder ermordet?'
> 'Warum haben die meine Eltern vergast?'[70]
>
> ['Why did you kill those children?'
> 'Why did they gas my parents?']

Summary

Although there is a very clear line between historical works that narrate verifiable facts and works of fiction that convey an otherwise unknowable story in its own right, recurring and memorable cultural representations nevertheless shape our notion of a historical period. At regular intervals, the popular imagery deployed p rovokes public discussions that focus on the key question of whether a particular representation of the historical past can be seen as appropriate in terms of historical causation, accuracy and probability.

---

68 Ibid., p. 293.
69 Ibid., p. 301.
70 Ibid., pp. 363–364.

Since these negotiations of discursive agreement equally apply to Jonathan Littell's novel *Les bienveillantes* [2006, *The Kindly Ones*] and Jörg Friedrich's study *The Fire: The Bombing of Germany, 1940–1945* (2002), two aspects must be noted. With a tacit understanding of the power of literature to shape collective memory, public discourses tend to limit the scope of literary privileges. This might explain the dominance of a realist mode of representation and of plot structures that are informed by studies such as Götz Aly's *Hitlers Volksstaat* and by scholarly catchphrases such as Christopher R. Browning's *Ordinary Men*. Then again, while they set their stories in Nazi or post-war Germany, contemporary German crime novels tend to shut out the Holocaust when they portray the years between 1933 and 1945. The oppression, deportation, exploitation and mass murder of European Jewry is referred to as an incontestable fact, but is marginalized in the diegetic world. Against the backdrop of 'moral' Allied bombing, these novels portray a frightened society that was not at all ideologically devoted to the murderous policy of the regime, but rather doubted the promised *Endsieg* [final victory]. It was greed and the prospect of career opportunities that drove the perpetrators. Instead of fanatical Nazis, the novels feature 'ordinary men' utilizing the leeway offered by a criminal regime to exploit forced labourers and European Jews. In general, the same holds true for those novels that ground current crimes in post-war Germany's failure to cope with the 'Third Reich' and its implications. At the same time, the retrospective historical crime novels discussed in this chapter favour family histories as a mode of emplotment, 'where love for the parent collides with horror upon learning of the parent's criminal past'.[71] Consequently, the transformation of distant historical knowledge into personal concern in the narrative pattern of family histories leads to the rediscovery of the wide range of Nazi atrocities for which the novels present perverted, false father and mother figures as perpetrators. Despite this politics of representation, the novels nonetheless distinguish the good German from the Nazi once again. In their diegetic worlds, detective characters may suspect the unacknowledged crimes of their parents and grandparents, but they regularly confirm that immediate involvement in the genocide of European Jews remains a dark secret in other family closets.

---

71 McGlothlin, *Second-Generation Holocaust Literature*, p. 205.

Sandra Beck

9 Blood, Sweat and Fears: Investigating the Other in Contemporary German Crime Fiction

The history of research on crime fiction confronts its readers with a methodological *tour de force*: from its structuralist beginnings in the 1960s to ideological readings and today's postcolonial approaches, the detective genre has served and 'serves as a kind of laboratory for testing various critical hypotheses and methodologies'.[1] The variety of research approaches therefore not only reprocesses current developments in the narrative macrostructure of the genre, it also attests to academic debates in the field of literary and cultural studies, which reach beyond the 'test case' and stimulate new readings of the genre and its history.

In discussing canonical texts and contemporary narrative experiments, inter-, multi- and transcultural studies arrive at conflicting understandings of the subject. In reference to the 'nonchalant racism'[2] that often pervades classic detective novels of the British Golden Age, critics dissect, on the one hand, a narrative pattern that is apologetic at best. Its implementation of a Eurocentric worldview and

1 Heta Pyrhönen, *Murder from an Academic Angle. An Introduction to the Study of the Detective Narrative* (Columbia, SC: Camden House, 1994), p.6.
2 Christine Matzke and Susanne Mühleisen, 'Postcolonial Postmortems. Issues and Perspectives', in *Postcolonial Postmortems. Crime Fiction from a Transcultural Perspective*, ed. by Christine Matzke and Susanne Mühleisen (Amsterdam/New York: Rodopi, 2006) pp. 1–16 (p. 4). Matzke and Mühleisen refer to Agatha Christie's *Murder on the Orient Express* (1934), *Murder in Mesopotamia* (1936), *Death on the Nile* (1937) and *Ten Little Niggers* (1939).

Note: This chapter is based on my article 'Zwei Welten, im Verbrechen überbrückt? Interkulturelles Erzählen in der deutschsprachigen Kriminalliteratur der Gegenwart', in *Gewissheit und Zweifel. Interkulturelle Studien zum kriminalliterarischen Erzählen*, ed. by Sandra Beck and Katrin Schneider-Özbek (Bielefeld: Aisthesis, 2015), pp. 7–40.

https://doi.org/10.1515/9783110426601-009

its politics of representation with regard to the criminal Other[3] prove to be deeply rooted in colonial discourses.[4]

> Beyond these fantasies of Orientalist wisdom and beneficent imperialism, however, classic detective fiction and its close cousin the spy story more typically align mystery conventions with anxieties over contamination, irrationality, and the threat posed to imperial modernity by unassimilated racial and cultural difference.[5]

On the other hand, critics propose that the introduction of the ethnic,[6] cross-cultural[7] or postcolonial detective[8] provides the narrative with the means to question an exclusive Western viewpoint and thwart the genre's dichotomous construction of identity and alterity, as well as the discursive strategies to usurp and appropriate the category of the 'Other'.[9] These opposing normative positions rely on the epistemological and ontological potential of crime fiction to both question and support a particular conception of reality as well as the premises of knowledge and interpretation on which a predefined socio-cultural order is based – whether it be (neo)imperialistic or multicultural. Consequently, the

---

3 Consequently, Teraoka notes: 'the detective became one means by which foreignness was criminalized and the safety of the body politic and England's identity as ruler of an empire were secured'; see Arlene A. Teraoka, 'Detecting Ethnicity. Jakob Arjouni and the Case of the Missing German Detective Novel', in *Investigating Identities. Questions of Identity in Contemporary International Crime Fiction*, ed. by Marieke Krajenbrink and Kate M. Quinn (Amsterdam/ New York: Rodopi, 2009), pp. 113–129 (p. 121). Teraoka is referring here to Ronald R. Thomas, 'The Fingerprint of the Foreigner. Colonizing the Criminal Body in 1890s Detective Fiction and Criminal Anthropology', *ELH* 61 (1994), 655–683.

4 See Caroline Reitz, *Detecting the Nation. Fictions of Detection and the Imperial Venture* (Ohio: The Ohio State Univ. Press, 2004), CD Rom.

5 Nels Pearson and Marc Singer, 'Introduction. Open Cases: Detection, (Post)Modernity, and the State', in *Detective Fiction in a Postcolonial and Transnational World*, ed. by Nels Pearson and Marc Singer (Farnham/Burlington: Ashgate, 2009), pp. 1–14 (p. 4).

6 Peter Freese, *The Ethnic Detective. Chester Himes, Harry Kemelman, Tony Hillerman* (Essen: Die Blaue Eule, 1992).

7 Margaret J. King, 'Binocular Eyes. Cross-Cultural Detectives', *The Armchair Detective* 13 (1980), 253–260.

8 *The Post-Colonial Detective*, ed. by Ed Christian (Basingstoke: Palgrave, 2001).

9 Accordingly, Fischer-Hornung and Mueller define ethnic detective novels as follows: 'ethnic detective novels address issues of personal and social identity that reflect the importance of the ethnic community for the particular detective. The intensity of the detective's negotiation of his or her ethnic identity tends to directly correlate with the distance that the detective's particular ethnic group has from "mainstream" society'; see Dorothea Fischer-Hornung and Monika Mueller, 'Introduction', in *Sleuthing Ethnicity. The Detective in Multiethnic Crime Fiction*, ed. by Dorothea Fischer-Hornung and Monika Mueller (Madison: Farleigh University Press, 2003), pp. 11–19 (p. 12).

genre can either affirmatively rehearse beliefs about being and knowing by successfully applying them to solving the murder at hand or demonstrate their contingency and expose epistemological gaps by means of red herrings.

> Many authors have thus broadened the theme of investigation to address issues of community, beliefs and identity constructions across geographic and national boundaries, including gender and race relations. Others have broadened the genre by inventing recognisable sub-categories which relate to the social, political and historical formations of their specific postcolonies.[10]

In the history of German crime fiction, questioning the social construction of reality dates back to the late 1960s. What is referred to as the *Neuer deutscher Kriminalroman* [New German Crime Novel] brought socio-political developments gone sour and the everyday problems of a modern multicultural society into the plot pattern of the genre. For Jeanne Ruffing, however, this functionalization of the genre often amounted to nothing more than a pejorative, 'pitying or even shuddering look at the fringes of national or world society'.[11] Thus, within the intercultural setting of crime fiction, the foreign is primarily an object of obsessive, meticulous observation. Critics agree that the appearance of the ethnic detective cuts across this questionable politics of representation, which perpetuates images of the criminal 'Other' by embodying pervading contemporary fears. With this figuration, crime fiction identifies coexisting or conflicting worldviews that reach well beyond the Western European notion of truth and reality. The genre thus comprises an impressive variety of themes, topics and narratives: we find subversive experiments de(con)structing 'a genre based on Western epistemology and ontology'[12] and novels that plumb the detective's hybrid soul or functionalize the narrative poetics of suspicion to comment on contemporary debates on migration, asylum policy, multiculturalism and interculturality, as well as rather conventional texts that rely on standardized narratives while using foreign countries 'both as sources of mystery and evil and as exotic backdrops'.[13]

Based on a closer reading of selected texts, this chapter highlights dominant tendencies in contemporary German crime fiction, which currently

---

10 Matzke and Mühleisen, 'Postcolonial Postmortems', p. 5.
11 Jeanne Ruffing, *Identität ermitteln. Ethnische und postkoloniale Kriminalromane zwischen Popularität und Subversion* (Würzburg: Königshausen & Neumann, 2011), p. 23.
12 Jeanne E. Glesener, 'The Crime Novel. Multiculturalism and Its Impact on the Genre's Conventions', in *Crime and Nation. Political and Cultural Mappings of Criminality in New and Traditional Media*, ed. by Immacolata Amodeo and Eva Erdmann (Trier: WVT, 2009), pp. 15–26 (p. 15).
13 Pearson and Singer, 'Introduction', p. 5.

focuses on the German-Turkish relationship, and discusses the possibilities and pitfalls of the structure of the genre from an intercultural perspective. The first sections present topical readings and analyse the ways in which the genre deals with the topics of 'honour killings' and terrorism. This discussion of the genre's capacity to question modern multicultural society and its social construction of reality is followed by an examination of contemporary attempts to shift the narrative emphasis from the tragic potential of intercultural encounters to the comic mode. The chapter concludes with a discussion of novels that dispatch their detective figures into foreign worlds, thus confronting them with the fragility of their Eurocentric interpretation of reality.

Killing in the name of honour

> The scandalous murders in the name of honour call upon us to give a clear answer to the question of whether immigrants from the Mediterranean region, whether men from tribal, patrilineal societies, whether Muslim men are compelled by their culture to kill members of their own family from time to time.[14]

Thomas Hauschild's rhetorical dismissal of a 'cultural defence' of 'honour killings' is not just a criticque of the 'blind culturalism' that supposedly resulted in an unacceptable 'cultural bonus for certain offenders'[15] in the 1980s and 90s.[16] Rather, his critical contribution to the discussion is, in fact, an explicit demand to side against these despicable excesses of a foreign culture and non-Western religion, and thus to take a firm stand regarding the cultural self-

---

14 'Nach der Skandalisierung von Morden im Namen der Ehre in den letzten Jahren sind wir aufgefordert, deutlich Antwort auf die Frage zu geben, ob Zuwanderer aus dem Mittelmeerraum, ob Männer aus tribalen, patrilinear organisierten Gesellschaften, ob muslimische Männer durch ihre Kultur genötigt sind, gelegentlich Mitglieder ihrer eigenen Familie zu töten'; see Thomas Hauschild, 'Ehrenmord, Ethnologie und Recht', in *Wider den Kulturenzwang. Migration, Kulturalisierung und Weltliteratur*, ed. by Özkan Ezli, Dorothee Kimmich and Annette Werberger (Bielefeld: Transcript, 2009), pp. 23–46 (p. 29).
15 Ibid., p. 42 and 27.
16 Sev'er speaks of 'patriarchal murders', because 'honour killings are a misnomer, an ugly façade that tries to cover up murders of women in patriarchal parts of the world. By attaching the word "honour" to brutal murders of women, people are erroneously led to believe that these are somewhat legitimized and culturally or religiously sanctioned practices'; see Aysan Sev'er, *Patriarchal Murders of Women. A Sociological Study of Honour-Based Killings in Turkey and in the West* (Lewiston, NY: Mellen, 2013), p. 21.

understanding of the German state. Similarly, public debates about an alleged 'Islam discount'[17] in 2014 made it perfectly clear that 'honour killings' are an emotionally and ideologically loaded topic that exacerbates discussions about 'parallel societies' and legitimizes claims made about the necessity of assimilation and integration by instrumentalizing the dead female body.[18]

In this tokenistic sense, 'honour killings' and their narrative aftermath are used as red herrings and as motives in German-language crime fiction. Consequently, these novels revolve around the obvious dichotomy between the (assumed) archaic rules of conduct to which the Muslim minority adheres and modern civilization's monopoly on power and punishment. The topic here is the incomprehensible and unbearable criminality of 'Others':

> Er [Staatsanwalt Suter] schüttelte traurig den Kopf [...]. 'Das ist der islamische Fundamentalismus', sagte er. 'Die Frau ist in dieser Kultur, wenn man es so nennen will, nichts weiter als ein Gebrauchsgegenstand, ein Tier, ein Hund. Die Frau wird gesteinigt, wenn sie einen fremden Mann auch nur anlächelt. [...] Das dürfen wir nicht zulassen, meine Herren. Da müssen wir durchgreifen. Und das ist die Aufgabe unserer Polizei'.[19]

> [He (attorney Suter) sadly shook his head (...). 'This is Islamic fundamentalism', he said. 'In this culture, if you want to put it that way, the woman is nothing more than a commodity, an animal, a dog. The woman is stoned to death for merely smiling at a stranger. (...) We must not allow that, gentlemen. We have to take drastic measures. And that is the task of our police'.]

Although Hansjörg Schneider's novel *Das Paar im Kahn* [1999, *The Couple in the Barge**] immediately reveals the categorization of Aische Aydin's death as an 'honour killing' to be a hasty, ersatz solution; the 'law and order' mentality quoted above, voiced in the name of women's rights, provides a fitting starting point – the idea of defending a morally legitimized order against the deadly, uncivilized and misogynist rule of a minority – for discussing the reflexive possibilities and structural pitfalls of the ways in which the genre deals with this topic.

---

17 [Anonym] 'So diskutiert das Netz über den Islam-Rabatt', in *Bild* (http://www.bild.de/news/inland/rechtsprechung/so-diskutiert-das-netz-ueber-den-islam-rabatt-35298338.bild.html).

18 See Elisabeth Bronfen, *Over Her Dead Body. Death, Feminity and the Aesthetic* (New York: Routledge, 1992).

19 Hansjörg Schneider, *Das Paar im Kahn. Hunkelers dritter Fall* (Zürich: Diogenes, 2011), p. 12.

Like other crime novels about 'honour killings',[20] Rose Gerdts's *Ehrenhüter* [2011, *Honour Keeper**] debates the insinuated 'clash of civilizations'[21] that takes place over the dead female body. With its cover, its title and its quotation of Surah 24:33, the text immediately suggests that the murder of Nilgün Cetin, a pregnant high-school student, is an 'honour killing'. The introduction of the crime scene deepens this suspicion by referring to the Bremer Bunker murder of 2003.[22] By citing the original verdict in this sensational case, commissars Frank Steenhoff and Navideh Petersen express existential incomprehension and moral outrage:

> 'Laut dem Vorsitzenden Richter sind die Beweggründe für diese Tat für uns Deutsche nicht nachvollziehbar. Es sei [...] beinahe anmaßend, ihre Beweggründe zu bewerten. Schließlich hätten die über Jahrzehnte erlittenen Grausamkeiten durch das türkische Militär den Volkscharakter der Kurden geformt. [...] Diese Urteilsbegründung werde ich nie vergessen'.
>
> 'Verständlich. Das ist doch ein Freifahrtschein für jeden vermeintlich kulturell begründeten Mord!' Navideh war empört.[23]
>
> ['According to the presiding judge, the motives for this crime are incomprehensible for us Germans. It would (...) be almost presumptuous to judge their motives. After all, the national character of the Kurds has been shaped by the atrocities they have suffered for decades at the hands of the Turkish military. (...) I will never forget these grounds for the judgment'.
>
> 'Stands to reason. That's a free pass for any murder allegedly committed for cultural reasons!' Navideh was outraged.]

With this explicit rejection of a cultural justification, the tone is set for the subsequent course of events: embedded in a reference system of personal, highly emotional dismay on the part of both investigators, the story of the investigation expands upon the characters' 'tiefste Verachtung'[24] [deepest contempt] – their rage paired with brutality in view of the 'abnormal' reaction of Nilgün's father to

---

20 For further reading, see Judith Arendt, *Unschuldslamm* (München: Ullstein, 2014); Roger Aeschbacher, *In der Hitze der Stadt* (Kassel: Exlibris, 2012); Ella Danz, *Rosenwahn* (Meßkirch: Gmeiner, 2012); Marcel Feige, *Kalte Haut* (München: Goldmann, 2012); Sabine Klewe, *Der Seele weißes Blut* (München: Goldmann, 2012); Sandra Lüpkes, *Todesbraut* (München: dtv, 2011); Christian Böhm, *Tod am Inn. Ein neuer Fall für Watzmann* (München/Zürich: Piper, 2009).
21 The phrase was coined by Samuel P. Huntington, *The Clash of Civilizations and the Remaking of World Order* (New York: Simon & Schuster, 1996).
22 See Dietrich Oberwittler and Julia Kasselt, *Ehrenmorde in Deutschland 1996–2005. Eine Untersuchung auf der Basis von Prozessakten* (Köln: Luchterhand, 2011), pp. 137–141.
23 Rose Gerdts, *Ehrenhüter* (Reinbek: Rowohlt Taschenbuch Verlag, 2011), p. 24.
24 Ibid., p. 55.

her body,[25] their rejection of 'vorsintflutlich'[26] [antediluvian] gender roles and their condemnation of the 'verdammte Familienehre'[27] [damn family honour]. These reactions, which reveal insurmountable incomprehension of the behaviour of the Cetin family, have a particularly strong effect on Steenhoff's conservative intellectual and emotional world.[28] Petersen, on the other hand, revises the notion of a uniform migrant body by pointing out the considerable socio-cultural differences and begins to contextualize the concept of honour. In debating the level of freedom women have been granted in patriarchal societies, she reveals a point of comparison between 'them' and 'us': 'Die Deutschen glauben immer, wer weiß wie fortschrittlich zu sein, aber all diese Errungenschaften im Verhältnis zwischen Männern und Frauen sind noch verdammt jung'[29] [The Germans like to think of themselves as being ever-so-progressive, but all of these achievements in the relationship between men and women are still damn young]. This passage marks a pivotal point from which the topographical and temporal demarcation of an archaic, parallel society could be questioned – but the novel fails to query these firmly entrenched stereotypes. Despite occasional hints at modern societies' concepts of honour, the detectives do not consider the possibility of a German perpetrator until the end of the story. Consequently, the novel leaves the explanation of his motives to the culprit, who confesses to having killed Nilgün Cetin for the 'honour' of his family:

> 'Mein Ruf wäre ruiniert gewesen. Ein junges, schwangeres Mädchen, noch dazu Türkin aus einfachsten Verhältnissen, stirbt im Haus eines angesehenen Bremer Hochschullehrers – es wäre immer etwas an mir und meiner Familie haftengeblieben. [. . .] Nein, ich musste es für ihn [Roman, seinen Sohn und Nilgüns Freund], für meine Familie tun. Das war ich ihnen schuldig. Unser Name sollte nicht öffentlich in den Dreck gezogen werden'.[30]

> ['My reputation would have been ruined. A young, pregnant girl, Turkish and of the humblest origins besides, dies in the home of a prestigious professor at Bremen University – something would have stuck to me and my family. (. . .) No, I had to do it for him (Roman, his son, Nilgün's boyfriend), for my family. I owed them that much. Our name should not be publicly dragged through the mud'.]

Due to the detective genre's policy of utilizing a strategy of disinformation by using red herrings to postpone the solution, the socio-cultural facts and

---

25 See ibid., p. 150 and pp. 95–96.
26 Ibid., p. 151.
27 Ibid., p. 170.
28 See ibid., p. 211.
29 Ibid., p. 153.
30 Ibid., p. 340 and 342.

circumstances of the case – that is, the importance of honour in terms of symbolic capital in modern mainstream society – are only touched on at the end of the novel, whereas the foreign value system is closely monitored and clearly rejected. Accordingly, the passages focalizing Nilgün and her younger sister Saliah constantly fuel the reader's suspicions regarding the male members of the Cetin family. Designated as authentic statements from an otherwise impervious, isolated world, both testify to the various forms of physical and psychological violence committed against women in their 'Parallelwelt'[31] [parallel world] and thus outline a pressing social problem that transcends this single murder case. On the other hand, the culprit's interpretation of the crime as an 'Unfall'[32] [accident] remains uncontested, rendering the murder a pitiable yet isolated case – not a societal problem. Although the text emphasizes German mainstream society's responsibility for 'honour killings', it scarcely breaks the binary demarcation between 'us' and 'them', between 'civilized' and 'archaic'; the German majority's interpretation of the world remains largely unquestioned. One seemingly causal passage reflects this by casting doubt on the (legal) distinction between (Turkish) 'honour killing' and (German) 'domestic murder':

> 'Ich musste hier vor Jahren mal zu einem Tötungsdelikt raus', sagte Steenhoff. 'Ein ziemliches Drama. Eine junge Frau war von ihrem eifersüchtigen Ehemann zu Tode geprügelt worden. Ihr ältester Sohn, ich glaube, er war vier oder fünf Jahre alt, hatte die Tat miterleben müssen'.[33]

> ['Years ago, I was called out to a homicide here', Steenhoff said. 'Quite a drama. A young woman had been beaten to death by her jealous husband. Her eldest son, I think he was four or five years old, had had to witness the deed'.]

Although the novel does not explicitly apply a litmus test by questioning the discursive differentiation between a (Turkish) 'honour killing' and a (German) 'family tragedy', it displays the potential of the genre to use its structure to query and observe the social construction of reality and the epistemological strategies on which it rests. In contrast to W. W. Domsky's scandalous novel *Ehre, wem Ehre ...* [2009, *Honour to whom Honour ...**], in which any concession to the customs of foreign cultures is understood as a defeat in the clash of civilizations, *Ehrenhüter* thwarts any detailed elaborations concerning the Turkish Others' concepts of honour – and thus leaves its readers to consider this questionable discursive surplus.

---

31 Ibid., p. 190.
32 Ibid., p. 340.
33 Ibid., p. 84.

Terrorism and its histories

Novels that investigate (supposed) 'honour killings' predominantly focus on the collapsing notion of intercultural understanding, assuming the adherence of Turkish men and women to the closed culture of an archaic, patriarchal, misogynist parallel society, where the punishment for crossing the frontier is death. German-language thrillers, in contrast, seem to be preoccupied with the figure of the male Muslim terrorist. As a popular literary means of both instigating and scrutinizing collective fears, the narrative of the thriller refers to the conflicting values, moral codes and religious beliefs of at least two characters, distorts them into extremist positions and translates them into a complex of events geared towards mutual destruction. The logic of the plot turns the symbolic struggle for interpretational sovereignty into an existential confrontation – perhaps most strikingly in the political thriller.[34] However, most contemporary texts alter this collective duel to the death: in accordance with the fundamental question of crime fiction – *Cui bono?* – these novels usually introduce a third party who secretly pulls the strings. To serve their economic and political agenda, they instrumentalize the threat of fundamentalist terrorist attacks in order to escalate intercultural tensions to civil war-like conditions. In Matthias Gibert's *Zirkusluft* [2009, *Circus Air**], for example, an alliance forged by the members of influential circles in the political and economic spheres arranges strategically planned contract murders to set 'die Türken gegen die Deutschen und umgekehrt'[35] [the Turks against the Germans and vice versa]. By creating an atmosphere of mutual hatred and distrust in this way, they stand to benefit immensely from the people's call for all-encompassing video surveillance. In Horst Eckert's novel *Sprengkraft* [2009, *Explosive Power**], in contrast, the bombing of a mosque turns out to be the result of a conspiracy, instigated by a control-obsessed official in the intelligence service:[36]

> 'Wer so viel weiß wie ich, kann das Gerede vom Miteinander der Kulturen nur für Träumerei halten. [...] Ohne Kontrolle wird das Dach, unter dem Sie so ruhig schlafen, einstürzen, noch bevor Sie richtig aufgewacht sind. Und dann herrscht Krieg. Das Ende der Moral'.[37]

---

34 See Hans-Peter Schwarz, *Phantastische Wirklichkeit. Das 20. Jahrhundert im Spiegel des Polit-Thrillers* (München: Deutsche Verlags-Anstalt, 2006).

35 Matthias P. Gibert, *Zirkusluft* (Meßkirch: Gmeiner, 2009), p. 266.

36 For an extensive reading of the novel, see Michael König, *Poetik des Terrors. Politisch motivierte Gewalt in der deutschen Gegenwartsliteratur* (Bielefeld: Transcript, 2015), pp. 261–286.

37 Horst Eckert, *Sprengkraft* (Dortmund: grafit, 2009), p. 375.

['For anyone who knows as much as I do, talk of the coexistence of cultures is nothing but a daydream. (. . .) Without control, the roof under which you are sleeping so peacefully will collapse, even before you have really woken up. And then it's war. The end of morality'.]

Pathologizing the lone perpetrator, whom the text diagnoses as paranoid, is one option with which to discuss the dubious role of the intelligence service. Other novels – for instance, Stefan Keller's *Kölner Totenkarneval* [2011, *Carnival of the Dead in Cologne**], Yassin Musharbash's *Radikal* [2012, *Radical**] or Hilal Sezgin's *Mihriban pfeift auf Gott* [2010, *Mihriban Gets on Without God**] – take a similar line. They paint a picture of an autocratic authority that redistributes the resources and power it has obtained 'unter dem Vorwand der Terrorbekämpfung'[38] [under the pretext of combating terrorism] within terrorist circles with the help of shady confidential informants: 'Das BKA [Bundeskriminalamt] hat einen Terroristen bezahlt [. . .]! Es hat ihm auch noch den Weg zu einer Sprengstoffquelle geebnet'[39] [The Federal Criminal Police Office has paid a terrorist (. . .)! It has even paved the way for him to find a source for explosives]. The plots link this reflection on the intelligence agencies' accumulation of power in the name of internal security to the idea of internal turmoil, which radical 'Verteidiger des Abendlandes'[40] [defenders of Western Christian civilization] try to unleash. Eckert's *Sprengkraft* and Musharbash's *Radikal* depict these nationalistic conspirators as members of a bizarre, elitist circle,[41] which nonetheless has extensive contacts in politics and economics.

In this nightmare scenario, the global threat of Islamist terror attacks and right-wing extremists fighting the alleged 'Islamisierung unserer Gesellschaft, den schleichenden Selbstmord unserer Kultur'[42] [Islamization of our society, the

---

38 Ibid., p. 406.
39 Yassin Musharbash, *Radikal* (Köln: Kiepenheuer & Witsch, 2001), p. 376.
40 Ibid., p. 197.
41 While in Musharbash's *Radikal* the inner circle calls itself 'Kommando Karl Martell' (ibid., p. 139), Eckert's *Sprengkraft* marks the financially powerful backers as passionate collectors of NS memorabilia who are in rapture at the sight of Borghild, a 'Nazisexpuppe' [NS sex doll] whose development 'Himmler Anfang der Vierziger [. . .] in Auftrag gegeben [hatte]' [Himmler had ordered in the early 1940s]. Eckert, *Sprengkraft*, p. 219.
42 Ibid., p. 60. In the novel, these words are uttered by Konrad Rolfes. This figure – 'Auschwitz-Überlebender und [. . .] international bekannter Schriftsteller' [a survivor of Auschwitz and (. . .) an internationally known writer] (ibid., p. 55), who coins the phrase 'die zweite Schuld' [the second guilt] (ibid., p. 60) – is obviously intended to be Ralph Giordano. With regard to Giordano's role as a 'critic of Islam', see Micha Brumlik, 'Das halbierte Humanum – Wie Ralph Giordano zum Ausländerfeind wurde', in *Islamfeindlichkeit. Wenn die Grenzen der Kritik verschwimmen*, ed. by Thorsten Gerald Schneiders (Wiesbaden: VS, 2009), pp. 469–475.

insidious suicide of our culture] plunge society into civil war. This setting depicts a divided civilization, whose multicultural self-understanding is forced into a state of emergency: 'Rechts und links waren als Begriffe der politischen Unterscheidung obsolet geworden. Ab heute sollte es nur noch den gemeinsamen Abwehrkampf gegen die islamistische Bedrohung geben'[43] [Right and left had become obsolete as terms of political distinction. As of today, all that would be left was the common defensive struggle against the Islamist threat]. Behind the brittle lacquer of peaceful multicultural coexistence, these novels envision a terrifying setting and dwell on the collective fear of a sudden crisis in intercultural relations, which would ultimately result in total surveillance in the name of internal security as the only feasible means to ward off the 'Diktatur der Mullahs'[44] [dictatorship of the mullahs].

In addition to this imaginary, fear-laden setting of internal escalation, in which Germany's parallel societies clash as implacable parties in a civil war[45] while the state treads a path towards totalitarianism, contemporary German thrillers also deal with foreign ethnic or nationalist racist conflicts. Due to processes of migration, the (armed) conflicts between Turks and Alevis, Turks and Cypriots, and the terrorism of the Pan-Turkish 'Grey Wolves' organization and the Kurdistan Workers' Party (PKK) continue within Germany. However, these novels do not primarily mirror collective fears. Instead, investigations on the diegetic level are supposed to inform the German readership about foreign conflicts by offering extensive explanations of the complex historical and political origins of these lethal confrontations. True to the motto '[l]esend lernte man'[46] [you learned by reading], H. Dieter Neumann's *Das Erbe der Wölfin* [2013, *The Legacy of the Wolf**] and Wilfried Eggers's *Paragraf 301* [2008, *Article 301**] highlight the need for differentiation within German debates over integration and assimilation:

> Schnell aber musste er feststellen, dass er für die Deutschen stets 'der türkische Änderungsschneider' bleiben würde. / Wie sollten sie auch verstehen, dass aus der Türkei nicht nur Türken nach Deutschland gekommen waren? Schließlich taten sich sogar in seinem Heimatland viele Menschen – und die Regierung sowieso – schwer

---

43 Eckert, *Sprengkraft*, pp. 185–186.
44 Ibid., p. 324.
45 This fear is fuelled on a whole new level in Pirinçci's notorious book *Deutschland von Sinnen*: 'There are now too many Muslims living in this country to get rid of those who cannot be civilized, without risking a civil war, if not a real war'; see Akif Pirinçci, *Deutschland von Sinnen. Der irre Kult um Frauen, Homosexuelle und Zuwanderer*, 4th edn (Waltrop/Leipzig: Manuscriptum, 2014), p. 41.
46 Eckert, *Sprengkraft*, p. 36.

damit, dass ihr Staatsvolk aus verschiedenen Ethnien bestand. / Dersim Bağdaş war Kurde.[47]

[He had quickly come to realize that he would always be 'the Turkish tailor' in the eyes of the Germans. / How could they be expected to understand that it had not only been Turks who had come from Turkey to Germany? After all, many people in his native country – and the government, in any case – had difficulties acknowledging that their national population consisted of different ethnic groups. / Dersim Bağdaş was a Kurd.]

Neumann's novel depicts the extremist, racist machinations of the *Bozkurtlar* [Grey Wolves], a Turkish nationalist organization of the radical right. It provides its readers with insight into the fascist manifestation of a Pan-Turkish ideology and implicitly suggests that the ideas of the 'türkischen Nazis'[48] [Turkish Nazis] arise from the same concepts of purity, homogeneity and superiority as the prevailing notion of the uniform, purely Turkish immigration culture that dominates German debates. While Neumann declines to further explain the political meaning of his Kurdish victim's given name, the name 'Dersim' runs like a common thread through the plot of Eggers's *Paragraf 301*. Turkish nationalism, the politics of Turkification and German asylum policy are condensed into this banned geographic term for the Turkish province of Tunceli: 'Diese Namen waren verboten jetzt. Alles hatte neue Namen, sogar die Menschen. Niemand durfte die alten erwähnen in der Heimat. Tunceli musste die Provinz [Dersim] genannt werden'[49] [Those names were forbidden now. Everything had a new name, even the people. Back home, no one was allowed to mention the old ones. The province (Dersim) must be called Tunceli]. With regard to the discrimination, persecution, coerced assimilation and murder of the Alevis, the book scrutinizes the formation of the Turkish Republic and its official political identity since the 1920s.[50] For the purposes of the twofold enlightenment outlined above, the novel uses the story of Heyder Cengi, an undocumented Alevi immigrant living in Germany, and his attorney, Schlüter, to depict the construction of national identity in Turkey 'in terms of race and language'[51] at the beginning of the twentieth century as well as its fatal implications for ethnic and religious minorities:

---

47 H. Dieter Neumann, *Das Erbe der Wölfin* (Stuttgart: Südwestbuch, 2013), p. 36.
48 Ibid., p. 54.
49 Wilfried Eggers, *Paragraf 301* (Dortmund: grafit, 2008), p. 50.
50 Poulton calls this process the '*Gleichschaltung* of political and cultural life'; see Hugh Poulton, *Top Hat, Grey Wolf and Crescent. Turkish Nationalism and the Turkish Republic* (London: Hurst, 1997), p. 129.
51 Ibid., pp. 109–110.

Aus Kurden, Zaza und Dersimi sollten brave Türken gemacht werden. Die Armenier hatte man umgebracht, danach die Griechen und die Lasen. [...] Zwanzig Millionen Kurden und sechs Millionen Zaza aber konnte man nicht umbringen. Man musste sie zwangsweise assimilieren. Sie würden sich in der Fremde mit den Türken vermischen und ihre Herkunft und Kultur vergessen. Wer von selbst ging, den musste man nicht mehr deportieren. Das, so erklärte Besê Adaman, sei türkische Politik seit Atatürk.[52]

[The Kurds, Zazas and Dersimi should be turned into good Turks. The Armenians had been killed, then the Greeks and the Lazes. (...) But twenty million Kurds and six million Zazas could not be killed. They had to be assimilated by force. Far from home, they would mix with the Turks and forget their origin and their culture. Those who left on their own did not need to be deported. That, declared Besê Adaman, had been the guideline of Turkish policy since Atatürk.]

While Schlüter's involvement in the political 'Nachrichten aus einem fernen Land'[53] [news from a foreign country] is introduced as a thirst for adventure, he decides to leave for Turkey because he feels an ethical need to document the 'unbekannteste[n] aller Völkermorde'[54] [most unknown of all genocides]. In order to interview the victims and their descendants, Schlüter's 'Reise in den Krieg'[55] [journey into a war zone] spatially and temporally retraces the history of the Alevis' persecution: starting in Sivas,[56] the scene of the most recent assault on the Alevi community, the route runs from Tunceli to the crime scenes of the massacre of 1938 and ends with a report from one of the last living eyewitnesses. In the name of the historiographical establishment of this other truth, the novel sharply criticizes article 301 of the Turkish Penal Code under which 'the denigration of Turkishness' or since its amendment in 2008 the 'denigration of the Turkish nation' respectively is a punishable offence. According to the novel, the elusiveness of the article is intentionally used to prosecute anyone who makes any objection to the official interpretation of national history. This law 'hielt die Wahrheit unter dem Teppich und den Türken ihre Völkermorde vom Gewissen [...]. Und er stopfte den letzten Zeugen den Mund'[57] [swept the truth under the rug and their genocides from the Turks' conscience (...). And it shut up the last witnesses]. In striding across the history of the national formation of the Turkish republic and its

---

52 Eggers, *Paragraf 301*, p. 383.
53 Ibid., p. 97.
54 Ibid., p. 165.
55 Ibid., p. 303.
56 The novel describes from different perspectives the arson attack on the Hotel Madımak on 6 June 1993, which caused the deaths of thirty-seven people; see ibid., pp. 61–70, 182–90, 220–223 and 325–327.
57 Ibid., p. 392.

politics of 'ethnic-linguistic homogenisation',[58] the novel discusses, on the one hand, the ignorance of the German people, who take every migrant from Turkey to be a Turk. On the other hand, it encourages its readers to reflect on the dark side of the mechanisms that produce national identities: by interweaving the story of the investigation with the rediscovery of an alternate history that is denied its place in official national memory, the novel discusses the processes of usurpation and exclusion in the construction of national identity. From this perspective, the PKK's terrorism is considered nothing but another attempt to usurp the Alevi minority.[59]

In contrast, Ulrich Noller and Gök Senin's novel *Çelik & Pelzer* (2010*) links the story of the Red Army Faction's forgotten children and the internal political escalation in Turkey in the 1970s with the discovery of a German-Turkish family history. Thus, the novel transcends two separate national historiographies by means of the mutual family history of Murad Çelik and Ines Pelzer. Their lives are intertwined due to the history of the Red Army Faction, which is usually interpreted as part of (intra-)German and thus Western European history. Despite living up to the requirements of the genre by identifying the culprit and hence solving the case, the end of the story of the investigation – the perpetrator's death by wrecking ball and the interlude at the bedside of Çelik and Pelzer's mother, who has been in a coma since an earthquake – emphasizes the emotional dimensions rather than hard-headed reasoning. While the murderer kills the former members of a terrorist cell, blaming them for the car accident that left his daughter an invalid, the investigators themselves suffer traumatic experiences. Thus, the novel primarily focuses on terrorism's emotional impact on parents and their children in terms of trauma, guilt and remorse. With Murad Çelik, it creates a character whose state of permanent liminality throughout the story of the investigation seems to be approaching resolution in the future brother-sister-relationship founded at their mother's bedside. In a letter, his mother not only begs his forgiveness, but also tells him about his sister: 'Verzeih mir, Murad, mein Alles; versprich mir, dass du mir verzeihst. Und dass du sie suchen wirst. Mein Sohn, du hast eine Schwester'[60] [Forgive me, Murad, my one and only; promise me that you forgive me. And that you will look for her. My son, you have a sister].

---

58 Gabriel Goltz, 'Die armenische Minderheit in der Türkei. Zu den Entwicklungen seit den EU-Anpassungsreformen 2002 und 2003', *Orient* 44.3 (2003), 413–435 (p. 413).
59 See Eggers, *Paragraf 301*, p. 78.
60 Ulrich Noller and Gök Senin, *Çelik & Pelzer* (Frankfurt a. M.: Eichborn, 2010), p. 222.

Comic interplay

Dorothy Sayers's 1935 Oxford lecture 'Aristotle on Detective Fiction'[61] presents detective fiction as a fitting enactment of the classical definition of tragedy in both plot and logic. The genre's predisposition towards the tragic mode may explain why novels dealing with 'honour killings' or with the collective fear of a clash of civilizations predominate in contemporary German crime fiction: the genre derives its narrative energy, above all, from the extradiegetic discourses of a multicultural society, which focus nonetheless on risky intercultural encounters. Reacting to current debates, the genre works through a fixed set of topics, including integration, assimilation and fundamentalism. Jakob Arjouni's Kayankaya novels burst into this sensitive political constellation:

> Sie hielt inne. Das Wörtchen 'wir' hallte lautlos nach, als wäre Katja Lipschitz ein Pups entfahren und sie hoffte nun, ich würde das Geräusch dem knarrenden Sessel zuordnen. Wir, die zivilisierten Europäer Lipschitz und Kayankaya, und er, der marokkanische Ben Baggermann? Oder doch eher ihr, die Orientalen, und ich, die große Blonde . . . ?
>
> [She stopped. The little word 'we' echoed soundlessly in the air, as if Katja Lipschitz had farted and was hoping, I'd put the sound down to the chair creaking. We, the civilised Europeans Lipschitz and Kayankaya, and he, the Moroccan Freddie the Flirt? Or more likely you two Orientals and I, the tall blonde . . . ?][62]

For scholars discussing German crime fiction from inter-, multi- and transcultural perspectives, Arjouni's novels might seem like a sight for sore eyes.[63] In their enthusiasm, some studies apparently miss the fact that the character of Kemal Kayankaya – if one relies on Stephen F. Soitos's definition – is an inadequate representative of the ethnic detective. However, he shares what is referred to as 'double-consciousness detection' with classic representatives of the recently proclaimed subgenre of ethnic crime fiction. To explain this term, Soitos cites W. E. B. Du Bois's *The Souls of Black Folk* (1903):

---

61 See Dorothy L. Sayers, 'Aristotle on Detective Fiction', *English*, 1.1 (1936), 23–35.

62 Jakob Arjouni, *Bruder Kemal* (Zürich: Diogenes, 2012), p. 45; *Brother Kemal*, trans. by Anthea Bell (Harpenden: No Exit Press, 2013), p. 41.

63 See Konstanze Kutzbach, 'The Hard-Boiled Pattern as Discursive Practice of Ethnic Subalternity in Jakob Arjouni's *Happy Birthday, Turk!* and Irene Dische's *Ein Job*', in *Sleuthing Ethnicity. The Detective in Multiethnic Crime Fiction*, ed. by Dorothea Fischer-Hornung and Monika Mueller (Madison, WI.: Fairleigh Dickinson Univ. Press and others, 2003), pp. 240–259; Thomas Kniesche, 'Vom Modell Deutschland zum Bordell Deutschland. Jakob Arjounis Detektivromane als literarische Konstruktion bundesrepublikanischer Wirklichkeit', in *Mord als kreativer Prozess. Zum Kriminalroman der Gegenwart in Deutschland, Österreich und der Schweiz*, ed. by Sandro M. Moraldo (Heidelberg: Winter, 2005), pp. 21–39.

> It is a peculiar sensation, this sense of always looking at one's self through the eyes of others, of measuring one's soul by the tape of a world that looks on in amused contempt and pity. One ever feels his twoness, – an American, a Negro; two souls, two thoughts, two unreconciled strivings; two warring ideals in one dark body, whose dogged strength alone keeps it from being torn asunder.[64]

Throughout the series of five Kayankaya novels, the provocative quick-wittedness of their main character,[65] together with the increasingly sarcastic emphasis on and grotesque exaggeration of images and stereotypes, yields comic effects, demonstrating the banality of everyday racism. Kayankaya's twofold disassociation from both the German majority and the Turkish minority as 'Türke mit deutschem Paß' [a Turk with a German passport][66] is fundamental to the representation and questioning of intercultural demarcations in Kayankaya's role-playing and his sarcastic narration. He combines a complex strategy of subversively mimicking and provocatively crosscutting the different notions of ethnicity and xenophobic prejudices against 'the' Turks with narration that sharpens observations into caricatures. The novels not only mock the obedient, xenophobic German administration and German philistinism, with its mandatory garden gnomes, but also ridicule those who respond to the announcement of a performance of 'Shakespeares Romeo und Julia [. . .] als moderne[m] oriental-existentialistische[m] Gegenentwurf zu herkömmlichen traditionell europäischen Interpretationsmodellen' [Shakespeare's Romeo and Juliet, in a modern, Oriental-Existentialist production that provides a corrective to traditional European models of interpretation][67] with a serious nod. Kayankaya's relentless opposition to the various strategies of usurpation and othering with which he is confronted climaxes in an encounter with Frau Beierle in *Kismet* – an encounter that is as amusing as it is alarming. When Frau Beierle hires the PI to bring back Susie, her lost German shepard, the novel finds a plausible subplot with which to stage the clash between the Islamic scholar – or rather, the Orientalist – and her 'object' of investigation, which is dominated by reciprocal strategies of usurpation: Kakyankay counters her 'Gewißheit, den Osmanen quasi erfunden zu haben' [belief that she had practically invented the

---

64 Cited in Stephen F. Soitos, *The Blues Detective. A Study of African American Detective Fiction* (Amherst: Univ. of Massachusetts Press, 1996), p. 33.

65 See Ruffing, *Identität ermitteln*, pp. 251–301.

66 Jakob Arjouni, *Ein Mann, ein Mord* (Zürich: Diogenes, 1993), p. 44; *One Man, One Murder*, trans. by Anselm Hollo (Brooklyn, NY: Melville House, 2011) p. 38.

67 Jakob Arjouni, *Happy birthday, Türke!* (Zürich: Diogenes, 2008), p. 56; *Happy birthday, Turk!*, trans. by Anselm Hollo (Brooklyn, NY: Melville House, 2011), p. 52.

Ottomans] not only with his performance as a 'Kulleraugentürke' [pop-eyed Turk],[68] but also with an equally exaggerated identification of his counterpart as a 'German' prototype: 'In Anlehnung an den bekannten Satz eines ehemaligen Politikers, mit Tugenden wie Pflichterfüllung, Treue und Gehorsam könne man ein KZ leiten, dachte ich, mit Frau Beierles Frisur auch' [As a former politician once famously said, you can run a concentration camp on virtues such as doing your duty, loyalty and obedience – and on Frau Beierle's hairstyle too, I was thinking].[69] Hence, the comic moments in Arjouni's *Kismet* can be summarized as a sarcastic unmasking and appropriation of the colonial strategies that Edward Said's classic study *Orientalism*[70] revealed in his discussions of the intimate relationship between 'Oriental studies' and imperial efforts to control the 'Oriental Other'.

Feridun Zaimoglu's *Leinwand* [2003, *Canvas**], Osman Engin's *Tote essen keinen Döner* [2008, *The Dead Don't Eat Doner Kebab**] and *1001 Nachtschichten* [2010, *1001 Night Shifts**], in contrast, link ethnicity discourses to the annulment of the macrostructure of the genre. On the one hand, Zaimoglu's novel relies on ironic dialogues between Commissar Seyfeddin Karasu and the intern Claudia Preetz; on the other hand, it literally blows up both the criminal plot and the investigators at the beginning of the investigation story – and gives the perpetrators the last word:

Remzi grunzt zufrieden. 'So, Alter. Jetzt ist Schluss mit Ermittlungen'.
Kemal nickt. 'Cooler Knall. Echt cool'.
[...] 'Ich hab n Scheißer gesagt, er soll mit m Scheiß aufhör'n'.
'Hört nich, der Scheißer'.
'Nu braucher nich mehr hör n'.
[...] 'Lass abklatschen'.
Remzi und Kemal klatschen ab.[71]

[Remzi grunts, satisfied. 'Hey, dude. The investigations are over now'.
Kemal nods. 'Cool bang. Really cool'.
(...) 'I told the little shit, he should stop doing this shit'.
'Didn't listen, the little shit'.
'Now he doesn't need to listen any more'.
(...) 'Let's high five'.
Remzi and Kemal high five.]

---

68 Jakob Arjouni, *Kismet* (Zürich: Diogenes, 2002), p. 110; *Kismet*, trans. by Anthea Bell (Brooklyn, NY: Melville House, 2010), p. 108.
69 Jakob Arjouni, *Kismet*, p. 228; *Kismet*, p. 219.
70 See Edward W. Said, *Orientalism* (New York: Vintage Books, 1978).
71 Feridun Zaimoglu, *Leinwand* (Hamburg: Rotbuch, 2003), pp. 158–159.

In contrast to Zaimoglu's *Leinwand*, which Tom Cheesman reads as a 'parody of hard-boiled police detective novels' because it 'mimics the standard, wise cracking dialogue-based style of the genre',[72] Engin's novels do identify the murderer, but are primarily concerned with the comic effects of the abductive fallacies and inappropriate behaviour of their ethnic detective: instead of exercising the 'tropes of black detection', which Soitos argues determine the investigations of ethnic detectives, Osman Engin, the novels' main character, imitates Western epistemological modes to form a hypothesis which he picks up from popular TV series. The improbable and implausible result of this process of ratiocination is evident to the reader; on the diegetic level, it prompts hysteria and whining. With its satirical digressions, the story of the investigation does not produce a definite story of the crime, but offers entertainment by way of abductive fallacy, by crushing every conjecture. Consequently, the end of the novel can be read as a comic variation on the anti-detective novel, in which the detective fails to fulfil his task:

> Bei Allah, was für ein glückliches Händchen ich doch als Detektiv habe! Zum ersten Mal in meinem Leben betätige ich mich als Scherlok Holms, und schon melden sich ein Dutzend Menschen freiwillig als Mörder. Wieso habe ich mir eigentlich all die Tage so viel Mühe gemacht und Tag und Nacht mein Leben riskiert, um den Mörder zu fassen? Ich hätte es mir vor dem Fernseher gemütlich machen und Tee trinken sollen.[73]

> [By Allah, I do have a knack for being a detective! For the first time in my life, I am acting like Sherlock Holms, and a dozen people are volunteering as murderers. Why did I put up with so much trouble for so long and risk my life day and night to catch the murderer? I should have made myself comfortable in front of the TV and had some tea.]

In this way, the detective's comic failure is bound to the inappropriate application of the plot and behavioural patterns that he has learned from TV shows to reality. Then again, the novel rewrites the traditional clash between reality and fiction as a clash between Engin's accentuated Turkishness and the foreign role of the detective of Western European provenance, which he tries to adopt. The comedic effect that the novel derives from this constellation climaxes in Engin masquerading as a xenophobic 'Polendeutscher'[74] [Polish German] and his first-hand investigation of the neo-Nazi scene. This self-characterization as 'Osman Wallraff'[75] leads to

---

72 Tom Cheesman, *Novels of Turkish German Settlement. Cosmopolite Fictions* (Rochester, NY: Camden House, 2007), p. 75.

73 Osman Engin: *Tote essen keinen Döner. Don Osmans erster Fall*, 4th edn (München: dtv, 2010), p. 227.

74 Ibid., p. 78.

75 Ibid., p. 119.

a passage of introspection, in which the exaggerated Nazi performance is linked to the basic predisposition of being of foreign descent in Germany:

> Es ist eine chronische Krankheit von uns Ausländern in Deutschland. Ständig sind wir in Argumentationsnot. Immer wieder müssen wir unsere Existenz begründen, erklären, entschuldigen und beweisen. Selbst ein atheistischer Iraner versucht hier dauernd zu erklären, warum er gar kein radikaler Islamist sein kann.[76]

> [We foreigners living in Germany suffer from a chronic illness. We are constantly being forced to justify ourselves. Again and again, we have to justify, explain, apologize for and demonstrate our existence. Here, even an Iranian atheist is constantly trying to explain why he cannot be a radical Islamist.]

With passages like this, the novel emphasizes the excessiveness of the German integration discourse through a peculiar, amusing distortion. Central to this serene tone, which conflicts with both the topic of the investigation – Engin is trying to solve the murder of a neo-Nazi – and the genre's affinity with the tragic mode, is the naïve, fussy narrative style of the first-person narrator, whose conclusions are always dead wrong. In contrast to the so-called metaphysical detective story, the possibility of a solution is not excluded from the narrative universe. Rather, the novel rewrites the classic dénouement of the Golden Age as a scene of collective confession: with the help of various self-accusations from family and friends, a clear causal sequence of events can be reconstructed. It starts not with the intent to kill, but rather with the idea of a warning shot, fired in order to preserve respectful (German–German) co-existence.

Orientalism in decay

While the genre's traditional certainty with regard to a single truth is undermined by the ethnic detective's competing system(s) of knowing, understanding and explaining, modernism's belief in one irrefutable truth is dismissed in the tradition of the metaphysical detective story; the macro-structure of the genre is now used

> to address unfathomable epistemological and ontological questions: What, if anything, can we know? What, if anything, is real? How, if at all, can we rely on anything besides our own constructions of reality? [. . .] Metaphysical detective stories – composed in equal parts of par-

---

76 Ibid., p. 80.

ody, paradox, epistemological allegory (Nothing can be known with any certainty), and in-soluble mystery – self-consciously question the very nature of reality.[77]

These novels reference the idea of a readable, understandable world, but keep deferring the solution or even withhold it entirely. Instead of providing the solution, they unfold a literary discourse which plumbs the depths of understanding by confronting divergent concepts of reality and knowledge. Modern fiction topographically represents this existential experience of being thrown into an opaque reality as entering into foreign sign systems,[78] in which attempts to interpret reality are always suspected of being paranoid readings. In an empirical reality of replaceable, relative truths, clinging to the idea of a definite, definitively relatable reality not only constitutes an anachronistic worldview, but also seems to be the result of a delusional assignment of meaning.

In contrast to crime novels like Edwin Klein's *Türkischer Wind* [2007, *Turkish Wind**], Jürgen Ebertowski's *Agentur Istanbul* [2007, *Agency Istanbul**] and Lena Blaudez's *Spiegelreflex* [2006, *SLR**], which set the conventional thriller plot against exotic backdrops, German-language literature offers challenging experiments – one might think of Linus Reichlin's *Die Sehnsucht der Atome* [2009, *The Atoms' Yearning**] or Wolfgang Herrndorf's *Sand* (2011) – which rely on crime fiction's narrative formula. While the genre's stories of investigation usually demonstrate a stable, consecutive production of meaning that ethnic detective fiction rewrites as the production of yet another meaning, Christoph Peters's *Das Tuch aus Nacht* [2003, *The Fabric of Night*] thwarts this very process: Peters's text disguises itself as detective fiction, but instead of identifying the 'true' imaginary of the foreign world, the novel stages an unsolvable, iconoclastic controversy in the cultural construction of (foreign) reality.

Drawing on the stereotypical setting of 'murder at the Bosporus', which may well be read as an Orientalist variation on the 'murder in the library', the novel confronts its readers with the life and death of the alcoholic sculptor Albin Kranz, who is convinced that he has witnessed the murder of the jeweller Jonathan Miller in Istanbul. This story is told by two conflicting narrators: while Olaf, a member of the student tourist group that Albin and his girlfriend

---

[77] Patricia Merivale and Susan Elizabeth Sweeney, 'The Game's Afoot. On the Trail of the Metaphysical Detective Story', in *Detecting Texts. The Metaphysical Detective Story from Poe to Postmodernism*, ed. by Patricia Merivale and Susan Elizabeth Sweeney (Philadelphia: Univ. of Pennsylvania Press, 1999), pp. 1–24 (p. 4).

[78] See, for instance, Andreas Höfele's *Das Tal* [*The Vale**], Adolf Muschg's *Baiyun oder die Freundschaftsgesellschaft* [*Baiyun or the Circle of Friends**], Bodo Morshäuser's *Tod in New York City* [*Death in New York City**], Gerhard Roth's *Der Plan* [*The Plan*] or Georg Klein's *Barbar Rosa**.

Livia meet during their stay, seeks to produce a progressive, factual, linear and causal reconstruction of the events, the passages narrated by Albin himself meander through his life and associations in the light of his impending death. Both narrators present stories of dissolution and extinction, affected by extrinsic yet opposing imaginaries, which can be described as a conflict between apocalyptic and entropic imaginaries. However, Olaf's analytical reconstruction of Albin's death, based upon eyewitness testimony, and Albin's own attempt to solve the enigma of his life are shattered by Messut Yeter – a figure who also remains inscrutable to the reader. Yeter evidently has command of twofold knowledge: on the one hand, he acts as a 'zwielichtige[r] türkische[r] Hotelportier' [shady-looking Turkish hotel clerk][79] with wide-ranging connections to the Istanbul underworld. Due to Yeter's knowledge of the diamond business, in which organized criminal elements are involved, Albin, whose perception is determined by the Orientalist fantasies of the Western films he watches as well as his own alcohol-induced paranoia, considers him to be the 'Pate von Istanbul' [godfather of Istanbul].[80] On the other hand – with its references to jinn, dervishes, voodoo and Sufism – the novel portrays Yeter as the representative of another system of knowledge, which its Western protagonists fail to understand:

> 'Welche Rolle Messut Yeter in der ganzen Angelegenheit spielt, weiß ich nicht. Jedenfalls ist er kein gewöhnlicher Portier. [...] Er kennt Bereiche, von denen wir keine Ahnung haben. Es wird Gründe geben, warum er seine Geheimnisse für sich behält.

> ['I have no idea what role Messut Yeter plays in this whole affair; in any case, he's no ordinary hotel clerk. (...) He's familiar with operations and activities we don't have the first clue about. There must be reasons why he's keeping his secrets to himself.][81]

Unlike traditional crime novels, which simply reel off the genre's typical detection plot even against exotic backdrops, and in contrast to novels in which ethnic sleuths provide insights into other concepts of being and knowing, Peters's novel confronts Olaf, Albin and its Western readers with the inaccessibility of a foreign sign system, embodied by Messut Yeter: the passages that scrutinize Yeter's motives and his knowledge of events contain extracts from the Qur'an in Arabic lettering, which neither Albin nor most of Peters's readers can decipher.[82] In the foreign reality of autumnal Istanbul, the novel thus stages the decomposition of Orientalism's imaginary. As a result, neither the characters in the diegetic

---

79 Christoph Peters, *Das Tuch aus Nacht* (München: Goldmann, 2003), p. 37; *The Fabric of Night*, trans. by John Cullen (New York: Nan A. Talese, 2007), p. 30.

80 Peters, *Tuch aus Nacht*, p. 197; *Fabric of Night*, p. 187.

81 Peters, *Tuch aus Nacht*, p. 289; *Fabric of Night*, p. 279.

82 See Peters, *Tuch aus Nacht*, p. 203; *Fabric of Night*, p. 193.

world nor the readers of the novel are able to decide whether 'sich diese Leute so [benehmen], damit sie unseren Klischees entsprechen, [. . .] oder haben wir die Klischees, weil sie sich so benehmen' [these people behave like this in order to correspond to our stereotypes, or (whether) we have the stereotypes because they behave like this].[83]

Instead of denouement

Contemporary German crime fiction refers, in different variations, to the diegetic setting of a modern multicultural society. The plots of most novels, however, focus on intercultural confrontations. By giving thematic priority to 'honour killings', a considerable body of texts deal with misogynist and extremist actions that violate professed beliefs of modern Western civilization. They thus participate in 'discourses that either scandalize or trivialize'[84] violence against women. Against the backdrop of a society divided into conflicting partial cultures, other novels act out contemporary fears by depicting extremist forces on both sides escalating everyday conflicts between the German majority and (among) the Turkish minority to the level of civil war. In this regard, German thrillers seem to be preoccupied with the task of defending a core of indisputable legal norms and untouchable cultural values. They feature investigators desperately seeking to protect democracy and the German constitution against attacks by fundamentalist Muslims, conspiracies in radical nationalist circles and the intelligence service's overabundance of power. The assessment of the latter in particular as the intrinsic birthplace of social paranoia provides exemplary insights into the potential of the genre to question the social construction of reality:

> 'Die polizeiliche Ermittlungsarbeit ermöglicht immer wieder tiefe Einblicke in die Interna gesellschaftlicher Gruppierungen und in persönliche Eigenarten, die uns sonst rein persönlich nicht interessierten. So gesehen erweitern wir unseren Horizont. Andere würden uns darum beneiden'.
> 'Deshalb lesen sie Kriminalromane'.[85]

---

83 Peters, *Tuch aus Nacht*, p. 151; *Fabric of Night*, p. 142.
84 Monika Schröttle, 'Gewalt gegen Frauen mit türkischem Migrationshintergrund in Deutschland. Diskurse zwischen Skandalisierung und Bagatellisierung', in *Islamfeindlichkeit. Wenn die Grenzen der Kritik verschwimmen*, ed. by Thorsten Gerald Schneiders (Wiesbaden: SV, 2009), pp. 269–87.
85 Zaimoglu, *Leinwand*, p. 79.

['Again and again, the investigative work of the police force enables in-depth insights into the internal affairs of social groups and into personal idiosyncrasies that would not be of interest to us personally. Viewed in this light, we are expanding our horizons. Others would envy us for that'. '
That's why they read crime novels'.]

On the other hand, ethnic detective characters who represent another body of knowledge or other tropes of detection are rare. In fact, the texts examined in this chapter prefer to deal with the 'double consciousnesses' of investigators of Turkish origin who live and work in Germany: 'Immer wieder holte ihn seine Herkunft ein. Er hatte es aber satt, sich zu rechtfertigen und klarzustellen, dass es zwei Welten in ihm gab. Mal war es der Türke in ihm, der sein Recht forderte, mal gewann der Münchner die Oberhand'[86] [Again and again his origins caught up with him. But he had had enough of justifying himself and of explaining that there were two worlds in him. Sometimes the Turk in him demanded his rights; sometimes the citizen of Munich gained the upper hand]. In Su Turhan's *Kommissar Pascha* [2013, *Detective Inspector Pascha**], for instance, the detective's hybrid soul is the real enigma to be solved: while the plot of the crime focuses on 'virginity' and 'femaleness', the story of the investigation, on the other hand, extensively explores Zeki Demirbilek's ethnic self-understanding in terms of 'Turkish' and 'German' 'maleness' and explicitly opposes the pressure to choose one side or the other. In this regard, Turhan's *Kommissar Pascha*, Musharbash's *Radikal*, Arjouni's *Kayankaya* novels, Engin's *Tote essen keine Döner*, Noller and Senin's *Çelik & Pelzer* and Sezgin's *Mihriban pfeift auf Gott* all defy the imposition of a distinct, unambiguous ethnic placement. In their attempts to take a stand against the logic of 'us' versus 'them', these novels conjure the state of emergency in their plots to observe the ways in which the German-Turkish demarcation – displayed as well as reversed in the hyphen between the words – is constantly constructed and destabilized, exaggerated and compromised in contemporary society.

---

86 Su Turhan, *Kommissar Pascha* (München: Knaur, 2013), p. 30.

Thomas Wörtche

10 Crime Fiction and the Literary Field in Germany: An Overview

The 'literary field', if one accepts Pierre Bourdieu's 'concept metaphor' (as Henrietta Moore calls it) as an explicative framework, is neither a static nor a peaceful place.[1] The positioning of an author, a setting, a form or a genre is historically variable, changing from the periphery to the centre and vice versa. At times, such positions are threatened with being ousted from the 'field' or having to fight for acceptance within it. The literary field is the battleground of aesthetic clashes, which are in turn inconceivable without political and social conflicts. The benefit of Bourdieu's concept is that it allows us to argue both diachronically and contextually – a method that is suitable for German-language crime literature, in which the differences in historical and current positions in the field can only be described multi-vectorially. The irony that Bourdieu himself sees crime literature rather statically positioned as one of the 'artes moyens'[2] confirms that the act of positioning is in no way free from the influence of external interests. German-language crime literature in particular is a pertinent and almost prototypical example of the dynamics that have to be considered in order to determine the provisional positioning of the genre.

Two essential factors must be considered from the start. Firstly, it is not possible to take a 'national literary' view of German-language crime literature. There is no 'autochthon' of German crime literature. Such literature has always existed in manifold, interdependent relationships with international crime literature. German crime literature is unthinkable without Edgar Allan Poe or French Pitaval literature. On this basis, the later differentiation between 'Verbrechensdichtung' – literature that incorporates an element of crime – and 'crime literature' sui generis initially plays no role. Secondly, crime literature is a trans-media event, which is why the English term 'crime fiction' is in some cases more useful. It allows us to consider the integration of other art forms that constitutively impact both the production aesthetics and the reception aesthetics of crime literature. This is helpful, for example, if

---

1 I refer here, as with all paraphrases of Bourdieu's 'field' concept, to this article: Boike Rehbein and Gernot Saalmann, 'Feld', in *Bourdieu Handbuch. Leben – Werk – Wirkung*, ed. by Gerhard Fröhlich and Boike Rehbein (Stuttgart/Weimar: Metzler, 2009), pp. 99–103.
2 See Pierre Bourdieu, *Die feinen Unterschiede. Kritik der gesellschaftlichen Urteilskraft* (Frankfurt a. M.: Suhrkamp, 1982), pp. 154ff.

https://doi.org/10.1515/9783110426601-010

one wishes to integrate Brecht's crime operas or Fritz Lang's pivotal film *M – Eine Stadt sucht einen Mörder* [1931, *M – A City Looks for a Murderer*] into the discourse, or to assess the effectiveness of earlier, momentous multi-media projects such as 'Fantômas' (not only the French *Fantômas* films by Louis Feuillade, but also the German *Phantomas* films produced between 1916 and 1920). A pure analysis of literature alone – without incorporating other examples, such as radio plays, comics or television – would lead to needlessly limited conclusions. The current references to German-language crime literature production in contemporary television series like *Tatort* [*Crime Scene**] will be discussed in more detail below.

Another reason to regard crime literature within the framework of Bourdieu's 'field' concept is his own historicizing approach. As Bourdieu sets out in *The Rules of Art. Genesis and Structure of the Literary Field*, the emergence of the literary field coincides with the genesis of crime literature in the middle of the nineteenth century.[3] The advent and, above all, assertion of new media options (the serialized novel, for example) and the accompanying schism of literature into 'literature intended to entertain' and 'serious literature' (which is quite different from the long, virulent differentiation between 'high' and 'low' subject matter that can be explored in literature – I will save myself the trouble of providing evidence of the history of this debate from the seventeenth and eighteenth centuries here) led to a conflict of assessment, which clearly arose from the realms of 'pure' aesthetics and had significant social and political implications. The concept of the field allows us to map the impact of these implications or 'conflicting forces' (in the sense intended by Kurt Lewin, who coined the term 'field'[4]) on literary production and its perceived merits. The construction of the literary field reflects not least the critical response to or the estimated worthiness of an aesthetic subject area, with all the implications this has in turn for the formation of the field construct, which is anything but a natural law. In order to connect this aspect more closely with the factors that constitute the field, Nele Hoffmann, in her study on the assessment of value, *A Taste for Crime*, made the very perceptive suggestion to integrate Georg Franck's *Ökonomie der Aufmerksamkeit* [1998, *Economy of Attention**][5] and the mechanisms negotiated there for the attainment of 'symbolic capital' into the field construct as a central component of

---

3 Pierre Bourdieu, *Die Regeln der Kunst. Genese und Struktur des literarischen Feldes* (Frankfurt a. M.: Suhrkamp, 2001), in particular pp. 83ff.

4 Cited from Rehbein and Saalmann, 'Feld', p. 99.

5 Cf. Georg Franck, 'The Economy of Attention', *Telepolis*, http://www.heise.de/tp/english/special/auf/5567/1.html (translation of an essay that appeared in German in *Merkur, Deutsche Zeitschrift für europäisches Denken*, 534/535 (1993), pp. 748–761).

assessment and appreciation.[6] It is an obvious suggestion, as one can read Franck's project as a contemporary, high-resolution modification of Bourdieu's dealings with the term 'symbolic capital', which is interchangeable with 'prestige'.[7] Both are central to any appraisal of crime literature. This somewhat abstract prelude is not a proposed outline, however, as it will now be dismantled. It merely sketches the frame for the following explanations and names the different vectors that need to be considered, without having to flag them up each time they occur.

There are good reasons for arguing that a specifically German-language crime literature starts only after the Second World War, in particular in the 1950s and 1960s. This was when it first intervened in the theoretical aesthetic discourse. This statement appears at first to be provocative. Nevertheless, its history up to that point had been fragmented, intermittent and disparate. More precisely, it was made up of a few interconnected particles and isolated authors. Above all, however, such a tradition constructed after the fact would be a tradition without any impact on production aesthetics. There were basically no 'canonical' or 'prototypical' texts that influenced the work subsequently produced with any conscious authority. Schiller's *Der Verbrecher aus verlorener Ehre* [1786, *The Criminal of Lost Honour*], Kleist's *Michael Kohlhaas* (1810) and E.T.A. Hoffmann's 'early' crime story and misunderstood artist novella *Das Fräulein von Scuderi* [1820, *Mademoiselle de Scuderi*] much later served as foundations for a tradition ex post, when an attempt was made to position German crime literature in the literary field without having to fall back on foreign paradigms. 'Tradition' was considered a factor that could propel crime literature out of the sub-literary into the literary. Authors who were deemed unsuitable for this strategy were left behind – authors such as Carl von Holtei and Jodocus Donatus Hubertus Temme (an exception who, through his collaboration with the illustrated family magazine *Die Gartenlaube* [*The Garden Arbour**], had attempted to make productive use of the new media situation in the mid-nineteenth century, as Julia Menzel shows in her detailed essay[8]). All of the other authors of this period who would later be viewed in terms of cultural

---

6 Nele Hoffmann, *A Taste for Crime. Zur Wertung von Kriminalliteratur in Literaturkritik und Literaturwissenschaft* (Salzhemmingen: Blumenkamp, 2012), in particular pp. 47ff. Hofmann's study also calls for an extensive bibliography on the value and canonization of crime literature.

7 Georg Franck, *Ökonomie der Aufmerksamkeit. Ein Entwurf* (Munich: Hanser, 1998).

8 Julia Menzel, "'Dies waren die Tatsachen". Kriminalliteratur und Evidenzproduktion im Familienblatt *Die Gartenlaube*', in *Kriminalliteratur und Wissensgeschichte. Genres-Medien-Technik*, ed. by Clemens Peck and Florian Sedlmeier (Bielefeld: transcript, 2015), pp. 31–53.

theory or folklore (as by Schönert and Hügel[9]) or as part of trivial literature, but certainly not in terms of aesthetic theory, were left out. Their supposedly lower literary quality, their serial publication methods and their less prestigious places of publication meant that their reception was blocked, both in terms of publicity and in a scholarly sense, based on their specific qualities – possibly with good reason, but that is not the point. More important is that, at this point, the assessment of quality had already intervened in crime literature's positioning within the field based on a few criteria, barring this kind of text entry into the field before a discussion of quality based on aesthetic parameters could take place. The question of who indeed has the 'power' to allow or refuse authors or texts entry into the literary field, which is raised at this point, cannot be discussed here. I will instead proceed heuristically on the premise that academic, public and wider reception factors played a role, though not with equal weight at that early stage. This is most relevant for the 'normal reader' of this kind of literature, who had an economic influence that could not (yet) be translated into symbolic capital. That would change in the twentieth and twenty-first centuries.

Up to this point, one term existed that allowed a work to move into the secure terrain of aesthetic theory: 'Verbrechensdichtung'.[10] This term refers to texts that, at first glance, seem related to crime literature because a crime is central to the story, but that have little in common with the other parameters of international crime literature in its purest sense, which had been gradually taking shape since the works of E.A. Poe, Emile Gaboriau and others. Annette von Droste-Hülshoff's *Die Judenbuche* [1842, *The Jew's Beech Tree*] belongs to this group, as does Jakob Wassermann's *Der Fall Mauritius* [1928, *The Maurizius Case*] and *Etzel Andergast* (1931), and Heimito von Doderer's *Ein Mord den jeder begeht* [1938, *Every Man a Murderer*].[11] Established as singular texts within the literary field (albeit as 'eccentric texts' within the author's entire oeuvre), but

---

9 *Erzählte Kriminalität. Zur Typologie und Funktion von narrativen Darstellungen in Strafrechtspflege, Publizistik und Literatur zwischen 1770 und 1920*, ed. by Jörg Schönert (Tübingen: Niemeyer, 1991); Hans-Otto Hügel, *Untersuchungsrichter, Diebsfänger, Detektive. Theorie und Geschichte der deutschen Detektiverzählung im 19. Jh.* (Stuttgart: Metzler, 1978).

10 The terms *Verbrechensdichtung* and *Kriminalroman* were particuarly virulent in Richard Gerber, 'Verbrechensdichtung und Kriminalroman', *Neue Deutsche Hefte* 111(1966), 101–117 – virulent because Gerber distinguished *Verbrechensdichtung* as more qualitatively valuable than crime literature.

11 For a more detailed analysis of *Ein Mord, den jeder begeht*, see Thomas Wörtche, 'Die Peinigung der Begriffe. *Ein Mord den jeder begeht*' in *Doderer, das Kriminelle und der literarische Kriminalroman. Zu Heimito von Doderers Ein Mord den jeder begeht*, ed. by Gerald Sommer and Robert Walter (Würzburg: Königshausen & Neumann, 2011), pp. 51–59.

strangely (or rather polemically) disassociated from crime literature or identified as a separate subgenre – the 'Krimi' – they were deliberately granted dignity as literary texts due to the prestige of their authors. Nevertheless, they would never achieve authoritative power or have any influence in terms of production aesthetics.

The positioning of Walter Serner and Friedrich Glauser is a little different. Both are the recipients of prizes: Radio Berlin-Brandenburg's Short Story Prize and the Prize of 'Das Syndikat', the German association for crime writers. Even if the prestige quotient is questionable in Glauser's case, the prizes show that both authors achieved entry into the literary field. At any rate, their positions have been posthumously transformed. Although they were both literary outsiders in their lifetimes (it is no coincidence that both had roots in the avantgarde movement of the time – read: 'Dada') and had written what would have been considered at the time to be 'unconventional' works (often short stories inspired by crime literature and uncategorizable novels by Serner, as well as unique, albeit bulky and rough novels by Glauser, which were somewhat inspired by the early works of Georges Simenon), they were pressed into service as representatives of a tradition of first-rate crime literature that would reflect positively on contemporary output. While the emphasis in Serner's work lies on the virtuosity of his miniatures, which by no means all have an affinity with crime literature, closer examination of Glauser has only taken place over the last few decades, more precisely since the new edition of his works,[12] leaving aside a few mentions made of him by Friedrich Dürrenmatt. With regard to Dürrenmatt, his 'crime novels' (*Der Richter und sein Henker* [1952, *The Judge and his Hangman*], *Das Versprechen* [1958, *The Promise*] and others) were long kept out of the general discourse on crime literature, regarded instead as 'Verbrechensdichtung', 'literary crime novels' or 'anti-crime novels' (viewed above all from a didactic position as the only good literary crime novels). Due to his dramatic works, Dürrenmatt was considered to be one of the established 'greats' in the literary field; his 'crime novels' were regarded more as meditations on the crime novel form and first received the label 'crime fiction' through the marketing strategies of their film adaptations. In brief, Serner (with limitations, since he still experiences 'rediscoveries' from time to time) and Dürrenmatt are two of the canonical authors of literary history, while Glauser's reputation is restricted to his Sergeant Studer novels. Viewed from the perspective of genre history, however, they are part of a particular tradition derived from Georges

---

12 Friedrich Glauser, *Gesammelte Werke in 4 Bänden*, ed. by Hugo Leber (Zurich: Die Arche, 1969–1997); Glauser, *Die Romane*, 7 vols., ed. by Bernhard Echte (Zurich: Limmat, 1995–1997).

Simenon's Maigret novels, following in the wake of the *romans policiers*, although I would like to quietly register my reservations as to whether the categorization of the Maigret novels as *romans policiers* is completely sound. The history of a work's reception sometimes proceeds in peculiar ways, which are not always conducive to a better understanding of the work, but are de facto reflected in the literary field, which is concerned with other matters. Apart from this, these examples merely demonstrate that the formation of a negotiable text corpus called 'the German-language crime novel' suffers from the problem of manufactured consistencies, which can only be produced with great difficulty and at the expense of consciously putting a certain slant on texts.

The significant output of crime literature in the Weimar Republic and the Third Reich – which has been rediscovered, bibliographically fixed and analysed in recent years by Carsten Würmann, Mirko Schädel, Herbert Kalbitz and Dieter Kästner, and in its multimedia aspects by Gabriela Holzmann in particular[13] – remains unaltered by the bigger picture. Excluding a few exceptions, such as Norbert Jacques and his 'Dr Mabuse' novels, this output consisted of low-profile or less innovative texts, content for the most part with modifying well-known international specimens. This was also where original contributions to crime literature culture outside of the crime novel took place – in the crime sonnets by Ludwig Rubiner, Friedrich Eisenlohr and Herbert August Livingstone Hahn, for instance, in which the relevant narratives were taken ironically and their topoi were parodied.

During this period – around the first half of the twentieth century – there was nevertheless an interesting intermediate step in the positioning of the crime novel in the German literary field, although not necessarily with regard to the German crime novel. Genuine literary studies research into crime literature was still fairly basic, and its academic influence was also quite modest. There was still hardly any journalism specializing in crime literature. But there were a few intellectuals, equipped with great reputations, who were interested in crime literature. I am referring to the frequently cited essays by Ernst Bloch,

---

13 Carsten Würmann, *Zwischen Unterhaltung und Propaganda. Das Krimigenre im Dritten Reich*, PhD diss (FU Berlin 2013); Mirko Schädel and Robert N. Bloch, *Illustrierte Bibliographie der Kriminalliteratur im deutschen Sprachraum von 1796 bis 1945* (Stollhamm-Butjadingen: Achilla, 2006); Herbert Kalbitz and Dieter Kästner, *Illustrierte Bibliographie der Leihbücher 1946–1976. Teil 1: Kriminalleihbücher* (Stollhamm-Butjadingen: Achilla, 2013); Gabriela Holzmann, *Schaulust und Verbrechen. Eine Geschichte des Krimis als Mediengeschichte 1850–1959* (Stuttgart: Metzler, 2001).

Bertolt Brecht and Siegfried Kracauer[14] (and others, including very different creative spirits, such as Walter Benjamin and Willy Haas), which were not among their most prominent works and were not primarily concerned with providing insights into crime literature. But by addressing the genre, they set it in relation to completely different contexts and removed it from its position in the field – away from the outer edges of trivial, mass literature and far from 'Verbrechensdichtung'. Measured against the international production of crime literature, the materiality of these texts was rather narrow and their knowledge was sparse, but they had a sense of the communicative potential of crime literature, which they understood as going far beyond 'pure entertainment'. One cannot overlook the pragmatism of the above-mentioned writers: thanks to his preoccupation with English mysteries, Brecht's relevant pieces (especially *Die Dreigroschenoper* [1928, *The Threepenny Opera*], *Aufstieg und Fall der Stadt Mahagonny* [1929, *Rise and Fall of the City of Mahagonny*] and *Arturo Ui* [1957]) take on dimensions that would have been inconceivable without his affinity for 'Krimis'. Conversely, 'crime fiction', which was mostly perceived as a prose event, emerged from its narrower framework of understanding through its association with Brecht's plays.

Siegfriend Kracauer, on the other hand, needed crime literature for his broader project of emancipating the popular cultures of his time (for him, crime literature was closely related to cinema) from the pejorative parameters of an elite understanding of art and culture – popular cultures, incidentally, that we today claim as our own. Ernst Bloch ultimately functionalized crime literature, because its handling of crime and its literary adaptation were welcome paradigms in his analysis of bourgeois capitalist society. Nevertheless, essays such as these significantly enhanced the attention paid to writers, as was the case for Georg Franck, and German crime literature (though not at the centre of these three authors' interests) would later benefit from this in its turn.

After the Second World War, German-language crime literature required more energetic help from outside, having been unable to establish itself independently in the literary field to a sufficient degree. Even if, as indicated above, there was a considerable quantity of German crime literature being produced (one cannot sweepingly say that there was a 'Krimi ban' under National Socialism, merely that its production and reception were, as it were, 'brought into line' and rigorously

---

14 Ernst Bloch, 'Philosophische Ansicht des Kriminalromans', in *Literarische Aufsätze* (Frankfurt a. M.: Suhrkamp, 1965), pp. 242–263; Bertolt Brecht, 'Über die Popularität des Kriminalromans', in *Schriften zur Literatur und Kunst 2* (Frankfurt a. M.: Suhrkamp, 1969), pp. 450–457; Siegfried Kracauer, *Der Detektiv-Roman. Ein philosophischer Traktat*, in *Schriften. Band 1* (Frankfurt a. M.: Suhrkamp, 1971).

screened), such works were detached from the best examples of the genre in international literature due to import restrictions, which affected the emerging American and British hard-boiled-school series from the 1930s onwards. Karl Anders (who, among other things, reported from the Nuremberg Trials and later founded the *Frankfurter Rundschau*) returned from his exile in London and broke through this reception barrier, which obviously impacted production aesthetics as well, by founding his publishing house, Nest Verlag, and publishing the Krähen series of translated crime works.[15] Works by Raymond Chandler, Dashiell Hammett, Eric Ambler and other important authors would appear for the first time in German in this series due to Anders's belief that literature of this kind should appear alongside literature about democracy and politics. The cultural and political climate, however, had not substantially changed. In the literary field, German continuity became apparent as a prime example of this agonal structure. Germane to the field metaphor is the librarian and cultural politician Wilhelm Müller's invocation of a kind of armed war, so to speak, against 'immoral crime novels' in the influential library magazine *Bücherei und Bildung* [Library and Education], which positioned such literature at the 'lower limit' of the literary field. He referred to this approach in 'Zur Topographie der *Unteren Grenze*' ['On the Topography of the Lower Limits'*], in which he issued a call 'to take up arms'[16] in order to inhibit this kind of crime literature. The counter attack came two years later. In 1953, Fritz Wölcken's pioneering study *Der literarische Mord. Eine Untersuchung über die englische und amerikanische Kriminalliteratur* [*The Literary Murder. An Investigation into English and American Crime Literature**] was published.[17] The book, subsidized by the German Research Foundation (a high prestige institution), took a genre blighted by the substantial suspicion of being trivial out of the usual research parameters of *Volkskunde* [folklore studies] and *Buchwissenschaften* [book studies] and discussed it using genuine literary studies arguments. Even if Wölcken's book has once more been forgotten, it played a considerable role in changing the position of crime literature in the field. But German-language output remained fragmented until the 1960s. Authors such as Frank Arnau and others delivered serialized works, and the emerging pulp-fiction industry oriented itself, without being original or innovative, towards the

---

15 See Patrick Rössler, *Anders Denken: Krähen-Krimis und Zeitprobleme. Der Nest-Verlag von Karl Anders* (Erfurt: Sutton Verlag, 2007).
16 'von der Waffe Gebrauch zu machen', WilhelmMüller, 'Zur Topographie der *Unteren Grenze*', *Bücherei und Bildung* 3 (1951), pp. 665–669.
17 Fritz Wölcken, *Der literarische Mord. Eine Untersuchung über die englische und amerikanische Kriminalliteratur* (Nuremberg: Nest Verlag, 1953), e-book published by Hamburg: edition Hamburg, 2015.

developing British and American tastes that were increasingly influencing all aspects of popular culture. A political thriller like *Es muss nicht immer Kaviar sein* [1960, *It Can't Always Be Caviar*] by Johannes Mario Simmel was a unique phenomenon. In the 1960s, however, the first flush of what could be described as 'autonomous' German-language crime literature germinated and took shape. This trend was known as the German *Soziokrimi* or 'sociological thriller'. However, this was also inspired by a foreign godfather. The *Soziokrimi* – with famous protagonists like – ky, Hansjörg Martin, Friedhelm Werremeier, Fred Breinersdorfer, Jürgen Alberts and Irene Rodrian (the validity of this grouping cannot be discussed here; the public, who are not always very discerning, make their own selections) – referred more or less explicitly to the ten-volume project of the Swedish author duo Maj Sjöwall and Per Wahlöö, who wanted to complete a kind of criminal-literary survey of Swedish society over the course of a decade (1965–1975) in what would later be called their Martin Beck series. Once again underlining the impossibility of a national literary approach, Sjöwall and Wahlöö based their project on the fifty-five novels about the eighty-seventh precinct of the fictional city of Isola, published regularly beginning in 1952 and written by the American author Ed McBain as a kind of *comédie humaine* about New York City. The two Swedes modified McBain's model by making the socio-critical analysis of social conditions the dominant factor in their novels. The German authors of *Soziokrimis* transposed this principle to German conditions and made German cities and provinces the scenes of everyday crimes. It could even be said that this was when the seed for the regionalizing of German crime literature in the late 1990s was planted. But in the beginning, the idea was principally that a popular genre combined with social critique could be an excellent and, where possible, broadly influential mechanism with an enlightened purpose. However, the (at the time) opinion-forming arts pages of major newspapers as well as other publications – weighty vectors in the literary field – seemed unimpressed by the new direction German crime literature was taking. One can understand this as a consequence of the frequent gaps between well-meaning intentions and their aesthetic unfolding. But one can also identify antagonistic aspects – the beginning of a defensive attack on inherited bourgeois concepts of 'culture' due to the suspicion surrounding the increasing popularity of a genre still generally considered to be trivial. Televised crime programmes, whose victory parade continues today, played an increasingly important role in this new popularity. Early conceptions such as *Stahlnetz* had attempted to incorporate German realities 'authentically' into a storyline dedicated to the police force; the famous three-parters (*Das Halstuch* [*The Scarf*, among others]), based on the model of the Englishman Francis Durbridge, were the blockbusters of their time. *Der Kommissar* [*The Detective Inspector**], in its primetime spot (airing Fridays at 8.15 pm on ZDF), penned by former SS war correspondent Herbert Reinecker, assured its audience that capable police officers could in principle solve crimes and that modern society had unfortunately lost its moral compass. Crime fiction – increasingly cherished in radio plays and, at the cinema, in the form of Edgar Wallace films – also made itself an economically interesting factor. But it was ARD's flagship *Tatort* project that ultimately prefigured the regionalization of German crime fiction and adopted the conceptual element of the *Soziokrimi*, which was manifest in the very first *Tatort*, aired in 1970. It was written by the aforementioned Friedhelm Werremeier, whose socio-critical intentions were already evident in his novels, with themes such as white-collar crime, German-German relations, the power of the media and German post-war justice. Media criticism, which has traditionally been closer to popular culture via cinema, took to television crime programmes much more quickly, while literary criticism remained reluctant to accept German crime fiction.

However, other ennobling powers influenced the literary field. In 1968, a two-part essay by the renowned Germanist Richard Alewyn appeared in *Die Zeit* and forced a renewed, genuinely literary studies approach to be taken towards the conversation on crime literature – fifteen years after Woelken's book was published. His 'Anatomie des Detektivromans', ['Anatomy of a Detective Novel'][18] codified the frequently cited differences between the 'detective novel' and the 'crime novel' (I will not go into the theoretical validity of this genre distinction here), but he limited himself primarily to foreign examples. Nevertheless, crime literature appears to him to be a manifestly self-contained, independent variety of literature that can be analysed using the tools of aesthetics. The publication of this essay in *Die Zeit* improved the position of crime literature considerably. In 1971, Jochen Vogt's *Der Kriminalroman. Zur Theorie und Geschichte einer Gattung* [*The Crime Novel. Theory and History of a Genre**],[19] now an indispensable collection of secondary texts, was published by Wilhelm Fink Verlag, a leading humanities publisher at the time, in two inexpensive editions in their UTB series. Vogt opens up frames of perception in which he decidedly references the international discourse on crime literature and shows that there had already been a long and far-reaching engagement with crime literature in all its forms, from Russian Formalism to (what were then) new cultural semiotic approaches (that of Umberto Eco, for example). Helmut Heißenbüttel further paved the way: in his essays on

---

18 Richard Alewyn 'Anatomie des Detektivromans', *Die Zeit* 47/48 (1968).
19 *Der Kriminalroman. Zur Theorie und Geschichte einer Gattung*, 2 vols., ed. by Jochen Vogt (Munich: UTB, 1971). A new, single-volume version with the subtitle *Poetik-Theorie-Geschichte* [*Poetics-Theory-History*] appeared in 1998.

crime literature,[20] he demonstrated other conceptual possibilities for interacting with the genre – for instance, by emphasizing its possible connections to the French *nouveau roman* and other forms of Pop Art.

Nevertheless, the Achilles heel endured for the time being: neither the *Soziokrimi* nor these secondary or essayistic endeavours equipped the German crime novel with sufficient symbolic capital to guarantee it more than a marginal position in the literary field. Single works that fell outside of the realm of the *Soziokrimi* and the usual run-of-the-mill output, and were specimens of the old-fashioned *Krimi* – namely, the books by Ulf Miehe and Jörg Fauser that were affiliated with the French tradition of the *roman noir* and therefore with the American hard-boiled detective novel, for example – might achieve a certain reputation as individual works (in the case of Ulf Miehe, who was a sensation at the time, this was reflected in his great success in the American market), but it was justified that they never managed to become paradigmatic of a kind of corporate 'German crime novel'.

The phrase 'German crime novel', to touch on this aspect briefly, primarily refers to crime novels from the Federal Republic of Germany, with a sidelong glance at Austria and Switzerland. In order to cover GDR crime novels, which enjoyed broad public interest and involved similar ways of different media working together as the West German scene (*Polizeiruf 110* [*Emergency Number*] and *Blaulicht* [*Blue Light*], among others) up until reunification, a focused discussion about a serious methodological problem needs to take place,[21] namely about whether, given the centrally controlled cultural and literary policies of the GDR, one can even speak of a 'literary field' freely influenced by various vectors. This is all the more problematic because there was no form of samizdat crime literature with radical subversive characteristics in the GDR. Even after the end of the GDR, very few literary crime texts emerged that had already been written, but had been supressed by the censors or written in secret, as occurred in Franco's Spain, for example; the *novela negra* had its heyday after the *transición*, and this dynamic owed much to opposition to the dictator, both in terms of its reception and production. In the case of the GDR, many authors integrated into the unified German market without any problems, even if a certain East-West divide, caused by the locations of publishers and general economic disruptions, can be observed. For all of these complex reasons, I must leave this aspect aside as a topic for specialist studies.

---

20 For example, see Helmut Heißenbüttel, 'Spielregeln des Kriminalromans', in *Über Literatur* (Olten/Freiburg/Breisgau: Walter, 1966), pp. 96–110.

21 See Brigitte Kehrberg, *Der Kriminalroman der DDR 1970–1990* (Hamburg: Kovac, 1998).

One could say, *cum grano salis*, that the successful, central positioning of a genre in the literary field happens in the moment when multiple strong vectors unite, so to speak, and exert their power. Readership, publicity and scholarship are examples of such vectors. From the end of the 1980s until the mid-1990s, there was such a moment. German crime literature, represented by authors such as Jakob Arjouni and Pieke Biermann,[22] not only achieved incredible sales numbers for the genre – in the range of six figures, despite being outside of the typical bestseller formats – it also received respectful coverage in the literary supplements of key media outlets, became the subject of academic works and was even translated into various other languages (another significant factor in the accumulation of symbolic capital). This new orientation was augmented over the course of these years – periodization is difficult, because this timeline continues into the 2000s – through a wealth of international novels, which increasingly made use of the formulas of the genre (whether a conversation about a 'formal corset' of crime literature since Hammett would be worthwhile is another question that cannot be discussed here). Key names that should be mentioned in this context include Joseph Wambaugh, Jerome Charyn, Paco Ignatio Taibo II, William Marshall, Walter Mosley, Jerry Oster, Derek Raymond, Liza Cody, Jean-Patrick Manchette, Helen Zahavi, Jean-Claude Izzo, Rubem Fonseca, Patricia Melo and many more whose work reached Germany, even if – as in Manchette's case – this was sometimes with a considerable delay. They were all more or less self-contained, each with their own poetic and aesthetic conceptions, not without tradition, but rather standing in dialogic, critical relation to their respective genre traditions. What united them, however, was their use of modern and postmodern narratives – polyphony, fragmentation, the juxtaposition of texts and the renunciation of the psychological realism of the nineteenth century, to name but a few – combined with plots and themes in such a way as to constitute, by definition, crime literature. In conjunction with their German colleagues, authors who joined this list over time with equally singular concepts (such as Frank Göhre, Friedrich Ani, Heinrich Steinfest, Wolf Haas and others) brought a disparate corpus of text into being – which, paradoxically, attained consistency through disparity. Whether it was the unified strength of this national and international 'New Wave' of crime fiction or whether one was a driving force for the others is probably impossible to determine. In any case, crime literature occupied a more central position in the literary field from then on. In other words, it had become, despite still being genre literature (and notwithstanding helpless

---

22 With regard to Pieke Biermann, see Hoffmann, *Schaulust und Verbrechen*, pp. 168–204.

constructions such as 'more than a *Krimi*' or 'literary crime novel'), state of the art. It was no longer possible to marginalize it using aesthetic arguments.

Wherever competition arises, defence mechanisms kick in. They can appear in completely different forms and are not necessarily recognizable as such at first glance. In the following considerations on the status quo of crime literature in the literary field, one can observe the 'competing forces' and their various directionalities.

In the 2000s and 2010s, the picture changed radically. Many developments that were set up in the 1990s have lasted until the present day: the opening up of the arts pages, for example, which more or less regularly contain 'Krimi Specials' or, like *Die Zeit*, include a 'Krimi-Bestenliste' ['Best of Crime Writing List']; the much-watched *Kultur Zeit* on the TV channel 3Sat, with its *Krimi Tips*, as a fixed slot in its programming; and the academic production of large numbers of theses and dissertations on the subject. Publishers of high literary prestige, such as Suhrkamp and Hanser/Zsolnay, have become active in the crime literature business. These developments initially strengthened the position of crime literature in the field significantly. However, on closer inspection, and putting aside the uncomfortable question of the professional competence of such undertakings, one can understand the separation of *Krimis* into brief columns and specials as an emergency *contre-coeur* reaction to the economic boom in crime literature, which is not insignificant when it comes to print media's advertising revenues. In universities, post-doctoral research on the subject is still rather rare, and the study of crime literature is still seen as 'eccentric' in terms of career and research strategies (read: funding). Institutionally organized research (such as a professorship, for example) on crime literature does not (yet) exist.

Things are quite different in terms of readership and therefore in the economic sector as well. At the moment, nearly every third book sold (the number is currently slightly in decline) is classified as a 'crime novel' or a 'thriller'. On television, over thirty crime series are shown on a daily basis, and the DVD and new media series market registers a substantial output of crime-related subject matter. *Krimi* radio plays (including the ARD series *Radio Tatort* [*Radio Crime Scene**]) are at epidemic levels. *Krimi* events, such as the Krimifestival München [Munich *Krimi* Festival] and Europe's largest international crime festival Mord am Hellweg, are among the largest literary events in existence for any genre. 'Krimi Dinners' and 'Krimi Roleplays' are regularly sold out. Around two hundred new crime novels and anthologies are published by German-language publishers every month. For years, 'crime novels' by Nele Neuhaus, Klaus-Peter Wolf, Charlotte Link, Bernhard Aichner and other German-speaking authors have regularly featured on the bestseller lists, but the authors from the 1990s mentioned above appear only rarely.

A brief historical review can perhaps explain this: these laborious texts with their advanced literary techniques have achieved significant cultural prestige in the field. Even if they were successful at the time, the wider readership prefers to return to more modest manifestations, which are aesthetically indebted to the premodern. Success of this kind of literature was furthered by the popularity of books by Donna Leon and the Wallander novels by Henning Mankell. In the case of Donna Leon, one can observe how she has managed to transform her image in a prototypical and economically successful way: the Zurich-based publisher Diogenes, which published her work in the German-speaking world (it is only here that she is regarded as a true great), acquired prestige by publishing volumes by authors such as Georges Simenon, Patricia Highsmith, Eric Ambler, Raymond Chandler and Dashiell Hammett as well as newcomers like Jakob Arjouni for decades, thus becoming a highly competent publisher of high-quality crime literature. On the basis of this high level of credibility, they were able to launch the aesthetically and conceptually modest works by Donna Leon (and, in a way, Ingrid Noll) into the market to generate much higher sales figures. One of the great ironies of the business is that a writer with an assured reputation for quality, like Eric Ambler, has been taken off the publisher's lists – but that is another matter. One should not speculate, but there is a suspicion that, at least in the beginning, the comparatively regressive manifestations of the genre, like those of Donna Leon, when compared to the aesthetic and epistemological possibilities of the crime novel in general, may not have thrived so easily had they been published elsewhere. The same is true of Henning Mankell, whose first Wallander novel was published in Germany by an obscure specialist publisher of books on medical topics. Since finding a home with Hanser/Zsolnay, his novels have been endowed with a literary prestige that can barely be detected in the unostentatious prose. Mankell, for his part, provides quality-assurance for the entire wave of northern *Krimis* (that they are kept afloat through the clever subvention policies of the Scandinavian states – with calculating publishers advertising them as 'Swedish *Krimis*', whether they are really from Sweden or not – is not public knowledge). Contemporary bestselling authors like Stieg Larsson and Jussi Adler-Olson still profit from the 'Wallander' effect. What is important for our considerations is taking into account that successful image transformations like these have made substantial contributions to the popularity of the genre, which has simultaneously made crime literature take a step back into simpler modes of storytelling, which in turn has had epistemological implications. What does this mean for our subtheme of antagonistic vectors in the field? The popularity of the genre based on its simpler manifestations means a significant increase in 'recognition', but a decrease in aesthetic prestige at the same time. Perhaps this dialectic explains why crime literature has garnered more media attention while being simultaneously penalized with cold disdain. Individual analyses in newspapers such as the *Frankfurter Allgemeine Zeitung*, the *Aargauer Zeitung*, the *Süddeutsche Zeitung*, *Die Zeit* and even *Die Tageszeitung* – which must uphold criteria of quality and competence when dealing with crime literature – easily confirm this suspicion.

The current large-scale (over)production of crime novels – there has presumably never before been such a flare up in the market – which also comprises a huge number of works by German authors,[23] can be classified into the following varieties: first is the *Regio-Krimi* or books labelled *Regio-Krimi*. Set within a precisely defined region (such as the 'Mosel', the 'Eifel' or 'Usedom'), these products are difficult to describe formally. The regions are mostly chosen by market-leading publishers (such as Emons, Gmeiner, KBV, Grafit and Leda) based on their attractiveness to tourists, and they are primarily marketed in connection with local events (such as the Krimifestival Vogtland). They distinguish themselves from other crime novels with a strong topographical reference (such as Ian Rankin and Edinburgh, Raymond Chandler and Los Angeles, Jerome Charyn and New York City), which has always been essential for crime literature. *Regio-Krimis* feature distinct paratexts and epitexts, a specific production design and different places of publication. Once again we see a transformation of image, albeit more banal: if Raymond Chandler can write *Los Angeles*, what is stopping Gabrielle Wollenhaupt from writing the 'Ruhrpott'? One might of course be tempted to carry out a patchwork and very limited 'ethnography' of the German-speaking regions, based solely on formulaic texts like these.

Second are the books referred to in publishing-speak as 'Schenkelklopfer' or 'thigh slappers'. These are novels mostly set in rural areas (such as the Allgäu), in which brute humour vaults over the elements of crime literature. Rita Falk and the duo of Kobr and Klüpfel are the market leaders in this area, having sold millions of copies. Derivations of these are 'funny *Krimis*', with anthology titles like *Mördchen fürs Örtchen* [*The Bathroom Massacres**] or *Mörderische Mandelhörnchen* [*The Murderous Almond Croissant**], or even more absurd variations, such as animal detective *Krimis* (featuring sheep, pig, cockroach or tortoise detectives) – which astonishingly are not categorized as children's *Krimis* – together with other highly marketable formulas, such as 'garden' or 'vegetable' *Krimis*.

Third is the 'thriller'. Even though there is no agreed-upon literary studies definition of the 'thriller', a colloquial shift has nevertheless taken place. This

---

23 'Das Syndikat', the *Krimi* genre's professional association, where by no means all German crime writers are registered, has around 800 members.

is especially true of the compound 'psycho-thriller'. These have long been understood as novels that can be clearly positioned within suspense literature, they are in many ways very difficult to categorize, and they are not required to follow any specific narrative conventions, apart from having central characters with clearly murderous dispositions and a narrative dissection of these characters. Names like Patricia Highsmith, Margaret Millar and Masako Togawa are examples of this sub-genre. Nowadays, the presence of a 'psychopath', a crazed serial killer, suffices to provide a quick understanding of the kind of book intended. These 'thrillers' may also include forensic scientists, pathologists or other criminologists as key protagonists who are occupied with the consequences of the actions of serial killers. Most do not imbue their text with contemporary discourse, but are content with the detailed description of 'autotelic' violence (in the vein of Jan Philip Reemtsma[24]). Patricia Cornwell, Thomas Harris, Mo Hayder and Karin Slaughter add such wares to the conveyor belt, while German authors such as Sebastian Fitzek, Wulf Dorn and Veit Etzold serve the national market with great or even, in some cases, remarkable success. Apart from a couple of exceptions (in a sense, Thomas Harris and his Hannibal Lector novels), texts such as these rarely play a role in the discourse on crime literature, but they make up for it by receiving significant attention from the broader reading public.

Fourth is the bestseller disguised as a *Krimi*. This category refers to texts by Charlotte Link and Nele Neuhaus, as mentioned above. The affinity between this kind of book and the *Krimi* is rather low, and the label 'crime novel' or 'thriller' conforms to the main current of presumed public taste. In addition to this, there are love story elements and other similar elements of genre literature (this is very apparent in Nele Neuhaus): horses, the aristocracy and depictions of high society from an uncritical point of view. To put it simply, such texts are the result of a general shift in the book market. They are a reassessment of what were once considered 'penny dreadfuls', with better presentation (in hardcover) and larger marketing budgets. The target audience for this promotional strategy is above all the broader public, which in this case we can also presume includes a strong female readership. The position of such books in the field is very clearly in the 'commercial' sector.

The kinds of texts listed above (which are, of course, only briefly outlined) account for around seventy percent of the current crime literature output; precise, dedicated statistical breakdowns are not available. The remaining thirty percent

---

24 Jan Philip Reemtsma, *Vertrauen und Gewalt. Versuch über eine besondere Konstellation der Moderne* (Munich: Pantheon, 2009), particularly pp. 106ff.

comprises detective *Krimis*, political *Krimis*, political thrillers, private detective novels, hard-boiled detective novels, *romans noir*, legal thrillers, gangster novels and other subgenres. In the case of detective novels – a makeshift term that takes into account the combination of cop novel and police procedural novel, two categories that are not always easy to differentiate –, these correspond to the traditional, pre-conceptual understanding of what a crime novel or a *Krimi* should be. They are characterized by the 'genre knowledge' of the public and can only be understood trans-medially. The German detective novel is greatly influenced by popular television series. This is why the investigating team is often a partnership between a detective and his or her assistant, helpfully supported by pathologists, forensic scientists or criminal psychologists. This constellation of personnel, which has existed since the German crime series *Der Kommissar* and has become practically canonical due to *Tatort*'s enormous success, now dominates many prose narratives. One must now assume that the public and many of the authors recreating this fictive television world (*Tatort* is praised for its 'realism', even though the police work portrayed in it is extremely unrealistic when compared with reality – almost all the characters would be discharged from the force within two minutes in real life) have confused it with the reality of detective work. Time and time again, the makers of these programmes put forward the argument that 'reality' – with its legal, regulated procedures – is boring and unsuitable for television or film dramaturgy. Of course, foreign series like *Homicide* and *The Wire* have already demonstrated incredible dramaturgical alternatives when dealing with police procedure, but the paradigm in Germany remains fixed (though there are certainly exceptions to the rule). What is of interest at this point is the strength of this kind of trans-media criminal narrative, having created a kind of fictional present through its ubiquity; its basic, constantly repeated format; and its acceptance as more realistic than reality. For narratologists interested in the fundamental permeation between fictional and nonfictional narratives such as Albrecht Koschorke,[25] this is the ideal field in which to examine the mechanisms behind our perception of reality. The detective novel not only shapes how a crime novel is understood, but also, because it proceeds in a realistic fashion, gives insight into the police (the detectives are usually good, though sometimes problematic characters) – in other words, into what a police officer may and may not do, and above all into the depiction of crime as something that can be countered narratively, from 'case open' to 'case closed'. If the belief that this simulated reality overshoots what one could simply call 'genre knowledge', and if at the very least it could be proven

---

25 Albrecht Koschorke, *Wahrheit und Erfindung. Grundzüge einer Allgemeinen Erzähltheorie* (Frankfurt a. M.: S. Fischer, 2012), particularly pp. 16–19.

that such realities and the courses of action they contain were not completely misplaced, then these narratives would have left the literary field and entered into the social field.

Let us return to the literary field. If they present the concept of crime as a single, solvable event rather than grasping it as constituting a continuum throughout all societies, and if they orient themselves more closely on Fritz Breithaupt's consideration that the 'world that opens up to people after they are driven out of paradise […] is a world of narrative ambiguity'[26] by taking affirmative regulatory positions and espousing official points of view, then crime novels of every stripe have it harder. As a result of refusing to serve as vehicles of meaningfulness and by avoiding the 'everything will be fine' topos, these authors are held in much lower regard in the eyes of a wider public desirous of somewhat evasive literature. This group of texts includes many international *romans noir* (such as those by Derek Raymond and Jean-Patrick Manchette), a wide range of subversive political thrillers (like those by Ross Thomas, Robert Littell and Eric Ambler) and a number of political crime novels (for example, D. B. Blettenberg, Merle Kröger, Zoë Beck, Lena Blaudez and Martin Burckhardt). This is why their literary and intellectual prestige is decidedly higher. In the literary field, one would have to understand their position as divided into two parts or as oscillating between these two poles. But this reveals nothing about the position of individual authors. For example, Zoë Beck, as we have been able to observe in the course of her literary career, has succeeded in making the journey from the 'commercial' sector into the sector of high literary prestige – which is visible in her brief sojourns with the publishers Bastei-Lübbe (of low literary prestige) and Heyne (of mid-level prestige) on her way to Suhrkamp (a publisher of high prestige).[27]

We can currently observe the following: regardless of the precisely definable position of 'crime literature' (meaning 'German crime literature') in the field, it has established itself as a strong player. The fight for this position is no longer a fundamental one, but rather primarily a battle for prestige. Carried over to the market, one could interpret this as a 'favourable climate' for the genre, whereby one could replace 'climate' with a vector in the literary field. This climate also allows small or even the smallest publishers with high prestige but little economic strength to gain the kind of attention to which pulp literature masters such as Alexander Verlag, Ariadne Verlag and Polar Verlag are

---

26 Fritz Breithaupt, *Kultur der Ausrede* (Berlin: Suhrkamp, 2012), p. 8, translated by Jen Calleja.

27 Similar kinds of publishing career trajectories include those of Friedrich Ani and Heinrich Steinfest.

accustomed. One might even dare to assume that German authors such as Miron Zownir and Merle Kröger are also able to profit from this situation.

This is one side of the crime literature economy of the 2010s. The other side threatens to gamble away the prestige of 'crime literature'. The production of pertinent texts runs the risk of bowing down to the dictates of the 'economic paradigm' – certainly in those places where economic interest dominates over all other considerations. Trying to recreate a 'model of success' is nothing new. For every bestseller, there will be a trail of clones; this is an old game that is played out in the publishing houses and is by no means reserved for genre literature. But talk of the crime novel as a 'form' (a great misunderstanding within literary scholarship, which confuses narrative convention with 'form' – another desideratum for research, incidentally) suggests that this form should go through as detailed a shaping process as possible in order to 'optimize' the text more precisely for the assumed or implied taste of the widest possible readership. Until computer programmes based on 'big data' supplied by the analysable reading habits of e-book readers have matured (the ultimate outcome being the generation of a tailor-made book for every customer), the marketing department will have to take on these small structural changes. Successful titles will no longer be cloned (Dan Brown is a good example, as is the wave of 'eco' thrillers that followed in the wake of Frank Schätzing's *Der Schwarm* [2004, *The Swarm*]); instead, discrete elements calculated to increase sales opportunities will be combined, while disturbing or disquieting elements will be removed prior to the production process. The large publishing groups (and the chain bookstores that influence what gets into publishers' programmes via their demands for more 'optimized' products) operate 'writing schools' and other similar enterprises that set the rules for what 'goes' and what 'does not go' in a crime novel. They are no longer guided by aesthetic, poetic or epistemological deliberations, but by what sells. One may absolutely be sceptical as to whether such dynamic specifications, bolstered by the (rather naïve) acceptance of a 'literary field', are within reach.

One must assume that the crime literature landscape will change completely during this period of fermentation, in terms of both its production and reception. The Internet plays a large role in this, with fan forums and specialized *Krimi* websites. In principle, what is being written there is what has always been written in traditionally published crime literature. In the decades when crime literature was marginalized in terms of publicity and university research (it is obvious that there has never been, still is no and – in the light of the new online availability of information – now will never be a reliable reference work on crime literature, let alone an accepted definition of what the genre is), more or less non- or semi-professional aficionados have undertaken the philological groundwork, maintained the archives and kept the genre memory alive – all the unspectacular, tedious, detailed work for which the appropriate public institutions are responsible in the 'mainstream' sector. A 'disparate archive'[28] has emerged and has largely relocated to the Internet. In the meantime, a few serious online feuilletons continue these increasingly professionalized traditions by contributing a handful of competent blogs at the highest level. Nevertheless, their number is surprisingly small – much less than those of the portals and communities (mainly on Facebook), for example, where it is easy to see the extent to which the marketing and advertising efforts of publishers generate new readerships for their products or increase their visibility. These communities and portals, if not directly or obviously operated by professional agencies for viral marketing on behalf of financially powerful publishers, are provided with more immediate and extensive materials – games, giveaways and more – than print media advertising, which is lacking in these respects. In return, the public reacts by gratefully reading even the most questionable products and suppressing all the texts that do not correspond to the specified format. If one wanted to be polemical, one could say that these are texts removed from literature for an audience removed from literature. This public often understands itself in opposition to the supposedly dominant tastes of the 'elites' (whatever might be meant by that term). Such a situation indicates a reading public that has presumably always existed but was previously invisible – one that considers Nele Neuhaus's trivial novels *which happen to include* murders as 'democratic' or 'subversive' alternatives to complex texts with higher contextual requirements, uncomfortable 'worldviews', and lacking the potential for identification. What is new in all this is that such positions are stridently and outspokenly supported (somewhat analogous to post-truth politics). It is also worth noting the irony that such a democratization of cultural politics (we have, as the reader can see, once again changed fields) is aligned with the spirit and the interests of the 'good old' culture industry. The 'dialectic of the Enlightenment'[29] has not yet become obsolete – *au contraire*.

One final remark: the rise of 'self-publishing' in recent years has fundamentally flooded the e-book market with a stream of crime literature texts that meet the style requirements in anticipatory obedience to the specified form (since, in exceptional cases, large publishers will recruit self-publishers and find ways of integrating this trend for profit) and from which the last remnants of literary

---

[28] Hoffmann, *Schaulust und Verbrechen*, p. 82.
[29] Cf. Max Horkheimer and Theodor W. Adorno, *Dialectic of Enlightenment*, trans. by John Cumming (New York: Seabury Press, 1972).

quality are absent. What does one do with texts like these in the 'literary field'? Devise new criteria for 'literariness'? Or declare the field obsolete?

After nearly two hundred years, crime literature has, to a certain extent, triumphed in a field defined by antagonism. Whether it has fought itself to death or can form itself anew, only time will tell.

Translated by Jen Calleja

William Collins Donahue and Jochen Vogt

11 Portal to the Humanities: Teaching German Crime Fiction in the American Academy

'I am tempted to posit a connection between Wittgenstein's longing for a clear view [eine übersichtliche Darstellung] and his passion for detective novels'.
– Toril Moi, *Revolution of the Ordinary. Literary Studies after Wittgenstein, Austin, and Cavell*[1]

While any literature teacher would do well to carefully consider his or her choice of texts, those of us who teach crime fiction are under a special obligation to do so, because the genre itself remains a target of considerable criticism. This may seem odd in light of the rise of cultural studies in US higher education; that trend would itself seem a brief for the study of popular culture. Being embattled may mean little to the readers of this volume, who very likely take this book in hand because of a prior interest in and commitment to the genre. But this is certainly not something we can take for granted – least of all in Germany. Yet we may be able to glean an advantage from this very challenge, for teaching what is in some quarters still a contested genre can – precisely because it is so – provide a number of benefits to students in German studies and beyond. In 2010, we co-taught a course at Duke University called 'The Poetics of Murder'. This essay draws on our experience as readers, researchers and perhaps above all as teachers of crime fiction. We have divided our reflections into three sections: first, we will briefly set out the beleaguered state of crime fiction in the university curriculum, responding specifically to the challenge of 'quality'. Second, we will argue for the particular contribution that crime fiction can make when teaching basic narratology, *Landeskunde* [German Regional and Cultural Studies] and, relatedly, matters of social critique. Finally, we will provide two brief case studies, one on Patrick Süskind's phenomenally successful novel *Das Parfüm* [1985, *Perfume*], the other on best-selling author Bernhard Schlink's Gerhard Selb trilogy. In discussing these two authors, whom we taught in the aforementioned course, we hope to exemplify and concretize the merits of teaching crime fiction elucidated elsewhere in the essay.

1 Toril Moi, *Revolution of the Ordinary. Literary Studies after Wittgenstein, Austin, and Cavell* (Chicago: University of Chicago Press, 2017), p. 51; cf. p. 247, n. 11.

https://doi.org/10.1515/9783110426601-011

The case against *Krimis* and the question of quality

Bashing crime fiction as unworthy of a university-level curriculum, let alone one for the schools, has a long tradition. In the United States, the perhaps best known of the genre's 'cultured despisers' was – seventy years ago – the *New Yorker* critic Edmund Wilson, who loved to hate detective fiction.[2] While the study of popular culture has generally gained a firm foothold in American higher education – a trend that would appear to authorize the inclusion of the genre in the curriculum – this is not universally the case. Eyebrows continue to be raised by colleagues who suggest that it is a regrettable concession to popular taste and one that crowds out the study of more challenging types of literature. Students have a limited number of courses, they argue, even in the relatively more capacious US liberal arts curriculum (compared to the European BA, for example), and if students substitute Shakespeare with a course on crime fiction, this is simply a loss.

Often cast as a desperate, even pandering attempt to attract students to the study of literature at a time of plummeting enrolments in the humanities, teaching crime fiction is frequently more tolerated than admired. One holds one's nose and wishes for the good old days of Chaucer, Milton, Keats and Shelley. Put in these rather stark terms, it is of course hard to disagree with this charge. Who would not want to keep the focus of attention on Shakespeare – if for no other reason than his dogged reappearance throughout contemporary culture? But rarely is the study of crime fiction in actuality such a crass, zero-sum game. It need not displace the classics, nor should it. Moreover, adding a course on a genre with which students are – as studies have shown – more likely to engage throughout their lives (if they read at all) offers a number of palpable advantages, as we discovered at Duke a number of years ago.

Undemanding, formulaic, lowbrow: we have heard these charges many times, and they appear to have lingered longer in Germany than in the US. This is of some importance when considering the inclusion of crime fiction within the German studies curriculum at a US college or university, for these departments are far more likely to be deeply connected to – and therefore influenced by – the longstanding German disdain for crime fiction. For that reason, it makes sense briefly to review the situation here.

---

2 Edmund Wilson, 'Who Cares Who Killed Roger Ackroyd?' in *The Art of the Mystery Story. A Collection of Critical Essays,* ed. by Howard Haycraft (New York: Simon & Schuster, 1946), pp. 390–397; and 'Why Do People Read Detective Stories?' *The Edmund Wilson Reader,* ed. and intro. Lewis M. Dabney (New York: DeCapo Press, 1997), pp. 595–598.

From the beginning, *Kriminalliteratur* led a dual life: popular within larger demographic groups, but disparaged or dismissed by the normative literary institutions of high culture, including literary critics, libraries and universities.[3] In Germany, the aesthetic and moral denigration of crime fiction goes hand in hand with the larger marginalization of *Unterhaltungsliteratur* or *U-Literatur* [entertainment literature] in favour of *ernste Literatur* or *E-Literatur* [serious literature], a distinction that harkens back to German classicism. This binary distinction, which simultaneously degrades genre literature as well as other forms of so-called *Trivialliteratur* [trivial literature], has remained much more durable in Germany than in other countries and literatures, above all the Anglo-American.

After World War II, Germany was focused on reviving a classical literary tradition, especially, but not only, within its school system. This made it difficult to find a market for German translations of classic British and American detective novels. Libraries, teachers and academic literary criticism exerted collective pressure through the end of the 1950s to limit the availability of this kind of *U-Literatur*. If there was a post-war hunger for translations, it was above all for those modernist works that had been banned during the Hitler period – not for crime fiction.

It was not until about 1970 that the breakthrough occurred, when British, American and West-European crime classics found an eager readership in Germany, a trend that was boosted by TV broadcasts of classics such as the *Schwarze Serie* [Film noir] and contemporary American crime shows. This was also a period that witnessed the first stirrings of the *Neuer deutscher Krimi* [New German Crime Novel], a more literary and thus more acceptable incarnation of the genre. Influential in this regard were the first crime series produced expressly for German television, above all the extremely popular *Tatort* [*Crime Scene**], which since 1970 has seen more than 1,000 instalments and will be discussed

---

3 In an unpublished lecture, 'Alles über den Krimi ... in zehn einfachen Sätzen', Jochen Vogt tells this anecdote that illustrates both the genre's abiding attraction as well as its questioned status in the academy: 'In meiner späteren Lehrtätigkeit habe ich das Thema "Krimi" aber weitgehend vermieden, nicht so sehr weil man sich damit in den Augen der Kollegen, die gerade in ihr Hölderlin-Seminar eilten, als Banause entlarvte. Sondern vor allem, weil ein 'Krimiseminar' ebenso unvermeidlich völlig überfüllt war [...]'. ['In my later teaching, however, I mostly avoided the topic of crime fiction, not so much because I would have revealed myself as a philistine to those of my colleagues who were just teaching their seminar on Hölderlin, but because a seminar on crime fiction would inevitably have been overrun by students'.] See also: Jochen Vogt, '"Modern? Vormodern? Oder Postmodern?" Zur Poetik des Kriminalromans und seinem Ort im literarischen Feld', in *Verbrechen und Gesellschaft im Spiegel von Literatur und Kunst*, ed. by Véronique Liard (Munich: Meidenbauer 2006), pp. 17–29.

below. Interestingly, it was *Tatort* that helped to set higher technical standards for German crime novels. Since then, we have witnessed a German-language crime literature that is more sophisticated both formally and qualitatively. With authors from not only Germany, but Austria and Switzerland as well, the best of germanophone crime fiction has proven attractive to an international readership.

Because it was for many years considered 'moralisch minderwertig' [morally inferior], crime fiction was rarely a candidate for inclusion in the literature curriculums of German schools and universities. The only exceptions to this rule were of course the classic *Criminalnovellen* [crime novellas], such as Friedrich Schiller's *Verbrecher aus verlorener Ehre* [1786, *The Criminal of Lost Honour*[4]], E. T. A. Hoffmann's *Das Fräulein von Scuderie* [1819, *Mademoiselle de Scudéry*], Annette von Droste-Hülshoff's *Die Judenbuche* [1842, *The Jew's Beech Tree*[5]] and Theodor Fontane's *Unterm Birnbaum* [1885, *Under the Pear Tree*]. Deployed as exemplars of various literary periods – elightenment/classicism (Schiller,), romanticism (Hoffmann) and realism (Droste-Hülshoff and Fontane) – these works proved useful in the classroom and remain of interest to this day. In addition to these, two crime novels by Friedrich Dürrenmatt were deemed acceptable for instructional purposes: *Das Versprechen. Requiem auf den Kriminalroman* [1958, *The Pledge. Requiem for the Detective Novel*] and *Der Richter und sein Henker* [1950–51, *The Judge and His Hangman*]. These works were thought to possess sufficient literary value in part due to the aura of the world-famous dramatist, Dürrenmatt, and because they presented opportunities to discuss philosophical matters of law and justice, as well as the roles of reason and chance in life.

Beginning in the 1970s – and much more so since the 1990s (when the genre experienced another blossoming) – crime fiction gained a firm foothold in the German classroom. This is particularly true of novels with literary ambitions, which are frequently taught in conjunction with other media formats, such as film, television, computer games and radio plays. In contrast to the United States, the *Hörspiel* [radio play] has flourished in Germany, particularly since the Second World War, and is itself an important factor in sustaining the

---

4 This title is usually rendered in English as 'Criminal of Lost Honour'. We have chosen to insert the perhaps more awkward 'because' to reflect the overt causal relationship suggested by the German word 'aus' in Schiller's title.

5 The English title of Droste-Hülshoff's novella is usually rendered 'The Jew's Beech Tree', i.e., in the singular; but this fails to capture the collective ownership of the eponymous tree by the Jewish community. See William Collins Donahue, '"Ist er kein Jude, dann verdiente er einer zu sein": Droste-Hülshoff's *Die Judenbuche* and Religious Anti-Semitism', *German Quarterly* 72.1 (1999), pp. 44–73.

genre of crime fiction in the broadest sense.[6] Another field that has begun to embrace crime fiction is that of creative writing: students at all levels are likely to be found writing *Krimis* – as stories to be read, as performances for the stage or screen, or in the context of more informal presentations (e.g. classroom skits). Sometimes they are even produced as radio plays and are occasionally filmed. It is at any rate an attractive pedagogical exercise – and one we adopted for our own class – that further attests to the inroads made by the *Krimi* (a catch-all term, originating in colloquial usage from the 1950s) into German schools and universities.

However, the old suspicions linger. In the summer of 2017, novelist Ulrich Woelk told Germanists gathered at the annual Notre Dame Berlin Seminar the story about his foray into the genre of crime fiction with his 2015 *Pfingstopfer. Kriminalroman* [*Pentecost Sacrifice. Crime Novel*]: one critic was so disappointed that Woelk had 'descended' to the level of the *Krimi* that, as a kind of punishment, the critic revealed the perpetrator in his review – depriving readers of the suspense of an unsolved riddle. Woelk, who acknowledged that this kind of critical condescension to the genre has economic consequences (readers, perhaps particularly of crime fiction, do not welcome plot spoilers), affirmed that the old distinction between *E-* and *U-Literatur* still plays a significant role in the German literary scene. Therefore, while much has changed since 1970, we should not be too sanguine about the acceptance of crime fiction *tout court*.

Thus far, we have only noted in a very general way the reserve, if not disdain, that many in cultural institutions retain. But there are specific – and frankly quite brilliant – theoretical challenges to the genre as well. To exemplify this, let us cast a glance at the powerful critique posed by Franco Moretti in his fascinating essay called 'Clues' that appeared in his 1988 book *Signs Taken for Wonders*. The point here is not to offer an exhaustive précis of – let alone a full response to – Moretti, but rather to provide a sense of the challenges posed by (a) theory that is deeply suspicious of crime fiction. This is, we think, intrinsically

---

6 One reason for this (on the production side) is the substantial incentive provided to authors by the annual 'Hörspielpreis der Kriegsblinden' [radio play prize awarded by those blinded in war], which is both prestigious and well endowed. Established in 1950 and presented annually (and in alternate years in the German Bundesrat or upper house of parliament), it has been awarded to some of the most notable German-language writers – including Günther Eich, Friedrich Dürrenmatt, Ingeborg Bachmann, Martin Walser, Robert Walser, Elfriede Jelinek, Walter Kempinski and many others. Writing for radio (which is publicly funded in Germany) in general is a relatively lucrative enterprise – as numerous writers affirmed at the 2017 and 2018 Notre Dame Berlin Seminar dedicated to the topic of the German *Literaturbetrieb* (see: www.notredameberlinseminar.org).

interesting, but also helpful to us in defining what we hold to be the most effective pedagogical approach to crime fiction.

Inspired by the Frankfurt School and Foucault, Moretti views detective fiction as a form of bourgeois ideology. It is fundamentally anti-individualistic (branding aberrant tendencies as both individualistic and criminal) and repressive of any suspicions about society and the means of production: 'Detective fiction', he writes, 'exists expressly to dispel the doubt that guilt might be impersonal, and therefore collective and social.'[7] The unquestioned status of the capitalist social order is an essential shibboleth of the genre, he claims: 'Because the crime is presented in the form of a mystery, society is absolved from the start: the solution of the mystery proves its [that is, society's] innocence'.[8]

Equally important to his critique is the view that the genre reinforces a kind of policing function. He asserts: 'Detective fiction is a hymn to culture's coercive abilities: which prove more effective than pure and simple institutional repression. Holmes's culture – just like mass culture, which detective fiction helped found – will reach you anywhere'.[9] Moretti's third major claim reinforces the other two; in declaring it a genre utterly opposed to *Bildung* [education, in the sense of a formative process, as shown in the Bildungsroman], he reiterates the genre's proclivity to affirm society and individuals fully within the status quo. He writes, '*Bildung*, expelled from [...] the narrative, is then evaporated by its relationship with the reader. One reads only with the purpose of remaining as one already is: innocent. Detective fiction owes its success to the fact that it teaches nothing'.[10]

---

7 See Franco Moretti, 'Clues' in *Signs Taken for Wonders. Essays in the Sociology of Literary Forms*, trans. by Susan Fischer (New York: Verso, 1988), pp. 130–156, (p. 135). Elsewhere to this point, Moretti observes: 'Money is always the motive of crime in detective fiction, yet the genre is wholly silent about production: that unequal exchange between labour-power and wages which is the true source of social wealth' (p. 139).

8 Moretti, 'Clues', p. 145.

9 Moretti, 'Clues', p. 143. Revealing his debt to Foucault, he elsewhere observes on this point: 'Every story reiterates Bentham's Panopticon ideal: the model prison that signals the metamorphosis of liberalism into total scrutability' (p. 143).

10 Moretti, 'Clues', p. 137–138. There is more, of course, to Moretti's case against detective fiction. A fourth point, and one that reflects his indebtedness to French linguistic theory, is the accusation that detective fiction serves essentially to quash the poetic individual, while shoring up the monotony of monovalent communication. He writes: 'This is also part of the criminal's guilt: he has created a situation of semantic ambiguity, thus questioning the usual forms of human communication and human interaction. In this way, he has composed an audacious poetic work. The detective, on the other hand, must dispel the entropy, the cultural equiprobability that is produced by and is a relevant aspect of the crime: he will have to reinstate the univocal links between signifiers and signifieds' (p. 146).

Teaching nothing, affirming the status quo, resolving systemic with individual responsibility – this is a genre Brecht should have hated. But he did not. On the contrary, he quite enjoyed it personally and wrote very accessible essays highlighting the genre's progressive potential.[11] We will resist assessing specific claims here. Rather, the point in summarizing one of the genre's most accomplished and better-known critics (Moretti) is to show that crime fiction is contested to the core. It is not just a matter of taste or even snobby condescension toward mass culture. For Moretti, promoting detective fiction is colluding in what the Frankfurt School termed bourgeois 'affirmative culture'.[12]

We would offer two general responses. First, it is always valuable to identify carefully the object of attack. Here it is not really 'detective fiction' (already a much narrower construction than the more capacious 'crime fiction') in general, but Arthur Conan Doyle in particular. Moretti takes virtually all of his examples from the Sherlock Holmes stories, asserting that all else follows suit, or he simply dismisses counter-examples as irrelevant – which for his purposes they surely are.[13] Umberto Eco and Fyodor Dostoyevsky – though both obviously famous for their crime fiction – are dispatched as far too divergent from the narrowly construed 'detective fiction' he wishes to consider. Dostoyevsky's Raskolnikov, for example, confesses his guilt from the outset, thus disqualifying the book – in Moretti's eyes – from consideration as appropriately 'detective'. This is all fine, but strikes wide of the mark. For we are working precisely with a much broader, more capacious conception of crime fiction. We are interested, as our course at Duke illustrated, in the genre broadly interpreted. We read everything from Poe and Schiller (the very *Verbrecher aus verlorener Ehre* mentioned above) to Chandler,

---

11 In class we lectured on Brecht's essay 'Über die Popularität des Kriminalromans' (*Große kommentierte Berliner und Frankfurter Ausgabe*, eds. Werner Hecht et al. [Berlin/Weimar: Aufbau Verlag, 1993], vol. 22, pp. 504–511. Readings for students (in English): Bertolt Brecht, 'Let's Get Back to Detective Novels', in: *Brecht on Art and Politics*, ed. by Tom Kuhn (London: Methuen, 2004), document #7, pp. 30–32; see also document #59, pp. 263–270.

12 See for example Herbert Marcuse, 'The Affirmative Character of Culture', in *Negations. Essays in Critical Theory*, trans. by Jeremy J. Shapiro (Boston: Beacon Press, 1968), 88–103.

13 In pointing out that Moretti bases his critique on Arthur Conan Doyle's Sherlock, we do not however concede the point. Even in his most insightful critique, Moretti is reductive when it comes to Conan Doyle. Overturning traditional categorizations (unfavourable to Conan Doyle), Toril Moi links Sherlock Holmes to Sigmund Freud in the promotion of 'conjectural knowledge' and a new 'evidential paradigm' (188). Elsewhere, she identifies Sherlock as one of 'the very poster-figures for the hermeneutics of suspicion' (178), which is not necessarily a compliment in her study, but nevertheless a richer contextualization than we find in Moretti. See her 'Looking and Thinking. Sherlock and Freud', in: *Revolution of the Ordinary*, pp. 185–188.

Eco and Süskind – including, of course, the 'classic' period in between, characterized by Conan Doyle and Agatha Christie.

Jochen Vogt (co-author of this article) has developed a helpful image for
thinking about the way in which the boundaries of crime fiction have changed
over time, namely that of an hourglass. It begins very broadly in the eighteenth
century and includes a wide array of works, including specimens like Schiller's
above-mentioned novella, which lack an actual detective (something that is impossible for Moretti). It narrows to a more predictable and, yes, relatively more
formulaic genre at the turn of the century (principally in the hands of Conan
Doyle and Agatha Christie), but then broadens out again, significantly by the
post-war period with the development – for example – of American 'hard-
boiled' detective fiction. Thomas Pynchon's postmodern *Inherent Vice* (2009) is
just one contemporary instance of the now much more variegated field of crime
fiction. The image of an hourglass captures well the way in which the genre has
varied significantly over time. In the context of our discussion of Moretti, however, it reminds us that theory's critique (and his in particular) often has
a much narrower and perhaps superannuated target in its sights – one that is
in the case of Moretti by no means coterminous with the relatively richer field
of crime fiction. Move away from Holmes in either direction – either earlier or
later in time – and one discovers a less uniform landscape of crime fiction. The
rich and variegated field of crime fiction defies the easy generalization that too
often constitutes the temptation and lure of theory.[14]

But this is not to argue that Moretti – or any of the other theorists antagonistic to crime fiction – is wrong on any particular point, at least within the restricted context of the examples that he cites. We expressly reject the defensive
option. First, it makes little sense to defend a whole genre. Of course, there are
specimens of relatively weaker or stronger works. How could it be otherwise?
And to attempt to defend an entire corpus of diverse works would in effect be to
commit the same error as some of those inimical critics – namely to take aim in-
discriminately at a whole assemblage of works, without attending to the merits
or demerits of particular ones and without applying a differential standard of
analysis, which could perceive potential strengths and weaknesses within
a single work. It can seem intoxicating and thrilling to possess a theory capable
of taking down an entire genre, and in this sense, Moretti's exposé of detective
fiction resembles the Frankfurt School's broadside critique of realism as bourgeois

---

14 On this point, see Moi's insightful discussion of the outsized role of theory in the humanities and within literary studies in particular: 'The Craving for Generality', in *Revolution of the
Ordinary*, pp. 92–99. Elsewhere (81), she characterizes this practice as a misbegotten, self-
congratulatory 'heroic activity'.

ideology. However, it may be time to reassess the lures of 'critique' and the unquestioned valorization of the hermeneutics of suspicion. We at any rate subscribe to the more capacious view, articulated forcefully by Rita Felski in her 2015 *The Limits of Critique*, that maintains a critical stance while remaining open to the local uses, pleasures and positive potentials of literature.

While Vogt's hourglass conception of crime fiction, as well as Felski's more welcoming, less sceptical approach to literature may blunt the effect of Moretti's onslaught, they do not invalidate any particular claim. Nor are they meant to do so. On the contrary, we see the questions of value and quality, which have so tenaciously adhered to the treatment of crime fiction, as deeply beneficial to literary pedagogy. Assessing aesthetic and social value is central to what we do whenever we teach literature. In the case of crime fiction, however, the battle lines have been drawn and redrawn with remarkable clarity and force. This proves quite useful in teaching. Students can readily grasp what is at stake and, given the typical lucidity with which these debates are conducted, engage directly with them. As in the case of narratology (see below), crime fiction can be used pedagogically as a training ground for skills that will serve students when (and if) they move on to related work in, say, the areas of modernism and modernist theory, where the arguments are typically murkier than in the debates on crime fiction.

Rather than simply defend crime fiction *in toto*, then, we thematized the debate within our course, as will become clear in our discussion of Schlink below. We did not merely recruit students to one side of the dispute; instead, we challenged them to see what part of the respective critique may or may not apply to a particular work. We read G. K. Chesterton ('A Defense of the Detective Story', 1902), Dorothy Sayers, Edmund Wilson, Raymond Chandler ('The Simple Art of Murder', 1944), Fredric Jameson ('On Raymond Chandler', 1970), Bertolt Brecht ('Notes on the Crime Novel' ['Über die Popularität des Kriminalromans', 1938]), Helmut Heißenbüttel ('The Rules of the Game of the Crime Novel' ['Spielregeln des Kriminalromans', 1963/1966]) and Patricia Highsmith ('Writing and Plotting Suspense Fiction', 1966), attempting to plot out areas of agreement, disagreement and uncertainty. Which charges go unanswered? Which ones are answered differently? Which are more (or less) convincing, based on our own reading experience?

In sum, then, we took the debates about crime fiction with us into the classroom. The 'value' of these works, no matter how much we may have deliberated beforehand in composing the syllabus, was not a matter that was settled in advance. Rather, we sought to use the ongoing discussion to practice the fundamentals of aesthetic and cultural analysis in the belief that airing these questions will equip students not only in their future encounters with crime fiction, but in all their interactions with art.

Crime fiction as narrative 'theory'

Krimis, in the broadest sense of the word, are virtually omnipresent in globalized contemporary culture. Variations abound and continue to proliferate to the extent that the *Krimi* has been called 'das Universalmedium des 21. Jahrhunderts' [the universal medium of the twenty-first century].[15] One can bemoan that fact or make use of it. We choose to do the latter. Indeed, for the purposes of literary pedagogy, students' widespread familiarity with *Krimis* can be a tremendous boon. In our experience, most of them in fact 'know' the essential criteria and elements of the genre without ever having formally articulated them to themselves, indeed without even being fully aware of their knowledge. The task, then, is Socratic: it is a matter of making explicit what is already latent. We help them identify and name the content, dramaturgy and *Erzählweise* [narrative presentation] of these stories in order to enrich their own reading and to enable classroom analysis.

The body of classic detective fiction can in fact serve as an effective primer on narratology or at least offer a set of particularly lucid examples of narrative technique and structure. Precisely because of their rather standardized, rule-bound form, the Sherlock Holmes stories of Arthur Conan Doyle and short novels of Agatha Christie are particularly useful in this regard. Their formulaic nature can be put to good use here to exemplify the basics of narration (progressive versus inverted narration, retrospective action, flashback, narrative perspective, stock characters, etc.).[16] Of additional pedagogical benefit is the fact that much of this transfers nicely to the study of film, which is of central concern to our course as well.

Not coincidentally, it is this very 'classic' form that has commanded the attention of those literary theorists who address themselves to the *Krimi* – as we have already seen in the case of Moretti above. However, numerous others as well – theorists of Russian Formalism, the Prague School, French structuralism

---

15 This oft-cited phrase is attributable to the philosopher and art historian Boris Groys (Karlsruhe). It is here quoted from: "Jochen Vogt, '(Fast) Alles über Krimis ... in 10 einfachen Sätzen', *literaturkritik.de*, no. 8, August 2016 (literaturkritik.de/public/rezension.php? rez_id=22330).

16 Jochen Vogt, ed., *Der Kriminalroman. Poetik, Theorie, Geschichte* (Munich: Fink, 1998).

and poststructuralism – are drawn to these specimens of the genre precisely because of the regularities of the narrative structure. They point above all to the 'inverted' form of narration, to the highly choreographed interplay of crime and discovery, to the stock repertoire of figures, to the multiple narrative perspectives and to much more. Even when they end up denigrating it, the detective story in its classic incarnation proves to be a highly productive object of study to theorists. Why not give our students this same opportunity to witness narrative technique in one of its clearest forms?[17]

Not all the theoretical approaches listed above will be productive for the classroom: some are unnecessarily complex and to some extent even obsolete; in other cases, crime fiction itself is mentioned only marginally. We recommend therefore that instructors work with excerpts chosen carefully for their relevance, for there is no intrinsic virtue in using long, unabridged essays of uneven quality. A short, accessible and still very insightful text is Bertolt Brecht's 1938 'Über die Popularität des Kriminalromans' ['On the Popularity of the Crime Novel'] – a small gem of theoretical reflection on the classical detective novel. Brecht's main point is to show the standardized form of the *Krimi*, especially the dialectic of schema and variation, that is, of repeated pattern and deviation.[18] It is precisely this 'Ästhetik der Wiederholung' [aesthetic of repetition], as the theorist Juri Lotman says, that distinguishes the detective novel from European and American literary modernism. Insofar as modernism is constitutionally hostile to traditional narration, it makes good pedagogical sense to work with a genre that embraces storytelling in order to illustrate its functions. But this does not render crime fiction essentially pre- or anti-modern. Quite the contrary: with its undeniable modern content, the detective novel actually gives us 'modernity without modernism': narratives that thematize the crises of modernity yet retain a commitment to plot and character.[19] As both an analyst

---

17 Beyond the specific course under discussion in this article, Vogt, who has focused and published on narratology for much of his career, has found the *Krimi* to serve as a particularly useful object for illustrating the basics of narrative in the classroom. See: Jochen Vogt, 'Mord im Hyde Park! Bauelemente und Strukturvarianten der Kriminalerzählung', in Jochen Vogt, *Wie analysiere ich eine Erzählung? Ein Leitfaden mit Beispielen* (Munich: Fink, 2011), pp. 70–87.

18 See note 14, above. Unfortunately, this particular essay is not yet, to our knowledge, available in English.

19 The phrase 'modernity without modernism' was coined by Vogt in: 'Modern? Vormodern? Oder Postmodern?', p. 23. But the argument itself, namely that the modern world is represented in texts that are not typically modernist, is to be found also in Robert Scholes, *Paradoxy of Modernism* (New Haven: Yale University Press, 2006), pp. 3–32, and in Peter von Matt, *Die Intrige. Theorie und Praxis der Hinterlist* (Munich: Hanser, 2006), pp. 453–465.

of modernity and an artist concerned with making art accessible to broad audiences, Brecht's fascination with crime fiction comes as no surprise.

However, the value of crime fiction in illustrating the building blocks of literary narration is not limited to its classical phase. On the contrary, one could take a step backward in time (to the top part of Vogt's 'hourglass', if you will) and use Schiller's *Verbrecher aus verlorener Ehre* story to demonstrate alternate characteristics of the genre and further facets of narratology in general. Schiller's narrative focuses on the criminal career of protagonist Friedrich Schwan, inquiring probingly into the socio-historical determinants of his behaviour. In so doing, the story does without a detective figure in the modern sense of the word. Despite its brevity, the story adopts a biographical format, showing that crime literature, broadly construed, can take other forms beyond the detective story per se. In recent times, it is the 'thriller' that has played a dominant role within the field, in some cases crowding out the detective strain, in others simply cannibalizing it by means of genre mixing.

For some readers, the merits of crime fiction as a vehicle for teaching narratology may remain unconvincing, not because the genre fails to lend itself to such an endeavour, but rather because the endeavour itself may seem in doubt. Narratology can seem a dusty, abstruse and old-fashioned thing. Can we really take its value for granted? Within a larger literary curriculum, the answer, we hope, should be a resounding 'yes'. Yet we believe the critical awareness that attends this enterprise has broader implications for students, beyond the benefits to students of literature. To become mindful of things that had formerly been taken for granted and to become alert to fundamental aesthetic questions: how is art made? How does it achieve the effects that we have experienced? What claims can it make on us? How and why does it change over time? These are all of fundamental educational value, we believe. Conducting this analysis in the context of literature that is, in many respects, already deeply familiar to our students provides the opportunity for cultural introspection. It helps us to live a more examined life, as it were, and can deepen the reading (and viewing) pleasure we already share.

Landeskunde and social critique

Contrary to Moretti, who holds that crime fiction (invested, as he claims it is, in the status quo) has essentially nothing to teach us, we contend that it is particularly well suited to teaching *Landeskunde* and to raising awareness of questionable social practices and arrangements. The Schiller story mentioned above asks us to consider the perpetrator, Friedrich Schwan (based on the historical person, Christian Wolf), as a victim of unjust social circumstances. The unhappy criminal is the casualty of deprivation and an inhuman penal code that does not stop short of torture. This is hardly culturally affirmative.

Psychological pathologies compound social injustice in many works, posing serious and enduring questions. If we skip to that other side of the Vogtian hourglass, moving into the more contemporary period, we arrive at one of the great German contributions to the genre of socially critical *Krimi* films, namely Fritz Lang's *M – Eine Stadt sucht einen Mörder* [1931, *M – A City Searches for a Murderer*], which memorably captured contemporary debates on the juridical culpability of mentally ill criminals. Peter Lorre's riveting portrayal of the child murderer Hans Beckert – particularly in his final monologue at the kangaroo court in which he repeatedly shrieks, 'Will nicht, muss!' ('I don't want to, but I must') – profoundly problematizes the easy assignment of guilt to a criminal whose actual crime is beyond doubt.

At what point does autonomy and human agency become biological determination and compulsion? Moreover, if we cannot know this with any confidence, what is the basis for a democracy that rests on the assumption of fully formed Kantian subjects? The image of the adult yet childlike Beckert is haunting in this regard – not only because he is a child murderer, but because his own status remains unresolved, perhaps unresolvable. This was not only a burning question for Germans experimenting with their first democracy (the Weimar Republic), but is also one of contemporary import. Almost ninety years later, *M* still speaks compellingly, giving us not a reductive, but a deeply unnerving conception of criminal behaviour. Furthermore, the example of *M* illustrates this key point regarding the discovery of the culprit: it does not – as many detractors claim – resolve all tensions, satiate all curiosity and close down further reflection. On the contrary, the 'solution' only raises more ominous questions. Lang's oft-criticized conclusion to the film, in which mothers are warned to watch their children more closely, is patently unsatisfying. For the film itself makes clear that in the working-class metropolis of Berlin, such a thing is hardly possible, and even if it were, it would not address the horrifying enigma of Beckert – and those like him who are still at large, let alone those who will come after him. *M* works very well in the classroom, particularly after students have mastered the basics of genre expectations.[20]

---

20 As background reading and preparation for discussion, we assigned Maria Tatar's substantive and readable chapter 'The Killer as Victim: Fritz Lang's *M*' from her book, *Lustmord. Sexual Murder in Weimar Germany* (Princeton: Princeton University Press, 1995), pp. 153–172.

What we have said about *M* is true of many specimens of the genre. The narrative 'skeleton' of crime fiction can be deployed to dramatize a great variety of social concerns, including white-collar crime, climate change, gender inequality, sexual identity, technological innovation (and its relationship to unemployment), medical and psychiatric issues, racism and prejudice, to name just a salient few. The question is not whether crime fiction can feature these issues – for it clearly does – but rather how well it can do so.[21] Again, the question should not be raised in the abstract, but should rather be asked of individual texts, films and TV shows. One will no doubt turn up numerous cases in which these issues serve primarily to 'adorn' or 'fill out' a suspenseful crime enigma that, once resolved, does not really seem very concerned with the very social issues it has allegedly raised. These are the cases in which serious matters of social justice and civic interaction are used (or, more accurately, abused) as titillating backgrounds for a simple 'who-done-it' plot that peaks and then suddenly melts away.

This, however, is a matter pertinent not only to crime fiction: the same, for example, could be said of novels like Hemingway's *For Whom the Bell Tolls,* in which the Second World War has been said to function as a kind of heightening mechanism for the drama of the foregrounded love story. The decisive factor in our view is the nature of the denouement. Has the reader's (or viewer's) attention been so focused upon the discovery of a particular criminal that this revelation alone neutralizes all further interest in the themes evoked throughout the story? Does the detection of the perpetrator absorb all of the reader's interest and energy, snuffing out, as it were, any further mode of engagement? Or, as in the case of a great Shakespearian comedy, does an allegedly 'neat' solution actually raise an abundance of other, fundamental and unsettling queries? Are we left with a plot-level resolution that unearths a whole host of unresolved issues, as in the case of Fritz Lang's *M,* in which the mystery is deepened at the very moment of superficial clarification?

If the answer to any of these latter questions is yes, then we are probably dealing with a work that takes its social concerns seriously. We can catch a glimpse of this in Germany's most popular and longest-running television

---

21 Tannert and Kratz argue that detective fiction is constitutionally predisposed to offer trenchant social commentary. 'The act of solving serious crimes', they argue, 'especially murder (and there is nearly always a murder in a detective story), involves not merely ratiocination applied to the physical evidence, but – even if unconsciously – also *the whole of a society's values with regard to justice and punishment*'. In Mary W. Tannert and Henry Kratz, eds, *Early German and Austrian Detective Fiction. An Anthology* (Jefferson, NC: McFarland Press, 1999), p. 7; emphasis in original.

crime series, *Tatort,* mentioned above.[22] With crime teams based in many German cities, among them Kiel, Munich, Leipzig and Freiburg, *Tatort* offers students learning German as a foreign language the opportunity to acquaint themselves with the rich variety of regional differences throughout Germany, a trend characteristic of German crime fiction since the 1990s.[23] Foregrounding diverse regions and dialects can serve to complicate foreign students' perhaps simplistic, touristic views of Germany that may be based on a very few well-known cities, such as Berlin, Heidelberg and Munich. Moreover, one should not assume that the relative complexity of the *Tatort* series (even native speakers will occasionally have trouble grasping bits of dialogue here and there) prohibits its use in a foreign language/culture classroom. The genre's characteristic penchant for repetition, summary and variation (discussed above) will come to the aid of the 'L2' *Deutsch als Fremdsprache* learner. Indeed, with proper pedagogical preparation, *Tatort* can prove a valuable 'text' for the German studies classroom.

But moving beyond the opportunities for a deeper, more differentiated sense of *Landeskunde, Tatort* provides numerous examples of serious social and political engagement. One of those is the episode 'Zwischen den Fronten' ['Between the Fronts'], produced by Austrian Television and first aired in 2013.[24] A bomb explodes as an American representative of the United Nations is arriving at an important conference in Vienna. It is immediately assumed that this is the work of a young Muslim suicide bomber, one Kásim Bagdadi, an Austrian of Iraqi ancestry. As the plot gradually unravels, it becomes clear that this is actually an Austrian, right-wing, white-supremacist conspiracy, staged to bring about the enactment of significant restrictions on civic freedoms and the exclusion of dark-skinned foreigners. Bagdadi (played by Samy Hassan) has been set up and then murdered, but because this 'attack' seems to fit the familiar narrative of a Muslim suicide bomber, it is widely believed. The detection process is complicated, delayed and almost fully obstructed by an ongoing rivalry between the Bundeskriminalamt (the German version of the FBI) and the Bundesamt für Verfassungsschutz und Terrorismusbekämpfung or *BVT* [Federal Office for the Protection of the Constitution and the Combat of Terrorism].

---

22 An attempt to explain to Americans the broad cultural import of *Tatort* can be found in Michael Kimmelman, 'German Viewers Love Their Detectives', *New York Times,* 27 August 2009.

23 For the many *Tatort* settings throughout Germany and Europe, see: http://www.daserste.de/unterhaltung/krimi/tatort/kommissare/die-kommissare-wer-ermittelt-wo-100.html.

24 For full citation, see: https://www.fernsehserien.de/tatort/folgen/863-zwischen-den-fronten-447494. See also: http://www.daserste.de/unterhaltung/krimi/tatort/index.html and: http://www.imdb.com/title/tt2372538/fullcredits/.

Ultimately, detection wins out: we learn that Kásim is the victim, not the perpetrator. However, this is hardly a comforting conclusion to the crime mystery.

Borrowing heavily from a John le Carré novel (*Absolute Friends*, 2003), the plot of 'Zwischen den Fronten' does little to restore order or reinforce the status quo (to name just two standard accusations against crime fiction).[25] On the contrary, viewers are left far more apprehensive than at the beginning, when they could at least comfort themselves with the familiar plotline of a suicide bomber. While the initial riddle is solved, it only introduces a far more portentous one. Who are those menacing political powers so intent upon restricting civil liberties? What political machinations make this conspiracy effective? How is this possible in an allegedly stable, first-world democracy? Is this abuse of power not as bad as – or in some ways worse than – the 'garden variety' of terrorism we have come to know? The naïve sense of closure so frequently associated with crime fiction is here nowhere to be found. While the series is not without occasional clichés, this sense of open-ended social critique is characteristic of numerous *Tatort* episodes.

Two case studies: Süskind and Schlink

Finally, let us consider two rather different novels from the perspective of their utility in the classroom. Both exemplify, albeit in different ways, the challenges and rewards of teaching German crime fiction. One is a classic detective novel, the other a celebrated 'cross-genre' text. But given the broadly construed notion of crime fiction deployed here, both fit squarely within the parameters of our topic.

The advantages of teaching Patrick Süskind's immensely popular *Das Parfum. Geschichte eines Mörders* [1985, *Perfume. The Story of a Murderer*] are manifold. It is an engaging, accessibly written novel that has gained wide cultural resonance. Having sold over 20 million copies worldwide, *Das Parfum* is both a bestseller and a *longseller*. Translated into almost fifty languages and made into a film in 2006 by the well-regarded director Tom Tykwer, Süskind enters the classroom, so to speak, as a known brand, and if he is not already

---

25 This is a widespread view of detective fiction in particular; the ultimate illumination is said to mark a return to the pre-criminal state of innocence and orderliness. See Nadya Aisenberg, 'Resolution and Irresolution', in *The Oxford Companion to Crime and Mystery Writing*, ed. Rosemary Herbert (Oxford: Oxford University Press, 1999), pp. 384–385.

recognizable to students, it is not difficult to get them interested. There is no shame in capitalizing on this asset in the literature classroom.

Despite the novel's popularity and acclaim, it is by no means pulp fiction. Rather, it constitutes a rich combination of various kinds of novel writing, including the historical novel, the artist novel and aspects of the *Bildungsroman*, not to mention aspects of the fantastic and the fairy tale. While not a classic detective novel strictly speaking (corresponding to that narrow 'neck' of the hourglass model discussed above), *Das Parfum* is certainly structured as a hybrid crime novel and is in this respect one of the best examples of the genre in its contemporary form. It offers students the opportunity to experience and learn to recognize diverse forms of writing all brought under the rubric of crime fiction.

Yet the novel is not merely a formal amalgamation, but is also structured in a manner that offers multiple levels of appreciation, beginning with an 'absorptive reading' of the crime story and escalating to the consideration of a complex web of subtle allusions to German and European art and literature. A careful assessment of these intertexts – one thinks, for example of Süskind's allusions to Heinrich von Kleist and E. T. A. Hoffmann – leads to a quite different, richer reading experience. This combination of entertaining prose with rich references to cultural history, dating at least to Umberto Eco's bestselling *The Name of the Rose* (1980), has been much commented upon in the secondary literature. As Judith Ryan has argued, Süskind's novel exemplifies the postmodern technique of 'double encoding', appealing simultaneously to multiple readerships with diverse backgrounds and assorted reading practices.[26] From a pedagogical point of view, this presents the opportunity to 'move' students from the absorptive approach to reading to one that entertains the novel's richly allusive textures.[27]

In Germany, Süskind has already entered the school canon, having become in the mid-1990s a standard text chosen for instruction in *Gymnasien* [college preparatory schools] – perhaps despite its crime fiction provenance. It will not surprise readers to learn that interpretive approaches to the novel differ quite dramatically. We have discovered that it is not in the least difficult to motivate

---

26 Judith Ryan, 'The Problem of Pastiche in Patrick Süskind's *Parfume*', *German Quarterly* 63.3/4 (1990), pp. 396–403. See also a more recent essay in which she compares Schlink and Süskind: Judith Ryan, 'Schlink's *Vorleser*, Süskind's *Parfum*, and the Concept of Global Literature', *Colloquia Germanica* 48.1–2 (2015) [published 2017], pp. 13–22.
27 But this is not to denigrate absorptive reading per se, which can be a rich and positive experience that is not necessarily opposed to reflection and critique, as opponents of crime fiction often claim. For a thoughtful reconsideration of the matter in the context of realism and compassion for the world, see Toril Moi, *Revolution of the Ordinary*, p. 234.

students to discuss their reading, given these interpretive possibilities. Will students become fascinated with the protagonist, Jean-Baptiste Grenouille, as a 'criminal genius'? Or will the novel's historical dimensions predominate? For better or worse, some have seen it as an allegory for Hitler – perhaps to be expected (regretted?) in an American German studies classroom.[28] The reception of *Das Parfum* seems to us at any rate destined to remain a dynamic affair. For reactions to this mass murderer of young girls – despite the murderer's indisputably deprived childhood – will depend to some extent upon rapidly changing social perspectives on gender and sexuality. This too is a pedagogical gain, providing teachers and students with the opportunity to observe how novels travel over time, that is, how they interact with multiple, diverse and evolving readerships. Crime fiction, like crime itself, is always to some extent in the eye of the beholder.

Let us conclude by taking a glance at an indisputable specimen of the detective genre, namely Bernhard Schlink's popular *Selbs Justiz* [1987, *Self's Punishment. A Mystery*], written with Walter Popp. A consideration of this novel (possibly along with the other two books in the trilogy, *Selbs Mord* [*Self's Murder*] and *Selbs Betrug* [*Self's Deception*]) prompts us to inquire both into the genre's limitations and possibilities with respect to social criticism. The trilogy features the lovable, ex-Nazi investigator Gerhard Selb (or Gerhard Self, in the English editions) who is called in to solve a number of high-level crimes. In the first instalment, *Self's Punishment*, the eponymous hero eventually uncovers the machinations of his evil brother-in-law, Korten, the murderous CEO of a major chemical company reminiscent of BASF. The novel plays out in postwar West Germany, with crucial flashbacks to the Nazi period, when both Selb and Korten served in the judiciary as junior *Staatsanwälte* [state prosecutors, or what Americans would call an assistant US attorney].

This is a snappily written, accessible novel that offers students a window onto central concerns of post-war West German society, above all, perhaps, insights into the problematic reintegration of ex-Nazis into the ruling establishment. In this way, Schlink provides instructors and students with an intriguing test case for the genre's contested 'literary quality'. Can we speak of serious social criticism that survives the decisive and deeply satisfying solution of the novel's mystery? Or does the post-war historical setting function more as

---

28 For a critique of the over-emphasis of this period/topic in the US German Studies curriculum, see Jochen Vogt, 'Steiniger Weg zu einer deutschen Normalität. Lektürenotizen zu Ulrich Herberts Geschichte Deutschlands im 20. Jahrhundert nebst der dringenden Empfehlung, diese selbst zu lesen', *andererseits. Transatlantic Yearbook of German Studies*, vol. 4 (2015), pp. 247–254, esp. pp. 247–248. http://andererseits.library.duke.edu/article/view/15449/6675.

a titillating backdrop to an intense drama that is essentially extinguished once Selb's 'justice' is meted out in the form of murdering Korten?

These competing options can make for quite effective classroom debate. Students can opt for or be assigned a position and are then pitted against each other in discussion. In our experience, this works exceptionally well in getting students to appreciate not two discrete, diametrically opposed positions, but rather two possible hermeneutic 'moments' that can in fact be held in tandem. If our lesson plan succeeds, students tend to leave class thinking that their opponents may have a point after all. If we can move them away from absolute positions to a perspective that assesses the relative 'weight' of selected scenes and episodes, we deem it a pedagogical gain, a higher level of differentiated aesthetic analysis.

In developing the second interpretive option mentioned above – that is, by maintaining that the very act of discovery tends to dispel rather than enhance narrative and readerly attention – we enable students to see the potential contribution made by Moretti and scholars like him, who offer sweeping indictments of the detective genre itself. In the case of *Selbs Justiz*, it happens to be Ernst Bloch who supplies the theory that gives us pause. He insists that all detective fiction (not, let us recall, all crime fiction) is organized around 'the darkness at the beginning', to which no one has access and of which no one (except the criminal himself) has adequate knowledge: 'In the detective novel the crime has already occurred, outside the narrative; the story arrives on the scene with the corpse [. . .]. The main point is always the same: the alpha, which none of the characters appearing one after another admits to have witnessed, least of all the reader, happens outside of the story like the fall from grace [. . .]'.[29]

If Gerhard Selb is, as Donahue argues, first and foremost a vehicle for 'coming to terms with the Nazi past' [*Vergangenheitsbewältigung*], then the very detective framework tends to exonerate contemporaries (readers and post-war figures alike) from this necessary work.[30] Like the novel's readers, these 'contemporaries' simply were not there. It is the genre itself that lets them (us) off the hook. The one who was there, the one who is 'discovered' to have been pulling the strings all along, meets his just demise. Indeed, once Korten is determined to be not only the novel's arch-villain, but also a kind of Hitler stand-in, a metonym

---

29 Ernst Bloch, 'A Philosophical View of the Detective Novel,' in E.B.,*Heritage of Our Times* (Cambridge: Polity Press, 1991), p. 219. ['Philosophische Ansicht des Detektivromans', in Vogt, ed., *Der Kriminalroman. Poetik, Theorie, Geschichte*, p. 38–51 (p. 45).

30 See William Collins Donahue, 'The Popular Culture Alibi. Bernhard Schlink's Detective Novels and the Culture of Politically Correct Holocaust Literature', *German Quarterly* 77.4 (Fall 2004): pp. 462–481.

for the entire model of elite Nazi culpability, his murder becomes an exceedingly satisfying solution that may substitute for rather than demand further *Vergangenheitsbewältigung*.

But is this the whole story? Becoming attentive to the way in which the detection formula itself can pre-determine meaning is a valuable insight – especially for life-long readers of crime fiction – and to us this is pedagogically as important as any of the lessons we wish to impart regarding narratology. Yet literature rarely adheres to the models theoreticians wish to impose upon it, and *Selbs Justiz* is no exception. Readers are of course equally entitled to attend to the foregrounded crime, which is the systematically concealed environmental pollution emitted by Korten's powerful chemical company. From this perspective, one is indeed more likely to appreciate not only the novel's deft portrayal of the post-war German *Wirtschaftswunder* [economic recovery], but also the social criticism implicit in *this* particular white-collar crime, namely the ability of highly placed, wealthy economic players to skirt the law and frankly do as they wish.[31] Seen in this light, Selb's 'punishment' of Korten – his dramatic vigilante-style justice at the novel's end – is not only a fantasy (and compensatory) form of coming to terms with the Nazi past, but also an indictment of an unjust capitalist society that installs its most 'successful' members as the overlords to rule over their employees, not as equal citizens, but as supplicants and servants. This is a searing criticism that is not extinguished with the murder of Korten, but one that survives his death, insofar as the conditions that gave rise to him (capitalist inequities, not just Nazism) persist into the present. Finally, Selb's heavy-handed references to his Nazi past can be read

---

31 'This compelling tale – the first of three, written with Walter Popp, a fellow lawyer – offers a sharp critique of German post-war society, and its refusal to confront its war time past. The seriousness of this underlying message does not detract from the novel's more entertaining qualities however' (Christina Koning, 'Fiction', *The Times*, 20 August 2005, p. 18[S3]). Beatrice Mall-Grob deems Schlink's prose a fruitful source of German *Landeskunde* as well as a serious treatment of German history and politics: 'Eine besondere Qualität fast aller Texte Schlinks liegt darin, dass sie brisante Themen der deutschen Zeitgeschichte auf eine brillante Weise verhandeln und gekonnt spannende Unterhaltung mit Tiefgang verbinden. Auch in den Kriminalromanen werden thematische Felder wie die deutsche Vergangenheit, das Verhältnis von Ost und West oder das Verhältnis von Deutschen und Juden auf eine Art und Weise angesprochen, die ihrer Komplexität gerecht wird' ['A particular quality that almost all of Schlink's texts feature is their ability to brilliantly negotiate controversial topics of German history, and that they manage to combine suspenseful entertainment with intellectual depth. As his other literary work does, his crime novels also address topics, such as the German past, the relationship between East and West Germany or the relationship between Germans and Jews, in ways that pay tribute to their complexity'.], in: 'Grossartiger Abgang einer literarischen Figur. Bernhard Schlinks neuer Roman *Selbs Mord*', *Der kleine Bund*, 11 October 2001.

not only as backhanded justifications, but (also) as an impeachment of post-war Germany's failure to oust ex-Nazis from the legal and governing establishment. Our sense of 'divine justice' or the putative return 'to an Edenic Great Good Place'[32] (as W. H. Auden would have it) at the novel's end is thus tempered by an eerie feeling of ongoing foreboding. Getting students to entertain both interpretive paradigms – simultaneously, if possible – will serve them well for their future interactions, not only with crime fiction, but also with art of all kinds.[33]

Teaching German crime fiction offers, in our estimation, a great portal to the humanities: it capitalizes on a literature that, as a genre at least, is both familiar and widely enjoyed, and uses it to teach the fundamentals of literary and filmic analysis that will stand our students in good stead for years to come. We embrace the rigorous interrogation of the genre, as we do the examination of all works of literature and film, but urge students to temper theory's sweeping indictments with careful consideration of individual works and of their broader, often layered, reception. These, too, are analytic practices that will travel well over time. Finally, we ask students to consider not two-dimensional figures and prefabricated plot lines, but characters – like Friedrich Schwan, Hans Beckert and Gerhard Selb – whose very ambiguity poses significant societal challenges that persist long after the respective mystery has been solved.

---

32 W. H. Auden, 'The Guilty Vicarage', *Harper's Magazine*, May 1948, pp. 406–412. See also: Nancy Ellen Talburt, 'Religion', *The Oxford Companion to Crime and Mystery Writing*, p. 383.
33 Classroom debate on these issues can be enhanced by including a screening and discussion of the film (that is closely based on the Schlink novel), *Der Tod kam als Freund* (1991, dir. Nico Hofmann). In translating the story for the screen, Hofmann adds a key scene to explicate Selb's younger years as a Nazi *Staatsanwalt* [state prosecutor], and focuses attention upon the Nazi period further by creating the role of 'Frau Weinstein', a survivor of the Holocaust who serves as an important 'reflector figure' for the older Selb. For further discussion, see William Collins Donahue, 'Resister After the Fact', in W.C.D.: *Holocaust as Fiction. Bernhard Schlink's 'Nazi' Novels and Their Films* (New York: Palgrave, 2010), pp. 21–49.

12 Contemporary German Crime Fiction Authors

Friedrich Ani *(Thomas W. Kniesche)*

According to some German literary critics and crime fiction experts, Friedrich Ani must be considered one of the best, if not the best German writer of crime fiction today. This assessment is borne out not only by the high esteem literary critics have for Ani and the commercial success of his books, but also by the numerous awards this writer has collected over the last two decades. Due to his specific way of shaping crime fiction by probing the psychological depths of his fictional characters, his work is often compared to the writing of the Swiss writer Friedrich Glauser, to that of Patricia Highsmith and, most significantly, to that of Georges Simenon. Ani is a prolific author. He has written scripts for many of Germany's most prestigious TV crime shows, such as *Ein Fall für Zwei* [*A Case for Two**], *Tatort* [*Crime Scene**] and *Rosa Roth*; he has collaborated with well-known directors, such as Dominik Graf and Martin Enlen, on television adaptations of his own novels; and he has written two theatre plays, a handful of literary stories, five volumes of poetry, seven young adult novels and seventeen radio plays.

Friedrich Ani was born in 1959 in a small town south of Munich. After finishing grammar school, he enrolled at the *Hochschule für Fernsehen und Film* [University of Television and Film] in Munich, made a living as a crime reporter and authored his first theatre and radio plays. Ani's books have been translated into several languages, such as French, Spanish, Dutch and Chinese, but none of them are available in English yet. His most distinguishing accomplishment is the way that he has enhanced the figure of the fictional investigator. The protagonists of his novels are usually police officers with the rank of *Hauptkommissar* [Detective Chief Inspector] who employ methods and ways of thinking that set them apart from their colleagues in more conventional crime fiction. This has important ramifications for the genre itself, since the gaze of Ani's protagonists is turned not only towards victims and perpetrators, but also towards society itself, which then becomes the focus of the investigation. In Ani's work, crime fiction becomes a critical assessment of post-industrialized, late capitalist society, and the mechanisms and structures that alienate people from others and from themselves.

The three novels starring *Hauptkommissar* Jonas Vogel (published between 2007 and 2010) follow a career police officer who loses his eyesight in an accident and thus has to quit the police force. Called 'der Seher' [the seer] by friends and colleagues, he cannot stop his habit of investigating crime, even

https://doi.org/10.1515/9783110426601-012

though he does not have official status anymore. He teams up with his reluctant son, who has followed in his footsteps into the police force and has taken over his position as chief investigating officer in the *Mordkommission* [homicide division]. The obvious oedipal constellation underlines the mythical dimensions of the investigator who doubles as the blind seer who, like Tiresias in Sophocles' *Oedipus Rex*, knows the truth when the perpetrator is still struggling to come to terms with the knowledge of his involvement in the crime.

Another series of three novels, written between 2006 and 2009, centres around another *Hauptkommissar*: Polonius Fischer is a former monk who is still following his catholic faith and is deeply concerned with the question of how it can be possible for somebody to commit murder. Fischer (his name, which translates as fisher or fisherman, is a biblical illusion to Saint Peter) and his eleven team members are called 'the twelve Apostles' at work because they have the habit of lunching together at a large table while one of the twelve reads a chapter from a novel or a philosophical work. Religious and philosophical questions and conundrums feature prominently in this series.

One of Ani's recent crime novels, *Der namenlose Tag* [2015, *The Nameless Day*], was advertised as the start of a new series. The novel follows the popular crime fiction model of investigating cold cases. Jakob Frank, a retired chief inspector, has at his disposal only old documents, archived texts and the fading memories of some of the people involved. But precisely because he takes up the case from a distance (here: after twenty years have passed), Frank is able to gain a new perspective on what happened when a young woman was found dead, supposedly having committed suicide. The past is always a reconstruction of what happened anyway, but here this process is even more mediated than in a regular investigation. What comes to light in the course of Frank's probing of the past is all the secrets the people involved are trying to hide, not because they are guilty of a crime, but because their egotism and negligence created an atmosphere or a situation in which death seemed like the only way out.[1]

Ani's most important and critically acclaimed contribution to crime fiction is the series of twenty-one novels (so far) featuring Tabor Süden, a Chief Inspector in the missing persons unit of the Munich police force. The first novel in the series, *Die Erfindung des Abschieds* [*The Invention of Farewell**] was published in 1998, the latest instalment, *Der Narr und seine Maschine. Ein Fall für Tabor Süden* [*The Fool and his Machine. A Case for Tabor Süden**] appeared in late

---

1 Another volume in this series is *Ermordung des Glücks* [*The Murder of Happiness**] (Berlin: Suhrkamp, 2017).

2018. The novels are set in the city of Munich, not only because the author resides there, but because Munich and its surroundings also provide a vital element of the aesthetics of the Tabor Süden series. As a vibrant commercial centre and cosmopolitan metropolis, Munich is a prime example of the vicissitudes of modern urban life. The topography of Munich, with its old and new neighbourhoods (Giesing, Schwabing, Milbertshofen, etc.) where people live according to their affiliation to certain social classes, is constantly invoked in the novels of the series.

Most of the novels are based on an unusual premise for a police procedural: in the beginning, there is *no* murder (or any other crime, for that matter), but a *Vermissung*, a case of a missing person. The fact that Ani does *not* adhere to the traditional genre convention is significant. Tabor Süden, who was himself traumatized by the early death of his mother and the subsequent disappearance of his father at the age of sixteen, is constantly confronted with the highly problematic microstructures of modern society: marriages break up after a long time, families fall apart for no apparent reason, individuals who seemed to have a normal life disappear into nowhere. It is Süden's task to dig into the past of these missing persons and find out what has happened to them. Invariably, the reasons for the disappearances have something to do with the overarching alienation brought about by modern life. The clash of traditional forms of life and modern developments results in what Theodor W. Adorno in the subtitle of *Mimima Moralia* has called 'a damaged life' ['das beschädigte Leben'],[2] and Süden's files are case histories of this plight.

A good example of this kind of throwing light on the seedier sides of life in contemporary Germany is *Süden und der Luftgitarrist* [2003, *Süden and the Air Guitar Player**] which tells the story of young Aladin, who begins a promising career as a soccer player and is signed on by international soccer powerhouse Bayern Munich. Due to a number of injuries, however, Aladin's soccer career is cut short, and he subsequently loses contact to his family, his girlfriend and all of his acquaintances. He ends up freezing to death in a parked car, having severed all bonds to his former life and being abandoned by everybody. Aladin's fate comes to light when his brother comes to Munich to participate in an air guitar contest in which Tabor Süden's best friend and colleague Martin Heuer is also a contestant. Playing air guitar, already alluded to in the title of the novel, is a powerful, if ambivalent metaphor: it could refer to people who have found a niche for themselves in which they can perform their otherwise hidden

---

2 Cf. Theodor W. Adorno, *Minima Moralia: Reflections From Damaged Life*, ed. and trans. E. F. N. Jephcott (London: Verso, 1978).

talents, or it could point towards the emptiness of their lives, indicated by the non-existent instrument they pretend to play.

At the end of *Süden und der Mann im langen schwarzen Mantel* [2005, *Süden and the Man in the Long Black Coat**], the tenth novel in the series, Süden quits his career as a police officer and takes a train to an unknown city somewhere in Germany. His author had decided not only to end the series, but to stop writing crime fiction altogether. The latter was reversed very soon and the Polonius Fischer and Jonas Vogel series were written. In 2011, however, Tabor Süden also came back in a novel simply called *Süden*. Just like his illustrious predecessor Arthur Conan Doyle, although arguably not for exactly the same reasons, Ani felt compelled to bring back his most popular fictional character. Unlike Holmes, who had to be brought back from the dead, Tabor Süden, who had not died at the end of what was meant to be his last case, was able to simply reappear – and so he did, as a private investigator working for a Munich detective agency and essentially doing what he had done before and does best: looking for missing persons.

Zoë Beck *(Thomas Wörtche)*

The terms *Kriminalroman* [crime novel] and *Thriller* are now little more than marketing labels. Their use satisfies reader expectations in a clear and targeted way and has led standard definitions of these concepts to become extremely narrow and limited. A crime novel is obviously much more than a story in which a police inspector investigates a case. A thriller need not involve a great deal of blood or serial killers, or women being stalked.[3]

This statement, made by Zoë Beck in a 2015 newspaper interview, could almost be regarded as an encoded reconstruction of her own literary career – and as a kind of personal poetics.

Born in 1975, Beck studied German and English literature after giving up her plans to become a concert pianist and went on to become a television producer and scriptwriter. She currently works as a dubbing director, as a translator from English into German and, since 2013, as co-director of the literary publisher *Culturbooks*. Since 2006, Beck's crime writing – the second strand of her biography – has established her as one of the most important contemporary German-language crime authors. However, this journey has

---

3 In an interview with Gerd Heiland: http://www.mittelhessen.de/hessen-welt/kultur-und-wissen/kultur_artikel,-Kein-Wellnessroman-_arid,463649.html.

not been without obstacles and is symptomatic of an industry in flux. Her first three crime novels, classic *Ermittlerkrimis* [investigative crime novels] set in Rostock, were commissioned by the publisher Bastei-Lübbe and appeared in 2006 and 2007 respectively.[4] While their themes drew on concrete, current and historical subjects (the Stasi [East German Ministry for State Security], Berlin Wall border guards, German-German relations, racism, football, neo-Nazis and the legacy of the Holocaust) rather than clichéd interpersonal conflicts (hate, greed, jealousy), they nonetheless adhered to the genre formulas and specifications that, even then, were increasingly being set by big publishing houses. Moreover, the publisher's cover designs and promotional materials suggested that the novels should be regarded as part of the wave of *Regionalkrimis* [regional crime novels] that were emerging at the time. Rostock is a 'normal' city with overseas connections, but the cover designs aimed to create a touristy Baltic Sea holiday feel. What was already apparent, however, was the novels' extraordinary linguistic quality – unusual for this type of *Krimi* – and the author's talent for smuggling narrative contraband into a predefined literary form. The success of the Rostock crime novels allowed the author to write four more novels for Bastei-Lübbe – with a change of setting to avoid the ever-increasing glut of regional crime novels – under the name of Zoë Beck, which she officially adopted at this point rather than just using it as a pen name. For a time, there were also forays into other genres – such as so-called 'chick lit'[5] and romance novels – under her real name, Henrike Heiland, and a secret pseudonym. Trying to make a living by writing literary texts generates a number of practical constraints, which crime fiction has always had to deal with as a historically unsubsidized genre – there are very few prizes that provide financial remuneration and hardly any of the grants or other funding mechanisms that 'high literature' enjoys. Beck's later crime novels are now mainly set in England and Scotland, where she went to school and studied, among other things. Her bilingualism has also led her to become a sought-after translator for challenging book projects.[6]

---

4 *Späte Rache* [*Late Revenge**] (Cologne: Bastei-Lübbe, 2006), *Zum Töten nah* [*Close to Death**] (Cologne: Bastei-Lübbe, 2007), *Blutsünde* [*Blood Sin**] (Cologne: Bastei-Lübbe, 2007).
5 Such as *Von wegen Traummann!* [*Dream Man? You Must be Joking!**] (Munich: Heyne, 2011).
6 Beck has translated Gary Dexter, *Der Marodeur von Oxford* [*The Oxford Despoiler*] (Berlin/Zurich: Diaphanes, 2013), Pippa Goldschmidt, *Weiter als der Himmel* [*Falling Sky*] (Bonn: Weidle, 2013), James Grady, *Die letzten Tage des Condor* [*The Last Days of the Condor*] (Berlin: Suhrkamp, 2016).

These four novels[7] are loosely linked by two protagonists – Ben, a journalist and the wealthy heir Cedric – although they do not necessarily appear as the main characters, instead remaining in the background of the plot to a greater or lesser degree. They are designed to function as a cipher for the 'investigative' element within the novels, rather than being classic investigators themselves. Nor do police investigations play a central role in the novels. Beck is interested in the dynamics between the main protagonists, although they are never depicted as purely 'psychological' (in the sense of nineteenth-century 'psychological realism'), but are always grounded in a socio-political reality. The opportunity for women to live a self-determined life can be identified as a leitmotiv here, although the minimal use of 'inner' dialogue in favour of an analytical and sometimes aloof, ironic linguistic style, together with the creation of characters along similar lines, impede the reader's search for an explicit 'message'.

Nor do these novels adhere conceptually to a standard crime fiction formula. Instead, their plots, characters and language have affinities with classic psychological thrillers like those of Patricia Highsmith, which, when viewed in formal terms, also forego the standard features of crime fiction and merit their inclusion in the genre only through their use of suspense and the murderous disposition of their characters. Oddly, the publisher chose to disrupt the chronological order of Beck's novels on less than convincing marketing grounds, altering the sequence after *Wenn es dämmert* [2008, *When Night Falls**]. In plot terms, *Der frühe Tod* [2011, *An Early Death**] should have been the next to appear, but *Das alte Kind* [2010, *The Old Child**] was brought forward instead, leaving some readers puzzled. By then, with the help of a 'viral marketing' agency, Beck had built up a considerable fan base through the skilful use of social media, which in turn generated pleasing sales figures. However, the dialectics of the cultural sector meant that the *Leitmedien* [the leading, most influential media] were initially very hesitant to draw attention to Beck's work. *Das alte Kind*, the third novel from this period, which dissects the neuroses of the upper-middle class, functioned as a kind of gateway to a different type of reading audience following a book discussion on the Deutschlandradio Kultur station.[8] *Das zerbrochene Fenster* [*The Broken Window**], Beck's final novel for Bastei-Lübbe, which received no marketing support from the publisher at all, made it onto the prestigious 'KrimiZeit-Bestenliste' [*Zeit* newspaper's 'Best of Crime Writing List'] in September 2012, thereby giving Beck a new level of visibility.

---

7 *Wenn es dämmert* (Cologne: Bastei-Lübbe, 2008), *Das alte Kind* (Cologne: Bastei-Lübbe, 2010), *Der frühe Tod* (Cologne: Bastei-Lübbe, 2011), *Das zerbrochene Fenster* (Cologne: Bastei-Lübbe, 2012).

8 Thomas Wörtche, Deutschlandradio Kultur, July 28 2010.

Unfortunately, we have no means of analysing or describing, as we do for voters in elections, something like a 'reader shift'. On a purely speculative level, I would conjecture that Beck lost some readers from her fan base, but gained a wider, more varied reading public from beyond the internet community in return.

The next big step for Beck came in 2013 when she switched to Munich's Heyne Verlag, which is part of Random House. Ironically, Beck's works ended up being categorized as 'women's suspense' there – a label typically used for a highly diverse set of products that are 'optimized' to suit broad reading tastes. In the face of some opposition from the publisher, the author produced two flawless political crime novels or *Polit-Thriller* [political thrillers]: *Brixton Hill* [2013*] and *Schwarzblende* [2015, *Fade to Black*].[9] Both were highly successful, helped in part by Beck's strengthened professional profile. *Brixton Hill* was on the 'KrimiZeit-Bestenliste' for three months (January, February, March 2014), while *Schwarzblende*, unusually, stayed on the list for four months (March to June 2015). Discussion about the novels in almost all leading media outlets contributed to and emerged from their success. Like the psychological thrillers of Highsmith, the classic political thrillers of Eric Ambler, Ross Thomas and others, they mostly unfold without the use of standard narrative techniques or narrative conventions that would allow for exact categorization. They are largely 'formula-free' and able to exploit all narrative possibilities without having to relinquish their membership in the genre. Beck adopts the same principle: *Brixton Hill* focuses on the particularly virulent problem of gentrification in the financial capital of London, which can be linked back to Thatcherism in particular and which, though a problem for all European cities to some extent, is especially acute there. Subplots involving the financial criminality endemic to the City and figures like the main protagonist Emma, who is depicted both as an individual and as a social entity, achieve a high level of complexity, which Beck communicates in elegant, precisely calibrated prose, without ever falling into the trap of inviting readers to identify with specific characters.

Beck's novel *Schwarzblende* is narrated even more coolly and precisely and gained a grim topicality through the terrorist incidents of winter 2014 and spring 2015. The novel is based on a real case: the murder of a British soldier by two Islamists, which was filmed and subsequently went viral on the Internet. Beck fictionalizes this murder and traces its effects and consequences in the British public sphere. In the process, the novel asks a number of key questions,

---

9 *Brixton Hill* (Munich: Heyne, 2013), *Schwarzblende* (Munich: Heyne, 2015); *Fade to Black*, trans. by Rachel Hildebrandt (Spartanburg/SC: Weyward Sisters Publishing, 2017).

but without ever offering facile solutions. How do societies deal with this kind of problem? In what ways are such cases instrumentalized for political gain? How do young people like these become radicalized? To what extent do police responses affect the social climate? What kinds of intelligence service interests might be involved? What role does the media gaze play (it is surely no coincidence that the main character is a cameraman)? The handling of these and other questions is not laboured, but rather an organic consequence of *Schwarzblende*'s thrilling plot. The *Süddeutsche Zeitung* wrote that 'fictionalizing a current political crisis and putting it into words' did not seem possible, but that Beck's 'sober tone' allowed the impossible to be realized.[10] It is precisely this fusion of an intellectual concept and sober, crystal-clear, emotion-free prose that led *Schwarzblende* to become a media event (with a flurry of positive reviews across the media[11]) and a hit with readers. Beck's subsequent change of publisher, this time to Suhrkamp Verlag, was the fundamentally logical outcome. Her latest novel, *Die Lieferantin* [2017, *The Supplier**], published in June 2017, has received even more attention than her previous works.[12]

A brief additional note: if one looks at Zoë Beck's numerous short stories down the years, the extent to which her condensed, compressed, often laconic narrative style has been able to develop – usually beyond formal conventions and at times outside the crime genre – becomes clear.[13] That she began her career as somebody who developed writing as a craft and is now, irrespective of genre, recognised as an important contemporary German writer is due to the quality of her literary work, which has increasingly moved beyond the constraints of the book industry.

Translated by Katharina Hall

Oliver Bottini *(Jochen Vogt)*

Oliver Bottini, born in 1965 in Nuremberg, attended the University of Munich in the 1990s, where he studied German, Italian and Psychology. He went on to work as a freelance lecturer and complete an apprenticeship as a family

---

10 *Süddeutsche Zeitung*, 13 April 2015. http://www.sueddeutsche.de/kultur/schauplatz-london-blut-im-handy-1.2418200.
11 For a collection of Beck's most important reviews, see https://zoebeck.wordpress.com/bucher/.
12 *Die Lieferantin* (Berlin: Suhrkamp, 2017).
13 For a prototypical short story, see Zoë Beck, 'Freundin' [Girlfriend*] in *Unter vier Augen. Sprachen des Porträts*, ed. by Kirsten Voigt (Bielefeld: Kerber, 2013), pp. 276–282.

therapist, and he lived in Berlin until 2008. The setting of his first five crime novels, which appeared almost annually between 2005 and 2010, is, however, predominantly the popular southwest German university city of Freiburg and the surrounding region, with which the author demonstrates his familiarity.

His novels are classic police procedurals, with the sturdy forty-year-old chief detective Louise Boní as their protagonist, who is employed by the homicide division in Freiburg, but hails from the French Alsace. She is characterized as wilful and stubborn in her investigative work, which is surely also due to her position among her mostly male superiors and colleagues. The pressures of her job – due not only to her day-to-day work in the endless struggle against both petty and large-scale crime, but also to difficult human and, in particular, romantic relationships – have apparently led to alcohol addiction. When she does overcome this addiction, she is unable to avoid the dangers of relapse. The interests of the author in psychological, spiritual and therapeutic questions manifest themselves in the depiction of the main character, whose development we can follow from case to case. (Oliver Bottini emerged after 2002 as a writer of serious fiction books on Zen, Buddhism and Qigong.)

A common pattern becomes apparent in the murder cases and other criminal cases with which *Hauptkommissar* [detective chief inspector] Boní is confronted: the idyllic surroundings that can be enjoyed in the Freiburg region and that the locals are proud of are disturbed by sinister or threatening incidents. For example, *Mord im Zeichen des Zen* [2005, *Murder Under the Sign of Zen**] features a Japanese monk, sparingly clothed, aimlessly wandering around Freiburg in the middle of winter. Who pursues him and why? Moreover, *Im Sommer der Mörder* [2006, *In the Summer of Killers**], why does a woodshed in Kirchzarten, halfway to the Black Forest, suddenly go up in flames? And who put a weapons arsenal beneath it? In *Im Auftrag der Väter* [2007, *On Behalf of the Fathers**], what does the armed man, who is hardly an ordinary burglar and who poses a strange ultimatum, want in the garden of the Niemann family? Finally, what happened to the missing Freiburg student in *Jäger in der Nacht* [2010, *Hunters at Night**]?

Such puzzling and disturbing introductions are then followed by further incidents and crimes, which bring Boní and her colleagues from the French side of the Rhine into the arena. It is almost always Louise who finds a larger, for her even threatening, context, such as in *Das verborgene Netz* [2010, *The Hidden Network**], which is often a conspiracy that stretches far back into somebody's personal history or the German past.

Throughout his police novels, Bottini works in elements of the thriller, which he very cleverly inserts within the context of the police novel, so that Boní's problems and sensitivities repeatedly become part of the story. In retrospect, however, even in these early novels, which received recognition among readers and critics from the outset and were honoured with crime fiction prizes, we can observe a subliminal affinity to the genre of the detective story or political thriller.

It is therefore indeed remarkable, but not entirely surprising, that Bottini emerged after a change of publisher with two extensive and complex political thrillers and gained a foothold in the hardcover segment of the crime novel market. With *Der kalte Traum* [2012, *The Cold Dream**] and *Ein paar Tage Licht* [2014, *A Few Days of Light**], he turned to the genre of – not only German – contemporary affairs, dealing with global or, at least, international problems and local crime. In *Der kalte Traum*, Bottini tells of the wars in former Yugoslavia in the 1990s and their extreme cruelty, even including genocide. But even those wars are part of the German past, which is not completely over. Thomas Cavar, high school graduate and the son of a Croatian *Gastarbeiter* [guest worker], grows up in the Swabian town of Rottweil, where his brother is even in charge of the local savings bank. However, Thomas, disoriented and adventurous, is caught up in the war – his Serbian girlfriend is powerless to stop him – and he disappears. Twenty years later, in 2010, he appears in a photo that shows him shooting defenceless prisoners. Tommy, a war criminal? A case for the tribunal in The Hague?

Now three hunters are on his trail: an inquisitive journalist who conjures up further mischief, a *Kommissar* [detective inspector] from Berlin who acts as the quintessential German 'friend and helper', and the shadowy agents of the Croatian secret service. What they are up to is revealed bit by bit, partly predictably, partly surprisingly, and leads to a conclusion that is as rapid as it is sad. Above and beyond brilliantly telling a story, Bottini is concerned with historically educating his readers about the almost forgotten downsides of those dark years. His personal commitment is clear, but it is seamlessly integrated into a political thriller, something that had not been achieved before in such political and literary quality in the German language. The fact that he has learned much from English veteran writer John le Carré does not diminish his accomplishment.

His subsequent novel, *Ein paar Tage Licht*, even exceeds the previous one with regard to story consistency and stylistic quality. Bottini manages to balance the divergent elements of a serious thriller – that is to say: suspense and realism, controversial political issues, and individual fates, locales and fictional characters. Moreover, he makes us highly aware of how tightly entangled local and global problems are today. This case deals with the dubious dealings of the German defence industry, more precisely, with tanks that do not even have to be delivered secretly to Algeria, because they will be built there. The novel shows that in one of the largest and richest countries in Africa, an aging authoritarian power elite is more interested in suppressing the internal contradictions afflicting the country than solving them; and it is getting by – but just barely. . The German manager who is supposed to direct production is kidnapped – by Al Qaeda, as the government in Algiers claims and the one in Berlin is only too happy to believe. However, the deal is controversial there, too, and Bottini traces with satirical sharpness the power plays and intrigue in the executive rooms and backrooms, at shooting festivals and in provincial brothels.

The hub of the action, however, is Algiers; the impassable mountain ranges of Kabylia become the setting for war. This is where the trail of the abductee leads, and a brave loner follows it, who is able to discover the true fronts behind lies and propaganda – without preventing the disaster. Ralf Eley is a member of the *Bundeskriminalamt* [Federal Criminal Police Office], i.e. the Central Crime Prevention Authority, which almost always comes off quite badly in German crime novels. The fact that he is playing at the highest level of risk is obvious; that he is still granted a small amount of private happiness at the end – we shouldn't grudge him that. This is a very accurate and well researched, atmospherically dense, instructive, suspenseful and, at the same time, touching political novel from the pen, or rather PC, of a German author – a real rarity and I therefore highly recommend it. The same is true of his most recent thriller, located in Romania, *Der Tod in den stillen Winkeln des Lebens* [2017, *Death in the Quiet Corners of Life**] which is based on a true story.

But what has happened to Louise Boní and East Germany while Bottini has been working on his political thrillers? She is actually still in commission, as her affectionate and curious readers almost surprisingly discovered in early 2016 when the sixth novel in the series, *Im weißen Kreis* [*In the White Circle**], was published. Boní has just ended a convoluted and difficult love affair and is therefore now living as a single woman, mourning her fatherly boss, but successfully, though not without temptation, keeping away from the bottle. Bottini thus takes us back to her and once again to the self-proclaimed 'green capital' of Germany. He remains highly political in the familiar genre of the police novel; it is commendable that he does not set his history of the Russian mafia, of murderous right-wing radicalism and the failure of the so-called protectors of the state in virtually stigmatized Saxony – which would have been a 'cheap move' – but in the green-red and subliminally Christian Democrat, liberal model state of Baden-Württemberg. Yes, there are violence and victims of homicide in this case – in particular an African visitor who reminds the self-satisfied city and the university of colonial injustice because he wants to bury the bones of his grandfather, which have rested in the ethnology basement of the university since the days of Kaiser Wilhelm, at home. The visitor becomes a target for the right-wing thugs who even eliminate their own henchmen when they become unreliable. In addition, the employees of the state protection force, who would like to sweep everything under the carpet due to their bad public image, quite uninhibitedly fire shots about the Cathedral Square at the end.

That it is 'sincere', 'upright' citizens who have created this evil network makes the reader think. The only thing that makes the story a little less credible is when they meet among the Black Forest pines wearing conical hats [Zipfelmützen] for a Ku Klux Klan party. However, Boní saw it and, after all, she is the only one that never gives up. At any rate, we are looking forward to see her again as soon as possible – although: maybe a new location would do her good?

Translated by Lily Rockefeller

Simone Buchholz *(Kirsten Reimers)*

Simone Buchholz, born in 1972 in Hanau, graduated from the Henri Nannen School for Journalism and spent fifteen years working as a journalist for various magazines. She is currently working as a freelance writer based in Hamburg. In addition to books for children and young adults, non-fiction works for adults, short stories and crime stories, she has written seven crime novels, the most recent of which was published in September 2018.

The main protagonist in Buchholz's crime novels is state prosecutor Chastity Riley, whose unusual name stems from her father, an American officer once stationed in Hessen. The novels are set in and around the Reeperbahn in St Pauli, Hamburg's nightclub and harbour district, and are told from Riley's perspective in the first person.

Buchholz's first crime novel, *Revolverherz* [Revolver Heart*], appeared in 2008 and features a serial murderer who kills and scalps dancers from the red-light district. The plot is largely unoriginal and frequently relies on coincidence to move along the action. *Knastpralinen* [2010, *Prison Pralines**] focuses on the issue of violence against women and is reminiscent of the 1980s *Frauenkrimi* [women's crime fiction], which increasingly thematized women's proactive resistance to violent attacks. Both *Revolverherz* and *Knastpralinen* give the impression of being constructed and artificial to some degree. In *Schwedenbitter* [2011, *Swedish Bitters**], the author turns her attention to contemporary social issues for the first time. Among other things, the novel depicts shady property dealings in Hamburg, which could undoubtedly take place in a similar way in real life. Organized crime also makes its debut. These first three crime novels differ greatly from one another in terms of their structure and themes. As Buchholz herself has noted, they gave her a means of testing out how she wanted to use the genre and what type of crime fiction she wanted to write.

Buchholz's subsequent crime novels place a stronger emphasis on socially relevant themes. *Eisnattern* [2012, *Ice Adders**] is about affluent, emotionally neglected youngsters and violence against the homeless. *Bullenpeitsche* [2013, *Bullwhip**] returns to the topic of organized crime, highlighting how politics, economics and criminality become entangled through property deals and corruption.

Buchholz is best known for her sixth crime novel, *Blaue Nacht* [2016, *Blue Night**]. While Droemer Knaur had published her earlier novels, *Blaue Nacht* was released by the literary publisher Suhrkamp. This move, together with other factors – such as a repositioning of the novel, the possible influence of a new editor and greater experience on the author's part – brought the novel increased attention and praise from critics and readers alike. *Blaue Nacht* was on the 'KrimiZeit-Bestenliste' (known since 2017 as the 'Krimibestenliste' ['Best of Crime Writing List']) – a highly regarded, monthly list of the best crime fiction, compiled by a panel of experts – for several months, including two months at number one. The novel was also awarded the Deutscher Krimi Preis [German Crime Fiction Prize], placing second in the 'national' category, and the 2016 Cologne Crime Award. It was published in English as *Blue Night* by London's Orenda Books in 2018. The novel focuses on the international drugs trade and the intersections between economics, politics and criminality, once again involving organized crime.

The crimes and cases that need solving in Buchholz's novels are sometimes overshadowed by the personal and day-to-day problems of the main characters and their neighbourhoods. As Buchholz herself admits, she is not particularly 'plotstark' [strong on plot],[14] but this is offset by her unusual protagonists with quirky friends and colleagues, who avoid seeming clichéd – though sometimes only just – thanks to the author's warm-hearted depictions and dry humour. As mentioned above, state prosecutor Chastity Riley is the central figure in the series. Like the author, she was born in Hessen and came to live in Hamburg's St Pauli district by chance, a place she now calls home. Riley shows no trace of Hanseatic reserve. In many respects, she resembles the hard-boiled characters of American crime novels in the tradition of Raymond Chandler: she smokes and drinks too much; she is quick-witted, but prone to melancholy and depression; she broods and fears commitment, especially in romantic relationships. Unlike the heroes of hard-boiled crime fiction, however, Chastity is not an isolated figure, as she has a reliable and mutually supportive social network of

---

14 Dr. Kirsten Reimers, Interview with the author, 17 June 2017.

friends and colleagues. Buchholz's novels are thus not simply about criminality, but about the value of friendship as well.

Another important role is played by the city of Hamburg, or more specifically the St Pauli district and port, which are depicted as a gateway for drugs and as a place where the interests of organized crime and Hamburg's trading world come into contact with one another. The district is so fundamental to the novels that it can almost be viewed as an independent character, with diverse facets and faces. The weather, the seagulls and birdlife, the asphalt, the industrial spaces, the harbour and its cranes – all of these form part of the area and are constantly thematized. Thus, rather than a realistic portrayal of the city or the district, we are shown an imaginary place – one that is sometimes greatly exaggerated – filled with longing and the promise of home.

St Pauli and its harbour also influence the plot development of Buchholz's later novels. The port is Hamburg's open flank, through which danger and threats – criminality – can force their way in. Chastity Riley and her troop of police colleagues and friends confront and try to hold these back but often only succeed to a limited extent. All does not end well in the novels: crime is not permanently eradicated, and organized crime is not driven from the city for good. Thus, Buchholz arguably writes *Großstadtkrimis* [urban crime novels] that, in structural terms, also resemble westerns.

Organized crime plays an increasingly significant role in these novels. Buchholz is keen to show that this type of crime does not just exist in far off places but affects the daily lives of ordinary citizens by infiltrating the housing market, city government, politics and trade. Buchholz takes her cue from real-life cases in Hamburg, but without writing *romans à clef*: organized crime's past and present links to Hamburg's most influential social circles provide the model, stimulus and catalyst for the novels, where they appear in a fictionalized and adapted form. As Buchholz notes, collaboration between the mafia and big business in Hamburg has an excellent chance of succeeding, as mafia DNA and Hamburg's DNA dovetail perfectly: although money is being made in this city, it is not openly discussed. In principle, these links are visible to everyone – one only has to read articles from different press outlets carefully and pay attention to the overlaps between them.

However, what interests the author are not just the links that organized crime has with the city, but the inner workings of such clans and male groups, and the fears that sustain them. In Buchholz's view, when cultures like those of organized crime (and other male societies) constantly feel the need to emphasize their fearlessness and strength, then there must be significant underlying fears about losing something or not measuring up to particular ideals.

Buchholz's novels are written from the main protagonist's perspective in a style that takes its lead from the spoken word. Buchholz likes dialogue and action; conversely, explanatory or narrative passages are rare. Her stylistic tone is almost flippant – cool and laconic, but also warm-hearted – and when the subject of friendship or St Pauli comes up, it sometimes threatens to tip over into pathos and kitsch, though it luckily never does. In spite of the melancholy that infuses the novels and the psyche of the main character, the stories are told with a light touch and extremely dry humour.

Simone Buchholz's crime novels have evolved from somewhat random, over-constructed, conventional plots into urban crime novels (or possibly urban westerns) that are anchored in reality, with narrative power and a shot of social criticism. One cannot help but wonder and look forward to how this series will develop in future.

Translated by Katharina Hall

Jörg Fauser *(Sandro M. Moraldo)*

Jörg Fauser was the *enfant terrible* of the German literary scene. Born in the Taunus town of Bad Schwalbach in 1944, he worked a number of different jobs (temporary worker, airport worker, night guard, journalist, author and rock songwriter). The night after his forty-third birthday, he died tragically and under mysterious circumstances when walking on the A94 highway between Feldkirchen and Riehm near Munich, where he was hit by a truck. It was only after his death that he became an iconic figure. In 1988, Das Syndikat, a group of German crime writers, awarded him the prestigious Ehrenglauser prize for crime fiction, named after the Swiss author Friedrich Glauser. Moreover, when in 1990, the Bochum-based Krimi-Archiv [crime fiction archive] ran a survey of critics, book dealers and authors intended to identify the best crime novels of all time, Fauser's first novel, *Der Schneemann* [*The Snowman*] made it into the top ten. Ranking as the best German title, it received more votes than Hans Werner Kettenbach's *Minnie*, which took fourteenth place, and Jakob Arjouni's *Happy birthday, Türke!* [*Happy Birthday, Turk!*], which placed sixteenth. However, *Der Schneemann*[15] is no classic crime novel, for it does not depict the process of solving an enigmatic crime that is necessary to convict and penalize the perpetrator(s). Instead, it is centred on one main character and the disasters he is entangled in. Fauser's crime novels are generally based on an almost

---

15 Jörg Fauser, *Der Schneemann* (Munich: Rogner & Bernhard, 1981).

stereotypical tragicomic constellation, i.e. the Don-Quixote-like struggle of an outsider against corrupt and greedy practitioners such as lawyers, politicians, artists and even representatives of the state authorities. In this respect, they are similar to Raymond Chandler's and Dashiell Hammett's hard-boiled novels, much admired by Fauser for breaking with the patterns of the traditional English crime story, e.g. its artificial rules and lack of realism.

It was in 1981, with the publication of *Der Schneemann*, that Fauser made his literary breakthrough. The book not only achieved critical acclaim but was also an economic success, and in 1984, director Peter F. Bringmann adapted it into a film starring Marius Müller-Westernhagen. *Der Schneemann* tells the story of small-time criminal and antihero Siegfried Blum, a man, as Fauser describes him, 'Ende dreißig, ein Bundesrepublikaner auf Abwegen, hat im Kunsthandel angefangen und es nie weiter gebracht als zum talentlosen Fälscher und Pornoheft-Händler'.[16] Blum just about manages to keep himself above water with obscure jobs, and when by accident he comes by five pounds of Peruvian Flake cocaine in Malta, he sniffs the opportunity of a lifetime. Without further ado, he launches himself into the drug business, hoping to finally fulfil his dream of leading a carefree life in the Bahamas. Yet he only manages to sell small amounts of the 'snow' that he keeps in Old Spice shaving foam cans. Things keep going wrong, making it impossible for him to close the real big deal. His dream quickly reveals itself to be a nightmare, and the locations on his journey – Munich, Frankfurt, Amsterdam and Ostend – become stops on an odyssey while Blum, hunting for fortune and happiness, himself become the hunted. Professional criminal organizations wrangle the dope off their unwanted competitor, and Blum is yet again the perennial loser. However, not only does he know how to make the most of things, he is also emotionally strong, cool and nitty-gritty enough to 'successfully' cope with this difficult situation.

Fauser again plays with typical elements of crime fiction in his 1985 novel *Das Schlangenmaul* [*The Snake's Mouth**],[17] which humorously describes sly and sometimes hypocritical characters as part of a grotesque pandemonium. In this novel, he once more proves himself to be a crafty narrator, who aptly tells incredible stories using laconic, unpretentious language. *Das Schlangenmaul* was probably inspired by the investigations that Fauser carried out in 1984 for

---

16 Jörg Fauser, 'Mit einem großen Bäng', in J.F., *Der Strand der Städte. Gesammelte journalistische Arbeiten 1959–1987*, ed. by Alexander Wewerka (Berlin: Alexander Verlag, 2009), pp. 1276–1287 (p. 1276). '[…] in his late thirties, a West German gone astray who has tried his luck in the art trade but amounts to nothing other than a talentless forger and porn magazine dealer'.

17 Jörg Fauser, *Das Schlangenmaul. Roman* (Frankfurt a.M./Berlin/Vienna: Ullstein, 1985).

a report on the disappearance of young women in West Berlin. It was published that same year under the heading *Spurlos verschwunden* [*Vanished Without a Trace**] in Berlin's city magazine *tip*.

In the novel, Heinz Harder, a former magazine reporter who now earns his living working as a 'Bergungsexperte für außergewöhnliche Fälle',[18] is engaged by Nora Schäfer-Scheunemann to search for her daughter Miriam, who has been missing for months. Harder's investigations take him straight into the concrete jungle of West Berlin where, amidst political and financial circles, he is confronted with an obscure sect and its mysterious snake cult. He manages to quickly solve the case and liberate Miriam from the grip of the sect, but the circumstances are so mysterious that, although the case itself may be over and done with, the entanglements between power and crime remain, and the real mastermind – an influential, dubious member of parliament – walks free. This is why the solution to the case does not feel like a triumph or a happy ending to Harder, instead disillusioning him. People who are on the fringes of society observing its potential decline can only rely on their own instincts and experience when it comes to morality. Harder may not be a cynical nihilist, but he only manages to survive the struggle against the entanglements between politics, crime and corruption because he is not a victim of his emotions.

In 1987, Fauser published *Kant*,[19] a 'Szene-Thriller' [cult thriller], as it presents itself in the subtitle. This novel once again takes up the motif of the kidnapped daughter that Faus er had already used in *Das Schlangenmaul*. In *Kant*, which is set in Munich instead of Berlin, this motif is combined with a blackmail story. *Kant* was originally conceived as a serial novel for the magazine *Wiener*, where it was published in six parts between May and October 1986. The protagonist is private investigator Hezekiel Kant, who describes himself as a 'freischwebender Ausputzer',[20] taking his work motto from his 'bekannten Namensvetter aus Königsberg': 'Ich übernehme alles mit einem kategorischen Imperativ'.[21] Action-loving crime enthusiasts will certainly get their money's worth as this rich, ironic thriller impresses with its fast, almost breathless rhythm. Although the case initially seems simple, it becomes more mysterious as investigations continue. The novel very gradually reveals a complex net of personal ties and entanglements, which are at the heart of the story's suspense.

---

18 Fauser, *Das Schlangenmaul*, p. 16. 'rescue expert for exceptional cases'.

19 Jörg Fauser, *Kant. Ein Szene-Thriller* (Munich: Heyne, 1987).

20 Jörg Fauser, 'Kant', in J.F., *Mann und Maus. Gesammelte Erzählungen und Prosa II. Werkausgabe in neun Bänden*, ed. by Alexander Wewerka (Zurich: Diogenes, 2009), p. 416. 'free-floating sweeper'.

21 Fauser, 'Kant', p. 408. 'famous namesake from Königsberg'; '[I take on everything with a categorical imperative'.

Kant brings light into connections that have to do with the world of prostitution and the personal past of the kidnapped girl's mother. The short novel is an eerie masterpiece about the fluid boundaries between good and evil, truth and lie. Ultimately, it depicts individuals in need of salvation, fighting for their existence in a small and shabby world in which commerce, a lust for life and artistry can merge into absurd and repugnant configurations. What remains is the protagonist's melancholic mood.

Fauser's novels do not introduce a serial hero, nor do they understand everyday reality as a consistent and rational chain of cause and effect, but they do succeed in drawing a truthful picture of the social situation in Western Germany at the time. Fauser was convinced that light fiction can diagnose moral ruptures and contradictions within society better than any other genre of fiction, and his novels attest to the shakiness of circumstances and the dubiousness of what we call reality in their very own specific tone. From the very beginning, Fauser did not just want to entertain; instead, he aspired to reflect social realities and their conflicts. In this context, he believed that crime fiction was the last possible literary genre dealing with the question of good and evil,[22] and his books illuminate all the different shades of grey in Germany, that land of mist,[23] as he once put it. At the same time, he did not write sociological case studies in the guise of crime fiction, and, luckily, his works completely lack that excessive, sometimes fake social criticism that dominated much of West German crime literature in the late 1960s and early 1970s. His books are more adequately described as brutally realistic crime novels whose characters – in search of the hidden truth[24] – set out to offer resistance to lies, corruption, indifference and malice.

Translated by Christine Henschel

22 Jörg Fauser, *Leichenschmaus in Loccum*, in Jörg Fauser, *Der Strand der Städte. Gesammelte journalistische Arbeiten 1959–1987* ed. by Alexander Wewerka (Berlin: Alexander Verlag, 2008), pp. 1176–1188, (p. 1177). '[. . .] in der die Frage nach Gut und Böse verhandelt wird'.
23 Jörg Fauser, *Die Ambler-Lektion*, in Jörg Fauser, *Der Strand der Städte/Blues für Blondinen. Essays. Werkausgabe in neun Bänden*, ed. by Alexander Wewerka, Band 8 (Zurich: Diogenes, 2009), pp. 252–258 (p. 256). '[. . .] mühsame Ausleuchten der Grautöne'; 'Nebelland'.
24 Jörg Fauser, *Auf der Suche nach der verborgenen Wahrheit*, in Jörg Fauser, *Der Strand der Städte/Blues für Blondinen. Essays. Werkausgabe in neun Bänden*. ed. by Alexander Wewerka, Band 8 (Zurich: Diogenes, 2009), pp. 30–34 (p. 34). '[. . .] auf der Suche nach der verborgenen Wahrheit'.

Monika Geier *(Kirsten Reimers)*

Monika Geier was born in Ludwigshafen in 1970. After completing her final school exams, she trained as a draughtswoman before studying architecture at Kaiserslautern University and working as a graduate in the field. She began writing crime fiction in her spare time, but eventually gave up her career in architecture to become a full-time author. She is currently a freelance writer based in the Palatinate region.

Geier's crime fiction debut, *Wie könnt ihr schlafen?* [1999, *How Can You Sleep?**], was published in 1999 by Ariadne, a Hamburg-based publisher specializing in feminist crime fiction. The novel was awarded the Marlowe crime prize by the Raymond-Chandler-Gesellschaft [Raymond Chandler Association] in 2000.

To date, Geier has published eight crime novels. Chief Inspector Bettina Boll plays a leading role in seven of them, while historian Richard (Rick) Romanoff appears in the eighth. Although the novels are constructed like classic 'whodunits', they go far beyond classic conventions in terms of their content and structure.

The novels featuring Chief Inspector Boll usually contain at least one murder, the motives for which appear to be personal. Geier's first novel *Wie könnt ihr schlafen?* is about rape and retribution; *Neapel sehen* [2001, *Seeing Naples**] explores abusive behaviour, resisting abuse and frustrated love; *Stein sei ewig* [2003, *Stone is Eternal**] and *Schwarzwild* [2007, *Wild Boars**] foreground financial issues and the topic of jealousy respectively. *Die Herzen aller Mädchen* [2009, *All the Girls' Hearts**] tells the story of the theft of an Ovid manuscript and insurance fraud; *Die Hex ist tot* [2013, *The Witch is Dead**] examines familial conflicts; while *Alles so hell da vorn* [2017, *Everything's So Bright Up There**] deals with forced child prostitution. In *Müllers Morde* [2011, Mller's Murders*], which features historian-detective Romanoff, at first glance, the murder seems to have been committed for financial gain.

However, the motives for these crimes go well beyond the personal, as the cases are often far more complex than they initially appear. Geier's perpetrators are never monsters or sick psychopaths. Instead, they are perfectly normal men and women from mainstream society, who, at a certain point in their lives, decide to solve their problems by committing a crime or by looking away, denying involvement or staying silent, thus becoming complicit in criminal acts. The characters' personal circumstances play a decisive role in this respect: they are often under some kind of pressure, although this only ever explains rather than excuses their crimes.

In this way, Geier depicts the crimes she writes about as individual decisions made in specific social contexts. In the process, she successfully reveals the interrelationships between society, the individual and criminality.

Her crime novels are set in a fictitious Palatinate region. As a rule, nearby towns and cities such as Ludwigshafen, Pirmasens and Mannheim are called by their real names, but the crime scenes are the author's own inventions. Real locations may have inspired these settings, but they are impossible to identify, as Geier's aim is not straightforward realism. Searching for recognizable local features in her work is thus a pointless exercise: the cities may keep their original names, but the squares, streets and buildings in them are disguised. As Geier herself notes in a personal interview on June 16, 2017, her works are set in a 'Paralleluniversum' [parallel universe]. This is one reason why her crime novels can never be classified as 'Regionalkrimis' [regional crime novels] – her works are considerably more complex, multifaceted and challenging.

Even the fictitious Palatinate region is not necessarily recognizable as such. The storylines could be transposed to any other region. Local colour is suggested by characters speaking the Palatine dialect, but even this does not tie the narrative down: the dialect could easily be substituted with a different one and function just as well.

The primary focus of Geier's crime novels is the characters and their depiction. With just a few words, the author succeeds in creating complex, vibrant figures who transcend the social and local contexts in which they are situated. Geier is a precise observer of human idiosyncrasies – and it is precisely this that sets her novels apart: they are peopled with often-quirky characters who, for all their peculiarities, never seem overly brash. Each novel is thus shot through with a unique mixture of the exaggerated and the down to earth, capturing reality in a trenchant way.

The novels' main protagonists illustrate this point: Bettina Boll is Chief Inspector with the Ludwigshafen K11, the 'Abteilung für Kapitalverbrechen' [Department for Serious Crimes]. Since becoming the main carer for her late sister's children, she works part time – probably the only investigator in German-language crime fiction to do so. Boll is depicted as slightly chaotic: always a little late, always a little disorganized, always dressed a little too casually. She compensates for this with her acute powers of observation and synthesis. Boll rarely immerses herself in detail, but looks at the bigger picture instead, allowing her to see the structures and spaces in which crimes occur. While she is portrayed as having a razor-sharp intellect, Boll retains an almost childlike sense of wonder that stops her from accepting things at face value and leads her to question everything. As a result, outsiders may view her as rather naïve. However, what might be misinterpreted as a type of artlessness on her part is actually a substantial and impartial thirst for knowledge. Equally, Boll's apparent intuition results from the rational synthesis of all she has seen and heard, her unconventional thinking, and the way she draws analytically on past experiences. The same is true of Rick Romanoff, a kind of intellectual 'Indiana Jones' figure, albeit more introverted and awkward, who unearths historical artefacts for obscure clients.

In this respect, Geier's main characters resemble those of her role model Agatha Christie. Like Christie, Geier equips her key players with a precise eye for human idiosyncrasy and the ability to synthesize facts in clever, complex ways. However, what Geier herself most admires is Christie's ability to condense multi-layered themes without losing their complexity. For Geier, Christie's crime novels are fundamentally mathematical in nature, as she explained in the interview in June, 2017.

Geier does not shy away from complexity either. Her crime novels reflect an architect's fascination with spaces and structures: complex edifices, intricate designs – elegant constructions suffused with light, with a compelling logicality that subordinates all else.

Narrative elements such as the characters' private lives thus only feature when they advance or impede the criminal investigation. Nor does their presence ever result, say, in a family member being placed in any crude kind of danger. The integration of family detail is much more subtle: for example, in *Alles so hell da vorn*, Boll questions a witness (who was initially dismissed as unimportant) only because her house lies on Boll's route home, where she is heading due to her part-time status and childcare responsibilities. This rather chance interview illuminates a new angle and contributes significantly to the solving of the case. There are no 'empty' situations or events in Geier's other novels either. Every element contributes to the action and supports the complex structure of the narrative.

These include depictions of the everyday sexism that Boll encounters working in a male-dominated profession. The Chief Inspector responds to her boss's insistence on calling her 'Böllchen' [little Boll] – as well as other forms of disrespect and being completely ignored – with repartee and clear boundaries, but without becoming strident. This is another of Geier's strengths: she includes into her stories the underlying or open sexism within the police force and in society – along with personal and socials responses to it – and she does this in a casual, understated and thus all the more effective way. None of this is related in a heavy-handed manner, nor is it not swept under the carpet.

Geier thus manages to combine elements that seem quite contradictory: her characters are quirky yet down to earth; the action is complex; none of her novels can be summed up in just a few words, as complicated spaces and interconnections keep opening up within the cases she depicts. However, for all its complexity her work remains rigorous and logical; her crime scenes are localized, without being tied to the region in which they are set; the narrative tone is both composed and pointed. This is made possible by Geier's writing style. She has great stylistic confidence, writing with a dry, black humour and clever, delicate irony. The subtlety of the latter sometimes means that her sentences build up their intellectual power only gradually, but once they do so, that power is all the more enduring. For these and many other reasons, Monika Geier is one of the most interesting and accomplished crime authors in the German-speaking world today.

Translated by Katharina Hall

Gisbert Haefs *(Thomas W. Kniesche)*

Gisbert Haefs, born in 1950, studied English and Hispanic languages and literatures at the University of Bonn. After completing his studies, he started his career as an author and translator. He has translated texts by Arthur Conan Doyle, Adolfo Bioy Casares, G.K. Chesterton, Georges Brassens, Mark Twain and Bob Dylan into German and has served as the editor and translator of the collected works of Rudyard Kipling, Ambrose Bierce and Jorge Luis Borges. He has written numerous historical, science fiction, and crime fiction novels and stories, a series of popular radio plays and a number of literary essays.

In his crime fiction writing, Haefs has covered the past, the present and the future by combining elements of crime fiction with the historical novel, the mystery novel and science fiction. His historical crime novels feature an investigator in the ancient city of Qart Hadasht (Carthage); his mystery novels set in contemporary Germany revolve around an amateur detective based in Bonn, the former capital of West Germany; and his science fiction novels and stories tell tales of crime investigations that take place on distant planets.

Haefs's historical crime novels were written after the publication of the first of his historical novels, *Hannibal*, in 1989. Haefs has authored an impressive number of historical novels, featuring historic personalities such as Alexander the Great (*Alexander. Der Roman der Einigung Griechenlands* [1992, *Alexander. Novel of the Unification of Greece**], *Alexander in Asien. Der Roman der Eroberung eines Weltreichs* [1993, *Alexander in Asia. Novel of the Conquest of an Empire**] and Gaius Julius Caesar (*Caesar*, 2007*). His other historical novels and historical crime stories are set in the ancient word (*Troja* [1997, *Troy**], *Alexanders Erben* [2013, *Alexander's Heirs**]), sixteenth-century Europe (*Die

Rache des Kaisers [2009, *The Emperor's Revenge**], *Das Labyrinth von Ragusa* [2011, *The Labyrinth of Ragusa**]) and late eighteenth-century India (*Raja*, 1999*).

If history is – as the saying goes – always told from the point of view of the victors, then Haefs does the reverse: in his historical novels, he often uses a neutral bystander as a narrator or focalizer. In *Troja*, for example, it is an Assyrian merchant who tells the story. Economic interests are identified as the real reason for the Greek attack on the city, not an alleged competition over Helena as female object of male desire. Christa Wolf's *Kassandra* [1983, *Cassandra*] comes to mind as a related project of demystifying historical events surrounding the Trojan War.

The historical crime novels about ancient Carthage follow a similar agenda. Haefs has written four novels in this series so far: *Hamilkars Garten* [1999, *Hamilkar's Garden**], *Das Schwert von Karthago* [2005, *The Sword of Carthage**], *Die Mörder von Karthago* [2010, *The Killers of Carthage**] and *Die Dirnen von Karthago* [2014, *The Prostitutes of Carthage**]. The novels cover the period from 230 BC to 228 BC and feature Bomilkar, the leader of the city's 'guardians' (its police force). He is supported by Laetilius, an unlikely ally who is sent to Carthage from Rome on several occasions.

In Haefs's Qart Hadasht (New City), as Carthage is called by its citizens, the city-state is ruled by two powerful political factions, the 'Old Ones' [die Alten] and the 'New Ones' [die Neuen]. The Old Ones want to make peace with the Romans at all costs and concentrate the city's sphere of influence in North Africa, while the New Ones recognize the continuing threat posed by Rome and work towards countering that threat. Bomilkar is a follower of the New Ones and their leader, Hamilkar Barkas. His antagonist is Hanno, the leader of the Old Ones. Conspiracies are at the centre of each novel. Bomilkar is the police chief of Qart Hadasht, but he also serves as spymaster for Hamilkar Barkas and, after his death, for his successor Hasdrubal.

In the first three novels, Hanno is the mastermind plotting in the background to further his own ambitions and defeat the party of his political opponents. The fourth and so far last novel in the series, *Die Dirnen von Karthago*, features the Libyans conspiring against Carthage. Hanno plays only a minor role, but it was his criminal and inhuman actions in the past that precipitated the wave of crime and war in the present.

Haefs presents Carthage as a multi-ethnic society where Carthaginians, Greeks, Numidians, Jews, Arabs and others live and work together. Although slavery exists in Qart Hadasht as well, the city-state is represented as an alternative to Rome, which stands for imperialism, colonization and the suppression of indigenous cultures. 'Rome' is depicted as the quintessence of everything that threatens a peaceful coexistence of the manifold peoples and cultures that comprise the *Oikumene*, the whole of the known/settled world. In this respect, Haefs is similar to Peter Tremayne (Peter Berresford Ellis), who, in his historical crime fiction featuring Sister Fidelma, lets 'Rome' stand for anything that threatens Ireland's specific form of Christian culture in the seventh century. The politics of the leaders of Haefs's Rome concerning their enemies is expressed succinctly in Cato the Elder's notorious demand, 'Carthago delenda est' ['Carthage has to be destroyed']. In contrast to this, the New Ones in Carthage, as Haefs sees them, follow a different approach: 'Feinde werden besiegt und eingegliedert, nicht vernichtet' [Enemies are conquered and integrated, not extinguished].[25]

The second group of texts, crime fiction that is set in the present, consists of detective novels with the amateur detective Baltasar Matzbach as the protagonist. Matzbach is modelled to some extent on Rex Stout's Nero Wolfe, but even more so on John Dickson Carr's fictional detectives Dr Gideon Fell and Sir Henry Merrivale, who combined certain characteristics of G.K. Chesterton, Winston Churchill and Carr himself. Like his literary forebears, Matzbach demonstrates an enormous capacity for devouring food and has an impressive girth. Due to an invention he came up with after studying philosophy and nuclear physics, and winning the lottery, he is financially independent and devotes his time to 'senseless learning'. He is the author of several works of obscure scholarship and is considered a 'universal dabbler' ['Universaldilettant'] who spends his ample free time investigating crime.

The first of the Matzbach novels, *Mord am Millionenhügel* [*Murder at Millionaire's Hill**] was published in 1981. *Finaler Rettungskuss* [*Final Kiss of Grace**], the ninth novel in the series, appeared in 2012, followed by a collection of Matzbach stories in 2013 (*Zwischenfälle* [*Incidents**]). *Mord am Millionenhügel* begins with Matzbach discovering an unknown toothbrush in his apartment and trying to find out whom it belongs to and how it got there. As in almost all the other Matzbach books, the novel is set in Bonn, back then the capital of West Germany. Haefs captures the atmosphere and the underlying forces driving the small city, 'where many things are possible and many impossible things become law'.[26] In the course of his investigations, Matzbach uncovers the seedy secrets of the wealthy and powerful and solves a murder case. This gives him abundant opportunity to level diatribes against the state, its bureaucracy and the many government institutions of the capital city. The fact that a murder

---

25 Gisbert Haefs, *Hamilkars Garten* (Munich: Heyne, 2000), p.193.
26 Gisbert Haefs, *Mord am Millionenhügel* (Munich: Goldmann, 1981), p. 8.

was committed at all is only revealed at the end, not at the beginning, as would befit a traditional detective story. In the second novel in the series, *Und oben sitzt ein Rabe* [*And Above There Sits a Raven, 1983], Matzbach believes that a husband accused of killing his estranged wife is innocent because the husband's pet raven is named 'Poe'.

In an interview, Haefs used the notion of wit ['Witz'] to describe his approach to writing crime fiction. He bemoaned that, with few exceptions (he recalls Heinrich Heine), wit, or intellectually challenging humour is missing in German literature.[27] In his novels featuring Baltasar Matzbach, he tried to emulate the tradition of 'learned wit' in the spirit of Rabelais, Laurence Stern and Voltaire. Consequently, the Matzbach novels are a cornucopia of parodies of literary and cultural traditions. Ludic elements abound, for example when Matzbach repeatedly and in more than one novel pays visits to a fictional 'Gesellschaft zur Stärkung der Verben' [Society for the Strengthening of Verbs] or when he and other characters engage in playful banter and witty dialogues that are more than once driven to the absurd. No fashionable trend is safe from this dismantling of stereotypical thinking. In *Ein Feuerwerk für Matzbach* [*Fireworks for Matzbach**, new edition 2013], one of his associates states: 'Wenn der Weg das Ziel ist, ist das Ziel weg' [If the path is the goal, then the goal is gone', 159]. Matzbach establishes himself as a defender of play ['Spiel'] and playfulness and exposes the rigidity of rules and regulations whenever and wherever he can. This mission includes government bureaucracies and the corruption and destruction they produce on a daily basis, but it also extends to the rules and conventions of crime fiction. The Matzbach novels offer an alternative to the dominant realist tradition in twentieth-century German crime fiction embodied in the *Soziokrimi* [sociological crime novel] and the vast production of *Regionalkrimis* [regional crime novels].

Haefs has also published a number of crime fiction stories and novels that are set in a distant future. *Die Reisen des Mungo Carteret* [2007, *The Travels of Mungo Carteret**] consist of stories that were published between 1989 and 2007 and feature the humorous and sometimes grotesque cases of an interstellar private detective. The *Dante Barakuda* trilogy comprises the novels *Pasdan, Gashiri* and *Banyadir*.[28] This science fiction series is set on the planet Shilgat after the downfall of humankind. Like the historical crime novels set in Carthage, the *Barakuda* trilogy features a set of anti-conspiracy thrillers. The nomadic

---

27 Jürgen Alberts, Frank Göhre, *Kreuzverhöre: Zehn Krimiautoren sagen aus* (Hildesheim: Gerstenberg, 1999), p. 161.
28 The series of novels was originally published in four volumes in 1986.

natives of Shilgat are peoples who gave up their highly developed technology a long time ago to lead a life of freedom, spirituality and oneness with nature. Fugitives from the collapsing 'Commonwealth of Humanity' came to Shilgat and are trying to force their ideologies on the pristine planet and its peaceful inhabitants. The protagonist, Dante Barakuda, chief of security for the Commonwealth authorities (in the first volume, he resigns at the end of the novel but stays on the planet), tries to save the indigenous peoples from the fanatics and their attempts at genocide. Each of the three volumes in the series features a conspiracy by a group of zealots that Dante Barakuda has to stop to save the planet. The series is a plea for tolerance, reason and peaceful coexistence and a warning against any kind of *Weltanschauung*, ideology, religion, or metaphysical belief system that sets out to violate a peaceful planet, its culture and its peoples. As in all of Haefs's work, 'Spiel' [game, play] is a key concept in these novels. In his science fiction novels, Haefs uses the idea of playfulness, embodied by the original inhabitants of the planet Shilgat and their system of (non-)government, to discredit any kind of political, religious or ideological system that makes claims to an absolute truth. Spiritual and political anarchy appears as the only viable system of humane existence.

Uta-Maria Heim *(Jochen Vogt)*

Since the early 1990s, the writer Uta-Maria Heim has toed the line between crime fiction and other novels, with about twenty titles on one side and about ten on the other – although marking the boundaries is not so simple. It must be mentioned for completeness's sake that Heim has also worked in other genres, such as poetry (published in 1985), short stories, children's books, essays and features. Nor should one fail to mention the dozens of plays and radio play adaptations (of detective novels as well) that she has written since 1990 as a freelance writer. Since 2006, she has also been working as a dramaturg and an editor at Südwestfunkradio, headquartered in Baden-Baden, producing radio plays and radio stories.

Due to its stylistic strengths, the creative use of the acoustic medium is also likely responsible for the impressive and effective design of the monologues, dialogues and polyphony in her novels. Uta-Maria Heim is thus not only an extremely versatile and prolific writer, but also full of literary ambition, as can be seen in her latest books in particular. The above-mentioned commuting between genres, especially between crime fiction and mainstream literature, like any balancing act, carries with it the risk of stumbling or toppling over. This danger can even be observed regarding the career of this author. If the aim of something is to bring about a deliberate subversion of literary life, it certainly has a price.

Uta-Maria Heim was born in the small town of Schramberg in the Württemberg part of the Black Forest, and she remains connected to south-west Germany even today, not just in terms of her life, but also in her work, in a kind of loyal love-hate relationship. While she was studying literature, linguistics and sociology in Freiburg and Stuttgart, Heim worked as a journalist for the leftist daily newspaper *die tageszeitung* in 1983, as a critic and author for the liberal *Stuttgarter Zeitung* and the Süddeutsche Rundfunk from 1987, and later for other newspapers and broadcasting institutions. From 1993 to 2002, she lived in Hamburg and Berlin, which is also reflected in her work. However, the southern German cities, particularly the capital and their Black Forest home, the Neckar Valley and Swabian Alb, are predominant as recurring settings in her detective novels.

Her first novels appeared with titles as unappetizing as *Das Rattenprinzip* [1991, *The Rat Principle**] and *Die Kakerlakenstadt* [1993, *Cockroach City**]. In the early 1990s, she was published in the legendary 'black series' of the Rowohlt paperback publishing house, winning critical acclaim and – twice – the Deutscher Krimipreis [German Crime Fiction Prize]. Then things got quieter for Heim, although almost every year she published a novel – some of them crime fiction, some of them mainstream literature – with different publishers. This must be understood as an indication of the difficulty of finding her own place within the literary field. That these books are now appearing at longer intervals is more beneficial to the substance of their content and their formal sophistication.

Uta-Maria Heim's crime novels – including the above and, among others, *Engelchens Ende* [1999, *Little Angel's End**], *Dreckskind* [2006, *Dirt Child**], *Wespennest* [2009, *Wasps' Nest**] and *Der Sieg des Rattenprinzips* [2009, *Victory of the Rat Principle**] do not form a series in the strict sense. One could call it a network or, as in French theory (which Heim knows and treats with ironic asides), a 'rhizome', in which, even over long periods of time, plotlines and fates are tracked, and some figures appear multiple times in a kind of small, Swabian, criminal *comédie humaine*. These include the journalist Udo Winterhalter, his long-time girlfriend Claudia Roth and her father, 'red Karl', a riotous old Communist with anarchic tendencies who always puts on ludicrous sideshows, which the author obviously finds amusing. These figures also include the investigators Anita Wolkenstein and Timo Fehrle of the Stuttgart criminal investigation department and the state police respectively, whose careers we often follow, along with their relationships and family problems. The murders and other criminal cases are bound to two major topics: on the one hand, opportunism, intrigue and corruption in journalism and cultural businesses, in local and regional politics, particularly the 'Spaetzle metropolis' Stuttgart and the police; and, on the other hand, family histories, often over several generations, which almost always feature the everyday abuse experienced by children and women that has been 'concealed' as a family secret. Violent crimes are often discovered late and are all the more difficult to detect; they often obscure further crimes and family secrets, so that out of the criminal investigation a historical inquiry is made and it becomes clear that the 'perpetrators' are not the only guilty ones. Most books broach (at their core or in a more glancing fashion) National Socialism and its aftermath in the attitudes and fates of individual characters and in familial contexts.

One example of how violence is transferred across generations is *Engelchens Ende*, which earned Uta-Maria Heim the Friedrich Glauser Prize in 2000 for the best crime novel of the year. Remarkably, this prize is awarded not by critics, but by fellow writers, who justified the award as follows:

> In ostensibly cool distance, the author describes an investigation into the murder of an eight-year-old girl. Heim writes confidently, without mannerisms, clearly yet sensually, with intelligent humour. Initially, this psychological thriller presents a multifaceted mirage. With the deep, ever more intensive exploration of the characters, the tension builds. The resolution of the puzzle creates only superficial clarity, while the mystery remains.[29]

Similarly structured books, though carried out in different formats, are *Dreckskind*, a gloomy family history spanning several generations, and *Totschweigen* [2007, *Hushing Up**], a classic case history, in which after more than twenty years the identity of a brutally murdered young woman and even the murder case itself are clarified in the end. The title itself, *Totschweigen*, is emblematic of many books by Heim, based on both secret family histories and the dark periods of the German past that famously 'do not want to pass'[30] – because they have to be 'hushed up'.

---

29 *Lexikon der deutschen Krimi-Autoren*, entry 'Heim, Uta-Maria' (http://www.krimilexikon. de/heim.htm). 'In nur scheinbar kühler Distanz beschreibt die Autorin Ermittlungen zum Mord an einem achtjährigen Mädchen. Heim erzählt souverän, ohne Manierismen, klar und dennoch sinnlich, auch mit intelligentem Humor. Anfangs präsentiert sich dieser Psychothriller als facettenreiches Trugbild. Mit der tiefen, immer intensiveren Auslotung der Figuren steigt die Spannung. Die Auflösung des Rätsels schafft nur vordergründig Klarheit, das Geheimnis bleibt bestehen'.

30 Cf. Ernst Nolte, 'Vergangenheit, die nicht vergehen will: Eine Rede, die geschrieben, aber nicht gehalten werden konnte', *Frankfurter Allgemeine Zeitung*, 6. Juni 1986. This essay triggered the *Historikerstreit* [Historian's Debate] in 1986/1987.

If first impressions do not deceive, these motifs, with which Heim connects crime fiction to a major theme of German post-war and contemporary literature, become more condensed in her later books. As a central symbol in several books, she makes use of the real institution of Grafeneck, the former summer palace of the King of Württemberg and, in the twentieth century, a mental health institute that was used by the Nazis in 1940 for the mass killing of intellectually disabled people – and thus the setting for a regional rehearsal of the Holocaust.

Structurally and stylistically, Heim's books stand out from the rest of the current German crime fiction output. This is because she makes use of common structures and writing techniques more forcefully and earlier than the rest of the genre. These originate from the arsenal of classic modernism, i.e. from the non-detective novel: breaking up and rearranging plot chronologies, changing narrative perspectives and, in particular, a 'polyphonic' narrative style, featuring multiple different narrators and character voices that complement or contradict each other. This mystifies events and goes well beyond the specific activity of traditional crime fiction reading, which usually consists in competing with the detective.

The polyphony of voices is reinforced by the emphasized use of the Swabian or Alemannic dialect, either when characters are speaking or in comments made by the narrator throughout the text, throwing a spotlight on regional traditions and regional mentalities and forming a unique, additional discursive and referential level. This should be regarded as a very conscious aesthetic device on the part of the author. However, it is undeniable, and many critical reactions from readers have confirmed, that this use of dialect presupposes a certain familiarity with the local language and, as such, may be an obstacle to its favourable reception that is hardly conducive to disseminating these texts. However, this effect seems to be almost deliberately provoked – to create wilful and poetic prose, or perhaps to hold up a fun house mirror to a literary scene that rewards the incomprehensible if it is only 'lofty' enough.

Characteristic of Heim's idiosyncratic and distinctive narrative style, particularly in her recent books, is the way she freely combines standard devices from various novel types: the police novel as the psychological thriller, but also the legal novel, the family novel, ultimately even the picaresque novel – the latter used in the satirical and grotesque *Heimstadt muss sterben* [2016, *Heimstadt Must Die**]. This story is about a small, semi-fictitious town in the Neckar region that is ruled by a gang of arms smugglers. The bizarre story interweaves current associations with German arms shipments to Mexico. As she has always done, the author also uses non-fictional paratexts as prefaces and epilogues, inserts historical or pseudo-historical documents, and uses explanatory footnotes like those found in scientific texts. These features can clearly be seen in the different combinations and emphases of two important recent novels.

Feierabend [2011, *After Hours**] is a montage of the monologues of three female characters and initially looks like a 'self-discovery story' from the women's literature of the 1980s, with a mother-daughter conflict at the heart of the plot. A petty theft at first causes uncertainty. But then, the family history leads to the question of the fate of 'Aunt Brunhilde', who was an intellectually disabled child, intended for death at Grafeneck. Was she a victim of the mass murder by poison gas, or did a well-meaning someone give her her 'own death'? This is not a case for the police, but the attentive reader-detective can find the answer. Whether or not it is the right answer? 'Nobody knows exactly', it says in the novel.[31]

Still more opaque are the characters and events in Heim's most ambitious (and best) novel so far, which has a Hölderlin quote in its title: *Wem sonst als Dir* [2013, *Whom Else But You**]. It begins as a judicial story and then leads into the abysses of German family histories and chronicles. The aging Judge K. is afflicted by a 'trial' almost to the same extent as his namesake in Kafka's world-famous novel. Twenty years ago, he charged the young teacher Schöller with the maximum sentence for allegedly stabbing his mother. Now K. is tormented by doubt: is he guilty of imprisoning an innocent person ? Then, Schöller breaks out of prison and the psychiatric ward and travels to Tübingen, where the mentally unwell poet Hölderlin, to whom he feels connected, lived and suffered. And what a burden Schöller carries! His mother was once a cook at the infamous Grafeneck, but she had always claimed that she knew nothing about what was going on there. His sister Irene slipped into left-wing terrorism in the 1970s and is supposed to have perished after the fall of the Berlin Wall in the former GDR. 'Nobody knows the exact truth' – again it is up to the reader to retrace the truth as much as possible. The various voices, not always clearly marked, make this investigation work as charming as it is difficult. Moreover, a network of intertextual references and allusions is used, both on the level of plot, again and again referring to Hölderlin, and on the layer of text, where, in addition to Kafka, the poet Paul Celan is quoted. The reader can appreciate how the author very purposefully questions the boundary between genre literature and so-called high literature, and even transcends it.

In choosing her literary forms and expressions, Heim treats the familiar genre conventions and the value associated with them if not with contempt,

---

31 Uta-Maria Heim, *Feierabend* (Meßkirch: Gmeiner Verlag, 2011), p. 222. 'Genaues weiß kein Mensch'.

then with irony. Her literary genre bending thus demonstrates artistic freedom and fearlessness, which risks losing its balance every now and then. We may put that to the test when reading her latest books, *Heimstadt muss sterben*, a highly satirical crime novel in a provincial setting, *Toskanische Beichte* [2017, *Tuscan Confession**] and *Toskanisches Feuer It soon becomes evident that the crimes, which form the starting point for all subs* [2018, *Tuscan Fire**], 'whodunits' with a good dose of comedy and a catholic priest from Lake Constance investigating at home and abroad (as the titles suggest).

Translated by Lily Rockefeller

Veit Heinichen *(Steffen Richter)*

In 1999, when Veit Heinichen first settled in Trieste, that seemingly peaceful city on the Adriatic had yet to establish its criminal credentials. But now, after eight novels about Inspector Proteo Laurenti, all doubts have been set aside. Despite the fact that the city has a low level of petty crime, its geographical situation and its chequered history show that it was predestined as a backdrop for crime fiction. It was inevitable that the crime writing that has gripped Trieste in recent years reflects many of the processes of European integration.

Veit Heinichen was born in 1957 in Villingen-Schwenningen in the Black Forest. He initially studied business and worked for the car giant Daimler-Benz, but switched to the book trade, where he worked for the publishing houses Ammann and S. Fischer. Together with Arnulf Conradi, he founded Berlin Verlag in 1994. In the first half of the 1990s, Veit Heinichen wrote crime fiction under the pseudonym Viola Schatten, which he shared with the journalist (and subsequent novelist) Elke Schmitter. Heinichen published five crime novels set in Frankfurt am Main, following the private detective Ruth Maria von Kadell. It was, however, only when writing the Trieste novels under his own name that Heinichen became one of the most successful crime writers in the German language.

Veit Heinichen is not the only non-Italian to have made Italy the setting for his crime fiction. The significant difference between Heinichen and, for instance, the British authors Michael Dibdin and Magdalen Nabb, or the American Donna Leon, is that Heinichen has, through the translation of his works, become part of the Italian literary scene, as well as due to his readings, his participation in public debates and his journalistic writing. Between 2003 and 2014, Veit Heinichen received several Italian prizes for his work. In 2003 and 2004, two of his novels were finalists in the Premio Franco Fedeli (a literary competition organized by the Italian police federation). Massimo Carlotto – one of the most prominent authors of Italian noir, inspired by the highest literary and political vision for the genre – has praised Heinichen's novels for the exceptionally important contribution that they make to debates on Italy's current severe problems. It is striking to note how little the novels of Heinichen draw on popular German myths about the Italians. While Heinichen does not ignore details of Italian gastronomy and tourism, his novels are far removed from the prevalence of such elements in the work, for instance, of Donna Leon. This has not prevented his work from being highly praised by German critics and greatly enjoyed by his German readers. This is reflected in the crime fiction prize he was awarded by Radio Bremen (2005) and in the film adaptations of several of his novels, which have featured star casts (Henry Hübchen, Barbara Rudnik, Götz George among others). His novels have been translated into many languages, among them French and Spanish, but not into English.

Heinichen's detective is Inspector Proteo Laurenti, deputy head of the Polizia Statale in Trieste. He is an amalgam of various classic detective figures, combining cerebral, intuitive and strong-arm methods. Laurenti began his police work in Salerno in the South before being transferred to Trieste. He is married and has three children, and his professional work frequently crosses paths with his family life. The fixed points in his work are provided by two women – his assistant and his secretary – and by the medical examiner Galvano, an old man bitterly resentful of having been forced into retirement. Laurenti's opponent for the first five novels is the Croatian Viktor Drakič, a key figure in the world of organized crime. After Drakič's death, his place is taken by a whole network of gangs and criminals.

Heinichen's novels are consistently marked by a high level of complexity in terms of both their plots and style. In his debut novel *Gib jedem seinen eigenen Tod* [2001, *To Each His Own Death**] Laurenti has to root out a gang of human traffickers, but his enquiries lead him to uncover criminal activities relating to the organization of EU aid in the wake of the Kosovo War. In *Die Toten vom Karst* [2002, *The Dead of the Karst**], the issues are the Italian exodus from Istria at the end of the war in 1945 and Italian-Croatian drug smuggling. *Tod auf der Warteliste* [2004, *Death on the Waiting List**] focuses on the international trade in human organs, in this case run from a Trieste beauty clinic. In *Der Tod wirft lange Schatten* [2005, *Death Casts a Long Shadow**], Laurenti solves an arms smuggling case that involves numerous secret service agencies and whose origins go back to the war crimes of 1939-1945. *Totentanz* [2007, *Danse Macabre**] deals with the pirating of luxury goods, together with illegal waste disposal and extortion on the black labour market. The collapse of the international financial markets creates the framework for Heinichen's next novel, *Die Ruhe des*

Stärkeren [2009, *The Repose of the Powerful**], and the ruthlessness of that world is mirrored in the sub-plot – the training of fighting dogs. *Keine Frage des Geschmacks* [2011, *Not a Question of Taste**] tells of the power of images and their manipulation, not just in pursuit of private blackmail, but in directing public opinion in the present and falsifying public understandings of the past. *Im eigenen Schatten* [2013, *In One's Own Shadow**] directs readers' attention to the problem of nationalism in South Tirol, in both its historical and its contemporary manifestations. This theme is interwoven with that of illegal trade across the recently opened frontiers between Italy, and Slovenia and Croatia. *Die Zeitungsfrau* [2016, *The Newswoman**], a novel featuring an art robbery, also illuminates the appalling living conditions in Trieste retirement homes and reaches back in time to the Falklands War. Heinichen's last novel to date, *Scherbengericht* [2016, *Ostracism**], tells the story of a series of murders in a gastronomic milieu against the background of a paradox: the xenophobia of Trieste, a city of migrants. In short: Heinichen has enriched crime fiction with one new novel every two years, and his unrelenting productivity has led to non-crime publications such as *Triest. Stadt der Winde* [2005, *Triest. City of Winds**], a travel and food book which he published with his wife, the celebrity chef Ami Scabar.

From the start, Heinichen has kept abreast of crime in all its most modern forms, constantly displaying his mastery of the craft of narration. His skills are evident in many features of his work, notably in the flawless coordination of the various strands of plot and setting, and in building tension as the story moves from one strand to the next. Heinichen has found a very satisfactory solution to one significant problem of his genre – the communication of background historical information, often in itself substantial and carefully researched. Heinichen achieves this by using Galvano – with his deep roots in Trieste's past – to put Laurenti, the newcomer who is not always familiar with aspects of the city's history, in the picture. Occasionally, critics have questioned the multiplicity of plots and characters and the frankly didactic approach to history that Heinichen adopts, suggesting that these aspects of his work reduce the excitement and confuse the reader. However, in fact, this complexity in narrative structure merely reflects the complexity of the novels' historical and geographical setting.

Trieste is situated on what was the most easterly point of what used to be called the West and shared a frontier with Yugoslavia. With the collapse of the Eastern Bloc, the city has become a heavily frequented corridor. The Iron Curtain was less than efficient, but the city's small catchment has expanded to include the whole area of Istria and the new states of Slovenia and Croatia. Trieste's identity had always been determined by its geostrategic position, and nowhere is that more evident than in its role as a centre of crime. In Western eyes, the enclave almost entirely surrounded by Slovenia represents, to quote Heinichen, 'a bridgehead of Europe to the middle east and Asia Minor',[32] whereas in the east, the city is regarded as the 'gateway to the west'.[33] That makes it a favoured conduit for smuggling drugs, human beings, organs and arms. 'While people in Brussels were debating the particular form of the extension of the EU', Heinichen writes sardonically, 'the European project had been anticipated by the Mafia and Camorra and had long since been up and running'.[34] At the same time, most criminality is a product of the city's history.

The city once served as Austro-Hungary's Adriatic port. It was Italianized after World War One, occupied by Jugoslav partisans after the Second World War and was not permanently restored to Italy until 1954. Hardly surprisingly, this frontier town with its changing national status is a place where Latin, Germanic and Slavic cultures overlap. Such cultural pluralism was a thorn in the side of the neo-fascist *Alleanza Nazionale* (1995-2009), whose representatives sat in Trieste's municipal parliament and aimed to create an ethnically homogenous region. In addition, Trieste is part of the Federal Republic of Padania, which was proclaimed by the separatists of the Lega Nord, who wish to separate the whole of the economically powerful north of Italy from the poorer Mezzogiorno and who are looking to cut Trieste off from the neighbouring states of Eastern Europe.

Heinichen's novels embark upon a very serious analysis of this politically confused situation. They examine the pronounced nationalism of the present and the past together with neo-fascism, the city's domestic policy towards illegal immigrants and various attempts to influence cultural and national symbolism by changing street-names and the like. That Heinichen's novels are not simply harmless fictions or casually constructed entertainment is proven by the attacks to which Heinichen has been subjected. One campaign in 2008/2009, carried out in anonymous letters, set out to brand him as a paedophile, and it was only the author's close collaboration with the police and the local newspaper that was able to put an end to it. As he explored the reasons for these attacks, Heinichen pointed to right-wing politicians and the economic power brokers of the city.

The success of Heinichen's crime fiction in German-speaking countries is due to more than the attractiveness of their Italian setting, although it may

---

32 Veit Heinichen, *Tod auf der Warteliste* (Munich: dtv, 2004), p. 32.
33 Veit Heinichen, *Totentanz* (Vienna: Zsolnay Verlag, 2007), p. 96.
34 Veit Heinichen, *Der Tod wirft lange Schatten* (Munich: dtv, 2007), p. 133.

have helped that they were marketed as *Regionalkrimis* [regional crime novels]. The persuasive linking of geography and crime certainly characterizes these novels and is the basis of their literary quality. As he conducts his investigations, Laurenti is continually forced to rely on what the anthropologist Clifford Geertz called 'local knowledge'. By this, Geertz referred to the understanding of the topographical determinants of various cultural practices, knowledge of the specific history of a place, the mentality of its inhabitants or of a particular dialect. It also makes sense to include Heinichen's work in the *noir méditerranéen* movement. The practitioners of this genre include the Spanish writer Manuel Vázquez Montalbán, the Algerian Yasmina Khadra, Massimo Carlotto from Italy and Jean-Claude Izzo from France. Despite the local differences between the port cities of Barcelona, Algiers, Marseilles and Trieste, the Mediterranean as a region remains the common denominator of their literary work. As the historian Fernand Braudel has shown, the scenic and cultural unity of this region initially depended on its climate; however, this is a region that declined in economic importance from the fifteenth century on, when the age of discoveries shifted the focus to the Atlantic and, with the opening of the Suez Canal in 1869, the city was reduced to being little more than a corridor.

Today it is hard to ignore the fact that Mare Nostrum has acquired new geopolitical importance in the wake of European unity. Within these often contradictory processes, with frontiers opening in the east while they are reinforced in the south, the Mediterranean is in part a unifying feature, in part a barrier to unity. This Mediterranean region is not simply 'the source of the culture which has nourished Europe'.[35] It is in the Mediterranean region that some of the world's most extensive money laundering takes place, and its waters feed the roots of a whole culture of crime. In Veit Heinichen, this region has one of its most perceptive literary chroniclers.

Translated by Hugh Ridley

Bernhard Jaumann *(Andreas Erb)*

Since the 1960s, the small mountain village of Montesecco in the Marche region of Central Italy has become increasingly depopulated due to economic recessions and migration to the cities, and the lives of its twenty-seven remaining

---

35 Georges Duby, 'Das Erbe', in *Die Welt des Mittelmeers. Zur Geschichte und Geographie kultureller Lebensformen*, ed. by Fernand Braudel, German trans. by Markus Jakob (Frankfurt a.M.: Fischer, 2005), pp. 171–189, (p. 173).

inhabitants have started to fall to pieces. Everyday life in Montesecco is no longer determined by bad harvests, lottery wins, deaths, births or village fairs, but by criminal cases that profoundly unnerve the village population. It is an intrinsic trait of Montesecco that the village community not only discusses all community-related matters, but also pervades and shapes the private lives of its citizens. It thus comes as no surprise that, in Bernhard Jaumann's trilogy of Montesecco novels, the village features as the true hero, but a hero who displays the obvious signs of dissolution. Its existence is incessantly being tested and must constantly be re-established and defended.

In *Die Vipern von Montesecco* [2005, *The Vipers of Montesecco**], *Die Drachen von Montesecco* [2007, *The Dragons of Montesecco**] and *Die Augen der Medusa* [2008, *Medusa's Eyes**], crimes fundamentally alter the societal system of this microcosm, illustrating how modern global powers act as a destabilizing factor that threatens the ultimately restorative local order. Beside the criminal case as such, which is almost put on the sidelines, another type of suspense is created, leaving the reader wondering about the survival and future of the village. Against the backdrop of this spatiotemporal and structural construction of Montesecco, Jaumann's novels unfold the outrageous. It soon becomes evident that the crimes, which form the starting point for all subsequent events, not only have to be uncovered, but also become instrumental in revealing underlying structures and unveiling just how penetrable the people's protective armour and how fragile communal life actually is. While the solution of the criminal case (potentially) restores the legal and moral order, the villagers' firm belief in the normative existence of the present is subverted or even shattered all the same.

Whenever a perpetrator is convicted in Montesecco, it does not happen due to the interventions of an outstandingly gifted or intuitive investigative first-person narrator, but is the task of the village as a whole. It is the community tackling the job, placing itself above official government authorities, which is most obvious in the last novel in the trilogy, *Die Augen der Medusa*. When the public system collapses, when politics comes to a standstill and are unable to restore justice, one has to take things into one's own hands, which is exactly what the villagers do in Jaumann's novels. In different acts of self-authorization, they analytically and practically take on the task of shedding light on the dark world of outrageousness and uncovering the facts and background of the crimes. In doing so, they unmask the public order as a corrupt and incapacitated system lacking any kind of legitimacy and sometimes even legality. At the same time, the role of the media is called into question, as it seems to ruthlessly focus on ratings alone, putting sensationalism before journalistic integrity and ethics. At the end of the novels, although the crime may be solved, the social order is shaken right down to its very foundations. The utmost form of disillusionment is orchestrated in Montesecco, with regard to not only the perpetrator, but also the idea of justice and morality as well as the village in itself. When the cases are solved, the village validates itself, its people move closer together while revealing Montesecco's anachronistic basic structure. In the end, the villagers come to realize that, with each new crime hitting Montesecco, their community is dissolving more and more.

While the three Montesecco novels constitute one dramaturgical unit, bound together by the unity of time, place and characters, Jaumann's first five works, published between 1998 and 2002, are set within a different thematic frame. The settings, located in very different regions of the world, are held together by the five senses, with each novel focusing on and characterized by one sense specifically. In *Hörsturz* [1998, *Sudden Deafness**], the sense of hearing is attributed to the city of Vienna; *Sehschlachten* [1999, *Vision Battles**] is set in Sydney and revolves around the sense of sight; *Handstreich* [1999, *Coup de Main**] focuses on the sense of touch, taking its readers to Mexico City; *Duftfallen* [2001, *Scent Traps**], set in Tokyo, is all about the sense of smell; and, finally, *Saltimbocca* (2002*) locates the sense of taste in Rome. However, these novels do not narrate simple linear stories. Just like in Montesecco, criminal cases lead to insights reaching far beyond the actual investigation. Jaumann composes his texts while making it very clear that they are indeed constructions, more precisely: narrative constructions. In particular, *Saltimbocca* takes the play with the diegetic form to new extremes, and 'narrative metalepsis' (G. Genette) characterizes the structure of the novel as a whole. In various places, *Saltimbocca* provides information on the empirical author and his previous novels. By revealing Jaumann's narrative methods and placing poetology directly beside pecuniary interests, the novel illustrates how symbolic capital competes with economic capital, and everything is kept within the 'bizarre' suspense of the narrative frame.

What Jaumann also showcases in his 'pentalogy of senses' is a specific way of dealing with cultural memory as it expresses itself fragmentarily and playfully in the course of the narrative. The texts bristle with quotations and allusions, demanding different types of attention from their readers than the solution of the cases does. As the policeman Leo Blum wanders around Vienna, we are reminded of Leopold Bloom's Dublin in James Joyce's *Ulysses*, and when, following the night's excesses, Leo finds that he has become a nobody in the cell of a mental institution, a cell with a one-eyed 'staring door', this is clearly an allusion to Polyphemus' cave in Homer's *Odyssey*. Just like the different crimes and terrorist attacks happening in Jaumann's novels, these subtexts form part of a mess that leads to destabilization. It becomes evident that subversion constitutes an undeniable part of the state of society, just as narrative does. Moreover, while some consider subversion to be a utopian foreshadowing ('utopischer Vorschein' according to E. Bloch),[36] others perceive it as something strange and disturbing that must be eliminated. In this way, Jaumann's crime novels become a stage, a platform for testing and studying the exploration and transgression of limits. Certainties such as chains of crime-perpetrator-guilt-justice are mere surface phenomena and, as such, ultimately insignificant. What remains is perturbation. It thus comes as no surprise that the truth is often accompanied by madness, which unexpectedly points to the solution, while normality makes people blind to the tremendousness of everyday life, be it consciously or not. Subversion and delusion undermine the authority and hegemonic strategies of (self-) assertion practiced by the bourgeois world. Jaumann's texts illustrate that it is possible for the crime novel as a genre to reveal this simple insight under the pretext of an unsettling crime.

The third group of Jaumann's works is composed of his three Namibia crime novels: *Die Stunde des Schakals* [2010, *The Hour of the Jackal*], *Steinland* [2012, *Rocky Land**] and *Der lange Schatten* [2015, *The Long Shadow**]. While the first two novels are set in Namibia alone and the third in both Namibia and Germany, all three of them feature, for the first time in Jaumann's works, a protagonist who is in charge of the investigation. She is Clemencia Garises, a black woman from the township of Katatura in Windhoek, who is given a clear voice in each of the novels. A well-educated, black female commissioner, Clemencia Garises represents the future of self-confident Namibian intellectuals who are at the same time deeply rooted in their background and family traditions. Her investigations reveal much about contemporary Namibian history.

The Hour of the Jackal is about the assassination of the white apartheid opponent and SWAPO member Anton Lubowski, who is killed in front of his Windhoek home on 12 September 1989. The unsolved circumstances of this murder as well as the involvement of both the South African Secret Service and possibly the SWAPO remain objects of different rumours, conjectures and conspiracy theories. Jaumann takes up this historical case and provides a possible explanation, but this is not the decisive aspect of this piece of crime fiction. What is more important is that he shows how the mechanisms of political and social repression and oppression work in post-apartheid Africa. As the novel reveals at the end, no court proceedings have been held on the Lubowski case up until the present day.

---

36 Cf. Ernst Bloch, *Geist der Utopie. Zweite Fassung* (Frankfurt a.M.: Suhrkamp Taschenbuch Verlag, 2000).

In *Rocky Land*, Jaumann deals with land reforms, a similarly controversial issue of current interest. Against the backdrop of Zimbabwean politics, the question of property and usage rights remains a politically and emotionally problematic issue that, after more than twenty years of independence, must urgently be settled, mainly for social reasons. Once again, under the guise of a fictional crime story (including a murder, an abduction, etc.), Jaumann manages to carve out the different discourses that ultimately pertain to the question of successful decolonization and are thus difficult to conciliate. The same holds true for *The Long Shadow*, published in 2015. This crime novel follows the same pattern employed in Jaumann's previous novels set in Namibia: a historical event is at the centre of the story – in this case, the Charité hospital in Berlin returning (for the first time) a skull to a high-level delegation from Namibia on 30 September 2011. About 3,000 preserved human specimens are probably still being held in German museums and hospitals, including some in Freiburg, an important sideshow in the novel. In this respect, the visit of the Herero delegation to Berlin was of great symbolic importance and served as a direct reminder of the Herero Genocide committed by the Germans. Jaumann takes up these real events and uses a hundred-year-long history as the background for his story, starting with genocide and closing with oblivion on the German side. However, he not only raises questions about German colonial history, but combines a critical view of historical processes with precise observations of Namibia as it presents itself today.

Like all of Jaumann's works, this text is dominated by the most profound uncertainty, which is revealed as the criminal investigation takes its course. What remains is the deepest distrust of all forms of government action. The solving of the case reveals abysses that make it impossible to ask further questions. In this sense, Jaumann's novels survey, under the surface of a crime story, the social realities of today's world. The initial disturbance in the guise of the criminal case that triggers this survey increasingly fades into the background, even as it keeps advancing the plot. What comes to the fore in its stead is the real disturbance, i.e. that of social order. The topographical peculiarities (be it village or metropolis) that characterize all of Jaumann's novels are only ever of secondary importance.

Translated by Christine Henschel

Merle Kröger *(Kirsten Reimers)*

Born in 1967 in Plön, Merle Kröger lives and works in Berlin as a freelance scriptwriter, filmmaker, film producer, artist, curator and crime author. In 2001, together with the filmmaker Philip Scheffner, she founded the media-art platform *pong*. Since then, they have made a number of outstanding documentary films, which have premiered at the Berlinale and other international film festivals.

Kröger has published four crime novels. The first three – *Cut!* (2003*), *Kyai!* (2006*) and *Grenzfall* [2012, *Borderline**] – form a series with a shared set of protagonists, while the fourth, *Havarie* [2015, *Collision*] is a standalone. From the outset, the novels generated an enormous response and substantial media praise. In 2007, *Cut!* was published in English under the same title by Katha Press in New Delhi, India. Both *Grenzfall* and *Havarie* have received numerous prizes. For example, *Grenzfall* was awarded first place in the 'national' category of the Deutscher Krimi Preis [German Crime Fiction Prize] in 2013. *Havarie* topped the 'KrimiZeit-Bestenliste' (a highly regarded 'Best of Crime Writing List', now known as the 'Krimibestenliste') for three consecutive months in 2015 and took first place in its annual round up of the best crime fiction. The novel also placed second in the 'national' category of the Deutscher Krimi Preis in 2016. In autumn 2017, *Havarie* was published in English with the title *Collision* by Unnamed Press in Los Angeles in the United States.

All four of Kröger's crime novels are constructed using multiple narrative perspectives. Events are depicted in short scenes from the viewpoint of individual characters, mostly in the third-person singular and the past tense. Dreams, memories and stream of consciousness are incorporated as well. In *Cut!*, passages told from the perspective of the main character, Madita Junghans, are written in the present tense using the familiar second-person 'Du' or 'you' form. References to pop culture play an important role in the first three novels. In the first two in particular, *Cut!* and *Kyai!*, allusions are made to the mechanics of filmmaking: directorial notes or instructions on camera work and editing ('cut', 'close-up', 'crossfade') are used to determine the structure of different scenes. On a thematic level, films, cinema and film production also play a significant role in both crime novels.

Kröger's novels are not conceived as classic investigative crime novels, which typically feature a police investigator or a detective. None of the protagonists have any criminalistic training, nor do their professions – cinema operator, DJ, director – equip them for investigative activities. They are just ordinary people who get involved in a situation, start digging and refuse to give up. In the course of her four novels, Kröger increasingly moves away from the conventions of investigative crime fiction and pushes its boundaries.

Cut! is characterized by its spare, highly visual language. Short scenes and frequent shifts in narrative perspective underscore the film-like construction of the book. The latter is emphasized by eight musical scenes, which rupture the text and are reminiscent of Bollywood productions. These filmic elements are mirrored in the novel's content, with the search for Madita's biological father leading to London and Bombay. Part of the storyline involves the 'Legion Freies Indien' [Free Indian Legion], also known as the Indian Legion, co-founded in 1941 by Subhash Chandra Bose, a former political ally and eventual rival of Gandhi. This fighting unit, whose ethnically Indian soldiers simultaneously fought for Hitler against Britain and against Gandhi during the Second World War, was under the control of the German Waffen-SS. In addition, the Indian film industry and its history feature in the novel, along with nuanced questions about identity and heritage.

Kyai! leads on from *Cut!*, skilfully weaving a wide range of themes and character storylines together. Among other things, *Kyai!* thematizes the participation of private or semi-private mercenaries and the Bundeswehr in the military conflicts of the mid-2000s, thereby exploring the privatization of war. In addition, the author tries to understand the romantic appeal of India in the 1980s and shows what became of former Bhagwan followers twenty years. The attempts made by various German states to offer themselves as film settings for Bollywood productions in the mid-2000s, with a view to attracting Indian tourists, provides a further backdrop. Other themes and character storylines are also woven into the narrative.

Grenzfall draws on a real-life case and, by fictionalizing it, turns it into a representative case study. Two Roma are shot at the German-Polish border while entering Germany illegally in the summer of 1992. As it is not possible to disprove the two perpetrators' claim that the killings were the result of a hunting accident, they both get off scot-free. These are not isolated incidents: 1992 was the summer when hostels housing Vietnamese contract workers were set alight in Rostock-Lichtenhagen and three people lost their lives in a racist arson attack in Mölln. The narrative spans the history of the Berlin Republic, from its beginnings to the present day. In seeking to understand the causes of xenophobic attacks, Kröger moves beyond a focus on the individual and on eastern German provinces to illuminate national and international contexts: unequal living conditions in Europe, the knock-on effects of economic grievances in various European states, the willingness of some to use violence and a fear of foreigners. In the process, she shows how extreme right-wing parties instrumentalize these for political gain and reveals the intersections between larger structures and individual ways of thinking.

Grenzfall arose from Kröger's research for the film *Revision*, which premiered in 2012 at the Berlinale film festival. As co-author and producer, she was heavily involved in the research process. The novel emerged as an additional project because a great deal of what she had experienced and learned could not be included in the film. It takes a different path from the film by developing plotlines up to and including the present day.

Kröger's fourth novel, *Havarie*, also came out of research for a film, which premiered with the same title at the 2016 Berlinale. The author's starting point was the Mediterranean as a border zone and the issue of what she terms 'vertical' borders: borders that can be safely crossed depending on one's financial status and the nationality of one's passport. *Havarie* is structured in a much more rigorous way than Kröger's previous novels. The style is extremely concise, many of the sentences are pared to their essentials, and events are concentrated into a forty-eight-hour period. Four vessels are shown crossing paths in the Mediterranean: a luxury cruise liner, a stricken dinghy carrying Algerian refugees, an old freighter sailing under a Ukrainian flag and an emergency rescue boat from Spain. Events are depicted from multiple perspectives in short scenes that cut swiftly from one another and which are all given equal status: no character is accorded a privileged position and there is no central protagonist. With just a few succinct strokes of the pen, the author describes the characters and their backgrounds and places them in their social, political and historical contexts. Each character embodies a different drama, which is not necessarily linked to the situation unfolding in the present. From the Ukrainian conflict to the Algerian War, from the Northern Irish Troubles to the brutal regime in Syria, from the Holocaust to the sinking of the Wilhelm Gustloff off the Pomeranian coast in 1945 – each character has experienced violence, crimes against humanity, war or has fled from conflict, but from diverse perspectives: as a perpetrator, victim or bystander. No one is completely without guilt, no one is completely good or bad, but no one is condemned either. Guilt does not lie solely with the characters: as in her previous novels, Kröger shows how individual actions are connected to larger structures and circumstances. There are also two deaths, but neither of these is investigated. Much more central is the question of how violence arises from the collision of different worlds, structures, hopes and pressures. *Havarie* is thus best viewed as a high-quality political thriller, which reads more like a documentary than fiction and makes the extremely complex connections between economics and politics visible, as well as their effects on abstract structures and real people. It is written with a great deal of anger, channelled into a rigorous, analytical form.

Merle Kröger's novels arise from incidents and events that are rooted in reality and combine historical engagement, individual experience and political analysis with elements of the crime novel and thriller. The author has a keen understanding of social fault lines and writes in a carefully researched, plausible manner, with a deft feel for dramatic composition and narrative tension. Her first three crime novels are also fast paced, featuring plenty of wordplay and situational comedy and, for all their exoticism, are free from cliché and folklore.

The violence Kröger explores in her novels is to a far greater degree contingent on structural factors than on individuals. Her main concern is exploring the effects of globalized capitalism and the ways these impact on the lives of individual people. While globalized capitalism may provide individuals with significant opportunities, the price that has to be paid for them, in her view, is very high.

Translated by Katharina Hall

Christine Lehmann *(Kirsten Reimers)*

Christine Lehmann was born in Geneva in 1958 and has lived in Stuttgart since 1963. Holding a doctorate in literature, she began writing crime fiction in the 1990s and is one of the most interesting crime authors in the German-speaking world. In addition to crime novels, Lehmann also writes children's books, romantic novels, non-fiction, radio plays, theatre plays, commentaries and essays, and has contributed to numerous anthologies. She is chair of the Baden-Württemberg Verband deutscher Schriftsteller/innen [Association of German Authors] and was a news editor for the SWR regional television channel for twenty-six years, leaving that role to become a Stuttgart city councillor in 2015.

Lehmann's first crime novel, *Kynopolis** was published by Goldmann in 1994. She went on to develop the series character Lisa Nerz, who is one of the most unusual female protagonists in German-language crime fiction and is still active today. Nerz, a reporter and the first-person narrator of the series, is self-assured, independent, rebellious, awkward and gruff. Her face, which is scarred, is not pretty, and she is rich. Nerz refuses to be categorized in any way – especially in relation to sexuality and gender. She is bisexual and rejects both male and female roles. The novels show her wearing suits and leather outfits, or sometimes mini-skirts and long boots, then skirts and blazers. Depending on the occasion, investigation or mood, she will appear as a man or as a woman and play with those roles. She resolves her internal gender conflict by refusing to be classified in a definitive way. Oscillating between genders, she has affairs with men and women and is unfaithful but very loyal. She refuses to be pigeonholed, questioning bonds, relationships, convictions, belief structures, values and institutions, as well as constantly questioning herself.

However, Nerz's non-conformity is not limited to questions of gender. When interacting with others, she often acts inappropriately with the aim of disrupting established patterns of behaviour. She creates chaos, as the author has noted in a personal interview on 23 June 2017, by acting irrationally or aggressively in order to disrupt and disturb situations with specific rules, so that conventional codes of behaviour no longer function. Nerz thus consistently breaks the rules and behaves in ways that subvert other people's expectations – and this principle holds equally true for Christine Lehmann's crime novels.

The novels are always very precisely situated in present-day social reality. Lehmann picks up on topical events, moods and social trends, and spins them into clever crime plots using razor-sharp language and a compelling logic. The novels are extremely witty and intelligent and are always researched with great care. Each novel's key themes play out on a number of different levels and in various social constellations. As a rule, opposing viewpoints on a particular social theme remain in tension with one another without a resolution being offered to the reader. As a result, the later novels in particular can be regarded as action-packed, fast-paced *Debattenkrimis* [crime novels that actively debate issues]. They never tip over into satire though: Lehmann takes care not to ridicule specific viewpoints, giving them equal weight and status in the text.

The first three crime novels featuring Lisa Nerz were published by Rowohlt: *Der Masochist* [1997, *The Masochist**], *Training mit dem Tod* [1998, *Training with Death**] and *Pferdekuss* [1999, *Horse's Kiss/Black and Blue**]. As the early novels were not selling well, it became clear during the writing of the third book that the series would not continue. *Pferdekuss* was therefore conceived as the last in a trilogy. For the fourth Liza Nerz novel, Lehmann moved to the feminist Hamburg publishing house Ariadne/Argument, where the first three novels were reissued in a newly edited form, meaning that all the crime novels in the series have now been published there.

Lisa Nerz makes her first appearance in *Vergeltung am Degerloch* [2006, *Vengeance in Degerloch**; the new edition of *Der Masochist*]. The novel focuses on a serial murderer who lies in wait for women at the final stop on public transport routes and kills them. The story is based on a real case and, according to the author, offers an explanation for Nerz's toughness: she is conceived in such a way that she would not only escape the perpetrator, but fight back as well. In *Gaisburger Schlachthof* [2006, *Gaisburg Slaughterhouse**; the new edition of *Training mit dem Tod*], Nerz investigates a death in a health club. The dominant theme is how individuals shape their bodies in ways ranging from fitness training to sex change operations; questions of identity thus also play a role. *Pferdekuss* (2008; a new edition of the 1999 novel of the same name) is set on a stud farm, focusing on the topics of reproduction, heredity and inheritance, as well as the accompanying issues of power, brutality and violence. *Harte Schule* [2005, *School of Hard Knocks**] is set in a school and describes a culture of abuse. This was the first of Lehmann's novels to appear with Ariadne/Argument and the first to be a commercial success. One reason for this breakthrough could be that a character like Lisa Nerz – and the questions raised by her identity and behaviour – were viewed as more acceptable in social discourses of the mid-2000s than they were in the late 1990s. Releasing the novels with a new publisher also allowed them to reach a different readership.

Höhlenangst [2005, *Fear of Caves**] is the only crime novel of Lehmann's not to incorporate a prominent socio-political dimension, focusing largely on murders committed in the caves of the Swabian Alps. *Allmachtsdackel* [2007, *Almighty Idiot**], her most successful crime novel to date, takes a very different form. This is a novel about Protestantism, set among the pietists of Baden Württemberg. It explores fanaticism while juxtaposing matriarchy and patriarchy from different angles, such as nature being much less patriarchal than is widely assumed. In *Nachtkrater* [2008, *Night Crater**], both author and protagonist leave Earth to investigate a murder in a space station on the moon. Elements of the fantastical and science fiction are present in all of Lehmann's novels, but most obviously so in *Nachtkrater*. Lehmann designed her fictitious space station with the help of Rene Laufer – formerly of the Deutschen Zentrum für Luft und Raumfahrt [German Centre for Air and Space Travel], currently Associate Research Professor at Baylor University's Centre for Astrophysics, Space Physics and Engineering Research – as well as astronaut Ernst Messerschmid. The crime novel *Mit Teufelsg'walt* [2009, *Devilish Violence**] is much more down to earth. It takes an uncompromising look at power relations and violence within families and welfare facilities and is politically resonant: it points to a legal loophole pertaining to children and young people taken into care by youth welfare services.

Malefizkrott [2010, *Malicious Toad/Malicious Child**] is based on the genuine case of young author Helene Hegemann, whose book, widely discussed in the arts pages, was later revealed to have been plagiarized. A sharply comic and richly allusive foray into the German-language literary scene, this novel examines questions relating to social communication. *Totensteige* [2012, *Walking with Death**] depicts a world apparently threatened by a remote murderer with telekinetic abilities, but is only superficially concerned with parapsychology. This thriller's organizing theme is the (print) media's power and its misuse of power as it constructs reality. *Die Affen von Cannstatt* [2013, *The Apes of Cannstatt**] violates the series' concept: here, Nerz is only a peripheral figure, while the novel's main protagonist is a woman who accuses the reporter of unjustly causing her arrest on suspicion of murder. The subject of matriarchy is again at the centre of this novel, partly refracted through the power structures in women's prisons and the social organization of bonobo apes. *Allesfresser* [2016, *Omnivores**] uses the question of which nutritional approach is best to compare and contrast beliefs about appropriate lifestyles, thereby thematizing fanaticism and extremism. Lehmann's most recent crime novel, *Die zweite Welt* [2019, *The Second World*] is focusing on misogyny and xenophobia in German contemporary society.

The language of Lehmann's first crime novels was highly dense and concentrated, with an idiosyncratic use of vocabulary sometimes reminiscent of Expressionism: roofs 'zacken' [spike] the sky; the television tower 'nadelt' [needles] the horizon; elsewhere a place is described as 'villaging' – 'es dörfelt'. This practice has lessened in the past few years, as the author eventually felt it was too mannered and intrusive, Lehmann explained in the interview mentioned above. Nowadays, Lehmann very rarely uses this kind of concentrated language as a stylistic device.

Lehmann's aim when writing is not so much to illuminate a particular theme or to create a particular atmosphere. Socio-political questions are at the heart of her crime novels. She interrogates how we live with one another, how we treat each another, the judgements we make about others. All of these are ruthlessly dissected, dusted and scrutinized. In the process, Lehmann consciously breaks rules in order to take her readers to the edge. This is seen regularly, for example, in her treatment of sexuality: almost all the Nerz novels contain fairly graphic sex scenes. The author's aim is to highlight the existence of sexual realities that do not fit neatly into current images or expectations, but which are rarely discussed. This is why Nerz refuses to be pinned down in terms of her sexuality. Nearly every novel shows her having an affair with a woman and often also with a man. The author is not trying to be provocative, instead showing that people's sexuality is complex and that sexual preferences can change. Her aim is to articulate realities beyond conventional models and to give them a means of expression.[37]

The principle of being unconventional and having a wide range of behaviours, tastes and orientations also applies to the structure of the crime novels. Here, too, Lehmann repeatedly breaks the rules. Time and again, there are

---

37 Interview with the author, 23 June 2017.

echoes of well-known subgenres. Some of the novels play with elements of the 'whodunit', the locked room mystery and the thriller – often simultaneously or consecutively in the same novel – only then to take delight in subverting expectations, dismantling well-known formulas and combining them in completely new ways. Sometimes the crime plot recedes noticeably into the background, but the novels do not suffer as a result, neither as novels nor as crime novels.

Lehmann is strict in only one respect: in the way that she deals with violence and murder. Most murders, according to the author,[38] are driven by a craving for power and control, and this is reflected in her novels: the male or female perpetrators that Lehmann describes use murder as a means of influencing relationships or situations in their favour – to resolve a conflict or to regulate relationships in such a way as to bring them under control. In other words, it is about power. Lehmann has said that all of her crime novels show an awareness of power structures and structures of domination, exposing them where possible as senseless and violent in nature.[39] The author takes murder very seriously. She has no sympathy for murderers or the act of murder, and therefore depicts the latter with as much objectivity and as little voyeurism as possible. In Lehmann's crime novels, the deed has nothing macabre about it – there is no playfulness involved, no death for death's sake, no murder as an elevated art form. The conflicts that lead to murder in her novels are therefore designed to inevitably escalate into violence. As a writer, Lehmann says,[40] she can use crime novels – with their inherent violence – to thematize the devastating consequences of violent acts.

Lisa Nerz is an experimental figure, whose fashion choices, sexuality and interactions with others are used to show, among other things, what happens when social expectations are broken rather than observed. The resulting novels are intelligent, intellectual, highly witty, fast-paced, liberating and go beyond the boundaries of the literary mainstream.

Translated by Katharina Hall

---

38 Interview with the author, 23 June 2017.
39 Interview with the author, 23 June 2017.
40 Interview with the author, 23 June 2017.

Ulrich Ritzel *(Hugh Ridley)*

Ulrich Ritzel was born in 1940 in the Schwäbische Alb, south-east of Stuttgart and studied law before becoming a journalist and court-reporter for regional and national newspapers. In 1980, he was awarded the prestigious Wächter Prize for his journalistic work, but at the age of sixty took up crime fiction writing and almost immediately established a major reputation.

Ulrich Ritzel's crime novels are packed into a short period. From his first, *Im Schatten des Schwans* [1999, *In the Shadow of the Swan**], to *Trotzkis Narr* [2014, *Trotzky's Fool**]) and the outstanding *Nadjas Katze* [2016, *Nadja's Cat*], one novel has appeared every couple of years. In each novel, the detective work is conducted by Hans Berndorf or his team, in Ulm or Berlin. The principal works are *Schwemmholz* [2000, *Driftwood**], *Die schwarzen Ränder der Glut* [2001, *The Black Edges of the Embers**], *Der Hund des Propheten* [2003, *Berndorf and his Dog**], *Uferwald* [2006, *Waterside Forest**], *Forellenquintett* [2007, *Trout Quintet**], *Beifang* [2009, *Ring of Blood**] and *Schlangenkopf* [2011, *Snake's Head**]. *Schwemmholz, Der Hund des Propheten* and *Beifang* have won significant prizes. In spite of this rapid sequence of quality texts, Ritzel does not write to a formula. In every element of his writing – apart from its intelligence and observational power – there is change and variety. Not only the settings and the type of case to be solved vary, but also the configuration of the detectives.

The crimes Ritzel chronicles share two features: first, crime is easy; people get used to it: it becomes an everyday reality. Secondly, taken together, his chronicles span fifty years of Federal Republic history. His experience covers the alienation of the student generation, urban guerrillas, environmental protests relating to nuclear power and the new runway at Frankfurt. His mindset has been shaped by the Auschwitz trials, the influential exhibitions of Wehrmacht war crimes, the Flick and Filbinger scandals, and the Guillaume affair.

In his first novel, Ritzel achieves that fusion between fiction and society at large at which Gruppe 47 had aimed. Heinrich Böll would have admired Ritzel's skill in linking the experiments conducted on concentration camp prisoners with a major post-war industrial and commercial corporation and his questioning of the foundations of West German affluence, nationally and locally. Ritzel's novels reveal a familiar picture: the greyness of terms such as justice, democracy and equality, the corrupting power of capital, the questionable aspects of 're-unification' and 'globalization' and the incomplete process of denazification.

The quality of texts that link the historical with fictional crime depends on the writing's integrity and the plausibility with which major events are embedded within everyday reality. It is here that Ritzel reveals his skill. He does not draw on popular themes, milking them for the sake of the drama that they can bring. Major themes are driven by small events, acutely observed in small towns and villages and in the metropolis. Ritzel has always made clear the personal touch to his novels, for instance the shot-up Wehrmacht jeep standing close to his grandmother's house in 1945, which features in *Der Schatten des Schwans*. He thus makes the major themes real to ordinary people.

It is not unusual for modern crime fiction writers to lay down their pen without full justice having been achieved. Brecht knew that feeling – the best we can achieve is 'a golden time, nearly of justice'.[41] Ritzel offers his readers even less comfort. *Beifang* – centrally concerned with issues of justice, also in German-Jewish relations – ends on a massively ambiguous note. The crimes are too big for justice; the past has been so alienated from true justice that guilt, remorse, personal integrity and the investigative tools of the law hardly have any effect on it. There is a cheap cynicism that some modern writing regards as fashionably 'tough', an acceptance of the evils of modern society. Berndorf keeps his faith in the importance of those few small justices which are possible.

Schlangenkopf, for instance, deals with the aftermath of the Yugoslav war of 1990. This war, with its ethnic cleansing and maltreatment of prisoners, awoke memories of earlier bloodshed. In particular, the generation that was old enough at the time will not forget a photograph that caught the world's imagination, showing emaciated prisoners behind a barbed wire stockade.

Ritzel's treatment of this picture is a *tour de force*. For a start, he knows the German press scene intimately, so the novel follows an authentic search for the photographer and how the picture came to prominence. (Ritzel does not write documentary novels; he simply, as a matter of course, gets the details right.) Slowly, the implications of the photo widen to include German parliamentarians and a shady arms company. It becomes clear that one prisoner in the picture can identify a Serbian military commander now sought as a war criminal and living under a new identity. Berndorf is drawn into politics through his own dogged determination to take seriously the small events in his backyard. Here he investigates the death of the tear-away son of a Turkish tailor on a shabby Berlin street. The construct offers a robust framework for concentric investigations and for *action*. In the end, the photograph appears in a very different light. The document turns into fiction, while the fiction ensures truth and offers what seems like the only framework in which justice can be achieved.

---

41 Bertolt Brecht, *Der kaukasische Kreidekreis* (Frankfurt a.M.: Suhrkamp Verlag, 1963 [edition suhrkamp 31]), p. 120. 'als einer kurzen/ Goldenen Zeit beinah der Gerechtigkeit'.

Ritzel comes closest to contemporary German fiction with *Beifang*. Berndorf is working on a murder case involving a young woman. He suspects that a ring that was owned by the dead woman, but was once in the possession of a Jewish family that was dispossessed and then murdered during National Socialism, could provide important clues. Berndorf uncovers political and industrial scandals – these scenes are among the most humorous and sharply observed in the novel – but also finds himself forced to confront the full scale of the murder and dispossession of the Jews of Eastern Europe, recognizing the absurdity of tracing one lost ring when the state stole millions during the Shoah. Why chase one murderer when thousands have gone free? He does not find it encouraging to observe how comfortably the murderers and thieves of those years have been re-integrated into West German society, mostly in the ranks of what Berndorf calls the 'state party' (i.e. CDU/CSU). It is not only Berndorf's search for truth, but the whole fabric of the detective story that is thrown into question by the mass crimes of the past. If Adorno challenged the writing of poetry in the shadow of Auschwitz, Ritzel's integrity challenges him to question the writing of detective fiction in that shadow.

Schlangenkopf plays out across a wide range of locations, but Berlin was starting to predominate among Ritzel's locations, following the shift of government to Berlin. There are two clear effects: one is affection for parts of Berlin – not just the hinterland, but small sections of the city itself – and perceptive critics have wondered if Ritzel is poised to become the writer of the new German capital. The other effect is an intense dislike of the false cosmopolitan gloss of a city contemptuous of so many of its ordinary citizens. As Zlatan struggles to find help at the start of *Schlangenkopf* and rings at the doors of his 'friends', all of them remain shut in his face. Berndorf's unease in Berlin fans out into occasional hatred of the city, built on corruption, the foundations of its glitzy buildings paid for by the laundered proceeds of every type of crime.

Nowhere is this dislike clearer than in Ritzel's last but one novel, *Trotzkis Narr* [2014, *Trotzky's Fool**]. The story is set in Berlin and its environs. Corrupt police and planning officials, neo-Nazi youths and careerist city politicians: Berlin walks over corpses. Yet two figures dominate Berndorf's case. There is Carmencita, a transgender woman who disappears in suspicious circumstances but is mourned by no one in liberal Berlin. In addition, there is the title figure, Brutus Finklin, living out in the sticks and embittered by the GDR for which he, as a Trotskyist, was too left-wing, although he is now endangered by the police of the new regime and is a target of the extreme right.

Ritzel's undramatic sympathies for the victims of intolerance feature strongly in all his novels. Tamar Wegenast fights her way through the police service, despite having 'come out' more publicly than she wished. Carmencita is neither normalized nor heroicized, but Berndorf insists that she deserves justice, as well as tolerance. Finklin himself is an appealing character, even though Berndorf loathes the jargon that he uses, just like the rehearsed phrases that the churches use to exercise their power and wealth. The only people who do not enjoy Berndorf's tolerance are those who do not need it.

It is clear that Ritzel is well acquainted with and admires detective stories written in English. Although they have more in common with the Simenon and Scandinavian traditions, his own books owe a debt to the English-language school but avoid its inherent class snobbery. Berndorf likes chess and crosswords (one of Ritzel's most diverting conceits is the creation of a crossword that can be answered differently depending on whether the person solving the puzzle comes from East or West Germany), and some of Berndorf's best work is carried out with a dog at his side, while he remains conspicuously loyal to his literary heroes, notably Lichtenberg and Brecht.

Ritzel's work has been rightly honoured in the German scene and has reached a wide audience without enjoying mass popularity. The critical response to his work has been highly positive. Inexplicably, however, none of his novels have been televised or filmed. This is probably due to their uncompromising attitude towards the establishment. Ritzel does not play to the gallery. Until crime fiction is recognized as a mainstream literary activity, no longer separated from 'proper' literature by irrelevant assumptions, Ritzel will likely stay out of the major headlines.

Ritzel's work is yet to be fully translated. Both the British and American markets have been slow to realize its appeal. Those looking to enjoy quality writing and a mind that takes pleasure in the complexities of human behaviour need go no further than Ritzel's work.

Bernhard Schlink *(Joachim Feldmann)*

In 1987, eight years before *Der Vorleser* [1997, *The Reader*], the novel that would make him world famous, Bernhard Schlink, a forty-three-year old professor of law at Bonn University, published his first book of fiction. It was a detective novel, whose title *Selbs Justiz* is a play on the term 'Selbstjustiz', which does not translate well into English,[42] but means 'taking the law into one's own hands'. This seems to be the reason why the name of the central character, a sixty-eight-year-old, widowed private detective and former public prosecutor

---

42 Bernhard Schlink, Walter Popp, *Selbs Justiz* (Zurich: Diogenes, 1987).

named Gerhard Selb, was changed into 'Self' for the English edition of the book which appeared under the title *Self's Punishment* in 2005. Schlink wrote the book together with his friend, the lawyer-cum-translator Walter Popp, within a period of three months in 1986 while he was teaching law at the University of Aix-en-Provence in Southern France. Both avid readers of crime fiction, the two decided to have a go at a detective novel. The result was an instant success. Its publisher Diogenes already enjoyed a reputation as one of the first addresses for crime fiction in the German speaking countries, its backlist including authors such as Raymond Chandler, Dashiell Hammett and Patricia Highsmith. *Selbs Justiz* can be considered a typical private eye novel, but with an unlikely protagonist: Gerhard Selb, who is still haunted by his Nazi-past, was an active party-member and cold-blooded public prosecutor before 1945. After the war, he refused to join the civil service again due to his repulsion for his former colleagues, who did not seem to feel any guilt at all. He started working as a private detective specializing in insurance fraud and white-collar crime, and has been on the job for more than 40 years now. Selb lives in Mannheim, a city of 300,000 in the industrial Rhine-Neckar region in south-west Germany. Like Michael Berg, the hero of *Der Vorleser*, Selb finds himself confronted with Nazi crime. However, unlike Berg, he is not one of the 'Nachgeborenen' [those born later] who is able to claim individual innocence. Selb is aware of this, but he does not come across as a guilt-ridden individual. He is a man of refined tastes, from the untipped Irish cigarettes he smokes to his love of good food and wine, who never forgets to mention the books he reads (Gottfried Keller), the films he watches on his VCR (*Heaven's Gate*) and the music he listens to (from Bach to Madonna). And he loves cats.

In the tradition of Chandler's Marlowe, Schlink's protagonist is a first-person narrator who cannot be accused of beating around the bush. Right at the beginning of *Selbs Justiz*, he describes his relationship to Ferdinand Korten, his brother-in-law who is the president of the (fictitious) Rheinische Chemiewerke in Ludwigshafen, just across the Rhine from Mannheim and (in reality) the home of BASF, one of the biggest players in the German chemical industry. Just like Selb, Korten started his professional career in Nazi-Germany, but he did not quit after 1945. On the contrary, he stayed with the company that he had joined in 1942 and worked his way up to the top. Since the death of Selb's wife Clara, the contact between the two men has been reduced to accidental meetings at cultural events. They still consider themselves 'old friends', but, as Selb expresses it, they "move in different circles".[43] Therefore, it comes as a surprise when Korten's secretary

---

43 Bernhard Schlink, Walter Popp, *Selb's Punishment*, trans. by Rebecca Morrison (New York: Random House, 2005), p. 4.

rings to make an appointment. Someone has been manipulating the computer system at Rheinische Chemiewerke, and Korten wants his brother-in-law to investigate, which seems a bit strange since Selb does not know anything about computing. However, it does not take the investigator very long to find the culprit – a systems administrator named Mischkey who used his expertise to play with the system. At least, that is what it looks like. But when Mischkey dies in a car accident some weeks later, Selb soon learns that the investigation is not over yet. The programmer's girlfriend, who also works for Korten's company, suspects foul play and offers Selb 10,000 marks to find out what really happened. The detective does not accept the money, but takes a closer look at the case, uncovering an environmental scandal of huge proportions. His investigation not only takes him back in time (and to America) but also confronts him with his own past. When he finally realizes that he has been set up twice (with murderous consequences), Selb resorts to the measure suggested by the title of the novel. Appalled by the cynicism of the man behind the plot, the detective pushes him off a cliff, a scene reminiscent of the showdown between the evil Harry Lime (Orson Welles) and the noble Holly Martins (Joseph Cotton) at the end of the film *The Third Man*.

However, Gerhard Selb's idea of justice leaves some doubts. Portrayed as a thoroughly likable character who has long repented the errors of his past, he is nevertheless a murderer, whose motive is not as noble as it may seem. The fact that Selb is aware of this does not make our moral judgement any easier. He knows that the world has not become a better place because a bad man without a conscience was killed, but he is not convinced that the West German legal system would have provided a just punishment either.

Selbs Justiz is an entertaining read. Bernhard Schlink and his collaborator Walter Popp display surprising narrative skill for a debut crime novel. Using typical patterns of the private eye-genre, they nevertheless manage to create an individual style that never tries to imitate the figurative language of the hard-boiled tradition. Gerhard Selb is not the kind of man who would decorate his narrative with far-flung similes. Like his creators, he has been trained to express himself in a factual way. However, his choice of words sometimes betrays his age. Blue jeans are 'Nietenhosen' and an undershirt is referred to as a 'Leibchen'.

The plot of *Selbs Justiz* spans almost a year, from spring to Christmas. It is probably set in the mid-1980s. About half a decade later, Gerhard Selb has not aged much. He is not seventy yet, although *Selbs Betrug* [1992, *Self's Deception*], the second novel featuring the private detective, is clearly set in the early 1990s.[44]

---

44 Bernhard Schlink, *Selbs Betrug* (Zurich: Diogenes, 1992).

Germany has just been re-unified, but this historic event hardly plays a role in this book. A man who calls himself Salger wants to find his daughter. The young woman, a student at Heidelberg University, has disappeared without a trace. It does not take the detective long to find out that Salger is working for the German secret service and that the girl he is looking for is not his daughter, but a member of a militant left-wing group planning attacks on the US Army in Germany – or so it seems. Once again, Gerhard Selb finds himself up against a powerful system and its representatives. Since there is no chance of winning this battle by legal means, he plays a trick on his adversaries that saves his skin. The third and final Selb novel, *Selbs Mord* [2001, *Self's Murder*] finds the detective in his early seventies, but not retired yet.[45] Even a heart attack cannot stop him from working. This time it is a case of money laundering in the aftermath of the German unification process. Selb manages to unravel the complicated plot, but once again, he has to come to terms with the sad fact that there is no justice in this world.

Although the second and the third Selb novels (which Schlink wrote on his own) seem like weaker variations on the theme established in *Selbs Justiz*, they can still be considered above-average mysteries due to their author's deft handling of plot and characterization. This quality also becomes obvious in Schlink's excursion into another popular genre – the espionage thriller. *Die gordische Schleife* [1988, *The Gordian Knot*] tells the story of Georg Polger, who gives up his career as a lawyer in Germany and moves to southern France, where he tries to make a living as a freelance translator.[46] His bad luck seems to change when he suddenly finds himself the owner of a translation agency specializing in technical manuals. It takes him a while before he realizes that he is part of a dangerous scheme involving secret plans for a new military helicopter. A mysterious young woman, with whom he desperately falls in love, complicates the matter. When she suddenly disappears, Polger starts looking for her and ends up in New York. *Die gordische Schleife* is less a thriller than the story of a man in search of himself. One interesting aspect of the book is its narrative structure. In the epilogue, the reader learns that the whole novel is a manuscript written by a friend of the protagonist, which allows Schlink to give the book a metafictional touch, but makes it look even more like a piece of literary juggling.

---

45 Bernhard Schlink, *Selbs Mord* (Zurich: Diogenes, 2001).
46 Bernhard Schlink, *Die gordische Schleife* (Zurich: Diogenes, 1988).

Contemporary German Crime Fiction: A Bibliography

Primary Literature

Aeschbacher, Roger, *In der Hitze der Stadt* (Kassel: Exlibris, 2012).

Arendt, Judith, *Unschuldslamm. Der erste Fall für Schöffin Ruth Holländer* (Munich: Ullstein, 2014).

Arjouni, Jakob, *Happy birthday, Türke!* [1985] (Zurich: Diogenes, 2008), [*Happy birthday, Turk!*, trans. by Anselm Hollo (Brooklyn, NY: Melville House, 2011)].

Arjouni, Jakob, *Mehr Bier. Ein Kayankaya-Roman* (Zurich: Diogenes, 1987), [*More Beer. A Kayankaya Thriller*, trans. by Anselm Hollo (Brooklyn, NY: Melville House, 2011].

Arjouni, Jakob, *Ein Mann, ein Mord. Ein Kayankaya-Roman* [1991] (Zurich: Diogenes, 1993), [*One Man, One Murder*, trans. by Anselm Hollo (Brooklyn, NY: Melville House, 2011)].

Arjouni, Jakob, *Kismet. Ein Kayankaya-Roman* [2001] (Zurich: Diogenes, 2002), [*Kismet. A Kayankaya Novel*, trans. by Anthea Bell (Brooklyn, NY, Melville House, 2010)].

Arjouni, Jakob, *Bruder Kemal. Ein Kayankaya-Roman* (Zurich: Diogenes, 2012), [*Brother Kemal. A Kayankaya Thriller*, trans. by Anthea Bell (Harpenden: No Exit Press, 2013)].

Beck, Zoë, *Brixton Hill* (Munich: Heyne, 2013).

Beck, Zoë, 'Freundin' [Girlfriend*] in *Unter vier Augen – Sprachen des Porträts*, ed. by Kirsten Voigt (Bielefeld: Kerber, 2013), pp. 276–82.

Beck, Zoë, *Schwarzblende* (Munich: Heyne, 2015), [*Fade to Black*, trans. by Rachel Hildebrandt (Spartanburg/SC: Weyward Sisters Publishing, 2017)].

Beck, Zoë, *Die Lieferantin* (Berlin: Suhrkamp, 2017).

Biermann, Pieke, *Herzrasen* (Berlin: Rotbuch, 1993).

Birkefeld, Richard and Hachmeister, Göran, *Wer übrig bleibt, hat recht* [2002] (Frankfurt a.M.: dtv, 2004).

Blaudez, Lena, *Spiegelreflex. Ada Simon in Cotonou* (Zurich: Unionsverlag, 2005).

Böhm, Christian, *Tod am Inn. Ein neuer Fall für Watzmann* (Munich, Zurich: Piper, 2009).

Borrmann, Mechtild, *Wer das Schweigen bricht* (Bielefeld: Pendragon, 2011).

Bosetzky, Horst, *Wie ein Tier. Der S-Bahn-Mörder* [1995] (Munich: dtv, 2009).

Bronsky, Alina, *Baba Dunjas letzte Liebe. Roman* (Cologne: Kiepenheuer & Witsch, 2016). [first ed. 2015; audiobook: *Sophie Rois liest Baba Dunjas letzte Liebe* (Bochum: tacheles! Roof Music GmbH, 2015)].

Chandler, Raymond, *The Big Sleep* [1939] (New York: Vintage Books, 1992).

Danz, Ella, *Rosenwahn* (Meßkirch: Gmeiner, 2012).

Ditfurth, Christian von, *Mann ohne Makel. Stachelmanns erster Fall* [2002] (Cologne: Kiepenheuer & Witsch, 2012).

Domsky, W.W. [i.e. Gabriele Brinkmann], *Ehre, wem Ehre...* (Leer: Leda, 2009).

Dostoevsky, Fyodor, *Crime and Punishment* [1866], transl. by Constance Garnett with an introduction by Joseph Frank (New York: Bantam Dell, 2003).

Dürrenmatt, Friedrich, *Werkausgabe in dreißig Bänden* (Zurich: Diogenes, 1980).

Dürrenmatt, Friedrich, *Selected Writings, Volume 2. Fictions*, ed. by Theodore Ziolkowski, transl. by Joel Agee (Chicago & London: The University of Chicago Press, 2006).

https://doi.org/10.1515/9783110426601-013

Dürrenmatt, Friedrich, *Selected Writings, Volume 3: Essays*, ed. by Kenneth J. Northcott, transl. by Joel Agee (Chicago & London: The University of Chicago Press, 2006).

Dürrenmatt, Friedrich, *The Inspector Bärlach Mysteries: The Judge and His Hangman and Suspicion*, trans. by Joel Agee (Chicago: The University of Chicago Press, 2006),

Dürrenmatt, Friedrich, *Das Versprechen. Reqiem auf den Kriminalroman* (Zurich: Arche 1958), [*The Pledge*, trans. by Joel Agee (Chicago: University of Chicago Press, 2006)].

Ebertowski, Jürgen, *Agentur Istanbul. Eugen Meuniers dritter Fall* (Berlin: Rotbuch, 2007).

Eckert, Horst, *Sprengkraft* (Dortmund: grafit, 2009).

Eggers, Wilfried, *Paragraf 301* (Dortmund: grafit, 2008).

Engin, Osman, *Tote essen keinen Döner. Don Osmans erster Fall* (Munich: dtv, 2010).

Engin, Osman, *1001 Nachtschichten. Mordstorys am Fließband* (Munich: dtv, 2010).

Ernst, Christoph, *Dunkle Schatten* (Bielefeld: Pendragon, 2012).

Fauser, Jörg, *Der Schneemann* (Munich: Rogner & Bernhard, 1981), [*The Snowman*, trans. by Anthea Bell (London: Bitter Lemon Press, 2004)].

Fauser, Jörg, *Das Schlangenmaul. Roman* (Frankfurt a.M., Berlin, Vienna: Ullstein, 1985).

Fauser, Jörg, *Kant. Ein Szene-Krimi* (Munich: Heyne, 1987).

Fauser, Jörg. *Der Strand der Städte. Gesammelte journalistische Arbeiten 1959–1987*, ed. by Alexander Wewerka (Berlin: Alexander Verlag, 2009).

Fauser, Jörg, *Der Strand der Städte/Blues für Blondinen. Essays. Werkausgabe in neun Bänden*, ed. by Alexander Wewerka, Band 8 (Zurich: Diogenes, 2009).

Feige, Marcel, *Kalte Haut* (Munich: Goldmann, 2012).

Gercke, Doris, *Weinschröter, du mußt hängen* (Hamburg: Galgenberg, 1988).

Gerdts, Rose, *Ehrenhüter* (Reinbek bei Hamburg: Rowohlt Taschenbuch Verlag, 2011).

Gerdts, Rose, *Morgengrauen* (Reinbek bei Hamburg: Rowohlt Taschenbuch Verlag, 2013).

Gibert, Matthias P., *Zirkusluft* (Meßkirch: Gmeiner, 2009).

Glauser, Friedrich, *Gesammelte Werke in 4 Bänden*, ed. by Hugo Leber (Zurich: Die Arche, 1969–1997).

Glauser, Friedrich, *Die Romane*, 7 vols., ed. by Bernhard Echte (Zurich: Limmat, 1995–1997).

Glauser, Friedrich, *Wachtmeister Studers erste Fälle*, ed. by Frank Göhre (Zurich: Arche Verlag, 1989).

Glauser, Friedrich, *Der Tee der drei alten Damen* (Zurich: Arche, 1989).

Glauser, Friedrich, *Sclumpf, Erwin, Mord* (Zurich: Limmat 1995), [*Thumbprint*, trans. by Kike Mitchell (London: Bitter Lemon Press, 2004)].

Glauser, Friedrich, *Fieberkurve* (Zurich: Arche, 1989), [*Fever*, trans. by Mike Mitchell (London: Bitter Lemon Press, 2006)].

Glauser, Friedrich, *Matto regiert* (Zurich: Arche, 1989), [*In Matto's Realm*, trans. by Mike Mitchell (London: Bitter Lemon Press, 2005)].

Glauser, Friedrich, *Der Chinese* (Zurich: Arche, 1989), [*The Chinaman*, trans. by Mike Mitchell (London: Bitter Lemon Press, 2008)].

Glauser, Friedrich, *Briefe 2 (1935–38)*, ed. by Bernhard Echte (Zurich: Arche Verlag, 1991).

Gross, Rainer, *Grafeneck* (Munich: Goldmann, 2010).

Gross, Rainer, *Kettenacker* (Bielefeld: Pendragon, 2011).

Gustmann, Jörg S., *Rassenwahn* (Meßkirch: Gmeiner, 2012).

Haas, Wolf, *Auferstehung der Toten* (Reinbek bei Hamburg: Rowohlt Taschenbuch Verlag, 1996), [*Resurrection*, trans. by Annie Janusch (Brooklyn/NY, London: Melville House, 2014].

Haas, Wolf, *Der Knochenmann* (Reinbek bei Hamburg: Rowohlt Taschenbuch Verlag, 1997), [*The Bone Man*, trans. by Annie Janusch (Brooklyn/NY, London: Melville House, 2013)].

Haas, Wolf, *Komm, süßer Tod!* (Reinbek bei Hamburg: Rowohlt Taschenbuch Verlag, 1998), [*Come, Sweet Death!*, trans. by Annie Janusch (Brooklyn/NY, London: Melville House, 2014)].

Haas, Wolf, *Silentium!* (Reinbek bei Hamburg: Rowohlt Taschenbuch Verlag, 1999).

Haas, Wolf, *Wie die Tiere* (Reinbek bei Hamburg: Rowohlt Taschenbuch Verlag, 2001).

Haas, Wolf, *Das ewige Leben* (Hamburg: Hoffmann und Campe, 2004).

Haas, Wolf, *Der Brenner und der liebe Gott* (Hamburg: Hoffmann und Campe, 2009), [*Brenner and God*, trans. by Annie Janusch (Brooklyn/NY, London: Melville House, 2012)].

Haas, Wolf, *Brennerova* (Hamburg: Hoffmann und Campe, 2014).

Hahn, Ulla, *Ein Mann im Haus* (Stuttgart: DVA, 1991)

Harsdörffer, Georg Philipp, *Der Grosse SchauPlatz Jämerlicher Mordgeschichte: Mit vielen merkwürdigen Erzehlungen/ neu üblichen Gedichten/ Lehrreichen Sprüchen/ scharffsinnigen Hoffreden/ artigen Schertzfragen und Antworten etc.* (Hamburg: Nauman, 1649).

Heim, Uta-Maria, *Feierabend* (Meßkirch: Gmeiner-Verlag, 2011).

Herrmann, Elisabeth, *Das Kindermädchen* [2005] (Munich: Goldmann, 2007).

Herrndorf, Wolfgang, *Sand* (Berlin: Rowohlt, 2011).

Hochgatterer, Paulus, *Das Matratzenhaus* (Vienna: Deuticke im Paul Zsolnay Verlag, 2010), [*The Mattress House*, trans. Jamie Bulloch (London: MacLehose Press, 2012)].

Höfele, Andreas, *Das Tal* (Munich, Zurich: Piper, 1975).

Isringhaus, Jörg, *Unter Mördern* [2010] (Berlin: Aufbau, 2011).

Isringhaus, Jörg, *Ein fremder Feind* (Berlin: Aufbau, 2013).

Kerr, Philip, *Prague Fatale. A Bernie Gunther Thriller* [2011] (London: Quercus 2012).

King, Stephen, *Misery* (New York: Viking Press, 1987).

Klausner, Uwe, *Das Eichmann-Syndikat. Tom Sydows fünfter Fall* (Meßkirch: Gmeiner, 2012).

Klein, Edwin, *Türkischer Wind* (Trier: Weyand, 2007).

Klein, Georg, *Barbar Rosa. Eine Detektivgeschichte* (Berlin: Fest, 2001).

Klewe, Sabine, *Der Seele weißes Blut* (Munich: Goldmann, 2012).

Komarek, Alfred, *Polt muss weinen* (Innsbruck: Haymon-Verlag, 1998).

Komarek, Alfred, *Blumen für Polt* (Innsbruck: Haymon-Verlag, 2000).

Komarek, Alfred, *Himmel, Polt und Hölle* (Innsbruck: Haymon-Verlag, 2001).

Komarek, Alfred, *Polterabend* (Innsbruck: Haymon-Verlag, 2003).

Komarek, Alfred, *Polt* (Innsbruck, Vienna: Haymon-Verlag, 2009).

Komarek, Alfred, *Alt, aber Polt* (Innsbruck, Vienna: Haymon-Verlag, 2011).

Komarek, Alfred, *Zwölf mal Polt* (Innsbruck, Vienna: Haymon-Verlag, 2015).

Kuhn, Krystyna, *Wintermörder* (Munich: Goldmann, 2007).

Kutscher, Volker, *Der nasse Fisch* (Cologne: Kiepenheuer & Witsch, 2007). [*Babylon Berlin*, trans. by Niall Sellar (Dingwall: Sandstone Press, 2016)].

Kutscher, Volker, *Der stumme Tod* (Cologne: Kiepenheuer & Witsch, 2009). [*The Silent Death*, trans. by Niall Sellar (Dingwall: Sandstone Press, 2017)].

Kutscher, Volker, *Goldstein* (Cologne: Kiepenheuer & Witsch, 2010). [*Goldstein*, trans. by Niall Sellar (Dingwall: Sandstone Press, 2018)].

Kutscher, Volker, *Die Akte Vaterland* (Cologne: Kiepenheuer & Witsch, 2012). [*The Fatherland Files*, trans. by Niall Sellar (Dingwall: Sandstone Press, 2019)].

Kutscher, Volker, *Märzgefallene* (Cologne: Kiepenheuer & Witsch, 2014).

Kutscher, Volker, *Lunapark* (Cologne: Kiepenheuer & Witsch, 2016).

-ky & Co., *Die Klette* (Reinbek bei Hamburg: Rowohlt Taschenbuch Verlag, 1983).

Lüpkes, Sandra, *Todesbraut* (Munich: dtv, 2011).

Martin, Hansjörg, *Gefährliche Neugier, Kein Schnaps für Tamara, Einer fehlt beim Kurkonzert*, omnibus edition (Reinbek bei Hamburg: Rowohlt Taschenbuch Verlag, 1990).

Molsner, Michael, *Die Schattenrose, Wie eine reissende Bestie, Rote Messe*, omnibus edition (Munich: Heyne, 1987).

Morshäuser, Bodo, *Tod in New York City* (Frankfurt a.M.: Suhrkamp, 1995).

Muschg, Adolf, *Baiyun oder die Freundschaftsgesellschaft* (Frankfurt a.M.: Suhrkamp, 1980).

Musharbash, Yassin, *Radikal* (Cologne: Kiepenheuer & Witsch, 2011).

Neuhaus, Nele, *Tiefe Wunden* (Berlin: List, 2009).

Neumann, H. Dieter, *Das Erbe der Wölfin* (Stuttgart: Südwestbuch, 2013).

Noll, Ingrid, *Der Hahn ist tot. Roman* (Zurich: Diogenes, 1993).

Noller, Ulrich and Gök Senin, *Çelik und Pelzer* (Frankfurt a.M.: Eichborn, 2010).

Peters, Christoph, *Das Tuch aus Nacht* (Munich: Goldmann, 2003). [*The Fabric of Night*, trans. by John Cullen (New York: Nan A. Talese, 2007)].

Reichlin, Linus, *Die Sehnsucht der Atome* (Frankfurt a.M.: Eichborn, 2008).

Ritzel, Ulrich, *Der Hund des Propheten* (Lengwil: Libelle, 2003), [*Berndorf and his Dog*, trans. by Hugh Ridley (Kindle)].

Ritzel, Ulrich, *Beifang* (Munich: btb, 2009), [*Ring of Blood*, trans. by Hugh Ridley (Kindle)].

Rossmann, Eva, *Freudsche Verbrechen. Mira Valensky ermittelt in Wien* (Bergisch Gladbach: Bastei Lübbe, 2003).

Roth, Gerhard, *Der Plan* (Frankfurt a.M.: Fischer, 1998). [*The Plan*, trans. by Todd C. Hanlin (Riverside/CA: Ariadne Press, 2012)].

Schätzing, Frank, *Tod und Teufel* (Munich: Goldmann, 2003), [*Death and the Devil*. trans. by Mike Mitchell (New York: William Morrow, 2007)].

Scharsich, Dagmar, *Die gefrorene Charlotte* (Hamburg: Ariadne, 1993).

Scharsich, Dagmar, *Verbotene Stadt* (Hamburg: Ariadne, 2002).

Schenkel, Andrea Maria, *Tannöd* (Hamburg: Edition Nautilus, 2006), [*The Murder Farm*, trans. by Anthea Bell (New York, London: Quercus, 2014)].

Schiller, Friedrich, *Der Verbrecher aus verlorener Ehre. Studienausgabe*, ed. by Alexander Košenina (Stuttgart: Reclam, 2014).

Schirach, Ferdinand von, *Der Fall Collini* (Munich, Zurich: Piper, 2011).

Schlink, Bernhard, Walter Popp, *Selbs Justiz* (Zurich: Diogenes, 1987), [*Self's Punishment*, trans. by Rebecca Morrison (New York: Vintage Books, 2005)].

Schlink, Bernhard, *Die gordische Schleife* (Zurich: Diogenes, 1988), [*The Gordian Knot*, trans. by Peter Constantine (New York: Vintage Books, 2010)].

Schlink, Bernhard, *Selbs Betrug* (Zurich: Diogenes, 1992), [*Self's Deception*, trans. by Peter Constantine (New York: Vintage Books, 2007)].

Schlink, Bernhard, *Selbs Mord* (Zurich: Diogenes, 2001). [*Self's Murder*, trans. by Peter Constantine (New York: Vintage Books, 2009)].

Schmöe, Friederike, *Bisduvergisst* (Meßkirch: Gmeiner, 2010).

Schneider, Hansjörg, *Das Paar im Kahn. Hunkelers dritter Fall* (Zurich: Diogenes, 2011).

Schorlau, Wolfgang, *Das dunkle Schweigen. Denglers zweiter Fall* (Cologne: Kiepenheuer & Witsch, 2011).

Sezgin, Hilal, *Mihriban pfeift auf Gott* (Cologne: DuMont, 2010).

Steinfest, Heinrich, *Cheng* (Munich, Zurich: Piper, 2007).

Steinfest, Heinrich, *Batmans Schönheit* (Munich, Zurich: Piper, 2010).
Turhan, Su, *Kommissar Pascha. Ein Fall für Zeki Demirbilek* (Munich: Knaur, 2013).
Waters, John (dir.), *Serial Mom* (USA 1994).
Weigand, Sabine, *Die Markgräfin. Roman* (Frankfurt a.M.: Fischer Taschenbuch Verlag, 2010).
[first ed. Frankfurt a.M.: Krüger Verlag, 2004].
Wiedergrün, Helene, *Blutmadonna* (Meßkirch: Gmeiner, 2013).
Wieninger, Manfred, *Der Mann mit dem goldenen Revolver* (Innsbruck, Vienna: Haymon, 2015).
Zaimoglu, Feridun, *Leinwand* (Hamburg: Rotbuch, 2003).
Zweyer, Jan, *Goldfasan* (Dortmund: grafit, 2009).
Zweyer, Jan, *Persilschein* (Dortmund: grafit, 2011).

Secondary Literature

Abt, Stefanie, *Soziale Enquête im aktuellen Kriminalroman. Am Beispiel von Henning Mankell, Ulrich Ritzel und Pieke Biermann* (Wiesbaden: Deutscher Universitätsverlag, 2004).
Aisenberg, Nadya, 'Resolution and Irresolution', in *The Oxford Companion to Crime and Mystery Writing*, ed. by Rosemary Herbert (Oxford: Oxford University Press, 1999), pp. 384–85.
Alberts, Jürgen and Frank Göhre, *Kreuzverhör: Zehn Krimiautoren sagen aus* (Hildesheim: Gerstenberg, 1999).
Alewyn, Richard, 'Anatomie des Detektivromans', in *Der Kriminalroman. Zur Theorie und Geschichte der Gattung*, ed. by Jochen Vogt, vol. 2 (Munich: Fink, 1971), pp. 372–404 [first published in *Die Zeit* 47/48 (1968)].
Aly, Götz, *Die Belasteten. ‚Euthanasie' 1939–1945. Eine Gesellschaftsgeschichte* (Frankfurt a.M.: S. Fischer, 2013).
Ammann, Wilhelm, '"Regionalität" in den Kulturwissenschaften', in *Periphere Zentren oder zentrale Peripherien? Kulturen und Regionen Europas zwischen Globalisierung und Regionalität*, ed. by W.A., Georg Mein, Rolf Parr (Heidelberg: Synchron 2008), pp.13–30.
[Anon.] 'So diskutiert das Netz über den Islam-Rabatt', in *Bild* (http://www.bild.de/news/inland/rechtsprechung/so-diskutiert-das-netz-ueber-den-islam-rabatt-35298338.bild.html).
Aristotle, *Poetics*, trans. by Anthony Kenny (Oxford: Oxford University Press, 2013).
Arnold, Silke, '"Ermordet?" Eine Kriminalnovelle von Auguste Groner', *Script: Frau Literatur Wissenschaft im alpen-adriatischen Raum*, 6 (1994), pp. 3–7.
Arnold-de Simine, Silke, *Leichen im Keller. Zu Fragen des Gender in Angstinszenierungen der Schauer- und Kriminalliteratur (1790–1830)* (St. Ingbert: Röhrig Universitätsverlag, 2000).
Aspetsberger, Friedbert and Daniela Strigl. eds, *Ich kannte den Mörder wußte nur nicht wer er war. Zum Kriminalroman der Gegenwart* (Innsbruck: Studien Verlag, 2004).
Auden, W. H., 'The Guilty Vicarage', *Harper's Magazine*, May 1948, pp. 406–12.
Aust, Hugo, *Der historische Roman* (Stuttgart, Weimar: Metzler, 1994).
Bachtin, Michail, *Literatur und Karneval. Zur Romantheorie und Lachkultur* (Frankfurt a.M.: Fischer, 1990).
Basseler, Michael and Dorothee Birke, 'Mimesis des Erinnerns', in *Gedächtniskonzepte der Literaturwissenschaft. Theoretische Grundlegung und Anwendungsperspektiven*, ed. by Astrid Erll and Ansgar Nünning (Berlin, New York: de Gruyter, 2005), pp. 123–47.

Baumberger, Christa, 'Glauser in Genf: Schauplatz literarischer Selbst(er)findung', *Quarto* 32 (2011), pp. 45–50.

Becker, Jens Peter and Paul Gerhard Buchloh, 'Ist der Kriminalroman im traditionellen englischen Sinn in Deutschland möglich?' in *Der neue deutsche Kriminalroman. Beiträge zu Darstellung, Interpretation und Kritik eines populären Genres*, ed. by Karl Ermert and Wolfgang Gast (Rehburg-Loccum: Evangelische Akademie Loccum, 1982), pp. 50–57.

Behrens, Cornelia, 'Verwischte Spuren. Die Detektivin als literarische Wunschfigur in Kriminalromanen von Frauen', *Weiblichkeit und Tod in der Literatur*, ed. by Renate Berger and Inge Stephan (Cologne, Vienna: Böhlau, 1987), pp. 177–197.

Bertens, Hans, Theo D'haen, *Contemporary American Crime Fiction* (Houndmills/Hampshire, New York: Palgrave, 2001).

Biamonthe, Gloria A., 'Funny, Isn't It? Testing the Boundaries of Gender and Genre in Women's Detective Fiction', in *Look Who's Laughing. Gender and Comedy*, ed. by Gail Finney (Amsterdam: Gordon and Breach, 1994), pp. 231–254.

Bloch, Ernst, 'Philosophische Ansicht des Detektivromans' [1960/1965], in *Der Kriminalroman. Poetik – Theorie – Geschichte*, ed. by Jochen Vogt (Munich: Fink 1998), pp. 38–51. [also in E.B., *Literarische Aufsätze* (Frankfurt a.M.: Suhrkamp, 1965), pp. 242–263; English trans.: E.B., 'A Philosophical View of the Detective Novel', in E.B., *Heritage of Our Times* (Cambridge: Polity Press, 1991)].

Blödorn, Andreas, '"Prodesse et delectare" oder Die Last mit der Lust. Der Soziokrimi als Experiment', Review of: Jürg Brönnimann, *Der Soziokrimi: ein neues Genre oder ein soziologisches Experiment? Eine Untersuchung des Soziokriminalromans anhand der Werke der schwedischen Autoren Maj Sjöwall und Per Wahlöö und des deutschen Autors -ky.* (Wuppertal: Nordpark 2004), *IASLonline* (March 19, 2005), (http://www.iaslonline.de/index.php?vorgang_id=1037).

Bodek, Janusz, 'Ein „Geflecht aus Schuld und Rache"? Die Kontroversen um Fassbinders *Der Müll, die Stadt und der Tod*', in *Deutsche Nachkriegsliteratur und der Holocaust*, ed. by Stephan Braese, Holger Gehle, Doron Kiesel and Hanno Lowey (Frankfurt a.M., New York: Campus, 1998), pp. 351–84.

Bourdieu, Pierre, 'The Market of Symbolic Goods', in P.B., *The Field of Cultural Production. Essays on Art and Literature*, ed. by Randal Johnson (New York: Columbia University Presse 1993), pp. 112–141.

Bourdieu, Pierre, *Die feinen Unterschiede. Kritik der gesellschaftlichen Urteilskraft* (Frankfurt a.M.: Suhrkamp, 1982.

Bourdieu, Pierre, *Die Regeln der Kunst. Genese und Struktur des literarischen Feldes* (Frankfurt a.M.: Suhrkamp, 2001).

Braun, Michael, *Die deutsche Gegenwartsliteratur* (Cologne, Weimar, Vienna: Böhlau Verlag, 2010).

Brecht, Bertolt, 'Über die Popularität des Kriminalromans', *Werke. Große kommentierte Berliner und Frankfurter Ausgabe*, ed. by Werner Hecht, Jan Knopf, Werner Mittenzwei, and Klaus-Detlef Müller, vol. 22 (Frankfurt a.M.: Suhrkamp, 1993), pp. 504–510 [also in B.B., *Schriften zur Literatur und Kunst 2* (Frankfurt a.M.: Suhrkamp, 1969), pp. 450–457]

Brecht, Bertolt, 'Let's Get Back to Detective Novels', in: *Brecht on Art and Politics*, ed. by Tom Kuhn (London: Methuen, 2004), pp. 263–70.

Breithaupt, Fritz, *Kultur der Ausrede* (Berlin: Suhrkamp, 2012).

Broich, Ulrich, 'Von Inspektor Field zu Sherlock Holmes. Die englische Detektivliteratur nach 1850 und die historische Realität', in *Literatur und Kriminalität. Die gesellschaftliche*

Erfahrung von Verbrechen und Strafverfolgung als Gegenstand des Erzählens.
Deutschland, England und Frankreich 1850–1880, ed. by Jörg Schönert (Tübingen:
Niemeyer, 1983), pp. 135154.

Brönnimann, Jürg, *Der Soziokrimi: Ein neues Genre oder ein soziologisches Experiment? Eine
Untersuchung des Sozialkriminalromans anhand der Werke der schwedischen Autoren
Maj Sjöwall und Per Wallöö und des deutschen Autors -ky* (Wuppertal: Nordpark, 2004).

Browne, Ray B., 'Historical Crime and Detection', in *A Companion to Crime Fiction*, ed. by
Charles J. Rzepka and Lee Horsley (Chichester: Wiley-Blackwell, 2010), pp. 222–232.

Browne, Ray B. and Laurence A. Kreiser, eds, *The Detective as Historian: History and Art in
Historical Crime Fiction* (Bowling Green: Bowling Green State University Popular Press,
2000).

Browning, Christopher R., *Ganz normale Männer. Das Reserve-Polizeibattalion 101 und die
„Endlösung" in Polen*, trans. by Jürgen Peter Krause (Reinbek bei Hamburg: Rowohlt,
1993). [*Ordinary Men. Reserve Police Battalion 101 and the Final Solution in Poland.*
New York 1992.]

Browning, Christopher R., *The Path to Genocide: Essays on Launching the Final Solution*
(Cambridge: University Press, 1992).

Brumlik, Micha, 'Das halbierte Humanum – Wie Ralph Giordano zum Ausländerfeind wurde', in
Islamfeindlichkeit. Wenn die Grenzen der Kritik verschwimmen, ed. by Thorsten Gerald
Schneiders (Wiesbaden: VS, 2009), pp. 469–75.

Bühler, Patrick, *Die Leiche in der Bibliothek. Friedrich Glauser und der Detektiv-Roman*
(Heidelberg: Winter, 2002).

Burgess, Michael, and Jill H. Vassilakos, eds, *Murder in Retrospect: A selective Guide to
Historical Mystery Fiction* (Westport: Libraries Unlimited, 2005).

Butler, Judith, *Antigone's Claim. Kinship Between Life and Death* (New York: Columbia
University Press, 2000).

Campbell, Bruce B., 'Justice and Genre: The *Krimi* as a Site of Memory in Contemporary
Germany', in *Detectives, Dystopias, and Poplit: Studies in Modern German Genre Fiction*,
ed. by Bruce B. Campbell, Alison Guenther-Pal and Vibeke Rützou Petersen (Rochester/
NY: Camden House, 2014), pp. 133–151.

Cheesman, Tom, *Novels of Turkish German Settlement. Cosmopolite Fictions* (Rochester/NY:
Camden House, 2007).

Christian, Ed, ed. *The Post-Colonial Detective* (Basingstoke: Palgrave, 2001).

Crocket, Roger, *Understanding Friedrich Dürrenmatt* (Columbia/SC: University of South
Carolina Press, 1998).

Dappert, Dagmar, 'Der historische Kriminalroman als hybrides Genre', in *Crimina. Die Antike
im modernen Kriminalroman*, ed. by Kai Brodersen (Frankfurt a.M.: Antike, 2004),
pp. 127–42.

De Groot, Jerome, *The Historical Novel* (London, New York: Routledge, 2010).

Dietze, Gabriele, 'Die verlorenen Schlachten der Männer und die Metamorphose der
Privatdetektive', *Das Argument* 37.1 (1995), pp. 19–33.

Dietze, Gabriele, *Hardboiled Woman. Geschlechterkrieg im amerikanischen Kriminalroman*
(Hamburg: Europäische Verlagsanstalt, 1997).

Donahue, William Collins, '"Ist er kein Jude, dann verdiente er einer zu sein": Droste-
Hülshoff's *Die Judenbuche* and Religious Anti-Semitism', *German Quarterly* 72.1 (1999),
pp. 44–73.

Donahue, William Collins, 'The Popular Culture Alibi: Bernhard Schlink's Detective Novels and the Culture of Politically Correct Holocaust Literature', German Quarterly 77.4 (2004): pp. 462–81.

Donahue, William Collins, Holocaust as Fiction: Bernhard Schlink's "Nazi" Novels and Their Films (New York: Palgrave Macmillan, 2010).

Düsing, Wolfgang, ed., Experimente mit dem Kriminalroman. Ein Erzählmodell in der deutschsprachigen Literatur des 20. Jahrhunderts (Frankfurt a.M., et. al.: Peter Lang, 1993).

Erll, Astrid, 'Literature, Film, and the Mediality of Cultural Memory', in Cultural Memory Studies: An International and Interdisciplinary Handbook, ed. by Astrid Erll and Ansgar Nünning, in collaboration with Sara B. Young (Berlin, New York: de Gruyter, 2008), pp. 389–98.

Ermert, Karl and Wolfgang Gast, Der neue deutsche Kriminalroman. Beiträge zu Darstellung, Interpretation und Kritik eines populären Genres (Rehburg-Loccum: Evangelische Akademie Loccum, 1982).

Fauser, Jörg, 'Leichenschmaus in Loccum', in Der Strand der Städte – Blues für Blondinen. Essays (Zurich: Diogenes, 2009), pp. 327–338.

Fiedler, Leslie, 'Cross the Border, Close the Gap', in A New Fiedler Reader (Amherst, N. Y.: Prometheus Books 1999) pp. 270–294.

Finney, Gail, ed., Look Who's Laughing. Gender and Comedy (Amsterdam: Gordon and Breach, 1994).

Franck, Georg, Ökonomie der Aufmerksamkeit. Ein Entwurf (Munich: Hanser, 1998).

Freese, Peter, The Ethnic Detective. Chester Himes, Harry Kemelman, Tony Hillerman (Essen: Die Blaue Eule, 1992).

Frei, Norbert, Vergangenheitspolitik. Die Anfänge der Bundesrepublik und die NS-Vergangenheit (Munich: Beck, 1996). [Adenauer's Germany and the Nazi Past. The Politics of Amnesty and Integration, trans. by Joel Gelb (New York: Columbia University Press, 2002)].

Friedlander, Henry, The Origins of Nazi Genocide. From Euthanasia to the Final Solution (Chapel Hill/NC; London: The University of North Carolina Press, 1995).

Gerard Genette, Paratexts: Thresholds of Interpretation, trans. by Jane E. Lewin (Cambridge: Cambridge University Press, 1997).

Gerber, Richard. 'Verbrechensdichtung und Kriminalroman', in Der Kriminalroman, ed. by Jochen Vogt, vol. 2 (Munich: Fink, 1971), pp. 404–420. [first published in Neue Deutsche Hefte 111(1966), pp. 101–117.]

Germer, Dorothea, Von Genossen und Gangstern. Zum Gesellschaftsbild in der Kriminalliteratur der DDR und Ostdeutschlands von 1974 bis 1994 (Essen: Verlag Die Blaue Eule, 1998).

Giordano, Ralph, Die zweite Schuld oder Von der Last Deutscher zu sein (Hamburg: Rasch und Röhring, 1987).

Glesener, Jeanne E., 'The Crime Novel: Multiculturalism and its Impact on the Genre's Conventions', in Crime and Nation. Political and Cultural Mappings of Criminality in New and Traditional Media, ed. by Immacolata Amodeo and Eva Erdmann (Trier: WVT, 2009) pp. 15–26.

Göring, Hermann, 'Görings Erntedankrede von 1942', in Volkes Stimme. Skepsis und Führervertrauen im Nationalsozialismus, ed. by Götz Aly (Frankfurt a.M.: S. Fischer, 2006), pp. 149–94.

Goltz, Gabriel, 'Die armenische Minderheit in der Türkei – zu den Entwicklungen seit den EU-Anpassungsreformen 2002 und 2003', *Orient* 44.3 (2003), pp. 413–35.

Gradinari, Irina, *Genre, Gender und Lustmord. Mörderische Geschlechterfantasien in der deutschsprachigen Gegenwartsliteratur* (Bielefeld: Aisthesis, 2011).

Griem, Julika, 'Beweisaufnahme: Zur medialen Topographie des "Tatort,"' in *Tatort Stadt. Mediale Topographien eines Fernsehklassikers*, ed. by J. G., Sebastian Scholz (Frankfurt a.M., New York: Campus 2010), pp. 9–28.

Haas, Wolf, *Sprachtheoretische Grundlagen der konkreten Poesie* (Stuttgart: Akademischer Verlag Stuttgart, 1990).

Hall, Katharina, 'The "Nazi Detective" as Provider of Justice in post-1990 British and German Crime Fiction: Philip Kerr's *The Pale Criminal*, Robert Harris's *Fatherland* and Richard Birkefeld and Göran Hachmeisters's *Wer übrig bleibt, hat recht'*, *Comparative Literature Studies* 50 (2013), pp. 282–313.

Hall, Katharina, 'Historical Crime Fiction in German: The Turbulent Twentieth Century', in *Crime Fiction in German: Der Krimi*, ed. by Katharina Hall (Cardiff: University of Wales Press, 2016), pp. 115–131.

Hauschild, Thomas, 'Ehrenmord, Ethnologie und Recht', in *Wider den Kulturenzwang. Migration, Kulturalisierung und Weltliteratur*, ed. by Özkan Ezli, Dorothee Kimmich and Annette Werberger (Bielefeld: Transcript, 2009), pp. 23–46.

Heißenbüttel, Helmut. 'Spielregeln des Kriminalromans', in H.H., *Über Literatur* (Olten and Freiburg/Breisgau: Walter, 1966), pp. 96–110. [also in Jochen Vogt, ed., *Der Kriminalroman. Poetik, Theorie, Geschichte* (Munich: Fink, 1998), pp. 111–120].

Herzog, Todd, *Crime Stories: Criminalistic Fantasy and the Culture of Crisis in Weimar Germany* (New York, Oxford: Berghahn Books, 2009).

Hett, Benjamin Carter, *Burning the Reichstag: An Investigation into the Third Reich's Enduring Mystery* (Oxford: Oxford University Press, 2014).

Hickethier, Knut, 'Der Alte Deutsche Kriminalroman. Von vergessenen Traditionen', *Die Horen* 144 (1986), pp. 15–23.

Hillich, Reinhard, 'Krimi in der DDR – DDR im Krimi', in *Die DDR im Spiegel ihrer Literatur: Beiträge zu einer historischen Betrachtung der DDR-Literatur*, ed. by Franz Huberth (Berlin: Duncker & Humblot, 2005), pp. 105–116.

Himmler, Heinrich, 'Rede vor den Reichs- und Gauleitern in Posen am 06. 10.1943', in *Heinrich Himmler. Geheimreden 1933 bis 1945*, ed. by Bradley F. Smith and Agnes F. Peterson (Frankfurt a.M., Berlin, Vienna: Propyläen, 1974), pp. 162–83

Hißnauer, Christian, Stefan Scherer, Claudia Stockinger, eds, *Zwischen Serie und Werk. Fernseh- und Gesellschaftsgeschichte im 'Tatort'* (Bielefeld: Transcript, 2014).

Hißnauer, Christian, Stefan Scherer, Claudia Stockinger, *Föderalismus in Serie. Die Einheit der ARD-Reihe 'Tatort' im historischen Verlauf* (Munich: Fink 2014).

Hoffmann, Nele, *A Taste for Crime. Zur Wertung von Kriminalliteratur in Literaturkritik und Literaturwissenschaft* (Salzhemmingen: Blumenkamp, 2012).

Holzmann, Gabriela, *Schaulust und Verbrechen. Eine Geschichte des Krimis als Mediengeschichte 1850–1959* (Stuttgart: Metzler, 2001).

Hügel, Hans-Otto, *Untersuchungsrichter, Diebsfänger, Detektive. Theorie und Geschichte der deutschen Detektiverzählung im 19. Jahrhundert* (Stuttgart: Metzler, 1978).

Huntington, Samuel P., *The Clash of Civilizations and the Remaking of World Order* (New York: Simon & Schuster, 1996).

Jäger, Manfred, 'Die Legitimierung der Unterhaltungsliteratur', in *Die Literatur der DDR*, ed. by Hans-Jürgen Schmitt, *Hansers Sozialgeschichte der deutschen Literatur vom 16. Jahrhundert bis zur Gegenwart*, vol. 11 (Munich: dtv 1983) pp. 229–260.

Jahn, Reinhard, 'Jesus, Buddha, der Müll und der Tod. Spurensicherung in Sachen Soziokrimi', *Deutschsprachige Literatur der 70er und 80er Jahre: Autoren, Tendenzen, Gattungen*, ed. by Walter Delabar and Erhard Schütz (Darmstadt: Wissenschaftliche Buchgesellschaft, 1997), pp. 38–52.

Jauß, Hans Robert, 'Über den Grund des Vergnügens an komischen Helden', in *Das Komische*, ed. by Wolfgang Preisendanz, Rainer Warning (Munich: Fink, 1976), pp. 103–132.

Kalbitz, Herbert, Dieter Kästner, *Illustrierte Bibliographie der Leihbücher 1946–1976. Teil 1: Kriminalleihbücher* (Stollhamm-Butjadingen: Achilla, 2013).

Karolle-Berg, Julia, 'The Case of the Missing Literary Tradition: Reassessing Four Assumptions of Crime and Detective Novels in the German-Speaking World (1900–1933)', *Monatshefte* 107.3 (2015), pp. 431–454.

Kehrberg, Brigitte, *Der Kriminalroman der DDR 1970–1990* (Hamburg: Kovac, 1998).

Keitel, Evelyne, 'Der weibliche Blick im amerikanischen Kriminalroman', *Das Argument* 37.1 (1995), pp. 35–51.

Kimmelman, Micheal, 'German Viewers Love Their Detectives', *New York Times*, August 27, 2009.

Klein, Kathleen Gregory, *The Woman Detective. Gender and Genre* (Urbana, Chicago/IL: University of Illinois Press, 1995).

Klein, Kathleen Gregory, *Diversity and Detective Fiction* (Bowling Green/OH: Bowling Green State University Popular Press, 1999).

Kniesche, Thomas, 'Vom Modell Deutschland zum Bordell Deutschland. Jakob Arjounis Detektivromane als literarische Konstruktion bundesrepublikanischer Wirklichkeit', in *Mord als kreativer Prozess. Zum Kriminalroman der Gegenwart in Deutschland, Österreich und der Schweiz*, ed. by Sandro M. Moraldo (Heidelberg: Winter, 2005), pp. 21–39.

Kniesche, Thomas, 'Gärgas: Die Kriminalromane von Alfred Komarek', *The German Quarterly* 79.2 (2006), pp. 211–233.

Kniesche, Thomas, '"Der Kommissar für die, die weg sind". Friedrich Anis Tabor-Süden-Romane und die Topographie des Traumas', in *andererseits. Yearbook of Transatlanic German Studies 3* (2013), pp. 125–145. Online version: http://andererseits.library.duke.edu/article/view/14941/6119.

Kniesche, Thomas, *Einführung in den Kriminalroman* (Darmstadt: Wissenschaftliche Buchgesellschaft: 2015).

Knight, Stephen, *Crime Fiction 1800–2000: Detection, Death, Diversity* (Houndmills, New York: Palgrave Macmillan, 2004).

König, Michael, *Poetik des Terrors. Politisch motivierte Gewalt in der deutschen Gegenwartsliteratur* (Bielefeld: Transcript, 2015).

Koning, Christina, 'Fiction', *The Times*, August 20, 2005, p. 18 [S3].

Korte, Barbara and Sylvia Paletschek, eds, *Geschichte im Krimi. Beiträge aus den Kulturwissenschaften* (Cologne, Weimar, Vienna: Böhlau, 2009).

Koschorke, Albrecht, *Wahrheit und Erfindung. Grundzüge einer Allgemeinen Erzähltheorie* (Frankfurt a.M.: S. Fischer, 2012).

Košenina, Alexander, ed., *Kriminalfallgeschichten*, Text + Kritik Sonderband (Munich: edition text + kritik, 2014).

Kotthoff, Helga, 'Vom Lächeln der Mona Lisa zum Lachen der Hyänen', in *Das Gelächter der Geschlechter. Humor und Macht in Gesprächen* von Frauen *und Männern*, ed. by Helga Kotthoff (Konstanz: Universitätsverlag, 1995), pp. 121–163.

Kracauer, Siegfried, *Der Detektiv-Roman. Ein philosophischer Traktat*, in S.K., *Schriften. Band 1* (Frankfurt a.M.: Suhrkamp, 1971).

Krajenbrink, Marieke, 'Austrian Crime Fiction: Experimentation, Critical Memory and Humour', in *Crime Fiction in Germany: Der Krimi*, ed. by Katharina Hall (Cardiff: University of Wales Press, 2016), pp. 51–67.

Kramlovsky, Beatrix, 'Show Your Face, oh Violence: Crime Fiction as Written by Austrian Woman Writers', *World Literature Today* 85.3 (2011), pp. 13–15.

Krause, Peter, *Der Eichmann-Prozeß in der deutschen Presse* (Frankfurt a.M., New York: Campus, 2002).

Kutch, Lynn M. and Todd Herzog, eds, *Tatort Germany: The Curious Case of German-Language Crime Fiction* (Rochester/NY: Camden House, 2014).

Kutzbach, Konstanze, 'The Hard-Boiled Pattern as Discursive Practice of Ethnic Subalternity in Jakob Arjouni's *Happy Birthday, Turk!* and Irene Dische's *Ein Job*', in *Sleuthing Ethnicity. The Detective in Multiethnic Crime Fiction*, ed. by Dorothea Fischer-Hornung and Monika Mueller (Madison/WI: Fairleigh Dickinson University Press et. al., 2003, pp. 240–259.

Laub Coser, Rose, 'Lachen in der Fakultät', in *Das Gelächter der Geschlechter. Humor und Macht in Gesprächen* von Frauen *und Männern*, ed. by Helga Kotthoff (Konstanz: Universitätsverlag, 1995), pp. 97–120.

Light, Alison, '"Young Bess". Historical Novels and Growing up', *Feminist Review*, 33 (1989), pp. 57–72.

Linder, Joachim, 'Feinde im Innern. Mehrfachtäter in deutschen Kriminalromanen der Jahre 1943/44 und der „Mythos Serienkiller"', *Internationales Archiv für Sozialgeschichte der deutschen Literatur* 28.2 (2003), pp. 190–227.

Little, Judy, *Comedy and the Woman Writer: Woolf, Spark, and Feminism* (Lincoln: University of Nebraska Press, 1983).

Little, Judy, 'Humoring the Sentence: Women's Dialogic Comedy', *Women's Comic visions*, ed. by June Sochen (Detroit: Wayne State University Press, 1991), pp.19–32.

Lorenz, Dagmar C.G., 'In Search of the Criminal – in Search of the Crime. Holocaust Literature and Films as Crime Fiction', *Modern Austrian Literature* 31.3/4 (1998), pp. 35–48.

Lovesey, Peter, 'The Historian, Once upon a Crime', in *Murder Ink: The Mystery Reader's Companion*, ed. by Dillys Winn (New York: Workman Publishing, 1977), p. 476.

Mall-Grob, Beatrice, 'Grossartiger Abgang einer literarischen Figur: Bernhard Schlinks neuer Roman *Selbs Mord*', *Der kleine Bund*, October 11, 2001.

Mankell, Henning, 'Introduction', in Maj Sjöwall, Per Wallöö, *Roseanna*, trans. Lois Roth (New York: Vintage Crime/ Black Lizard, 2008), pp. vii–x.

Mann, Jessica, *Deadlier than the Male. An Investigation into Feminine Crime Writing* (London: David & Charles, 1981).

Marcuse, Herbert, 'The Affirmative Character of Culture', in *Negations: Essays in Critical Theory*, trans. by Jeremy J. Shapiro (Boston: Beacon Press, 1968), 88–103.

Matzke, Christine and Susanne Mühleisen, 'Postcolonial Postmortems: Issues and Perspectives', in *Postcolonial Postmortems. Crime Fiction from a Transcultural Perspective*, ed. by Christine Matzke and Susanne Mühleisen (Amsterdam, New York: Rodopi 2006) pp. 1–16.

McChesney, Anita, 'The Case of the Austrian Regional Crime Novel', in *Tatort Germany: The Curious Case of German-Language Crime Fiction*, ed. by Lynn M. Kutch and Todd Herzog (Rochester/NY: Camden House, 2014), pp. 81–98.

Menzel, Julia, '"Dies waren die Tatsachen". Kriminalliteratur und Evidenzproduktion im Familienblatt *Die Gartenlaube*', in *Kriminalliteratur und Wissensgeschichte. Genres-Medien-Technik*, ed. by Clemens Peck and Florian Sedlmeier (Bielefeld: transcript, 2015), pp. 31–53.

Merivale, Patricia and Susan Elizabeth Sweeney, 'The Game's Afoot: On the Trail of the Metaphysical Detective Story', in *Detecting Texts. The Metaphysical Detective Story from Poe to Postmodernism*, ed. by Patricia Merivale and Susan Elizabeth Sweeney (Philadelphia: University of Pennsylvania Press, 1999), pp. 1–24.

Meyer-Krentler, Eckhardt, '"Geschichtserzählungen". Zur >Poetik des Sachverhalts< im juristischen Schrifttum des 18. Jahrhunderts', in *Erzählte Kriminalität. Zur Typologie und Funktion von narrative Darstellungen in Strafrechtspflege, Publizistik und Literatur zwischen 1770 und 1920*, ed. by Jörg Schönert (Tübingen: Niemeyer, 1991), pp. 117–157.

Miquel, Marc von: "Explanation, Dissociation, Apologia. The Debate over the Criminal Prosecution of Nazi Crimes in the 1960s", in *Coping with the Nazi Past. West German Debates on Nazism and Generational Conflict, 1955–1975*, ed. by Philipp Gassert and Alan E. Steinweis (New York, Oxford: Berghahn, 2006), pp. 50–63.

Moi, Toril, *Revolution of the Ordinary: Literary Studies after Wittgenstein, Austin, and Cavell* (Chicago: University of Chicago Press, 2017).

Moretti, Franco, 'Clues' in F.M., *Signs Taken for Wonders: Essays in the Sociology of Literary Forms*, trans. by Susan Fischer (New York: Verso, 1988), pp. 130–156.

Müller, Wilhelm, 'Zur Topographie der *Unteren Grenze*', *Bücherei und Bildung* (3) 1951, pp. 665–669.

Müller-Funk, Wolfgang, *Komplex Österreich. Fragmente zu einer Geschichte der modernen österreichischen Literatur* (Vienna: Sonderzahl, 2009).

Munt, Sally R., *Murder by the Book? Feminism and the Crime Novel.* (London, New York: Routledge, 1994).

Murphy, Bruce F., *The Encyclopedia of Murder and Mystery* (New York: St. Martin's Press, 1999).

Naftali, Timothy, 'The CIA and Eichmann's Associates', in *U.S. Intelligence and the Nazis*, ed. by Richard Breitman, Norman J.W. Goda, Timothy Naftali and Robert Wolfe (Cambridge, Mass. et al.: Cambridge University Press, 2005), pp. 337–74.

Neale, Sue, 'Crime Writing in Other Languages', in *A Companion to Crime Ficiton*, ed. by Charles J. Rzepka and Lee Horsley (Chichester: Wiley-Blackwell, 2010), pp. 296–302.

Neuhaus, Volker, 'Die Schwierigkeiten der Deutschen mit dem Kriminalroman', in *Mord als kreativer Prozeß: Zum Kriminalroman der Gegenwart in Deutschland, Österreich und der Schweiz*, ed. by Sandro M. Moraldo (Heidelberg: Universitätsverlag Winter, 2005).

Nindl, Sigrid, *Wolf Haas und sein kriminalliterarisches Sprachexperiment* (Berlin: Erich Schmidt Verlag, 2010).

Nusser, Peter, 'Kritik des neuen deutschen Kriminalromans', in *Der neue deutsche Kriminalroman. Beiträge zu Darstellung, Interpretation und Kritik eines populären Genres*, ed. by Karl Ermert and Wolfgang Gast (Rehburg-Loccum: Evangelische Akademie Loccum, 1982), pp. 19–32.

Nusser, Peter, *Der Kriminalroman* (Stuttgart: Metzler, 2009).

Oberwittler, Dietrich and Julia Kasselt, *Ehrenmorde in Deutschland 1996–2005. Eine Untersuchung auf der Basis von Prozessakten* (Cologne: Luchterhand, 2011).

O'Brien, Traci S., 'What's in Your Bag'?: "Freudian Crimes" and Austria's Nazi Past in Eva Rossmann's *Freudsche Verbrechen*', in *Tatort Germany: The Curious Case of German-Language Crime Fiction*, ed. by Lynn M. Kutch and Todd Herzog (Rochester/NY: Camden House, 2014), pp. 155–174.

O'Brien, Traci S., 'Note to Self? Postmodern Criminality and (Feminist) Consciousness in Eva Rossmann's *Freudsche Verbrechen*', *Woman in German Yearbook* 31 (2015), pp. 122–146.

Ott, Paul, *Mord im Alpenglühen: Der Schweizer Kriminalroman. Geschichte und Gegenwart* (Essen: Nordpark Verlag, 2005).

Pailer, Gaby, '"Die Blutspur habe ich bereits aufgewischt." Zu den Romanen Ingrid Nolls', *Script. Zeitschrift für Literatur im Alpen-Adriatischen Raum*, 1 (1995), pp. 28–30.

Pailer, Gaby, '"Weibliche" Körper im "männlichen" Raum. Zur Interdependenz von Gender und Genre in deutschsprachigen Kriminalromanen von Autorinnen', *Weimarer Beiträge* 4 (2000), pp. 264–581.

Pailer, Gaby, 'Das komische Scheitern der Wiedervereinigung: Zum Verhältnis von Komik und Kriminalroman am Beispiel zweier deutschsprachiger Frauenkrimis der 90er Jahre', in *Gelegentlich: Brecht. Jubiläumsschrift für Jan Knopf zum 15jährigen Bestehen der Arbeitsstelle Bertolt Brecht (ABB)*, ed. by Birte Giesler, Eva Kormann, Ana Kugli and Gaby Pailer (Heidelberg: Winter, 2004), pp. 197–227.

Pailer, Gaby, 'Verführung und wahre Gewalt. Der Fall la Chapelle / Birnbaum und seine Dramatisierung durch Christiane Karoline Schlegel', *Kriminalfallgeschichten*, ed. by Alexander Kosenina, *Text & Kritik. Zeitschrift für Literatur. Sonderband*, 5 (2014), pp. 42–57.

Pailer, Gaby, 'Frauen im Turm: Geschichtserzählung und Geschlechterverhältnis bei Felicitas Hoppe, Viola Roggenkamp und Sabine Weigand', in *Romanhaftes Erzählen von Geschichte: Vergegenwärtigte Vergangenheiten im beginnenden 21. Jahrhundert*, ed. by Daniel Fulda and Stephan Jaeger, in collaboration with Elena Agazzi (Berlin: de Gruyter, 2019) (in press).

Palmer, Jennifer S., 'Mysteries of the Ages. Four Millenia of Murder and Mayhem in Historical Mysteries', *The Armchair Detective*, (30) 1997, pp. 156–164.

Paravasini, Lizabeth, Carlos Yorio, 'Is It or Isn't It? The Duality of Parodic Detective Fiction', in *Comic Crime*, ed. by Earl F. Bargainnier (Bowling Green: Bowling Green State University Popular Press, 1987), pp. 181–193.

Pasche, Wolfgang, *Friedrich Dürrenmatts Kriminalromane. Interpretationshilfen* (Stuttgart: Klett, 1997).

Pearson, Nels and Marc Singer, 'Introduction. Open Cases: Detection, (Post)Modernity, and the State', in *Detective Fiction in a Postcolonial and Transnational World*, ed. by Neal Pearson and Marc Singer (Farnham, Burlington: Ashgate, 2009) pp. 1–14.

Pellin, Elio, '*Matto regiert* – Eine Figur emanzipiert sich vom literarischen Text', in *'Es gibt kein größeres Verbrechen als die Unschuld' Zu den Kriminalromanen von Glauser, Dürrenmatt, Highsmith und Schneider*, ed. by Peter Gasser, Ellio Pellin and Ulrich Weber (Göttingen, Zurich: Wallstein, Cronos, 2009), pp. 39–51.

Pier, John, 'Metalepsis', *the living handbook of narratology* (http://www.lhn.uni-hamburg.de/article/metalepsis-revised-version-uploaded-13-july-2016).

Pirinçci, Akif, *Deutschland von Sinnen. Der irre Kult um Frauen, Homosexuelle und Zuwanderer* (Waltrop, Leipzig: Manuscriptum, 2014).

Plener, Peter and Michael Rohrwasser, '"Es war Mord": Zwischen Höhenkamm, Zentralfriedhof und Provinz: Österreichs Krimiszene', *Der Deutschunterricht*, 2 (2007), pp. 57–65.

Polt-Heinzl, Evelyne, 'Frauenkrimis – Von der besonderen Dotation zu Detektion und Mord', in *Ich kannte den Mörder wußte nur nicht wer er war. Zum Kriminalroman der Gegenwart*, ed. by Friedbert Aspetsberger and Daniela Strigl (Innsbruck: Studien Verlag, 2004), pp. 144–170.

Poulton, Hugh, *Top Hat, Grey Wolf and Crescent. Turkish Nationalism and the Turkish Republic* (London: Hurst, 1997).

Preisendanz, Wolfgang and Rainer Warning, eds, *Das Komische* (Munich: Fink, 1976).

Priesching, Doris, 'Erfolgreich, werbewirksam, trivial. Anmerkungen zum österreichischen Fernsehkrimi', in *Ich kannte den Mörder wußte nur nicht wer er war. Zum Kriminalroman der Gegenwart*, ed. by Friedbert Aspetsberger and Daniela Strigl (Innsbruck: Studien Verlag, 2004), pp. 221–239.

Priestman, Martin, *Crime Fiction from Poe to the Present* (Plymouth: Northcote House, 1998).

Pyrhönen, Heta, *Murder from an Academic Angle: An Introduction to the Study of the Detective Narrative* (Columbia/SC: Camden House, 1994).

Reddy, Maureen T., *Detektivinnen. Frauen im modernen Kriminalroman* (Mühlheim: Guthmann-Petersen, 1990).

Reemtsma, Jan Philip. *Vertrauen und Gewalt. Versuch über eine besondere Konstellation der Moderne*. Munich: Pantheon, 2009).

Rehbein, Boike and Gernot Saalmann, 'Feld', in *Bourdieu Handbuch. Leben – Werk – Wirkung*, ed. by Gerhard Fröhlich and Boike Rehbein (Stuttgart, Weimar: Metzler, 2009), pp. 99–103.

Reilly, John M., 'Milieu' in *The Oxford Companion to Crime and Mystery Writing*, ed. by Rosemary Herbert (New York, Oxford: Oxford University Press, 1999), pp. 289–290.

Reitz, Caroline, *Detecting the Nation: Fictions of Detection and the Imperial Venture* (Ohio: The Ohio State University Press, 2004). CDRom.

Renz, Werner, ed., *Interessen um Eichmann. Israelische Justiz, deutsche Strafverfolgung und alte Kameradschaften* (Frankfurt a.M.: Campus, 2012).

Rix, Walter T., 'Krimis in der DDR: Sozialistischer Seiltanz', *Die Horen* 144 (1986), pp. 71–77.

Rix, Walter T., 'Wesen und Wandel des Detektivromans im totalitären Staat', in Paul G. Buchloh, Jens P. Becker, *Der Detektivroman. Studien zur Geschichte und Form der englischen und amerikanischen Detektivliteratur* (Darmstadt: Wissenschaftliche Buchgesellschaft, 1989).

Rössler, Patrick, *Anders Denken. Krähen-Krimis und Zeitprobleme. Der Nest-Verlag von Karl Anders* (Erfurt: Sutton Verlag, 2007).

Rosenfeld, Gavriel D., *The World Hitler Never Made. Alternate History and the Memory of Nazism* (Cambridge, New York: Cambridge University Press, 2005).

Rosenfeld, Gavriel D., *Hi Hitler! How the Nazi Past is Being Normalized in Contemporary Culture* (Cambridge: Cambridge University Press, 2015).

Rüsen, Jörn, 'Was ist Geschichtskultur? Überlegungen zu einer neuen Art, über Geschichte nachzudenken', in *Historische Faszination: Geschichtskultur heute*, ed. by Klaus Füßmann, Heinrich Theodor Grütter and Jörn Rüsen (Cologne, Weimar, Vienna: Böhlau, 1994), pp. 3–26.

Rüsen, Jörn, 'Geschichtskultur', *Geschichte in Wissenschaft und Unterricht* (46) 1995, pp. 513–521.

Ruedi, Peter, *Dürrenmatt oder Die Ahnung vom Ganzen. Biographie* (Zurich: Diogenes, 2011).

Ruffing, Jeanne, *Identität ermitteln. Ethnische und postkoloniale Kriminalromane zwischen Popularität und Subversion* (Würzburg: Königshausen & Neumann, 2011).

Russegger, Arno, 'Ortspiele. Wortspiele. Aspekte kriminalistischen Erzählens in der österreichischen Gegenwartsliteratur', in *Mord als kreativer Prozess. Zum Kriminalroman der Gegenwart in Deutschland, Österreich und der Schweiz*, ed. by Sandro M. Moraldo (Heidelberg: Universitätsverlag Winter, 2005), pp. 75–98.

Rusterholz, Peter, 'Der Ausbruch aus dem Gefängnis. Wandlungen des Schweizer Kriminalromans', *Quarto* 21/22 (2006), pp. 29–39.

Rutledge, Christopher, 'Crime and Detective Literatur for Young Readers', in *A Companion to Crime Ficiton*, ed. by Charles J. Rzepka and Lee Horsley (Chichester: Wiley-Blackwell, 2010), pp. 321–331.

Ryan, Judith, 'The Problem of Pastiche: Patrick Süskind's *Das Parfum*', *German Quarterly* 63.3/4 (1990), pp. 396–403.

Ryan, Judith, 'Schlink's *Vorleser*, Süskind's *Parfum*, and the Concept of Global Literature', *Colloquia Germanica* 48.1–2 (2015) [published 2017], pp. 13–22.

Said, Edward W., *Orientalism* (New York: Vintage Books, 1978).

Sandrock, James P., 'Understanding Heimatliteratur: An Approach to Traditional Regional Literature', *Die Unterrichtspraxis* 14.1 (1981), pp. 2–8.

Saner, Gerhard, *Friedrich Glauser. Eine Biographie.* vol. 1 (Zurich: Suhrkamp, 1981).

Saner, Gerhard, *Friedrich Glauser. Eine Werkgeschichte*, vol. 2 (Zurich: Suhrkamp, 1981).

Saupe, Achim, *Der Historiker als Detektiv – der Detektiv als Historiker. Historik, Kriminalistik und der Nationalsozialismus als Kriminalroman* (Bielefeld: transcript, 2009).

Sayers, Dorothy L., 'Aristotle on Detective Fiction', *English*, 1.1 (1936), pp. 23–35.

Scaggs, John, *Crime Fiction* (London and New York: Routledge, 2005).

Schädel, Mirko, Robert N. Bloch, *Illustrierte Bibliographie der Kriminalliteratur im deutschen Sprachraum von 1796 bis 1945* (Stollhamm-Butjadingen: Achilla, 2006).

Scholes, Robert, *Paradoxy of Modernism* (New Haven: Yale University Press, 2006).

Schmidt, Jochen, *Gangster, Opfer, Detektive. Eine Typengeschichte des Kriminalromans* (Hillesheim: KBV, 1999).

Schmitz, Helmut, 'Representations of the Nazi past II: German wartime suffering', in *Contemporary German Fiction. Writing in the Berlin Republic*, ed. by Stuart Taberner (Cambridge/NY et al.: Cambridge University Press, 2007), pp. 142–58.

Schmuhl, Hans-Walter, *Rassenhygiene, Nationalsozialismus, Euthanasie. Von der Verhütung zur Vernichtung „lebensunwerten Lebens" 1890–1945* (Göttingen: Vandenhoeck & Ruprecht, 1987).

Schönert, Jörg, ed., *Literatur und Kriminalität. Die gesellschaftliche Erfahrung von Verbrechen und Strafverfolgung als Gegenstand des Erzählens. Deutschland, England und Frankreich 1850–1880* (Tübingen: Niemeyer, 1983).

Schönert, Jörg, ed., *Erzählte Kriminalität. Zur Typologie und Funktion von narrativen Darstellungen in Strafrechtspflege, Publizistik und Literatur zwischen 1770 und 1920* (Tübingen: Niemeyer, 1991).

Schönert, Jörg, 'Kriminalgeschichten in der deutschen Literatur zwischen 1770 und 1890. Zur Entwicklung des Genres in sozialgeschichtlicher Perspektive', in *Der Kriminalroman. Poetik, Theorie, Geschichte*, ed. by Jochen Vogt (Munich: Wilhelm Fink Verlag, 1998).

Schreckenberger, Helga, 'The Destruction of Idyllic Austria in Wolf Haas's Detective Novels', in *Crime and Madness in Modern Austria: Myth, Metaphor and Cultural Realities*, ed. by Rebecca S. Thomas (Newcastle: Cambridge Scholars Publishing, 2008), pp. 424–443.

Schröttle, Monika, 'Gewalt gegen Frauen mit türkischem Migrationshintergrund in Deutschland. Diskurse zwischen Skandalisierung und Bagatellisierung', in *Islamfeindlichkeit. Wenn die Grenzen der Kritik verschwimmen*, ed. by Thorsten Gerald Schneiders (Wiesbaden: SV, 2009), pp. 269–87.

Schulz-Buschhaus, Ulrich, 'Die Ohnmacht des Detektivs – Literarhistorische Bemerkungen zum neuen deutschen Kriminalroman', in *Der neue deutsche Kriminalroman. Beiträge zu Darstellung, Interpretation und Kritik eines populären* Genres, ed. by Karl Ermert and Wolfgang Gast (Rehburg-Loccum: Evangelische Akademie Loccum, 1982), pp. 10–18.

Schulze-Witzenrath, Elisabeth, 'Emile Gaboriau und die Entstehung des roman policier', in *Literatur und Kriminalität. Die gesellschaftliche Erfahrung von Verbrechen und Strafverfolgung als Gegenstand des Erzählens. Deutschland, England und Frankreich 1850–1880*, ed. by Jörg Schönert (Tübingen: Niemeyer, 1983), pp. 155–183.

Schwarz, Hans-Peter, *Phantastische Wirklichkeit. Das 20. Jahrhundert im Spiegel des Polit-Thrillers* (Munich: Deutsche Verlags-Anstalt, 2006).

Sev'er, Aysan, *Patriarchal Murders of Women. A Sociological Study of Honour-Based Killings in Turkey and in the West*. (Lewiston/NY et. al.: Mellen, 2013).

Sherman, Jon, 'Plurality and Alternity in Wolf Haas's Detective Brenner Mysteries', in Kutch, Lynn M. and Todd Herzog, eds, *Tatort Germany: The Curious Case of German-Language Crime Fiction* (Rochester/NY: Camden House, 2014), pp. 61–80.

Soitos, Stephen F., *The Blues Detective. A Study of African American Detective Fiction* (Amherst: The University of Massachusetts Press, 1996).

Stangneth, Bettina, *Eichmann vor Jerusalem. Das unbehelligte Leben eines Massenmörders* (Hamburg, Zurich: Arche 2011), [*Eichmann Before Jerusalem: The Unexamined Life of a Mass Murderer*, trans. by Ruth Martin (New York: Alfred A. Knopf, 2014)].

Stewart, Faye, 'Girls in the Gay Bar: Performing and Policing Identity in Crime Fiction', in *Tatort Germany. The Curious Case of German-Language Crime Fiction*, ed. by Lynn M. Kutch and Todd Herzog (Rochester, NY: Camden House, 2014), pp. 200–222.

Stierle, Karlheinz, 'Komik der Handlung, Komik der Sprachhandlung, Komik der Komödie', in *Das Komische*, ed. by Wolfgang Preisendanz and Rainer Warning (Munich: Fink, 1976), pp. 237–268.

Sturm-Trigonatis, Elke, 'Der Wiener Privatdetektiv Markus Cheng – Charlie Chan in Österreich?' *Journal of Austrian Studies* 45.1/2 (2012), pp. 69–92.

Talburt, Nancy Ellen, 'Religion', in *The Oxford Companion to Crime and Mystery Writing*, ed. by Rosemary Herbert (Oxford: Oxford University Press, 1999), pp. 383–384.

Tannert, Mary W. and Henry Kratz, eds, *Early German and Austrian Detective Fiction: An Anthology*, (Jefferson/NC and London: McFarland, 1999).

Tatar, Maria, *Lustmord: Sexual Murder in Weimar Germany* (Princeton: Princeton University Press, 1995).

Tekolf, Oliver, ed., *Schillers Pitaval. Merkwürdige Rechtsfälle als ein Beitrag zur Geschichte der Menschheit, verfaßt, bearbeitet und herausgegeben von Friedrich Schiller* (Frankfurt a.M.: Eichborn Verlag, 2005).

Teraoka, Arlene A., 'Detecting Ethnicity: Jakob Arjouni and the Case of the Missing German Detective Novel', in *Investigating Identities. Questions of Identity in Contemporary International Crime Fiction*, ed. by Marieke Krajenbrink and Kate M. Quinn (Amsterdam, New York: Rodopi, 2009), pp. 113–29.

Thielking, Sigrid, [Introduction], in *'Beinahekrimis'- Beinahe Krimis?* ed. by S. T. and Jochen Vogt (Bielefeld: Aisthesis 2014), pp. 7–19.

Thüring, Hubert, 'Die Erfahrung der Psychiatrie. Friedrich Glausers *Matto regiert*', in *'Es gibt kein größeres Verbrechen als die Unschuld'. Zu den Kriminalromanen von Glauser, Dürrenmatt, Highsmith und Schneider*, ed. by Peter Gasser, Ellio Pellin and Ulrich Weber (Göttingen, Zurich: Wallstein, Cronos, 2009), pp. 13–37.

Todorov, Tzvetan, 'The Typology of Detective Fiction', in *The Poetics of Prose*, trans. by Richard Howard (Ithaca/NY: Cornell University Press, 1977), pp. 42–52.

United States Holocaust Memorial Museum, 'Holocaust Encyclopedia', (https://www.ushmm.org/wlc/en/article.php?ModuleId=10007327).

Viehoff, Reinhold, 'Der Krimi im Fernsehen. Überlegungen zur Genre- und Programmgeschichte', in *MedienMorde. Krimis intermedial*, ed. by Jochen Vogt (Munich: Fink 2005), pp. 89–110.

Vogt, Jochen, ed., *Der Kriminalroman. Zur Theorie und Geschichte einer Gattung*, 2 vols. (Munich: UTB, 1971).

Vogt, Jochen, ed., *Der Kriminalroman. Poetik, Theorie, Geschichte* (Munich: Fink, 1998).

Vogt, Jochen, ed. *MedienMorde. Krimis intermedial* (Munich, Fink, 2005).

Vogt, Jochen, '"Tatort" – Der wahre deutsche Gesellschaftsroman', in *MedienMorde. Krimis intermedial*, ed. by J. V. (Munich: Fink 2005), pp. 111–129.

Vogt, Jochen, 'Modern? Vormodern? Oder Postmodern? Zur Poetik des Kriminalromans und seinem Ort im literarischen Feld', in *Verbrechen und Gesellschaft im Spiegel von Literatur und Kunst*, ed. by Véronique Liard (Munich: Meidenbauer 2006), pp. 17–29.

Vogt, Jochen, 'Krimis, Antikrimis, "Gedanken"-Krimis'. Wie Friedrich Dürrenmatt sich in ein gering geschätztes Genre einschrieb', in *Dürrenmatt und die Weltliteratur. Dürrenmatt in der Weltliteratur*, ed. by Véronique Liard and Marion George (Pieterlen/CH: Martin Meidenbauer, Peter Lang, 2011), pp. 215–235.

Vogt, Jochen, 'Mord im Hyde Park! Bauelemente und Strukturvarianten der Kriminalerzählung', in Jochen Vogt, *Wie analysiere ich eine Erzählung? Ein Leitfaden mit Beispielen* (Munich: Fink, 2011), pp. 70–87.

Vogt, Jochen, 'Steiniger Weg zu einer deutschen Normalität. Lektürenotizen zu Ulrich Herberts Geschichte Deutschlands im 20. Jahrhundert nebst der dringenden Empfehlung, diese selbst zu lesen', *andererseits: Transatlantic Yearbook of German Studies*, vol. 4 (2015), pp. 247–54. [http://andererseits.library.duke.edu/article/view/15449/6675].

von Matt, Peter, *Die Intrige. Theorie und Praxis der Hinterlist* (Munich: Hanser 2006).

Walker, Nancy A., *What's so funny? Humor in American Culture* (Wilmington/ Del: Scholarly Resources Inc., 1998).

Walker, Nancy A., 'Toward Solidarity: Women's Humor and Group Identity', in *Women's Comic Visions*, ed. by June Sochen (Detroit: Wayne State University Press, 1991), pp. 57–81.

Wallace, Diana, *The Woman's Historical Novel. British Woman Writers, 1900–2000* (Basingstoke: Palgrave McMillan), 2005.

Wallace, Diana, '"The Haunting Idea": Female Gothic Metaphors and Feminist Theory', in *The Female Gothic. New Directions*, ed. by Diana Wallace and Andrew Smith (Basingstoke: Palgrave McMillan, 2009), pp. 26–41.

Weber, Ulrich, *Friedrich Dürrenmatt. Von der Lust, die Welt nochmals zu erdenken* (Bern: Haupt, 2006).

Werlen, Benno, *Sozialgeographie alltäglicher Regionalisierungen*, 3 vols. (Stuttgart: Steiner, 1995, 1997, 2007).

Weingart, Peter, Jürgen Kroll and Kurt Bayertz, eds, *Rasse, Blut und Gene. Geschichte der Eugenik und Rassenhygiene in Deutschland* (Frankfurt a.M.: Suhrkamp, 1988).

Welzer, Harald, Sabine Moller and Karoline Tschuggnall, *„Opa war kein Nazi".
Nationalsozialismus und Holocaust im Familiengedächtnis* (Frankfurt a.M.: Fischer, 2002).
Wieninger, Manfred, 'Heimatliteratur ohne Kitsch', *Wiener Zeitung Online* September 16, 2011.
(http://www.wienerzeitung.at/themen_channel/wz_reflexionen/kompendium/397240_
Heimatliteratur-ohne-Kitsch.html).
Wilke, Sabine, 'Wilde Weiber und dominante Damen: Der Frauenkrimi als postfeministischer
Verhandlungsort von Weiblichkeitsmythen', *Literatur für Leser*, 3 (1995), pp. 151–163.
Wilson, Edmund, 'Who Cares Who Killed Roger Ackroyd?' in *The Art of the Mystery Story:
A Collection of Critical Essays*, ed. by Howard Haycraft (New York: Simon & Schuster,
1946), pp. 390–97.
Wilson, Edmund, 'Why Do People Read Detective Stories?' *The Edmund Wilson Reader*, ed. and
intro. Lewis M. Dabney (New York: DeCapo Press, 1997), pp. 595–98.
Winks, Robin W., ed., *The Historian as Detective: Essays on Evidence* (New York et. al.: Harper
& Row, 1968).
Wirtz, Irmgard, 'Verbrechen auf engstem Raum', *Quarto* 21/22 (2006), pp. 51–60.
Wittgenstein, Ludwig, *Tractatus Logico-Philosophicus*, trans. by C. K. Ogden (London: Kegan
Paul, Trench, Trubner; New York: Harcourt, Brace & Company, 1922).
Wölcken, Fritz, *Der literarische Mord. Eine Untersuchung über die englische und
amerikanische Kriminalliteratur* (Nuremberg: Nest Verlag, 1953) [e-book: Hamburg:
edition Hamburg, 2015].
Woeller, Waltraud and Bruce Cassiday, *The Literature of Crime and Detection: An Illustrated
History from Antiquity to the Present* (New York: Ungar, 1988).
Wörtche, Thomas: 'Krimis zwischen Dessous und Jägerzaun. Die Dialektik des Marketing'
[2003]. http://www.kaliber38.de/woertche/einzelteile/jaegerzaun.htm.
Wörtche, Thomas, 'CrimeWatch No. 80', *Freitag* 52, December 19, 2003.
Wörtche, Thomas, 'Zivile Notwehr. Manfred Wieningers Marek-Miert-Romane', *Literatur und
Kritik* 417/418 (2007), pp. 74–78.
Wörtche, Thomas, *Das Mörderische neben dem Leben. Ein Wegbegleiter durch die Welt der
Kriminalliteratur* (Lengwil: Libelle, 2008).
Wörtche, Thomas, 'Die Peinigung der Begriffe – Ein Mord den jeder begeht', in *Doderer, das
Kriminelle und der literarische Kriminalroman. Zu Heimito von Doderers* Ein Mord den
jeder begeht, ed. by Gerald Sommer and Robert Walter (Würzburg: Königshausen &
Neumann, 2011), pp. 51–59.
Würmann, Carsten, 'Zum Kriminalroman im Nationalsozialismus', in *Verbrechen als Passion.
Neue Untersuchungen zum Kriminalgenre*, ed. by Bruno Franceschini and Carsten
Würmann (Berlin: Weidler Buchverlag, 2004), pp. 143-186.
Würmann, Carsten, *Zwischen Unterhaltung und Propaganda. Das Krimigenre im Dritten Reich*.
diss. FU Berlin 2013.

Online Publications and Resources

www.bokas.de.
www.culturmag/crimemag.
www.daserste.de/unterhaltung/krimi/tatort/.
www.emons-verlag.de/programm/krimis/historischer-krimi.
www.fernsehserien.de/tatort/folgen/.
www.gereonrath.de/.
www.gmeiner-verlag.de/zeitgeschichtliche-krimis.html.
www.histo-couch.de/historische-kriminalromane-ueber-das-mittelalter.html.
www.kbv-verlag.de/18.html.
www.kaliber38.com.
www.krimi-couch.
www.krimilexikon.de.
www.lovelybooks.de/stoebern/empfehlung/historischer%20kriminalroman/.
www.randomhouse.de/Webtags/Historischer-Kriminalroman/9050.rhd.
www.rowohlt.de/themen/belletristik-und-verwandte-gebiete/kriminalromane-und-mystery/
    historische-kriminalromane.
www.verlagshaus24.de/krimis-und-romane/historische-romane/.
www.zeit.de/krimizeit-bestenliste.

Contributors

Sandra Beck is a Postdoctoral Associate in the Department of German Studies at the University of Mannheim. Her research and publications focus on literature and terrorism, cultural memory studies, expressionistic poetry, contemporary German literature and crime fiction. Funded by the *Studienstiftung des Deutschen Volkes*, her PhD thesis examined the interplay between crime fiction and (post-)modern German literature by discussing the genre's essential narrative patterns – confession, testimony, detection – and their rewritings in 'highbrow' literature. Her study *Narratologische Ermittlungen. Muster detektorischen Erzählens in der deutschsprachigen Literatur* was published in 2017. Her current research project analyses the opportunities and limitations of a transnational literary history.

William Collins Donahue is the Director of the Nanovic Institute for European Studies, Cavanaugh Professor of the Humanities and Concurrent Professor of Film, Television and Theatre at the University of Notre Dame. He is author of *Holocaust as Fiction. Bernhard Schlink's 'Nazi' Novels and their Films* (published in German as *Holocaust Lite. Bernhard Schlinks 'NS' Romane und ihre Verfilmungen*); as well as of *The End of Modernism*, which was awarded the 2002 Scaglione Prize of the Modern Language Association.

Andreas Erb teaches in the program 'Literatur und Medienpraxis' at the University of Duisburg-Essen in Germany. His areas of research are contemporary German literature, travel writing, image-text relationships, and literature and media. Together with Christof Hamann, he was the co-editor of the recent issue ... *immer steigend, kommt Ihr auf die Höhen. Bergübergänge* (vol. 266, 2017) of the journal *die horen*.

Joachim Feldmann is a teacher of German and English, a book reviewer working in different media (*Freitag, Culturmag.de* and others) and specializes in crime fiction. He is also a co-editor of the literary journal *Am Erker* and a member of the jury for the Deutscher Krimi Preis [German Crime Fiction Prize].

Katharina Hall is a Germanist, editor and freelance translator. She is Honorary Research Associate in the Department of Modern Languages at Swansea University and the editor of *Crime Fiction in German. Der Krimi* (2016). She recently established her own company, Peabody Ink.

Thomas W. Kniesche is Associate Professor of German Studies at Brown University. He has written on Günter Grass, German-Jewish literature, mystery novels and German Science Fiction. His latest books are *Einführung in den Kriminalroman* (2015) for the series *Einführung in die Germanistik*, published by Wissenschaftliche Buchgesellschaft, Darmstadt, and *Büchermorde – Mordsbücher* (2016).

Sandro M. Moraldo is Associate Professor of German Linguistics, Literature and Culture at Bologna University (Italy) and of Comparative Literature at Catholic University of the Sacred Heart of Milan (Italy). He was educated in Germany, earning his PhD at Heidelberg University, where he was Visiting Professor within the excellence initiative in Winter 2014/15. In spring 2017, he was the Max Kade Distinguished Visiting Professor at the University of Rhode Island (Kingston, RI). His books include *E.T.A. Hoffmann. Vita e opera. Vol. 1: Vita, romanzi, fiabe* and *Vol. 2: Tutti i racconti* (2015 and 2017) and *Wandlungen des Doppelgängers: Shakespeare*

https://doi.org/10.1515/9783110426601-014

– *E.T.A. Hoffmann – Pirandello. Von der Zwillingskomödie zur Identitätsgefährdung* (1996). He has also been the editor of several other books, including *Mord als kreativer Prozess. Zum Kriminalroman der Gegenwart in Deutschland, Österreich und der Schweiz* (2005), *Das Land der Sehnsucht. E.T.A. Hoffmann und Italien* (2002) and *Leonardo Sciascia. Annäherungen an sein Werk* (2000).

Gaby Pailer received her PhD in 1992 from the Universität Karlsruhe/TH, Germany. From 1992–2001 she served as lecturer, research associate, and assistant professor in Karlsruhe. In 2001 she was appointed Associate Professor at the University of British Columbia, Vancouver BC, Canada, and promoted to Full Professor in 2010. Her research foci include gender and canon critical studies of German literature from early modern to contemporary, from a cultural comparative perspective. She has published articles and books on drama and theatre, narrative prose, poetry, Nietzsche's literary reception, Holocaust drama and crime fiction. Since 2017, she has been carrying out a major project on Charlotte Schiller. Recent book publications include Charlotte Schiller, *Literarische Schriften* (eds. G. Pailer, A. Dahlmann-Resing, M. Kage, 2016), *Fremde – Luxus – Räume* (eds. J. Eming; G. Pailer; F. Schößler; J. Traulsen, 2015) and *Scholarly Editing and German Literature* (eds. L. Jones, B. Plachta, G. Pailer, C.K. Roy, 2015).

Kirsten Reimers is a Hamburg-based independent scholar and literary critic. She is a co-editor of the critical edition of the works of Ernst Toller and the annotated edition of Toller's letters. Her other areas of expertise are crime fiction, the history of crime fiction and literary criticism.

Steffen Richter is coordinator of the DFG research project 'Ästhetische Eigenzeiten' at the Free University Berlin. His main interests are the literary aesthetics of technology and nature, the theory of the Anthropocene and contemporary literature/contemporary literary institutions. His book *Infrastruktur. Ein Schlüsselkonzept der Moderne und die deutsche Literatur 1848–1914* was published by Matthes & Seitz, Berlin, in 2018. He is the editor of the magazine *Dritte Natur. Technik – Kapital– Umwelt*.

Hugh Ridley is Professor Emeritus at University College Dublin. Among his numerous book publications are *'Relations stop nowhere': The Common Literary Foundations of German and American Literature 1830–1917* (2007), *Thomas Mann* (together with Jochen Vogt, 2009) and *Wagner and the Novel* (2012). His latest book is *Eine kleine Geschichte der Vogelmalerei in Deutschland* (2016).

Gonçalo Vilas-Boas is a member of the Institute for Comparative Literature at the Faculty of Arts of the University of Porto, where he was Professor of German and Comparative Literatures. His main fields of expertise are Swiss- German literature, myths and the labyrinth, travel literature (in particular Annemarie Schwarzenbach) and crime fiction. His most recent books are *Macht in der Deutschschweizer Literatur* (Gonçalo Vilas-Boas /Teresa Martins de Oliveira, eds., 2012), *Revisitar Annemarie Schwarzenbach* (2016) and *As Serras e os Vales. Ensaios sobre Literatura Suíça* (2018).

Jochen Vogt is Professor emeritus at the University of Essen, where he taught from 1973 to 2008. He has held numerous visiting professorships at universities in Europe and the US. His main areas of research are German twentieth-century literature, narratology, and international crime fiction. He edited the volume *Der Kriminalroman* [The Crime Novel, first edition 1972], which has become a standard work on the theory and history of crime fiction. As a literary critic and book reviewer he continues to track the development of the genre.

Thomas Wörtche is a critic, journalist and literary scholar. He writes on books, images and music for print, radio and online media, with a focus on international crime fiction in all media and on literature from Latin America, Asia, Africa and Australia/Oceania. *Berlin Noir*, an anthology of crime stories edited by Thomas Wörtche, was published in 2018 by Akashic Books. Thomas Wörtche is a member of the 'Weltempfänger' and other juries. He directs the online feuilleton CULTURMAG/CrimeMag and has his own crime fiction series with Suhrkamp Verlag. He lives and works in Berlin.

Index

https://doi.org/10.1515/9783110426601-015